SHORTHAND DICTATION STUDIES

SIMPLIFIED

BY

WALLACE B. BOWMAN

SECOND EDITION

PUBLISHED BY

SOUTH-WESTERN PUBLISHING COMPANY

CINCINNATI   NEW ROCHELLE   CHICAGO   DALLAS   SAN FRANCISCO

E47

H655

Printed in the United States of America

PREFACE TO THE SIMPLIFIED EDITION

This Simplified Edition represents a change in the shorthand plates only. It is believed that during the transition from the Standard Gregg to the Simplified Gregg many schools will face the problem of having in the same dictation class both Standard writers and Simplified writers. With this thought in mind, the author has retained, as far as possible, a page-for-page similarity between the two editions of SHORTHAND DICTATION STUDIES. In some few cases, to meet theory revisions, it has been necessary to change word lists in those lessons devoted to theory review. The reading and writing material in the two books, however, remains identical.

In the preparation of SHORTHAND DICTATION STUDIES, Second Edition, every effort has been made to present a book that would be of maximum value to both student and teacher. All the basic features of the earlier edition have been retained. Business information, business correspondence, and business practices—all appearing in the first edition—now appear in revised form as Parts 2, 3, and 4 of the various dictation studies. Parts 1 and 5 are entirely new.

Part 1 of each dictation study is devoted to a review of brief forms or theory principles. Brief forms are emphasized in every third dictation study, beginning with Dictation Study I. The commoner rules of punctuation are also reviewed in Part 1; and both punctuation review and theory review are correlated in specially prepared reading and dictation exercises.

Part 5 of each dictation study consists of a Progress Checkup that introduces the student to the writing of new material through the use of familiar subject matter and a familiar vocabulary. Although the student has the opportunity of practicing such material, he does so without the aid of a vocabulary preview. The teachers' manual contains similar dictation material to which the student has no

iii

access. Beginning with Dictation Study XXXI, the Progress Checkup letters appear only in the teachers' manual (with the exception of Dictation Studies XXXV and XL), and the student is thrown entirely on his own resources in the handling of this dictation material.

There has been a growing attitude toward the use of office-style dictation in the classroom, with the thought of orienting the student to the type of dictation that he will meet in the office. Although some teachers have used dictation of this type in their classes, little or no attempt has been made to present an organized plan to assist the student in meeting the problems involved. Consequently, beginning with Dictation Study XXVI, nine of the last fifteen studies are devoted to the development of techniques in handling dictation that includes pauses, changes, corrections, deletions, and insertions. SHORTHAND DICTATION STUDIES gives the student a definite plan of handling these problems in taking dictation. Similar methods have been employed in the use of voice-writing machines and shorthand machines. SHORTHAND DICTATION STUDIES, however, offers the *shorthand* student a simple means of applying tested practices to office problems that might otherwise prove exceedingly difficult.

Other elements that give this second edition added value include an increased vocabulary range, the use of cross references for the phrases in the General Vocabulary at the back of the book, word discriminations wherever homonyms add to the problems of transcription, an increased number of attractive models, and an increase in the number of longer articles and letters. A suggested reading rate goal has also been indicated at the end of each shorthand plate.

The author feels deeply indebted to the many teachers and students who have helped to develop the plan of the book. Without their help this publication would not have been possible.

The shorthand plates in this book were written by Grace A. Bowman

W. B. B.

CONTENTS

DICTATION STUDY I

DICTATION STUDY II

DICTATION STUDY III

DICTATION STUDY IV

DICTATION STUDY V*

DICTATION STUDY VI

DICTATION STUDY VII

DICTATION STUDY VIII

DICTATION STUDY IX

---

*In the longer dictation studies, Part 4, Business Practices is omitted.

DICTATION STUDY X

DICTATION STUDY XI

DICTATION STUDY XII

DICTATION STUDY XIII

DICTATION STUDY XIV

DICTATION STUDY XV

DICTATION STUDY XVI

DICTATION STUDY XVII

DICTATION STUDY XVIII

DICTATION STUDY XIX

DICTATION STUDY XXX

DICTATION STUDY XXXI*

DICTATION STUDY XXXII

DICTATION STUDY XXXIII

DICTATION STUDY XXXIV

DICTATION STUDY XXXV

---

*Part 5, Progress Checkup is omitted from the remaining dictation studies except in Dictation Studies XXXV and XL.

TO THE STUDENT

When you apply for a stenographic position after graduation, your prospective employer will expect you to be able to write shorthand at a satisfactory rate of speed for a length of time varying from a few minutes to several hours. He will also expect you to become quickly familiar with whatever vocabulary his dictation may include. The required vocabulary and the rate of dictation will depend both on the kind of business and on the type of employer. Not many stenographers can predict the particular kind of office in which they will work. It is therefore necessary for the advanced training in school to build a suitable vocabulary and a sufficient speed of writing to meet the needs of any position for which the students may be eligible.

Basic Skills. The parts called "Basic Skills" are given to assist you in strengthening your knowledge of shorthand theory. Not all principles are reviewed, but so-called trouble spots in shorthand writing are given a great deal of attention. You have already found that correctly written shorthand is easy to read. Brief forms and brief-form derivatives are repeatedly emphasized because their prompt and accurate use is of material assistance in developing speed of writing. The punctuation pointers and English aids are included to assist you in developing the ability to make your shorthand of practical value. In order to enable you to study your shorthand with the least possible interference, punctuation is studied only in connection with Part 1 of each dictation study.

Vocabulary Building. Many special or technical words you will have to learn on the job. For that reason you should continue to practice and study shorthand even after you find employment. *Shorthand Dictation Studies*, however, will supply you with a vocabulary large enough to meet the requirements of beginning employment and sufficient for all the needs of many offices. When practicing the outlines for the words in the vocabulary previews, give attention to the common, easy words: they are the ones you will meet most frequently. When you encounter an outline that you cannot write easily, try writing it slowly and smoothly at first. Then be sure that you can write it rapidly and smoothly before proceeding to the next word.

Spelling. Although *Shorthand Dictation Studies* is devoted primarily to the development of shorthand skills, it does offer you an excellent opportunity, through the shorthand previews, to learn the spelling of many words that should become a permanent part of your spelling vocabulary. In the business office you will be expected to use a dictionary for the spelling of any word about which you are uncertain; however, you cannot waste either your own or your employer's time by referring to the dictionary for words that you should really know. Make it a point to give some attention to spelling each day.

Reading. The shorthand plates in *Shorthand Dictation Studies* serve two purposes: First, they keep you in touch with accurately written shorthand and assist you in improving your own style of writing; second, they give you an opportunity to strengthen your shorthand reading ability. When you can read shorthand with ease, you can give full attention to other elements of transcription and thus, in the transcription class and in the office, attain your best transcription rate of typing. We have set a reading-rate goal ranging from 125 to 150 words a minute. Such a speed of reading is sufficient for all good shorthand purposes. Be sure to maintain this rate in all your plate reading.

Speed Building. Shorthand writing is very much like swimming or running or any other skill in which speed is an element. Unless you can swim rapidly for a short distance, you cannot swim rapidly for a long distance. Unless you can run rapidly for a short distance, you cannot run rapidly for a long distance. Unless you can write shorthand rapidly for a short time, you cannot write shorthand rapidly for a long time. It is therefore necessary that rapid writing be given constant attention, no matter whether you are practicing words, phrases, sentences, paragraphs, complete letters, or articles. Of course, you should always try to write with accuracy, and you should practice any outline with which you are not thoroughly familiar; but you should never leave a lesson until you have made a real effort to write it rapidly.

Shorthand Dictation Studies provides ample material for a satisfactory speed development in both spurt and sustained writing. If you will prepare your assignments conscientiously and properly, you will reach your goal without loss of time. All but a few of the business letters are taken from the files of actual businesses; they represent, in a large measure, the kinds of letters you will have to write when you are employed as a stenographer. The articles on business information and office practices will help you do your work intelligently and economically. Put your best effort into your study of shorthand, and it will pay you rich dividends.

Word Division. The vocabulary previews of the various letters and articles supply the printed forms of words as well as the shorthand outlines for the words. In the printed forms marks are used to show the points at which the words may be divided at the end of lines of typing.

Word divisions are never desirable but are sometimes necessary. The best division is always the one that is in keeping with typewriting efficiency and that interferes least with ease of reading. The following rules will help you to decide when and where divisions may be made:

1. Words should be divided only between syllables.

    Right: prod/uct   *Wrong*: pro/duct
           ship/ping   shipp/ing

2. A one-letter syllable at the beginning of a word should not be separated from the rest of the word.

    Right: about   *Wrong*: a/bout
           agree   a/gree

3. A one- or two-letter syllable at the end of a word should not be separated from the rest of the word.

    Right: noisy   *Wrong*: nois/y
           wanted   want/ed

4. Words containing hyphens should be divided only at the hyphens.

> *Right*: one-/sided
> mother-/in-/law

5. A syllable that does not contain a vowel should not be separated from the rest of the word.

> *Right*: didn't   *Wrong*: did/n't
> haven't   have/n't

Some word divisions are permitted where necessity is concerned; but it is better to observe the following practices:

6. If possible, proper names should not be divided, and initials and titles should not be separated from names.

7. When two medial vowels come together and are sounded in separate syllables, the preferred division is between the vowels.

> anxi/ety   is better than   anx/iety
> continu/ation   is better than   continua/tion
> vari/eties   is better than   varie/ties

8. Medial syllables consisting of single vowels are preferably placed on the first line.

> presi/dent   is better than   pres/ident
> apolo/gize   is better than   apol/ogize
> *but*
> polit/ical   is better than   politi/cal
> sal/able   is better than   sala/ble

9. Compound words are usually better divided between the elements of the compound.

> turn/over   is better than   turno/ver
> under/estimate   is better than   underes/timate
> *but*
> underesti/mate   is also better than   underes/timate

10. Awkward or misleading divisions that cause difficulty in reading should be avoided.

> annoy/ance   is better than   an/noyance
> carry/ing   is better than   car/rying
> often   is better than   of/ten
> re/ality   is better than   real/ity
> re/admit   is better than   read/mit

You are not expected to remember all word divisions. When you are in doubt as to the proper division of a word, consult a dictionary.

DICTATION STUDY I

PART 1. BASIC SKILLS

Brief-Form Review

Directions. Do you know your brief forms? The brief forms are among your best shorthand friends. When you know them thoroughly, you can write them without hesitation and read them accurately. The following paragraphs contain 50 different brief forms and brief-form derivatives. Do you know them? Read this exercise until you can read at the rate of at least 125 words a minute—better still, 150 words a minute. A satisfactory reading time is indicated at the end of the article. When you have reached your reading goal, copy the exercise twice in shorthand—once for accuracy of outline, and once for ease and speed of writing.

1

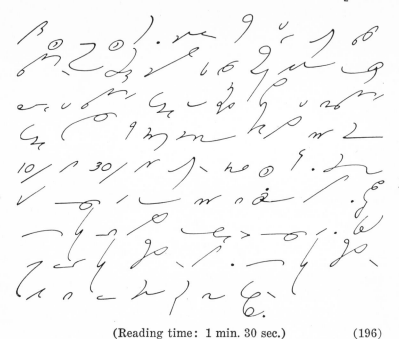

(Reading time: 1 min. 30 sec.)   (196)

Punctuation Pointer

The following punctuation pointer is given to explain the use of all the commas in the foregoing article. Ordinarily, medial punctuation is not written during dictation unless the punctuation itself is dictated; but a good stenographer must understand the correct use of punctuation in order to make her services of maximum value to her employer. Study the punctuation pointers and their application as given in the various lessons on basic skills.

1. The *comma* is used to separate introductory and intermediate parenthetical expressions from the rest of the sentence.

Of course, prices on these goods are subject to change.

As a matter of fact, there is ample argument for such action.

As a result of the storm, the building was closed for repairs.

Our opinion, as a matter of fact, is the result of careful study.

You must realize, however, that we cannot grant your request.

We cannot, unless otherwise directed, accept the goods for exchange.

PART 2. BUSINESS INFORMATION

Directions. Practice the following vocabulary preview until you can write the shorthand outlines smoothly and easily. Then write the article on "Collections" twice in shorthand. Try to develop the ability to pass promptly from one outline to the next, losing no time between outlines. You will need to know the spellings and the meanings of homonyms appearing in dictation material. Two such homonyms are discussed immediately following this vocabulary preview.

Vocabulary Preview

ad/dress
agree with this
ap/peal

ap/pli/ca/tion
busi/nesses
care/less

col/lect
con/ven/ient
cor/po/ra/tion

cor/re/spond/ence
cus/tom/er's
dic/tated

dis/hon/est
dou/ble
dras/tic

fail/ure
fol/low/ing
for/mula

greater
how/ever
in/di/vid/ual

ir/re/spon/si/ble
let/ters
mat/ter

mul/ti/graphed
ne/ces/si/tate
nu/mer/ous

of/fer
one-/sided
out/stand/ing

per/sonal
printed
prob/lem

rather
rep/re/sents
sat/is/fac/tion

se/ries
set/tling
those

through
types
typ/ist

un/for/tu/nate
uses
weight

writer
writ/ten

Correspondence ～_ℓ_   **Correspondents** ～_ℓ_ /

Correspondence refers to letters or the act of writing letters.

> Our correspondence with you has been most interesting.
> We have referred to this matter several times during our correspondence with you.
> We prefer to handle this matter directly rather than through correspondence.

Correspondents refers to persons who write letters.

> Our correspondents must complete a training program before they are permitted to handle company business without supervision.
> The entire matter was handled by two of our youngest correspondents.

Collections

This set of correspondence is rather one-sided, as the writer is trying to collect money. Collection [20] letters, like claim letters, offer a double problem: one, of settling the matter to the satisfaction of the [40] business that the correspondent represents; the other, of trying to keep the customer's good will.

One [60] corporation uses the following formula for collection letters:

Some men do not pay because they are careless; [80]

Some men do not pay because they are unfortunate;

Some men do not pay because they are irresponsible;

But [100] no men are dishonest.

The letters of this series show the application of this formula; however, not [120] all businesses agree with this creed. In any case, drastic steps usually follow the failure to collect [140] through letters.

Collection letters are of two types: those dictated and written to cover individual cases; [160] and multigraphed or printed form letters in which the typist need type only the name and the address of the [180] customer. Dictated letters usually have greater weight in the collection of money because they have [200] a personal appeal, but numerous outstanding accounts necessitate the use of the more convenient form [220] letters.   (221)

PART 3. BUSINESS CORRESPONDENCE

between

AMERICAN SHIRT COMPANY   NORRIS CLOTHING COMPANY
1028 Chestnut Street   *and*   718 Marshall Street
Baltimore 4, Maryland   Frederick, Maryland

Directions. Practice the vocabulary preview of Letter 1 until you can write the outlines smoothly and rapidly. Then read the letter until you can read at the rate of at least 125 words a minute—better still, 150 words a minute. A satisfactory reading time (salutation to closing) is indicated at the end of the letter. Finally, make two copies of the letter—one for accuracy of outline, and one for fluency of writing. Apply the same procedure to Letters 2 and 3.

Many students have difficulty in deciding whether or not to use a hyphen in such expressions as *worth-while*. To help you understand when the hyphen is used and when it is omitted, a number of illustrations follow the vocabulary preview of Letter 1.

LETTER 1

ac/count	Nor/ris
Amer/i/can	op/por/tu/nity
buy	orig/i/nal
cloth/ing	part
con/sider	prof/its
cus/tom/ers	re/ceived
didn't	ship/ping
en/tered	de/part/ment
ex/cel/lent	shirts
for/got	sup/pose
Fred/er/ick	to do so
in/tended	we had
is/sued	we should
lost	have
mail	won't
Mar/shall	worth-/while
Mary/land	yours

Worth-while *nO*   Worth while *nO*

The hyphen is used only when the adjective precedes the noun it modifies.

If this order cannot be shipped promptly, we may lose a worth-while account.

We have studied the plan carefully, and his suggestions seem well worth while.

The stenographer should set a worth-while goal and strive to attain it.

The student will not gain the most from his practice unless he believes the exercise is truly worth while.

October 1, 19—

AMERICAN SHIRT COMPANY, John H. Davis, Manager

(Reading time: 45 sec.)   (111)

American Shirt Company

1028 Chestnut Street   Baltimore 4, Maryland

October 1, 19--

Norris Clothing Company
718 Marshall Street
Frederick, Maryland

Gentlemen

        If you intended to send us your check
for $43 but forgot to do so; if you issued
this check but forgot to mail it--just
consider:

        Suppose we received your original order
for the shirts but forgot to ship them! Or
suppose we had entered the order but forgot
to send it to the shipping department!

        Your customers would have lost an op-
portunity to buy some excellent shirts; you
would have lost some good profits; and we
should have lost a worth-while account.

        We didn't forget--we shipped the shirts
on the day the order was received. We did
our part. Now, won't you do yours?

                        Very truly yours

                        AMERICAN SHIRT COMPANY

                        John H. Davis

                        John H. Davis
                        Manager

JHD:RT

MODEL 1—MODIFIED BLOCK LETTER WITH OPEN PUNCTUATION
A well-arranged, accurately written letter is a good advertisement for both
the stenographer and the business for which she works.

LETTER 2

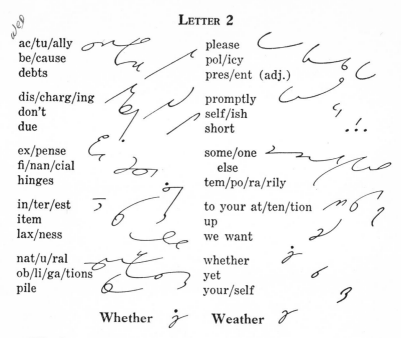

ac/tu/ally	please
be/cause	pol/icy
debts	pres/ent (adj.)
dis/charg/ing	promptly
don't	self/ish
due	short
ex/pense	some/one
fi/nan/cial	else
hinges	tem/po/ra/rily
in/ter/est	to your at/ten/tion
item	up
lax/ness	we want
nat/u/ral	whether
ob/li/ga/tions	yet
pile	your/self

Whether   **Weather**

Whether indicates a choice or alternative.

I do not know whether I shall go tomorrow or wait until early next week.

Let us know whether you like the materials or prefer other samples.

Weather refers to the state or condition of the atmosphere.

The weather has been very changeable for the past week.

The paper predicts a favorable change in the weather tomorrow.

November 3, 19—

AMERICAN SHIRT COMPANY, John H. Davis, Manager
(Reading time: 1 min.)   (148)

LETTER 3

an/swer	re/fusal
changed	re/ply
check	rep/u/ta/tion
cour/tesy	re/spect
credit	res/pite
dearly	sit/u/a/tion
dif/fer/ence	still
dif/fi/cult	tem/po/rary
en/close	though
faith	we are sure
grant	weak/en/ing
No/vem/ber	why not
owe	

December 1, 19—

AMERICAN SHIRT COMPANY, John H. Davis, Manager
(Reading time: 50 sec.)   (120)

PART 4. BUSINESS PRACTICES

Directions. Practice the first vocabulary preview until you can write the outlines smoothly and accurately. Then write the article on "Pen or Pencil" twice in shorthand to develop accuracy and fluency.

Proceed in the same manner with the second vocabulary preview and the article "The Notebook." Try always to pass from one outline to the next without hesitation.

Vocabulary Preview

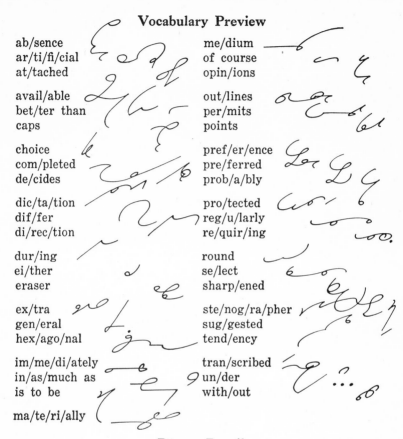

ab/sence
ar/ti/fi/cial
at/tached

avail/able
bet/ter than
caps

choice
com/pleted
de/cides

dic/ta/tion
dif/fer
di/rec/tion

dur/ing
ei/ther
eraser

ex/tra
gen/eral
hex/ago/nal

im/me/di/ately
in/as/much as
is to be

ma/te/ri/ally

me/dium
of course
opin/ions

out/lines
per/mits
points

pref/er/ence
pre/ferred
prob/a/bly

pro/tected
reg/u/larly
re/quir/ing

round
se/lect
sharp/ened

ste/nog/ra/pher
sug/gested
tend/ency

tran/scribed
un/der
with/out

Pen or Pencil

The choice of pen or pencil for note-taking lies with the stenographer. Writers differ very materially [20] in their opinions as to which is better.

If a pencil is to be used, the writer should be very [40] careful to select one with a medium hard lead. A round pencil is better than the hexagonal shape; and a [60] pencil without an eraser is to be preferred to one with an eraser attached, inasmuch as the [80] absence of an eraser makes possible a point at either end of the pencil. Of course, the pencils should be sharpened [100] regularly. When they are not in use, the points may be protected by means of metal caps.

If the [120] stenographer decides to use a pen, she should select one with a medium fine point that permits light, easy outlines; [140] that has a regular flow of ink; and that is not too heavy. It is suggested that the cap of the pen be [160] laid aside during the writing because it adds extra weight to the pen.

For general office work the tendency [180] lies in the direction of the pencil because pencils are available at every desk and probably [200] make greater speed possible. Then, too, the notes are usually transcribed immediately after the [220] dictation has been completed. For work requiring the reading of notes at night or under artificial light, the [240] pen has the preference as it makes clear, regular outlines that are more readable than pencil outlines.   (259)

Vocabulary Preview

ad/van/tage
also
al/though

al/ways
av/er/age
bits

blank
cal/cu/la/tion
cen/tral

close
col/umns
com/pletely

con/nec/tion
es/pe/cially
es/sen/tial

ex/pen/sive
fairly
filled

im/por/tance
in/flex/ible
in/structed

it is not

it might be
nar/row
non/sense

note/book
num/ber
per/ti/nent

prac/tice
proper
pur/pose

qual/ity
re/peat
re/port/ers

re/pos/i/tory
re/vers/ing
scrib/bled

short/hand
should not be
stu/dent

thicker
urged
ver/ti/cal

The Notebook

A good quality of paper is just as essential for proper note-taking as a good pen or pencil, and [20] the ruling of this paper is also of great importance. For general office work a notebook with fairly [40] close lines is to be preferred. A central vertical line will help the stenographer keep her writing in narrow [60] columns.

In buying notebooks, the stenographer should consider the cost in connection with the number of [80] pages and the number of lines to the page. It is not always the thicker notebook that permits the greater amount [100] of writing. Although many shorthand writers, especially reporters, use a notebook with an inflexible [120] cover, this type is rather expensive for general use and serves the purpose of the average stenographer [140] to no better advantage.

The student has probably been instructed in the proper use of the notebook; [160] but it might be well to repeat here that good practice requires writing in narrow columns on only one side of [180] the sheet until the notebook has been completely filled one way, then reversing the notebook and filling in the blank [200] sides of the sheets.

The student is urged to use the shorthand notebook for shorthand notes and pertinent information.[220] It should not be made a repository for bits of calculation or scribbled nonsense.   (236)

PART 5. PROGRESS CHECKUP

Directions. The following letter will give you the opportunity of writing shorthand without the benefit of a vocabulary preview. The words have all been used in the material of this dictation study. Use the general vocabulary beginning on page 617 for any outline about which you are doubtful. The progress-checkup letters are not intended as tests. They will give you the opportunity of determining the extent to which you are learning your shorthand vocabulary. The frequency with which you must refer to the general vocabulary is an indication of how much you are remembering.

LETTER PC-1

Norris Clothing Company
718 Marshall Street
Frederick, Maryland

Gentlemen

Your check for $43 has not been received, and we are wondering why not. When the matter [20] was called to your attention, we supposed you would answer our letter and send us a check promptly. Business courtesy [40] requires that customers pay their debts when due. We are sure you will agree with this.

Your failure to pay your account [60] will necessitate the application of a drastic collection policy that we should prefer to use [80] for irresponsible accounts. We know you don't want to be considered dishonest.

We suggest that you pay your [100] present obligation so that you will not weaken your credit reputation. Won't you write us now and send us [120] a check?

Yours very truly　　　(125)

AMERICAN SHIRT COMPANY

JHD:RT　　　　　　　　John H. Davis, Manager

DICTATION STUDY II

PART 1. BASIC SKILLS

Theory Review

Directions. All the $\overline{\text{O}}$ and $\overline{\text{OO}}$ hook words given in this review are used in the shorthand plate that follows. Read these words until you can read them fluently. Use the key if you need it. After you have learned to read the words without hesitation, write each word at least once. When writing the words, be sure to keep the hooks deep and narrow. Don't permit them to spread out like *k* or *r*.

The $\overline{\text{O}}$ Hook

Key: no—know, most, show, owes, close, so, notebook, homework, only, draw, thought, cautioned, although, brought, of, job, what, collecting, knowledges, obtaining, nonsense, following, opportunities, policy

The $\overline{\text{OO}}$ Hook

Key: wish, way, world, you—your, to—too, student, school, clue, pull, push, looking, number, another, up, sufficient, luck, pluck

Directions. Read the following shorthand plate until you can read it at the rate of at least 125 words a minute— better still, 150 words a minute. A satisfactory reading time is indicated at the end of the article. When you can read

15

the article easily, make two shorthand copies of it—one for accuracy of outline, and one for speed and ease of writing.

The application of the second punctuation pointer, which is explained on page 17, is indicated by the figure 2 written above the encircled comma.

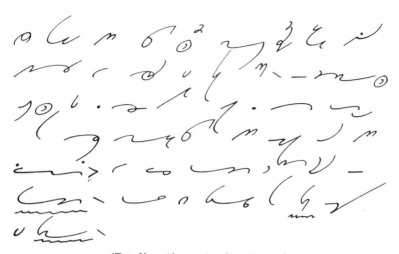

(Reading time: 1 min. 25 sec.)   (195)

Punctuation Pointer

The following punctuation pointer, together with the one given on page 2, will explain the uses of all the commas in the foregoing article. The number 2 placed above a comma indicates that the punctuation pointer of this part applies at that particular point.

2. The *comma* is used after dependent introductory clauses.

If the enclosed statement agrees with your own records, please let us know at once.

In case you cannot be with us, you can give us your answer by mail.

Although you cannot attend the meeting, we feel that you should provide a substitute.

When you arrive at the home office next Monday, please notify me promptly.

Whether you need the shipment this month or next, you should place an immediate order.

PART 2. BUSINESS INFORMATION

Directions. Practice the following vocabulary preview until you can write the outlines smoothly and easily. Then make two shorthand copies of the article "Problems Resulting from an Error." As you practice such articles from day to day, give some thought to the information contained in them. These articles will help you to understand the business correspondence that follows. The well-informed stenographer is a valuable stenographer. For that reason, you should never miss an opportunity to learn.

Vocabulary Preview

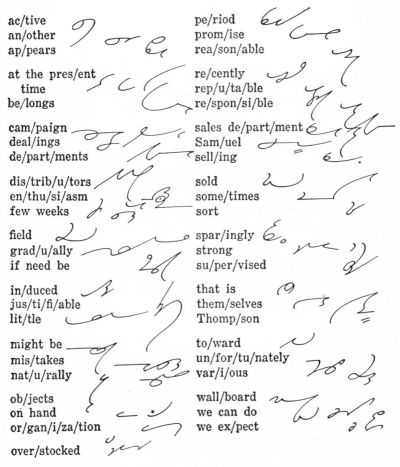

ac/tive	pe/riod
an/other	prom/ise
ap/pears	rea/son/able
at the pres/ent time	re/cently
	rep/u/ta/ble
be/longs	re/spon/si/ble
cam/paign	sales de/part/ment
deal/ings	Sam/uel
de/part/ments	sell/ing
dis/trib/u/tors	sold
en/thu/si/asm	some/times
few weeks	sort
field	spar/ingly
grad/u/ally	strong
if need be	su/per/vised
in/duced	that is
jus/ti/fi/able	them/selves
lit/tle	Thomp/son
might be	to/ward
mis/takes	un/for/tu/nately
nat/u/rally	var/i/ous
ob/jects	wall/board
on hand	we can do
or/gan/i/za/tion	we ex/pect
over/stocked	

Problems Resulting from an Error

One of our salesmen has recently induced Samuel Thompson & Company to serve as distributors of [20] our wallboard in their territory. In the enthusiasm of his success, he unfortunately overstocked [40] the company and made the careless promise that this stock might be paid for after it was sold. Sometimes a promise [60] of this sort is justifiable, especially when the customer has an active territory; but such [80] a promise should be made sparingly to a new distributor who does not have a strong selling organization.[100]

As reputable business houses hold themselves responsible for mistakes made by their field agents, we expect [120] to take our loss if need be. We should make some effort, however, to collect from the customer and still be [140] fair in our dealings.

A bill is the first step toward collection. Naturally, the customer objects to [160] making payment at the present time because he sees a large stock of wallboard on hand and little chance of selling [180] within the next few weeks. Hoping to move this stock gradually over a reasonable period, Samuel [200] Thompson & Company offer to settle with a ninety-day note without interest. This appears to be the [220] best we can do; so we agree.

We now have another problem on hand; that is, to help our customer sell his [240] stock so that he may remain a customer. But that job belongs to our sales department, and all the collection [260] department can do is to suggest a mail campaign to be supervised by the sales organization. You see [280] it is necessary for the various departments of a big business to keep in touch with one another.[300]   (300)

PART 3. BUSINESS CORRESPONDENCE

between

WEBBER WALLBOARD CORPORATION
909 Clifton Street
Boise, Idaho

and

SAMUEL THOMPSON & COMPANY
866 Overland Street
Watertown, South Dakota

Directions. In the letters that follow we have a two-way correspondence. The letters in shorthand are outgoing letters and those in type are incoming letters. This is similar to the office situation in which the stenographers see type-written letters in the incoming mail and shorthand records of the outgoing mail. Always practice the vocabulary preview of a letter before making two shorthand copies of the letter. Complete each letter before proceeding to the next. Always read the shorthand plates before copying them. Never be satisfied with your reading until you reach a reading rate of from 125 to 150 words a minute. A satisfactory reading time is indicated at the end of each shorthand letter.

LETTER 4

ac/cept/ing
col/lec/tion de/
   part/ment

gen/tle/men
hear from you
how much

Jan/u/ary
monthly
Over/land

reg/u/lar

set/tle
shows
South Da/kota

state/ment
sta/tus
stock

Wa/ter/town
we should like
   to know

Web/ber

February 8, 19—

WEBBER WALLBOARD CORPORATION, Collection Department

(Reading time: 25 sec.)   (55)

WEBBER WALLBOARD CORPORATION

909 CLIFTON STREET   *BOISE, IDAHO*

February 8, 19--

Samuel Thompson & Company

 866 Overland Street

  Watertown, South Dakota

Gentlemen:

 The enclosed regular monthly statement shows
the status of your account on January 31. Before
accepting your offer to settle this account with
a ninety-day note, we should like to know just how
much stock you have on hand at this time.

 May we hear from you promptly?

  Very truly yours,

   WEBBER WALLBOARD CORPORATION

   G. L. Wright

   Collection Department

GLW:MA

Enc.

**MODEL 2—DOUBLE-SPACED INDENTED LETTER WITH A
FULL COMPANY SIGNATURE**

The usual signature consists of the typewritten name of the business,
the handwritten name of the dictator, and the typewritten name of the
dictator, of the dictator's position, or of his department.

LETTER 5

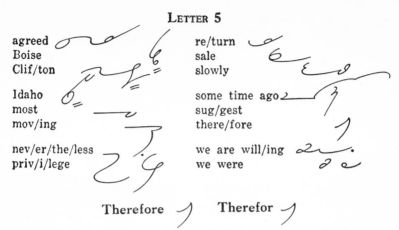

agreed	re/turn
Boise	sale
Clif/ton	slowly
Idaho	some time ago
most	sug/gest
mov/ing	there/fore
nev/er/the/less	we are will/ing
priv/i/lege	we were

Therefore   Therefor

Therefore means for that reason, because of that, consequently.

Your letter arrived this morning. I was, therefore, able to complete the work without delay.

Therefor, used chiefly in legal work, means for that or for it.

If he committed the crime, he should be punished therefor.

February 12, 19—

Webber Wallboard Corporation
909 Clifton Street
Boise, Idaho

Gentlemen

As we wrote you some time ago, our stock of wallboard is moving very slowly, and we still have most [20] of it on our hands.

When we agreed to take this stock, we were given the privilege of paying for it at the [40] time of sale. Nevertheless, we are willing to settle for the full stock through a note and therefore suggest that you [60] send us a ninety-day note filled in for the account as it now stands. We shall return the note promptly.

Yours very [80] truly   (81)

SAMUEL THOMPSON & COMPANY

ST:AL   President

LETTER 6

as/sist/ance
busi/ness
con/di/tions

dated
dis/pose
Feb/ru/ary

in the mean/
  time
lo/cal

ma/tur/ing
rep/re/sent/a/tive
we hope that

February 17, 19—

WEBBER WALLBOARD CORPORATION, Collection Department
(Reading time: 40 sec.)   (89)

LETTER 7

after
con/clude
en/ti/tled

long
ma/tu/rity
prop/erly

ref/er/ence
scratched
value

we no/tice
your in/ten/tion

February 25, 19—

WEBBER WALLBOARD CORPORATION, Collection Department

(Reading time: 40 sec.)   **(87)**

LETTER 8

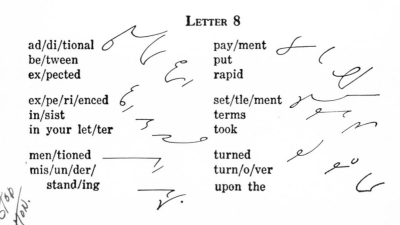

ad/di/tional	pay/ment
be/tween	put
ex/pected	rapid
ex/pe/ri/enced	set/tle/ment
in/sist	terms
in your let/ter	took
men/tioned	turned
mis/un/der/	turn/o/ver
stand/ing	upon the

March 3, 19—

Webber Wallboard Corporation
909 Clifton Street
Boise, Idaho

Gentlemen

It was our intention not to pay interest on the note mentioned in your letter of February [20] 25. Of course, we want to do the fair thing; but we feel that we should be put to no additional expense [40] in the settlement of this account.

The misunderstanding in terms was between you and your representative,[60] who turned this stock over to us on the condition that we might pay for it when we sold it. It is true that [80] we expected a much more rapid turnover than we have experienced, but we took the same chance that you took.[100]

We hope you will not insist upon the payment of this interest.

Yours very truly   (116)

SAMUEL THOMPSON & COMPANY

ST:AL   President

LETTER 9

ad/dresses	names
at once	peo/ple
build/ing	po/si/tion
cir/cu/lar/ize	re/sult
con/fi/dent	some of the
con/se/quently	start
en/cour/age	sum/mer
ex/pressed	ter/ri/tory
list	use
March	within the

March 10, 19—

[shorthand outlines]

WEBBER WALLBOARD CORPORATION, Collection Department

(Reading time: 45 sec.)   (99)

PART 4. BUSINESS PRACTICES

Directions. Practice the vocabulary preview until you can write the outlines smoothly and easily. Then make two shorthand copies of the article "Care of the Typewriter."

Vocabulary Preview

ap/plies
as far as pos/si/ble
as/signed

back and forth
both
brush

car/riage
cleaned
cloth

com/mon
con/di/tion
cor/rect/ing

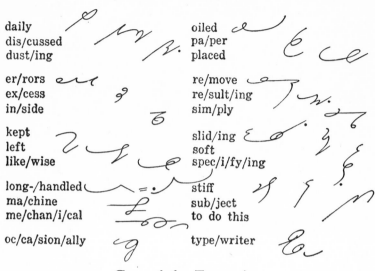

daily
dis/cussed
dust/ing

er/rors
ex/cess
in/side

kept
left
like/wise

long-/handled
ma/chine
me/chan/i/cal

oc/ca/sion/ally

oiled
pa/per
placed

re/move
re/sult/ing
sim/ply

slid/ing
soft
spec/i/fy/ing

stiff
sub/ject
to do this

type/writer

Care of the Typewriter

Unfortunately, not every office stenographer has the privilege of specifying the make or [20] quality of typewriter she
is to use in the office. This applies likewise to the student
stenographer.[40] Both have, however, one common duty;
that is, to keep the machine assigned to them in the best
possible [60] mechanical condition. This means that the machine should be cleaned daily and oiled regularly.

The cleaning of [80] the typewriter includes dusting with
a soft cloth, cleaning the type with a stiff brush, and occasionally cleaning [100] inside the typewriter by means of a
long-handled brush. The typewriter should be kept free of
pieces of eraser [120] and bits of paper resulting from erasing. (The subject of erasing and correcting errors is discussed [140] in another lesson.)

The proper oiling of the typewriter requires simply the
oiling of the carriage [160] rails. To do this, the typist should
move the carriage as far as possible to the right, then place
a drop of oil to [180] the left of the carriage on the carriage
rail or rails. The carriage should then be moved as far as
possible to the [200] left, and a little oil placed to the right
of the carriage on the carriage rail or rails. After sliding
the carriage [220] back and forth a few times, the typist

should remove with a cloth any excess oil collecting at the ends of the [240] carriage rails.

When not in use, the typewriter should be kept covered. Good work can best be done through the use of good tools.[260]

(260)

PART 5. PROGRESS CHECKUP

Directions. The following letter will give you practice in writing shorthand without a vocabulary preview. All the words in the letter have been used in the material of this and the preceding dictation study. Refer to the general vocabulary beginning on page 617 for any outline about which you are doubtful.

LETTER PC-2

Webber Wallboard Corporation
909 Clifton Street
Boise, Idaho

Gentlemen

When your representative was in our territory, he induced us to overstock with Webber [20] wallboard by giving us the privilege of paying for the wallboard after selling it. Of course, we had expected [40] a more rapid sale than we have had, but that is a chance we both took.

If we could have sold this stock promptly, we [60] could have made a settlement of our account with you. As we are still overstocked with Webber wallboard and it is [80] moving very slowly, we cannot settle the account at the present time. We are willing to sign a note in [100] the amount of $285.35, payable in 90 days without interest.[120]

We hope that you will agree to this offer.

                    Yours very truly   (132)

                    SAMUEL THOMPSON & COMPANY

ST:AL   President

DICTATION STUDY III

PART 1. BASIC SKILLS

Theory Review

Directions. Read the following blend words until you can read them with ease. Use the key if you need it. Then write each word at least once, and give special attention to any word that you cannot write smoothly and without hesitation. All these words are used in the shorthand plate that follows. Make the TEM-DEM blend decidedly longer than the TEN-DEN blend.

The TEN-DEN Blend

Key: intentions, unfortunately, continued, between, circumstance, distance, standards, attained, maintained, sustained, captain, student, tendency, attendant, evident

The TEM-DEM Blend

Key: sometimes, temporary, attempt, tomorrow, victim, item, ultimate, estimate, random, medium, seldom, wisdom

29

Directions. Read the following shorthand plate until you can read it at the rate of from 125 to 150 words a minute. A satisfactory reading time is indicated at the end of the article. Make two shorthand copies of it—one for accuracy of outline, and one for speed and ease of writing. This article contains all of the foregoing blend words. How well do you know your shorthand theory? The numbers 3 and 4 appearing above some of the commas refer to the punctuation pointers explained on page 31.

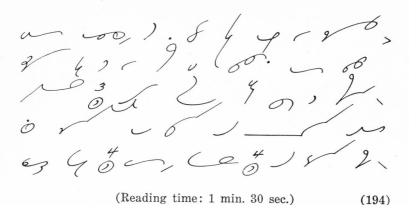

(Reading time: 1 min. 30 sec.) (194)

Punctuation Pointers

The following punctuation pointers and those of previous lessons explain the uses of the commas in the foregoing article. The number placed over a comma refers to the particular punctuation pointer involved in this study.

3. The *comma* is used between clauses connected by the co-ordinate conjunctions *and, but, or,* etc. No comma is used if the sentence contains only one subject.

This isn't so simple as it sounds, but our business is to sell shingles.

A great deal of thought seems to have been given to this drawing, and I shall probably adopt some of the ideas.

We can ship the goods on the 10th, or we can hold them until the 25th.

We had hoped to pay this bill in full and regret that we cannot do so at this time.

4. The *comma* is used to separate words or groups of words arranged in a series. Careful writers use the comma before *and* or *or* when such a conjunction precedes the last element of the series.

Our advertising department, sales department, and art department co-operate to build sales.

I needed a tube of cream, a bottle of lotion, and a box of talcum.

He rushed around the corner, into the store, and up to the counter.

He expected his employees to be on time, to remain on the job, to render efficient service.

This work could be done by our filing clerk, by our billing machine operator, or by one of our stenographers.

PART 2. BUSINESS INFORMATION

Directions. In practicing the following vocabulary preview, give special attention to those outlines that you cannot write smoothly and easily. When you feel sure of your ability to handle the words in the list, make two shorthand copies of the article "National Advertising."

Vocabulary Preview

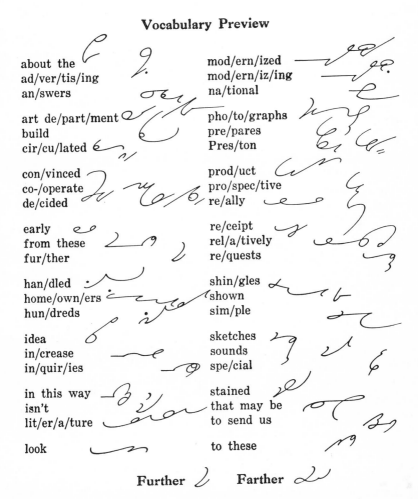

about the
ad/ver/tis/ing
an/swers

art de/part/ment
build
cir/cu/lated

con/vinced
co-/operate
de/cided

early
from these
fur/ther

han/dled
home/own/ers
hun/dreds

idea
in/crease
in/quir/ies

in this way
isn't
lit/er/a/ture

look

mod/ern/ized
mod/ern/iz/ing
na/tional

pho/to/graphs
pre/pares
Pres/ton

prod/uct
pro/spec/tive
re/ally

re/ceipt
rel/a/tively
re/quests

shin/gles
shown
sim/ple

sketches
sounds
spe/cial

stained
that may be
to send us

to these

Further   **Farther**

Further refers to theoretical distance, time, quantity, or degree.

We shall be glad to give further consideration to your request.

Farther refers usually to actual distance.

Philadelphia is farther from Washington than from New York.

National Advertising

The Preston modernizing idea makes it possible for homeowners to make over their old homes at [20] relatively little cost by simply applying Preston stained shingles over the old siding. This isn't quite so [40] simple as it sounds, but our business is to sell Preston shingles.

National advertising brings, through the daily [60] mail, hundreds of requests for further information about the Preston idea. Our answers to these requests [80] encourage homeowners to send us photographs of their homes. In return, our art department prepares from these [100] photographs sketches showing what the same houses would look like if they were modernized with Preston shingles. In this way [120] our advertising department, sales department, and art department co-operate to build Preston sales.

Of course,[140] not all inquiries result in sales. We follow up these leads, however, until we are convinced that the prospective [160] customer has really decided not to buy; then we either drop his name or place it on our general [180] mailing list for the receipt of any special literature that may be circulated from time to time.[200]

Much of the early correspondence resulting from our national advertising is handled through the medium [220] of form letters; but personal letters must follow the increase of interest shown by some of the homeowners [240] who inquired about our product.   (246)

PART 3. BUSINESS CORRESPONDENCE

between

PRESTON STAINED SHINGLE COMPANY   MR. CHARLES W. SAVAGE
177 National Street   *and*   123 Cameron Avenue
Buffalo 5, New York   Duluth 13, Minnesota

123 Cameron Avenue
Duluth 13, Minnesota
September 26, 19--

Preston Stained Shingle Company
177 National Street
Buffalo 5, New York

Gentlemen:

In answer to a recent request for information
about Preston shingles, I received a booklet and a
form letter inviting me to send you one or two
photographs of my home. You suggested that you
might prepare some sketches to show improvements
that would be made possible by the use of stained
shingles.

The enclosed photograph, unfortunately, does
not show the entire front of the house; but it may
give you all necessary information. The roof is a
hip roof, pitching all four ways. The entire front
of the second story is a sleeping porch. The main
roof of the house covers the porch on the same line
as the cornice shown in the picture.

I am planning to shingle this house either this
fall or next spring and should like all the information you can let me have.

Yours very truly,

Charles W. Savage

Charles W. Savage

Enclosure

MODEL 3—MODIFIED BLOCK PERSONAL BUSINESS LETTER

This style of arrangement may be used for letters of application and for
other personal business letters. The indented style of arrangement
is also acceptable.

Directions. In the following correspondence the letters printed in shorthand are outgoing letters, and those printed in full form are incoming letters. Practice the vocabulary preview of each letter before making two shorthand copies of the letter. Complete each letter before proceeding to the next. Always read the shorthand plates before copying them. Never be satisfied with your reading until you reach a reading rate of from 125 to 150 words a minute. A satisfactory reading time is given at the end of each shorthand letter.

LETTER 10

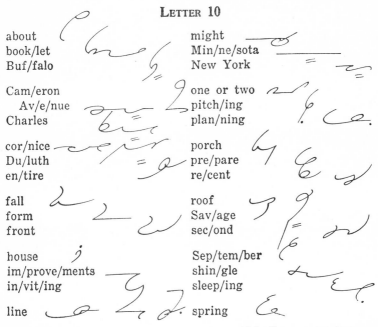

about	might
book/let	Min/ne/sota
Buf/falo	New York
Cam/eron	one or two
Av/e/nue	pitch/ing
Charles	plan/ning
cor/nice	porch
Du/luth	pre/pare
en/tire	re/cent
fall	roof
form	Sav/age
front	sec/ond
house	Sep/tem/ber
im/prove/ments	shin/gle
in/vit/ing	sleep/ing
line	spring

123 Cameron Avenue
Duluth 13, Minnesota
September 26, 19—

Preston Stained Shingle Company
177 National Street
Buffalo 5, New York

Gentlemen

In answer to a recent request for information about Preston shingles, I received a booklet [20] and a form letter inviting me to send you one or two photographs of my home. You suggested that you [40] might prepare some sketches to show improvements that would be made possible by the use of stained shingles.

The enclosed [60] photograph, unfortunately, does not show the entire front of the house; but it may give you all necessary [80] information. The roof is a hip roof, pitching all four ways. The entire front of the second story is a sleeping [100] porch. The main roof of the house covers the porch on the same line as the cornice shown in the picture.

I am planning [120] to shingle this house either this fall or next spring and should like all the information you can let me have.

Yours [140] very truly   (143)

Charles W. Savage

Enc.

LETTER 11

ap/pear/ance	out/side
at/trac/tive	paint
beauty	pleas/ure
car/pen/ter	pre/served
col/lat/eral	quote
cooler	re/al/ity
cre/ates	re/gard/ing
emer/gency	strik/ing
frac/tion	that can be
fuel	up-/to-/date
in/ex/pen/sive	warmer
in/vest/ment	we may be sure
lum/ber	we should like
mer/chant	to have
or/di/nary	win/ter

October 3, 19—

[Shorthand content]

PRESTON STAINED SHINGLE COMPANY, Wm. H. Lloyd, Sales
    Department

(Reading time: 1 min. 30 sec.)   (194)

LETTER 12

adopt	I thank you
clear	pre/vi/ous
de/sir/ous	sin/cerely
draw/ing	spent
ex/plained	thought
great deal	to have been
ideas	to make
I may have	

Adopt   Adapt   Adept

Adopt means to accept and use as one's own without
change.

If we adopt this idea, what will our indebtedness be?

Adapt means to change or to adjust in order to make
suitable.

We cannot adapt this idea to our needs.

Adept means proficient, expert.

She is exceedingly adept in high-speed shorthand writing.

123 Cameron Avenue
Duluth 13, Minnesota
October 8, 19—

Preston Stained Shingle Company
177 National Street
Buffalo 5, New York

Gentlemen

I thank you most sincerely for the effort spent in preparing the sketch showing suggested changes [20] for the

improvement of my home. A great deal of thought seems to have been given to this drawing, and I shall probably [40] adopt some of the ideas, if not all.

As I explained in my previous letter, I am very [60] desirous of having this work done this fall; but I may have to wait until next spring. I shall let you hear from me when [80] I can see my way clear to make the change.

Yours very truly　　　(91)

Charles W. Savage

LETTER 13

again		of/fice	
ap/ply/ing		re/ac/tion	
few		sid/ing	
hes/i/tate		tell/ing us	
if there is		to serve you	
it will be		to write us	
mi/nor		you can give	
Oc/to/ber			

Minor　　　　Miner

Minor means of little or less importance.

A few minor changes in your house will make a great difference in its appearance.

He plays professional baseball in one of the minor leagues.

Miner refers to a person who mines or digs for ores, coal, precious stones, etc.

A coal miner may have to go thousands of feet into the earth.

October 12, 19—

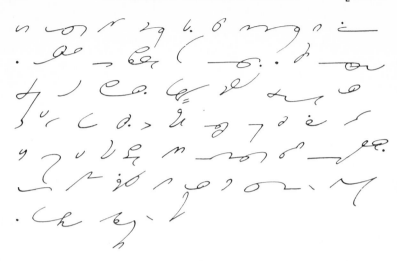

PRESTON STAINED SHINGLE COMPANY, Wm. H. Lloyd, Sales
Department

(Reading time: 40 sec.)   (96)

LETTER 14

ap/pre/ci/ate		lot	
bother		morn/ing's	
con/tent/ment		of this let/ter	
con/trib/ut/ing		owner	
doubt/less		re/marks	
en/ve/lope		re/tail	
folks		shoul/der	
fully		side walls	
hap/pi/ness		some/how	
"hom/ier"		stamped	
I am go/ing		truth	
if you could have		we have had	
last/ing		when I was	
let us know		words	
		writ/ing	

PRESTON STAINED SHINGLE COMPANY

177 NATIONAL STREET
BUFFALO 5, NEW YORK

November 12, 19--

Mr. Charles W. Savage
123 Cameron Avenue
Duluth 13, Minnesota

Dear Mr. Savage

You doubtless think that I am going to a lot of
bother in writing you all these letters about a few
stained shingles for your side walls. The truth of
the matter is that every time a homeowner modern-
izes with Preston stained shingles, we folks up here
feel that we have had a hand in contributing happiness and contentment.

If you could have looked over my shoulder half an
hour ago when I was reading the morning's mail, you
would fully appreciate what I am trying to put into
words. It means a great deal to feel that we have
had a hand in helping to make someone's home "homier"
and in helping to create a thing that will give such
lasting pleasure.

Of course, stained shingles are what you really buy
from us through your retail lumber merchant, but
somehow we have a way of thinking that what we sell
you is satisfaction.

Won't you let us know what you are planning to do?
Use the enclosed stamped envelope, and pencil your
remarks on the back of this letter.

                Yours very truly

                Wm. H. Lloyd

                Wm. H. Lloyd, Sales Department

                PRESTON STAINED SHINGLE COMPANY

WHL:DC

Enc.

**MODEL 4—MODIFIED BLOCK BUSINESS LETTER
WITH A PERSONAL SIGNATURE**
When the "I" element is stronger than the "we" element, the writer's
name frequently precedes the name of his company in the signature.

41

November 12, 19—

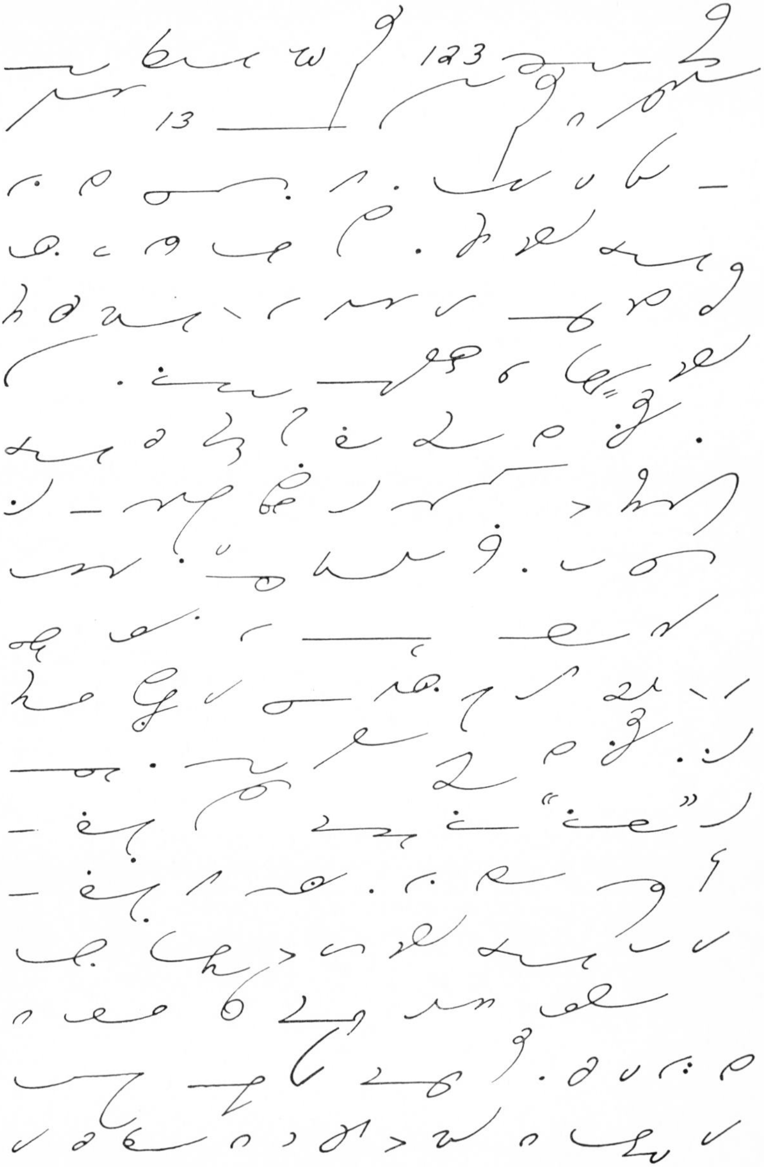

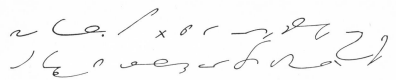

Wm. H. Lloyd, Sales Department, PRESTON STAINED SHINGLE
    COMPANY
            (Reading time: 1 min. 20 sec.)   (179)

LETTER 15

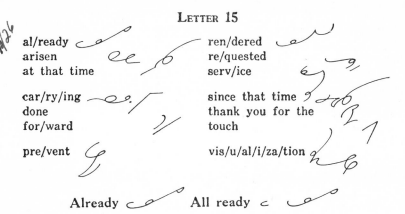

al/ready	ren/dered	
arisen	re/quested	
at that time	serv/ice	
car/ry/ing	since that time	
done	thank you for the	
for/ward	touch	
pre/vent	vis/u/al/i/za/tion	

Already   All ready

Already means prior to a particular or specified time.

They had already left when we arrived at the office.
We have already registered to vote in the next primary.
The information requested in your letter of June 10 has already been sent to you.

All ready means all prepared.

We are all ready to go.
The machines are all ready to be installed.
They were all ready for a picnic, but rain upset their plans.

                              123 Cameron Avenue
                              Duluth 13, Minnesota
                          •   November 19, 19—

Preston Stained Shingle Company
177 National Street
Buffalo 5, New York

Gentlemen

When I requested you to prepare a visualization sketch
to suggest changes for modernizing [20] my home, I fully

expected to have the work done at once; but since that time conditions have arisen [40] to prevent my carrying through these plans just now.

I am interested in Preston improvements, however, and [60] am looking forward to having the work done early next spring. At that time I shall get in touch with you again.

Thank [80] you for the service you have already rendered me.

Yours very truly   (93)

Charles W. Savage

PART 4. BUSINESS PRACTICES

Directions. Practice the vocabulary preview until you can write the outlines smoothly and easily. Then make two copies in shorthand of the article "Dating the Notebook." The business practices discussed in the various chapters will bring to your attention many ideas that will help make your stenographic work more effective. Unless your teacher instructs you to the contrary, try to apply these practices in your daily school work.

Vocabulary Preview

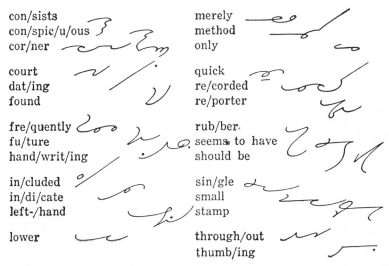

con/sists	merely
con/spic/u/ous	method
cor/ner	only
court	quick
dat/ing	re/corded
found	re/porter
fre/quently	rub/ber.
fu/ture	seems to have
hand/writ/ing	should be
in/cluded	sin/gle
in/di/cate	small
left-/hand	stamp
lower	through/out
	thumb/ing

Dating the Notebook

All notes written in shorthand should be carefully recorded under proper dates so that quick reference can be [20] made to the material in the notebook. A court reporter frequently uses one or more books for a [40] single case. An office stenographer, however, may find it necessary to use only a small part of her [60] notebook on any one day. As a result the office stenographer should have numerous dates appearing [80] throughout her book.

The dating method that seems to have preference in the office consists of placing a date in the [100] lower left-hand corner of the notebook, in conspicuous handwriting or by means of a rubber stamp. When this [120] method is used, the letters written on a single date may be found by merely thumbing the pages.

When the [140] notebook has been filled, the stenographer should indicate on the cover the dates included in the writing, and should [160] then file the notebook for possible future reference.   (170)

PART 5. PROGRESS CHECKUP

Directions. The following letter will give you practice in writing shorthand without a vocabulary preview. All the words in the letter have been used in the material of this and preceding dictation studies. Use the general vocabulary for any outline about which you are doubtful.

LETTER PC-3

Mr. Charles W. Savage
123 Cameron Avenue
Duluth 13, Minnesota

Dear Mr. Savage

We are confident that the enclosed visualization sketch will please you. The suggested [20] improvements that can be made in your home at little expense will give you a feeling of satisfaction and [40] happiness.

When a home is modernized by the Preston plan, we feel that we have helped to create a thing of lasting [60] beauty. Our morning's mail is filled with letters from homeowners who have experienced the satisfaction that [80] modernizing will give.

By simply applying Preston shingles over the old siding of your house, you can make your [100] house cooler in summer and warmer in winter. Then, too, the saving in the cost of outside paint will be a pleasure [120] to you.

Do not hesitate to write us if we can be of assistance to you in carrying out your plans [140] for the improvement of your home.

Yours very truly   (149)

PRESTON STAINED SHINGLE COMPANY

WML:DC   Sales Department
Enc.

DICTATION STUDY IV

PART 1. BASIC SKILLS

Brief-Form Review

Directions. The following article contains 60 different brief forms and brief-form derivatives. Do you know them? Read the shorthand plate until you can read at the rate of from 125 to 150 words a minute. Then make two shorthand copies to develop accuracy and fluency in your writing.

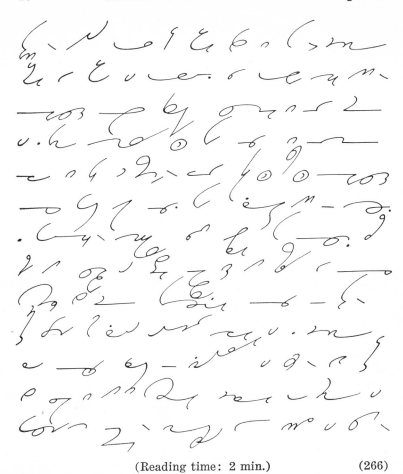

(Reading time: 2 min.)   (266)

No new punctuation pointer is given in this lesson. All the commas used in the foregoing article are explained by rules previously given. Review these rules if you don't already know them.

PART 2. BUSINESS INFORMATION

Directions. Practice the vocabulary preview, giving special attention to those outlines that you find troublesome. Then make two shorthand copies of the article "Free Goods."

Vocabulary Preview

ac/quaints	in/tro/duc/tion
at least	lim/ited
at the same time	look/out
ben/e/fits	low/er/ing
buyer	magic
by the	or/ders
cer/tainly	pack/ages
charged	per/sons
com/bi/na/tion	prices
com/pe/ti/tion	prod/ucts
con/cerned	profit
con/stantly	pub/lic
cut/ting	pur/chase
def/i/nite	sal/able
de/mand	sea/sons
dull	skin
food	spe/cials
get/ter	spe/cific
here's	stim/u/lates
in/creased	store
in/def/i/nitely	tal/cum
in/tro/duce	that will

Free Goods

Well, here's a business getter—at least, for a time. The free-goods plan certainly brings in orders during dull seasons [20] and has the additional advantage of helping us introduce new products to the public.

Business houses [40] are constantly on the lookout for ideas that will help them meet increasing competition. Unfortunately,[60] no one idea, however good, will work indefinitely; consequently, persons with salable [80] ideas are in demand in the business field.

Our free-goods plan is really a combination of two plans. In [100] one case we offer a definite number of free talcum packages to firms placing an order for a [120] specific number of packages. This offer is made with the idea of stocking a store with our goods and [140] cutting out competition. The buyer benefits by the increased profit or by the opportunity of [160] lowering his prices and advertising "specials."

Our second free-goods plan is concerned with the introduction of [180] Magic Skin Food, a new product. Under this plan we offer the public, through the merchant, the privilege of [200] getting one free tube of Magic Skin Food with each purchase of men's talcum. This offer stimulates the sales of men's [220] talcum and, at the same time, acquaints the public with the benefits of Magic Skin Food. This plan runs for a limited [240] time only, and the cost is charged to the advertising department.   (253)

PART 3. BUSINESS CORRESPONDENCE

between

FULLER CHEMICAL COMPANY		ANDREW BAKER & COMPANY
2441 Lake Street	*and*	3801 Thompson Street
Cleveland 15, Ohio		Pittsburgh 2, Pennsylvania

Directions. Once again we have a set of two-way letters. The incoming letters are printed in full form, and the outgoing letters are presented in shorthand plates. Proceed with these letters as previously instructed. Always complete all the work on one letter before beginning the next.

LETTER 16

al/low/ance	chem/i/cal
al/low/ing	dis/trict
An/drew	dozen
ar/ti/cles	equiv/a/lent
asked	fea/ture
Baker	free of charge
bo/rated	Fuller
bring	gross
buy/ers	larger

man/ager

mer/chan/dis/ing

Penn/syl/va/nia

Pitts/burgh

prop/o/si/tion

smaller

stand/ard

tube

un/able

un/doubt/edly

units

you will be

July 8, 19—

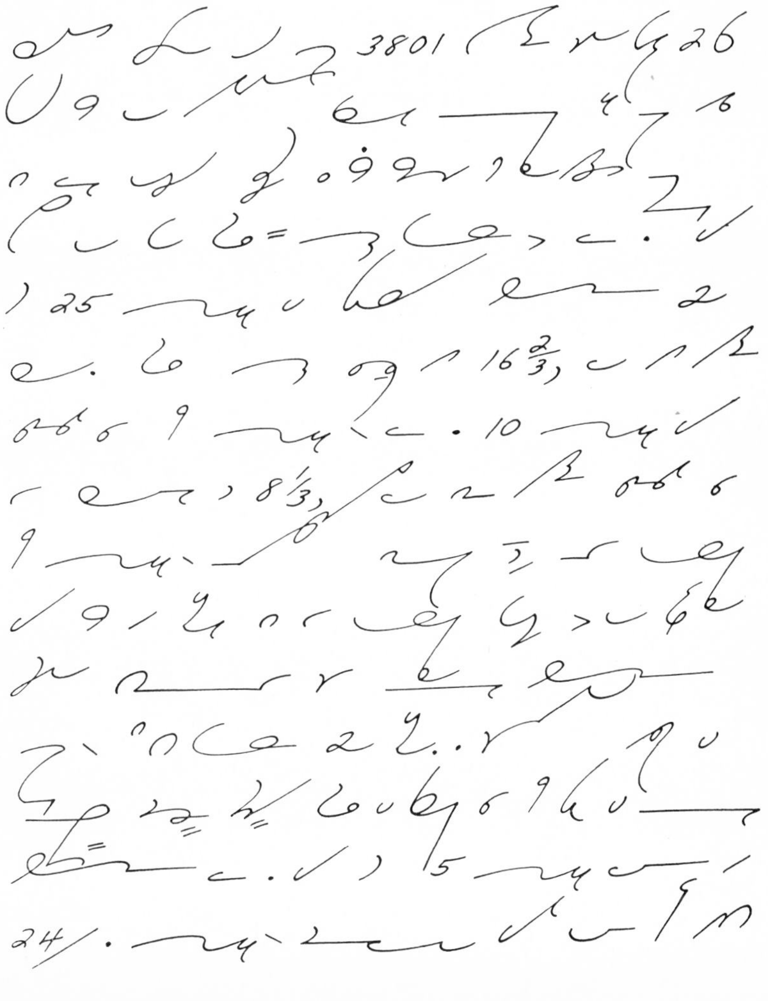

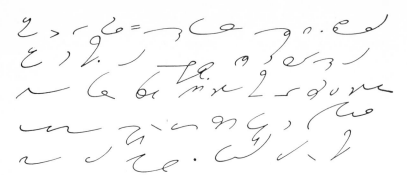

FULLER CHEMICAL COMPANY, Sales Department
(Reading time: 1 min. 30 sec.)   (207)

LETTER 17

ahead		fel/low	
can/not be		has not yet been	
ex/pi/ra/tion		over/looked	

July 15, 19—

FULLER CHEMICAL COMPANY, Sales Department
(Reading time: 40 sec.)   (88)

LETTER 18

ap/ply		hold/ing	
as well as		July	
Au/gust		ma/te/rial	
Cleve/land		Ohio	
de/liv/ery		out/lined	
en/ter	...	re/main/ing	
han/dle		we under/stand	

July 17, 19—

Fuller Chemical Company
2441 Lake Street
Cleveland 15, Ohio
Gentlemen

Please enter our order for forty gross of borated talcum under the free-goods plan outlined in [20] your letter of July 8. We shall be unable to handle all this material at this time and shall [40] appreciate your shipping twenty-five gross to us at once and holding the remaining fifteen gross for delivery [60] on August 15.

We understand that your free-goods offer for a twenty-five gross order will apply to [80] the fifteen gross as well as to the twenty-five gross that you are to ship now.

Yours very truly   (97)
ANDREW BAKER & COMPANY

JWJ:JC   Purchasing Agent

LETTER 19

alone		en/able	
bang		lib/erty	
be/yond		news/pa/per	
bought		sam/ple	
con/tin/u/ing		to/day	
copy		to/gether with	
		the	
counter			
dis/plays		we have taken	

July 19, 19—

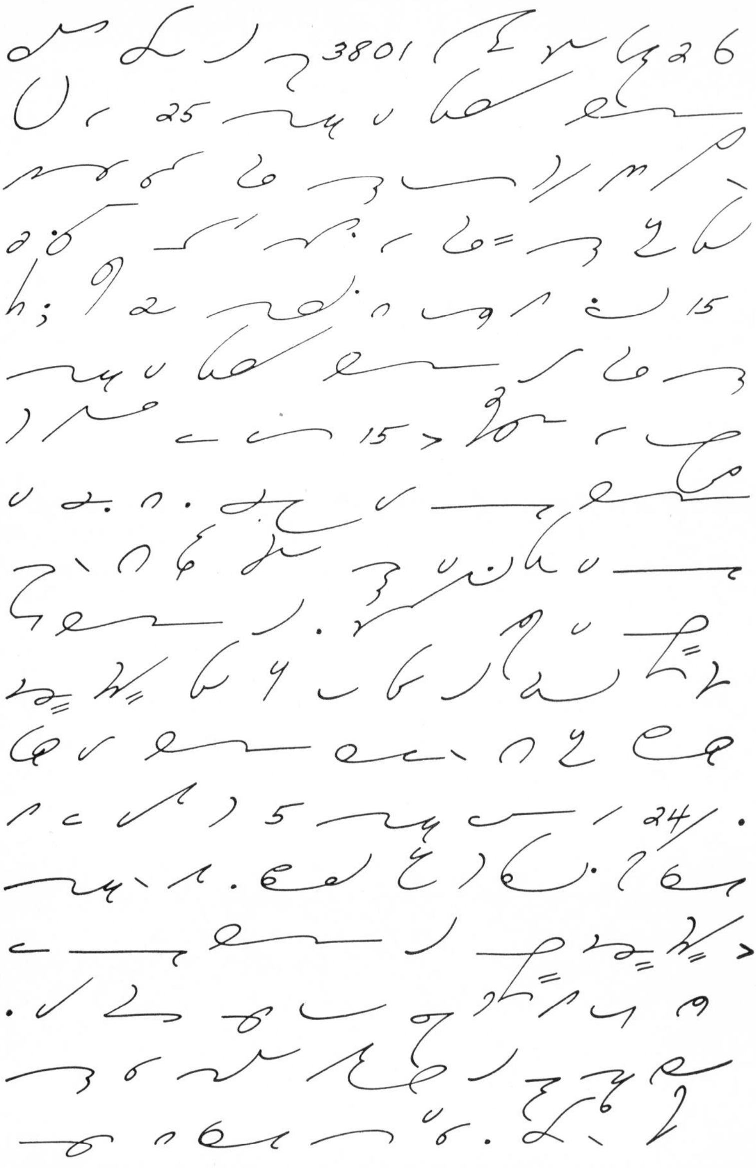

FULLER CHEMICAL COMPANY, Sales Department

(Reading time: 1 min. 20 sec.) (168)

Fuller Chemical Company

2441 LAKE STREET • CLEVELAND 15, OHIO

July 19, 19--

Andrew Baker & Company
3801 Thompson Street
Pittsburgh 2, Pennsylvania

Gentlemen

The twenty-five gross of borated talcum, together
with the free goods, will go forward to you today.
We had not intended continuing the free-goods offer
beyond July; however, we are granting your request
to hold fifteen gross of borated talcum and the free
goods for delivery on August 15.

We have taken the liberty of sending you a sample of
the men's talcum combination. This special feature
consists of a box of men's talcum and a standard tube
of Magic Skin Food, both of which are bought and sold
for the price of the talcum alone. This offer applies
to all orders for five gross or more at $24 a gross.
It is an excellent opportunity for building up sales
on men's talcum and Magic Skin Food.

An order from you now will enable us to rush these
goods with counter displays and newspaper copy that
will make your sales go over with a bang.

Yours very truly

FULLER CHEMICAL COMPANY

T. J. Cameron

Sales Department

TJC:GH

MODEL 5—FULL BLOCK LETTER

Strictly speaking, the date line in a full block letter should be typed flush
with the left margin. Such a position, however, gives an unbalanced
appearance to the letter; therefore, the position shown here is preferred.

PART 4. BUSINESS PRACTICES

Directions. Prepare the vocabulary previews and the articles "The Elastic Band" and "The Indication of Transcribed Material" as previously instructed. Unless otherwise directed by your teacher, apply these suggestions to your classwork.

Vocabulary Preview

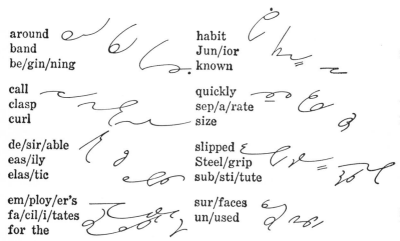

around	habit
band	Jun/ior
be/gin/ning	known
call	quickly
clasp	sep/a/rate
curl	size
de/sir/able	slipped
eas/ily	Steel/grip
elas/tic	sub/sti/tute
em/ploy/er's	sur/faces
fa/cil/i/tates	un/used
for the	

The Elastic Band

It is very desirable in shorthand work to keep the used pages separate from the unused pages so [20] that clean writing surfaces may be found quickly. This purpose may be well served by an ordinary elastic [40] band of proper size to fit easily around the notebook without causing the pages to curl. Each page that has [60] been transcribed, or at the end of the day all filled pages, should be slipped under the elastic band so that a clean [80] writing surface will be left for the beginning of the next day's work.

The habit of using an elastic band [100] facilitates the stenographer's answering promptly the employer's call for dictation. A good substitute [120] for the elastic band is a large metal clasp known as the Junior Steelgrip.

(134)

Vocabulary Preview

as many as

col/umn

di/ag/o/nally

ex/tended

help/ful

hour

in/di/ca/tion

in/ter/rupted

in the

lunch

may be given

passed

proc/ess

proves

re/sume

sim/plify

sys/tem/atic

through the

where

Passed　　　Past

Passed is the past tense and past participle form of the verb *to pass.*

Years have passed since I saw him.

I passed your office this morning, but no one seemed to be there.

The hours passed far too slowly while we waited.

Past, when used as a noun or adjective, refers to a former time.

In the past it has been our policy to declare dividends every six months.

During the past year our business has been unusually good.

Credit will be extended to you in the future as in the past.

The Indication of Transcribed Material

In the business office, where sometimes as many as fifty letters may be given in one dictation, it is [20] quite necessary for the stenographer to have a systematic method of keeping the work in her notebook.[40] In addition to dating and the use of an elastic band, another aid in this direction is the [60] indication of material that has already passed through the process of transcribing. A very simple [80] method consists in drawing a line diagonally down the column through the transcribed material. This proves [100] especially helpful when the stenographer has taken a number of letters from dictation and has had [120] her transcription interrupted by the lunch hour. The diagonal line permits the stenographer, after lunch [140] or after any other extended interruption, to resume her work promptly. A blank line between letters [160] will simplify this method.

(165)

PART 5. PROGRESS CHECKUP

Directions. All the words in the following letter have been used in this and previous dictation studies. Refer to the general vocabulary for any words about which you are doubtful.

LETTER **PC-4**

Andrew Baker & Company
3801 Thompson Street
Pittsburgh 2, Pennsylvania

Gentlemen

We are wondering why you have not yet placed your order for the various products called to your [20] attention in our letters of July 8 and 15. The men's borated talcum and the Magic Skin Food are [40] selling well this month, and you will certainly want to keep ahead of all competition.

The free-goods plan, as outlined [60] in our previous letters, should appeal to you. It offers you a good profit and an opportunity of [80] advertising special material that will bring customers to your store. This material helps to build business,[100] and you owe it to yourself to mail your order promptly. The proposition is temporary and will close [120] early in August.

Why not write us at once and place an immediate order for these attractive goods? They should [140] be in stock for summer customers.

Yours very truly   (150)

FULLER CHEMICAL COMPANY

JHH:AC   Sales Department

DICTATION STUDY V

PART 1. BASIC SKILLS

Theory Review

Directions. Read the following blend words until you can read them without hesitation. Use the key if you need it. Then write each outline at least once. Make the EMT-EMD blend considerably longer than the ENT-END blend.

The ENT-END Blend

Key: confronted, doesn't, printed, current, countless, eventually, applicant, granted, inventory, warrants, lenient, entire, shorthand, handle, hundreds, assigned, individual, planned, around, telephoned, and, render, find, point

The EMT-EMD Blend

Key: promptness, exempt, empty, seemed, blamed, dreamed, ashamed

Directions. All the foregoing blend words are used in the following article. Read the shorthand plate until you can read at least 125 words a minute. A satisfactory reading

59

time is given at the end of the article. Then make two shorthand copies of the article to develop accuracy and fluency of writing.

(Reading time: 1 min. 30 sec.)   (219)

Punctuation Pointer

In the foregoing article a figure 5 is used to indicate the beginning of each clause said to be "restrictive." Such clauses are discussed in Punctuation Pointer 5. The various commas appearing in the article are explained by punctuation pointers previously given.

5. When a relative clause cannot be omitted without materially affecting the thought of the sentence in which the clause appears, the relative clause is said to be "restrictive." A restrictive clause is *not* separated from the rest of the sentence.

The man whom I saw yesterday was here again today.
Please get me the book that you will find on the desk.
I do not know anyone who would be willing to make such a statement.
He is a man who can be trusted.
The fact that you are going makes a great deal of difference.

PART 2. BUSINESS INFORMATION

Directions. Practice the vocabulary preview until you can write the outlines rapidly and accurately. Then make two shorthand copies of the article "Borrowing Money."

Vocabulary Preview

ac/cept	at/ti/tude
ad/dressed	banks
against	be/liev/ing
agrees	bor/row/ers
ar/bi/trary	charg/ing
at/ten/tion	com/pro/mise

con/ces/sion
con/sid/ers
con/trol

de/fense
def/i/nitely
dis/ad/van/tage

dis/count
dis/lik/ing
en/ti/tle

ex/change
fact that
fa/vor/able

fi/nally
5%
great many

has been
in/sists
in/stead

in/ter/ested

in this mat/ter
just as much
mer/chan/dise

of that
Pol/lard
prin/ci/ple

pros/per/ous
re/duces
re/fuses

re/spec/tive
sac/ri/fice
sat/isfy

se/cu/rity
sem/i/per/sonal
strongly

Terry
typ/i/cal
un/fair

wish/ing

Accept   Except

Accept means to receive as a gift; to agree to; to believe.

She accepted the book with joy and expressed her appreciation.
I am willing to accept your point of view.
His theory is quite generally accepted.

Except means to leave out, to exclude; also excluding, rejecting.

All members are invited to attend, but we shall have to except those who have not paid their dues.
I was able to get all the books except one.
Everyone except the president should vote on the motion.

Principle   Principal

Principle means a fundamental truth, a basic law.

The principle of the problem was correct, but the answer was wrong.

When a man believes in a definite principle, he will sometimes defend it with his life.

Principal means chief, main; a leader or head; chief sum.

The principal speaker of the evening was an outstanding college athlete.

The principal of the school was ill for several months.

The principal in the note need not be paid at this time, but the interest should be kept up to date.

Borrowing Money

Mr. Terry and Mr. Pollard treat their correspondence in a semipersonal way, although the matter [20] definitely concerns their respective companies. When two persons know each other well, this semipersonal [40] style is sometimes used even in business correspondence. A disadvantage lies in the fact that letters addressed [60] to an individual are frequently held for that individual in case he is absent from the office.[80] A better method is to address the letter to the company for the attention of the individual.[100]

Persons who "buy" money from banks are just as much interested in getting a good price as are buyers [120] of merchandise. Most of us can do little to control the price of money, and banks appear arbitrary; but [140] in prosperous times "buyers," or borrowers, of large sums of money who have good security can borrow on [160] very favorable terms.

Mr. Pollard feels that the amount of business he has given the bank should entitle [180] his company to a lower rate or "price," and therefore suggests a discount rate of 5% instead of [200] the 5½% that the bank has been charging. The bank, wishing to satisfy a good customer,[220] reduces the discount rate to 5¼%; but Mr. Pollard, disliking what he considers a [240] compromise, refuses to accept the substitute. The bank finally agrees to the 5% rate; but Mr.[260] Pollard, believing that the bank has made the concession much against its will, now insists on the original [280] discount rate of 5½% in preference to a rate that the bank considers unfair. So, after [300] the exchange of nine letters, the matter remains as it was originally set.

Mr. Pollard's attitude [320] in this matter is typical of that of a great many businessmen who believe strongly in some principle [340] and are willing to sacrifice much in the defense of that principle. No compromise or substitute will [360] satisfy such men.   (363)

PART 3. BUSINESS CORRESPONDENCE

between

MR. JAMES N. TERRY, Cashier   MR. STEWART POLLARD
Western National Bank   *and*   Pollard & Wynne, Distributors
Roswell, New Mexico   South Spring, New Mexico

Directions. Prepare the following letters according to the instructions given in the preceding dictation studies. Always complete the work on one letter before proceeding to the next. Do not forget to check your reading rate.

LETTER 20

cash/ier
cred/ited
I am aware

it seems to me
mar/ket
New Mex/ico

pro/ceeds
Ros/well
sim/i/lar

Stew/art
west/ern

January 3, 19—

Mr. James N. Terry, Cashier
Western National Bank
Roswell, New Mexico

Dear Mr. Terry

I notice that you have credited our account with the proceeds of our January 2 [20] note at 5½%. It seems to me that under present market conditions we are entitled to [40] a 5% rate. I am aware, too, that such a rate has been given on paper of a similar kind very [60] recently.

Will you give this matter your attention and let me hear from you.

Cordially yours   (77)

SP:HEG   Stewart Pollard

LETTER 21

as you know
de/tail
en/deav/ors

Ful/ton
I be/lieve
lib/er/ally

lunch/eon
marked
re/duc/tion

South Spring
wishes
Wynne

January 4, 19—

JAMES N. TERRY, Cashier

(Reading time: 50 sec.)   (125)

LETTER 22

at the ear/li/est
　pos/si/ble
　　mo/ment

care/fully
fixed

i.e. (that is)
in my opin/ion
in/vite

jus/ti/fied
pre/fer

January 5, 19—

Mr. James N. Terry, Cashier
Western National Bank
Roswell, New Mexico

Dear Mr. Terry

Thank you for your letter of January 4, which I have carefully read.

I should prefer [20] to let the matter stand according to the original discount—i.e., at $5\frac{1}{2}\%$ instead [40] of at the compromise rate of $5\frac{1}{4}\%$—for even the latter rate, in my opinion, is too [60] high. Please talk the matter over with Mr. Fulton, who you think fixed the original rate, and then let me know [80] whether you feel we are justified in our request.

It is good of you to invite me to luncheon, and it is [100] a pleasure to accept. I shall call on you at the earliest possible moment.

Cordially yours　　　(118)

SP:HEG　　　　　　Stewart Pollard

LETTER 23

agree/able
con/sid/ered
dis/cuss

granted

per/fectly
per/son/ally
spoke

to him

January 6, 19—

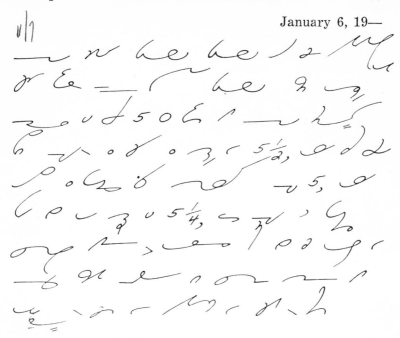

JAMES N. TERRY, Cashier
(Reading time: 40 sec.)   **(91)**

LETTER 24

ac/corded		for many years	
any/thing		low/est	
ar/gu/ment		ques/tion	
en/gage/ment		war/rants	

January 10, 19—

Mr. James N. Terry, Cashier
Western National Bank
Roswell, New Mexico

Dear Mr. Terry

My absence from the office has delayed an answer to your letter of January 6.[20]

Please do not feel that I am demanding anything to which we are not entitled. I have felt confident for [40] many years that our business with you warrants the lowest market rate and that such should be accorded us without [60] question. I certainly do not wish to believe that the rate on every note is a matter for argument.[80]

I am still hoping to keep that luncheon engagement.

Cordially yours　　　(92)

SP:HEG　　　　　　　　Stewart Pollard

LETTER 25

amount	nei/ther
cir/cum/stances	never
closed	on our books
deems	par/tic/u/lar
eq/ui/ta/ble	press
I do not wish	pre/sume
in/ci/dent	re/ferred

February 3, 19—

Mr. James N. Terry, Cashier
Western National Bank
Roswell, New Mexico

Dear Mr. Terry

In checking over the statement of our company, I found credited to our account the [20] sum of $10.20, which I presume is the amount referred to in your letter of January [40] 4 —that is, the amount resulting from a reduction of 1/4% from the 5 1/2% discount [60] charged on our note of January 2.

In my letter of January 5 I wrote that I should prefer,[80] under the circumstances, to have the rate remain at 5 1/2% ; but you asked me in your letter [100] of January 6 to let the matter rest until we had a chance to talk it over.

I still feel that [120] neither 5 1/2% nor 5 1/4% was an equitable rate at the time. I shall, therefore,[140] appreciate your charging to our account the $10.20, as we have never credited it on [160] our books. Then let us consider that particular incident closed, for I do not wish to press a request that [180] your bank deems unfair—and I hate compromises.

                                 Cordially yours   (191)

SP:HEG   Stewart Pollard

LETTER 26

agree with you	of/ten	
ap/pro/ba/tion	pleas/ant	
as/sure you	re/la/tions	
con/cur/ring	re/lieved	
ex/ist/ing	stigma	
hon/est	views	
mem/o/ran/dum		

February 5, 19—

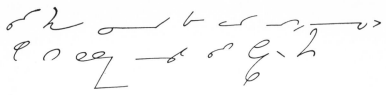

JAMES N. TERRY, Cashier
                    (Reading time: 50 sec.)   (125)

LETTER 27

af/fect		learned
con/sci/en/tiously		mine
dif/fer/ent		re/al/iz/ing
en/joy		re/in/state
gen/er/ous		some/thing

Affect   Effect

Affect means to influence; to feign or to pretend.

Climate often affects one's health.
Your attitude will not affect our pleasant relations.

Effect means intent; result; fact; goods or possessions
(in the plural) ; to bring about or to accomplish.

Mr. Hampson said that he would handle all the details, or
something to that effect.
What effect will this plan have on the success of our
business?
Will your suggestion effect a definite saving in our operating costs?

February 6, 19—

Mr. James N. Terry, Cashier
Western National Bank
Roswell, New Mexico

Dear Mr. Terry

Your letter of February 5 seems to indicate a misunderstanding.

When I learned [20] of the rate of discount on our note of
January 2, I felt that 5½% was too much,[40] particularly
as I knew of similar paper discounted at 5%. I therefore

wrote you my views,[60] realizing, of course, that the bank might have ideas different from mine.

It was very good of you to offer [80] the ¼% reduction some time ago, and generous of you to make a further reduction now. I [100] should much prefer, however, to have your bank reinstate the original rate, as I cannot conscientiously [120] accept something to which your organization feels I am not entitled.

I can assure you that this [140] incident will not in any way affect the pleasant relations we enjoy with one another.

Cordially yours [160]   (160)

SP:HEG   Stewart Pollard

Letter 28

ad/just   ob/li/ga/tion
de/tailed   rec/ords (n.)
en/try   run/ning

February 7, 19—

James N. Terry, Cashier

(Reading time: 35 sec.)   (81)

PART 4. BUSINESS PRACTICES

Directions. Part 4 is omitted from this dictation study because of the length of the correspondence series in Part 3.

PART 5. PROGRESS CHECKUP

Directions. The following letter will give you practice in writing shorthand without a vocabulary preview. All the words have been used in this and the preceding dictation studies.

LETTER PC-5

Mr. Stewart Pollard
Pollard & Wynne, Distributors
South Spring, New Mexico

Dear Mr. Pollard

We do appreciate the business you have been giving us for so many years, and we would [20] do a great deal to prompt your continuing approbation of our business policy. That is why we desire [40] to make a concession in your discount rate. We are writing to offer you a reduction of ¼% [60] from the original rate of 5½% on your present note with us.

We know you object to a [80] compromise, and we agree with you; but this is not intended as a compromise. Rather, we are sincerely [100] desirous of meeting your views in reference to a fair discount rate.

It is suggested that you accept this [120] rate reduction on the present note and then let the matter rest until we can discuss it again when you meet [140] me for luncheon. At that time we can decide on a rate to apply to future notes.

Yours very cordially   (159)

James N. Terry
JNT:GL   Cashier

DICTATION STUDY VI

PART 1. BASIC SKILLS

Theory Review

Directions. With the aid of the key, if necessary, read the following diphthong words until you can read them easily from the shorthand outline; then write each word at least once. In writing the diphthongs, be sure to maintain the proper circle size and keep the hook deep and narrow.

The U Diphthong

Key: use, used, unit, uniform, humanity, human beings, cure, excuse, few, view, fuel, confusion, graduation, purely, peculiarly

The OW Diphthong

Key: outlines, outstanding, ounce, however, somehow, now, doubtless, undoubtedly, proudly

Directions. All the foregoing words are used in the following article. Read the shorthand plate until you can read it at the rate of 125 to 150 words a minute. Then make two shorthand copies of it—one for accuracy of outline and one for fluency of writing. There is no better way of learning to be a good writer than by conscientiously copying good notes. If you know your diphthong words, the reading and writing should be easy for you.

73

(Reading time: 2 min. 15 sec.)   (283)

No new punctuation pointer is given in this lesson. All the preceding pointers, however, have been reviewed in the foregoing article. Remember: No commas are needed with restrictive clauses.

PART 2. BUSINESS INFORMATION

Directions. After you have practiced the vocabulary preview, make two shorthand copies of the article "Credit Information." Never write shorthand carelessly.

Vocabulary Preview

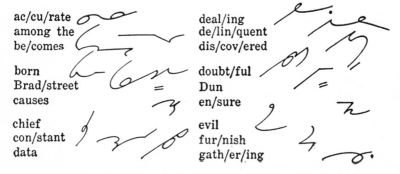

ac/cu/rate	deal/ing
among the	de/lin/quent
be/comes	dis/cov/ered
born	doubt/ful
Brad/street	Dun
causes	en/sure
chief	evil
con/stant	fur/nish
data	gath/er/ing

him/self	re/course
if the	re/li/a/bil/ity
in many cases	re/quired
in spite	re/spon/si/bil/ity
it may not be	sources
le/gal	stand/ing
le/ni/ent	sus/tained
losses	that might have
mem/bers	been
oc/ca/sional	threat/en/ing
opened	too much
op/por/tu/ni/ties	usu/ally
pa/tience	vir/tue
pro/cras/ti/na/tors	will give
rec/om/mend	

Ensure   **Insure**

Ensure means to make sure, to guarantee.

Careful packing will ensure the safe arrival of the goods.
Legal steps are often necessary to ensure the collection of money.

Insure means to give, take, or obtain insurance.

It will cost approximately three dollars a year to insure your furniture against fire.
A young man can insure his life for $1,000 at a cost of less than $30 a year.

Credit Information

It is often said that patience is a virtue, and it certainly proves to be a virtue among the members [20] of a collection department who are dealing with delinquent accounts. Too much patience sometimes becomes a business [40] evil and causes the loss of accounts that might have been collected if the collection department had been [60] a little less lenient.

Before an account is opened for a new customer, a business has recourse to [80] numerous sources of information regarding the customer's financial responsibility. If the [100] customer's business is in another city, the salesman's report may be of some value. In many cases [120] Dun & Bradstreet,

Inc., will give accurate information; and very frequently the customer [140] himself will be required to furnish satisfactory credit references. Banks are usually excellent [160] sources of information about the reliability of businesses.

In spite of the many [180] opportunities offered for the proper gathering of financial data, but because of the great desire to [200] make sales in the face of competition, salesmen recommend and business houses grant credit to customers of [220] doubtful standing. This, of course, is not the only cause for losses sustained by business houses, and it may not be [240] the chief cause; but it is one cause. Some persons, it seems, are born procrastinators; and when they are discovered,[260] constant threatening and occasional legal steps are necessary to ensure collections.   (276)

PART 3. BUSINESS CORRESPONDENCE

between

THE MONROE COMPANY, INC.		THE NELSON CORPORATION
12 Harrison Street	*and*	742 Hamilton Avenue
Indianapolis 3, Indiana		Muncie, Indiana

Directions. Unless otherwise instructed, follow in all future lessons the procedures already outlined in previous dictation studies.

LETTER 29

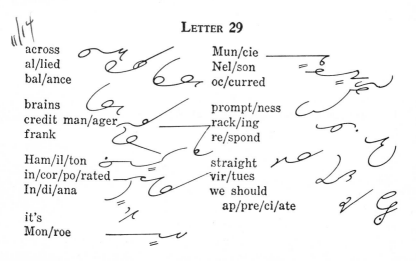

across
al/lied
bal/ance

brains
credit man/ager
frank

Ham/il/ton
in/cor/po/rated
In/di/ana

it's
Mon/roe

Mun/cie
Nel/son
oc/curred

prompt/ness
rack/ing
re/spond

straight
vir/tues
we should
ap/pre/ci/ate

It's   Its

It's is a contraction for "it is" and is written with an apostrophe both in longhand and in shorthand.

It's a good machine; you'll like it.
We know it's going to meet your needs.

Its is a possessive pronoun and is written without an apostrophe.

The book has lost its cover.
He mentioned promptness and its allied virtues.

December 8, 19—

THE MONROE COMPANY, INC., Credit Manager

(Reading time: 40 sec.)   (90)

LETTER 30

abil/ity
ap/proval
cap/i/tal

con/tinue
coun/try
De/cem/ber

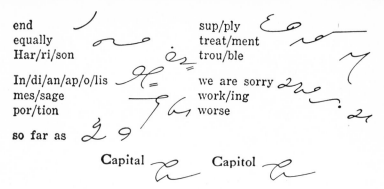

end   sup/ply

equally   treat/ment

Har/ri/son   trou/ble

In/di/an/ap/o/lis   we are sorry

mes/sage   work/ing

por/tion   worse

so far as

Capital   Capitol

Capital, as an adjective, means main, important; as a noun, it means a governing city or the value of property owned by a person or business.

This topic is of capital importance.

Washington is the capital of the United States.

The business failed because of insufficient capital.

Capitol, when written with a capital letter, usually refers to the building that houses Congress in Washington; when not capitalized, it refers to a building in which any state legislature meets.

The Capitol is one of the most beautiful buildings in Washington.

Many of the state capitols are similar to the Capitol in Washington, D. C.

December 12, 19—

The Monroe Company, Inc.

12 Harrison Street

Indianapolis 3, Indiana

Gentlemen

Your letter of December 8 certainly put your message across so far as we are concerned, and [20] we are sorry you have been put to so much trouble with our account.

Conditions in this part of the country,[40] especially in connection with collections, were never worse; and as our supply of working capital is [60] limited, our ability to meet our own obligations is naturally affected. We have always given [80] your requests for payment equally favorable treatment with others, and we shall continue to do so.[100]

We will send you a check for a good portion of this account before the end of the month. We hope this plan will meet [120] with your approval.

Yours very truly   (127)

THE NELSON CORPORATION

HJH:AW   Treasurer

LETTER 31

ac/com/mo/da/tion		ex/ten/sion	
ac/cord/ingly		files	
ac/tion		in/debt/ed/ness	
al/lot/ted		in/ten/tions	
as/sured		moved	
easy		to re/duce	
ex/pired		we have not heard	
ex/tend		whether or not	

January 9, 19—

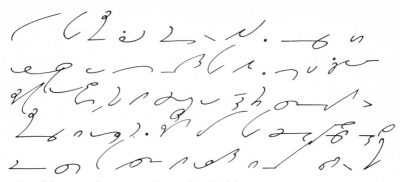

THE MONROE COMPANY, INC., Credit Manager

(Reading time: 1 min. 5 sec.)   (147)

LETTER 32

mid/dle   of this week
of next week

January 16, 19—

The Monroe Company, Inc.
12 Harrison Street
Indianapolis 3, Indiana

Gentlemen

Your letter of January 9 must have been on its way to
us when we mailed you our check for [20] $64.59, reducing
our balance to $126.

We had hoped to send [40] you another check before the
end of this week, but it appears now that we shall be unable
to make any [60] further payment until the middle of next
week.

May we request a further extension of your patience?

Yours [80] very truly   (82)

THE NELSON CORPORATION

HJH:AW   Treasurer

LETTER 33

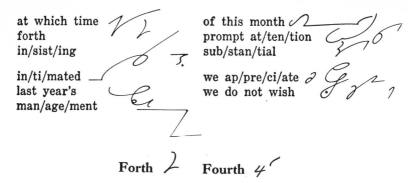

at which time
forth
in/sist/ing

in/ti/mated
last year's
man/age/ment

of this month
prompt at/ten/tion
sub/stan/tial

we ap/pre/ci/ate
we do not wish

Forth   **Fourth**

Forth means forward.

     We should put forth more effort to increase our sales.
     He stepped forth and volunteered his services.

Fourth indicates numerical position or order; as, first, second, third, fourth.

     You should receive the goods by the fourth of September.
     The first seat in the fourth row has been reserved for you.
     The Fourth National Bank is two blocks down the street.

February 4, 19—

THE MONROE COMPANY, INC., Credit Manager
(Reading time: 1 min.)   (127)

LETTER 34

at/tor/ney	passes
com/pelled	per/form/ance
co-/operation	rec/og/nize
de/serves	surely
duty	un/de/sir/able
ex/ceeded	un/less
fair/ness	un/paid
lack	un/pleas/ant
nearly	your re/mit/tance

February 19, 19—

THE MONROE COMPANY, INC., Credit Manager
(Reading time: 1 min.)   (130)

PART 4. BUSINESS PRACTICES
Vocabulary Preview

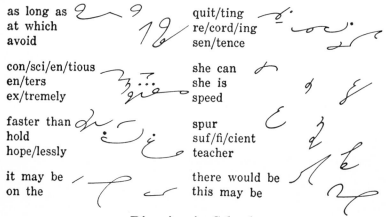

as long as	quit/ting
at which	re/cord/ing
avoid	sen/tence
con/sci/en/tious	she can
en/ters	she is
ex/tremely	speed
faster than	spur
hold	suf/fi/cient
hope/lessly	teacher
it may be	there would be
on the	this may be

Dictation in School

When a student enters the dictation class, she may find
that the dictation speed frequently becomes too fast. This [20]
may be due to the fact that the teacher is trying to give a
spur to the student's recording speed, or it may [40] be due
to the lack of sufficient practice on the particular dictation
material. In either case [60] the student should avoid the

extremely undesirable habit of putting her pencil down and quitting.[80]

Recording speed can be increased only through conscientious effort. If the teacher were to dictate no faster than [100] the student could write easily, there would be little gain in recording speed, even over a long period.[120] The writer should hold on to the dictation as long as she can. When she finds that she is getting hopelessly lost,[140] she should drop the sentence and begin again at the point at which the teacher is dictating.   (156)

Vocabulary Preview

above them	re/place
con/tin/ued	some other
dic/tion/ary	this does not
en/cir/cle	trou/ble/some
even/tu/ally	un/til
ex/ceed/ingly	un/wise
im/prove	vo/cab/u/lary
in/cor/rect	will find

Troublesome Outlines

The shorthand writer will find, as she proceeds with her work, that many of her shorthand outlines are incorrect. To [20] improve her work, she must check these incorrect outlines and, by means of assistance from others or from a [40] dictionary, replace the incorrect outlines with correct ones. This does not mean that she should erase the incorrect [60] outlines, for it is exceedingly unwise to erase shorthand written from dictation. Rather, she should encircle [80] the incorrect outlines and write the correct ones above them.

Corrections should be made during the reading of the [100] notes or at some other time when the writer has an opportunity to learn a correct form. If this practice [120] is continued, the writer will find the number of incorrect outlines becoming smaller and smaller, until [140] eventually most of the words in common use will be a definite part of her shorthand vocabulary.[160]   (160)

PART 5. PROGRESS CHECKUP

Directions. All the words in the following letter have been used in this and previous dictation studies. Therefore you will not need a vocabulary preview. If any word in the letter should bother you, the correct outline may be found by referring to the general vocabulary at the back of this book.

LETTER PC-6

The Monroe Company, Inc.
12 Harrison Street
Indianapolis 3, Indiana

Gentlemen

We are sorry that we have been unable to send you a check for the amount due you. We did expect [20] to be in position to make this payment by the first of last month; but business conditions have not been good [40] in this part of the country, and we have had trouble in collecting our own outstanding money.

We do hope that [60] you will realize that we are not holding up payment of this account purposely to avoid such payment. It [80] is our hope and intention to continue buying goods from you. We are desirous, therefore, of improving our [100] credit standing with you.

If you can see your way clear to show a little further patience with our account, we are [120] sure that we can send you a check to close the matter within a month. Won't you help us settle this account without [140] too much sacrifice for us. We shall put forth every effort to make future payments promptly.

Yours very truly   (160)

THE NELSON CORPORATION

HJH:AW   Treasurer

DICTATION STUDY VII

PART 1. BASIC SKILLS

Brief-Form Review

Directions. The following article contains 93 different brief forms and brief-form derivatives. Proceed in the usual manner.

As explained under the heading "Punctuation Pointers" on page 89, the figures 5, 6, 7, and 8 are used to explain certain punctuation practices. Do not confuse these figures with others that are a part of the subject matter of the article itself.

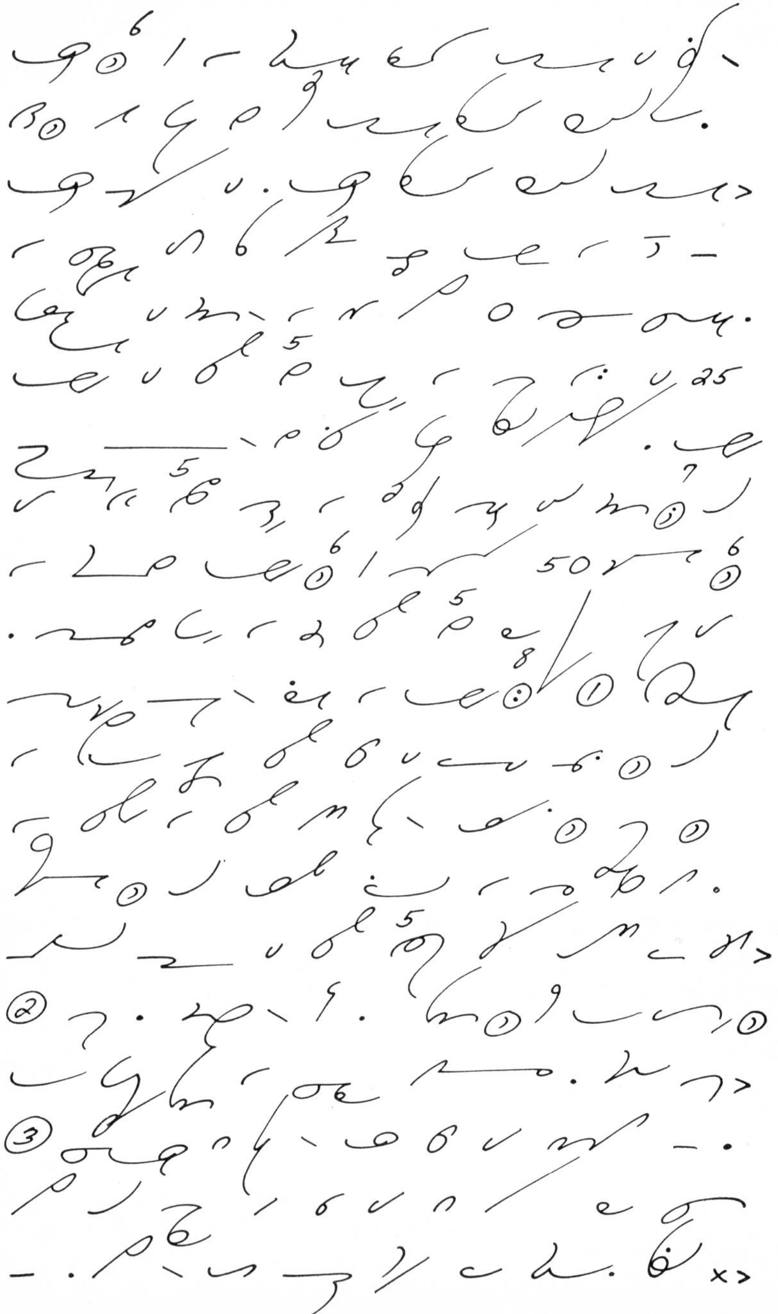

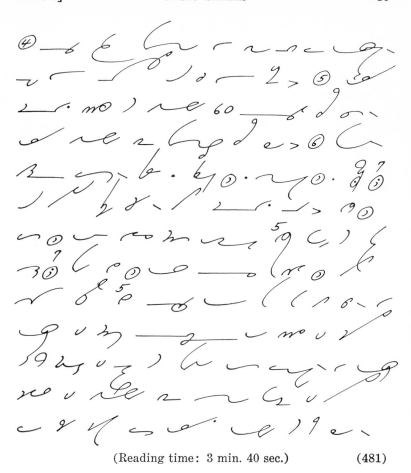

(Reading time: 3 min. 40 sec.)   (481)

Punctuation Pointers

In the foregoing article almost all the previously used pointers are reviewed, but only pointers 5, 6, 7, and 8 are marked. Pointer 5 refers to restrictive clauses, which require no commas. Pointer 6 refers to nonrestrictive clauses, for which commas are necessary.

6. The *comma* is used to separate nonrestrictive clauses from the rest of the sentence. A nonrestrictive clause may be omitted without materially affecting the thought of the sentence. (See Restrictive Clauses on page **61**.)

The Empire State Building, which is in New York City, is the tallest building in the world.

Our Main Street store, which is now having its annual sale, is open from 9.00 a.m. to 6.00 p.m.

During the week of March 30, which is the end of our fiscal year, we shall take our annual inventory.

7. The *semicolon* is used between co-ordinate clauses that contain commas.

I have been in conference with Mr. Green, who is here now; and we both agree that the plan can be used.

There is no doubt, as a result of your investigation, that the territory is well covered; but it seems to us that Clark shoes, which are our best seller, are not being given proper publicity.

8. The *colon* is used after formal introductions to quotations and to lists of items.

We quote from our letter of June 10: "All requests for payment must be submitted in duplicate."

The enclosed check is intended to cover the cost of the following items:

PART 2. BUSINESS INFORMATION

Vocabulary Preview

agen/cies
al/pha/bet
al/pha/betic

as/sume
at/tempt
bear/ing

by means of
can/ning
card

col/lec/tion
con/ven/ience
cop/ies

cred/i/tor
dic/ta/tor
du/pli/cate

ef/fec/tive
ex/pe/di/ent
fig/ures

here is
iden/ti/fi/ca/tion
in/i/tials

in/ter/preted
in which case
in which the

Jud/son
key/ing
le/gally

main/tain
man/u/fac/tur/ers
may be done

name
of these let/ters
or/gan/i/za/tions

Pa/cific
pow/ers
pro/ceed/ings

pros/e/cute   sys/tem
re/sort   third
sake   thou/sands

serv/ices   thus
sta/tion/ery   type/writ/ten
sup/pos/edly

Prosecute   Persecute

Prosecute means to sue legally; to institute legal action.

The district attorney will prosecute the case against the gangster.

The company will prosecute its competitor for infringement of copyright.

Persecute means to cause to suffer; to afflict, harass, or annoy.

In the history of the world there are numerous examples of the attempts of certain groups to persecute other groups.

Stationery   Stationary

Stationery refers to writing materials.

At a stationery store one may buy pens, pencils, writing paper, ink, rulers, and related materials.

Stationary means fixed in a certain place; unmovable; unchanging.

A stationary engine is usually fastened to a permanent base.

Economic conditions are constantly changing, never stationary.

Form Letters

Here is a real set of form collection letters that may be used in either of two ways: These letters may be [20] either multigraphed or printed by the thousands, in which case the typist need fill in only the name and the address [40] of the customer; or copies of these letters may be kept in a form-letter book, in which case the typist [60] makes full typewritten copies of the letters. The second method is more effective but less expedient.

In [80] order to avoid the sending of duplicate letters, it is very necessary to keep an accurate [100] record of the form letters sent to a customer. This is frequently done by means

of a card file in which the [120] key to a particular letter and
the date on which the letter was sent are recorded under
the customer's [140] name. The keying of the letters may be
done through the use of the alphabet or figures. An alphabetic [160] system is shown in the following:

MJ:NA   MJ:NB   MJ:NC   MJ:ND   MJ:NE [180]

In this particular system the initials (supposedly those
of the dictator and the stenographer) [200] are interpreted to
be the initials of the dictator (MJ), the identification of
the [220] particular series used (N), and the order of the letter in the series (A). Thus, a letter bearing the [240] initials
"MJ:NC" may be the third letter in a collection series (N)
signed by Marshall Judson.

As [260] a last step before legal proceedings, many business
organizations resort to the services of [280] collection agencies
in the attempt to close out old accounts. These collection
agencies have no special legal [300] powers, but they may
prosecute legally at the request of the creditor. For the
sake of convenience and [320] because of the high rate charged
by some collection agencies, many large business houses
maintain their own [340] collection agencies. These agencies
assume special names and have special stationery. The
Manufacturers [360] Collection Agency is in reality one department of the Pacific Canning Corporation.   (379)

PART 3. BUSINESS CORRESPONDENCE

between

PACIFIC CANNING CORPORATION   MESSRS. SPAIN & WEEKS
2532 Morgan Street   *and*   453 High Street
Portland 4, Oregon   Salem, Oregon

and

MANUFACTURERS COLLECTION AGENCY
888 Pullman Building
Portland 2, Oregon

LETTER 35

bear in mind 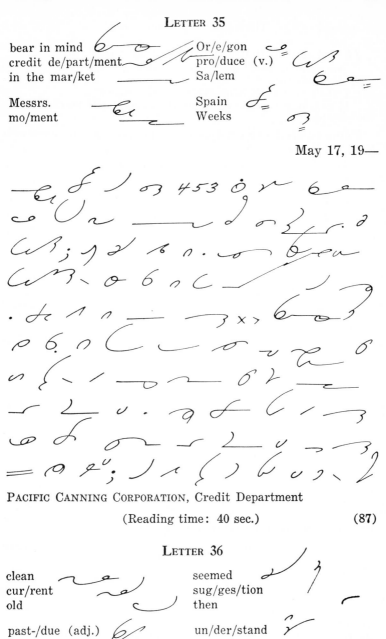   Or/e/gon
credit de/part/ment   pro/duce (v.)
in the mar/ket   Sa/lem

Messrs.   Spain
mo/ment   Weeks

May 17, 19—

PACIFIC CANNING CORPORATION, Credit Department

(Reading time: 40 sec.)   (87)

LETTER 36

clean   seemed
cur/rent   sug/ges/tion
old   then

past-/due (adj.)   un/der/stand

Then   ⌐   Than   ⌐

Then means at that time; next; in that case; accordingly.

The accident could not have happened at four o'clock. I was in the office then.

I shall go to the bank; then, to the meeting.

If you have been on vacation, then you should be in the best of health.

Than is used after adjectives and adverbs in comparison; it also expresses choice.

This is more easily planned than executed.

I would rather go than stay.

This, more than any other factor, brought the matter to a climax.

May 30, 19—

PACIFIC CANNING CORPORATION, Credit Department

(Reading time: 40 sec.)   (84)

LETTER 37

agency

draft

law/yers

prompted

June 12, 19—

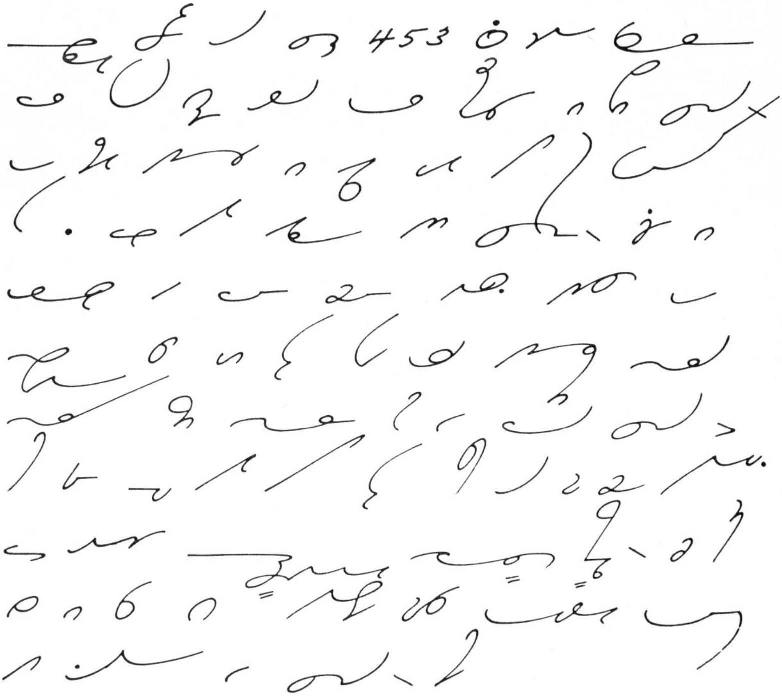

Pacific Canning Corporation, Credit Department

(Reading time: 50 sec.) (108)

Letter 38

cli/ent
con/trary
em/bar/rass

en/ter/tain
in/structs
no/tify

our/selves
please under/stand
rea/son

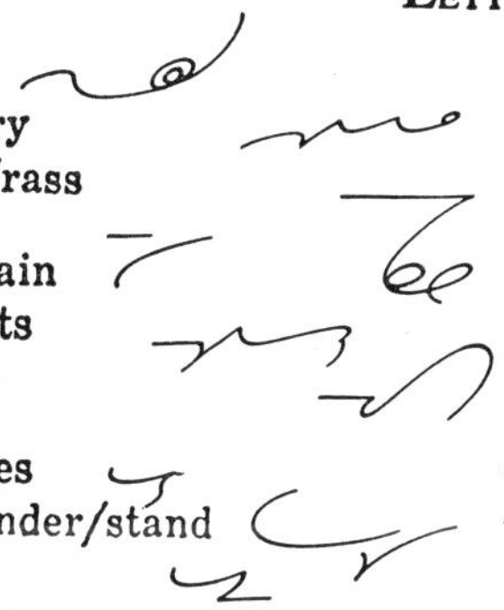

reg/is/tered
steps
tend/ing

to/gether
to pre/clude
to pro/tect

valid
will/ing/ness

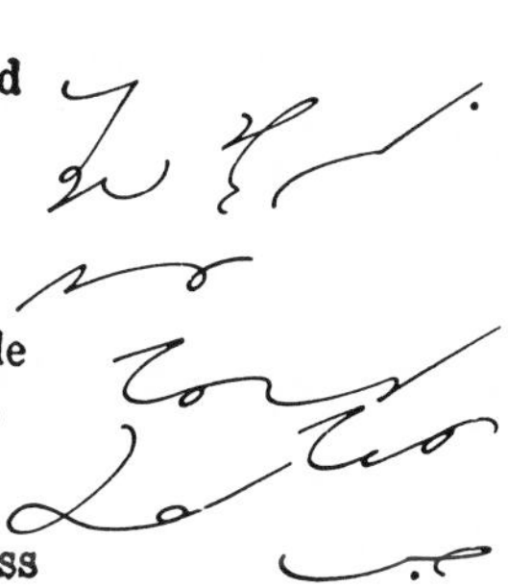

June 15, 19—

MANUFACTURERS COLLECTION AGENCY, Robert Green, Manager
(Reading time: 1 min. 10 sec.)   (150)

PART 4. BUSINESS PRACTICES

Vocabulary Preview

ac/cus/tomed
be/fore they
break

clearly
cor/rectly
dis/tract

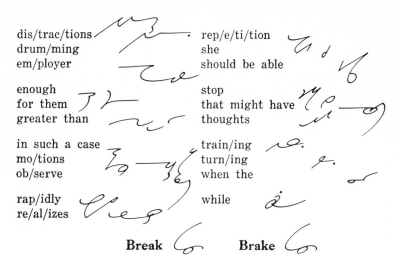

dis/trac/tions
drum/ming
em/ployer

enough
for them
greater than

in such a case
mo/tions
ob/serve

rap/idly
re/al/izes

rep/e/ti/tion
she
should be able

stop
that might have
thoughts

train/ing
turn/ing
when the

while

Break   Brake

Break means to interrupt; to separate suddenly into two or more parts. (There are other meanings too numerous to mention here.)

A stenographer should avoid doing anything that might break the dictator's line of thought.

Some pencil points seem to break very easily.

Brake refers to a device for slowing or stopping motion.

Modern automobiles have a brake on each wheel.

Office Dictation

Until the stenographer becomes accustomed to the work of a particular business, the dictation may [20] occasionally be given at a rate greater than that at which she can write. Of course, if she has had sufficient [40] training, she should be able to keep up with any dictation given in the office. The desire to write [60] rapidly, however, does not help much when the stenographer realizes that the dictator is speaking [80] at far too great a rate. In such a case she should stop the dictator before he has gone far enough to make a [100] repetition of the material necessary.

Although much of the responsibility for the proper [120] recording of dictated material rests with the dictator, the stenographer, too, has her [140] responsibilities and she should observe them carefully. While the employer is in the act of collecting his thoughts,[160] the stenographer should avoid drumming on the desk, turning pages, or making other motions that might have a [180] tendency to distract his attention. Good dictators plan a whole letter before they start the dictation; and [200] these little distractions often break their line of thought, making it difficult for them to dictate either correctly [220] or clearly.   (223)

Vocabulary Preview

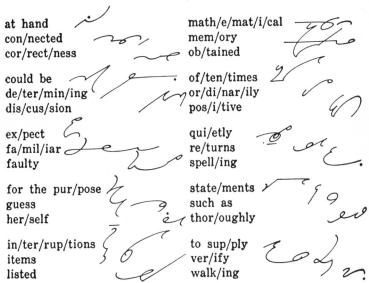

at hand	math/e/mat/i/cal
con/nected	mem/ory
cor/rect/ness	ob/tained
could be	of/ten/times
de/ter/min/ing	or/di/nar/ily
dis/cus/sion	pos/i/tive
ex/pect	qui/etly
fa/mil/iar	re/turns
faulty	spell/ing
for the pur/pose	state/ments
guess	such as
her/self	thor/oughly
in/ter/rup/tions	to sup/ply
items	ver/ify
listed	walk/ing

Office Dictation (Concluded)

During interruptions in the dictation, the stenographer should sit quietly at the desk and wait until [20] her dictator returns to the material at hand. Unless she has been instructed to go on with some other [40] work, she can use this time in reviewing her notes, correcting faulty outlines, or making herself thoroughly [60] familiar with the subject under discussion.

During the dictation the stenographer should not interrupt [80] the dictator for the purpose of getting the correct spelling of a name or the correct amount expressed by [100]

During a pause in the dictation, the stenographer should sit quietly at the desk until her dictator returns to the material at hand. If an interruption is extended, the time may be used for the insertion of punctuation and the correction of notes.

some particular figures. Such information may well be obtained at the close of the letter. The dictionary [120] should be used for determining the proper spelling of words.

The stenographer should not expect her employer [140] to be a walking store of information. Her own interest in and attention to the business with which [160] she is connected will enable her oftentimes to supply, from memory, information that ordinarily [180] could be obtained only from reference to the files. She must never guess, however, but must be positive [200] of the correctness of any statements made in letters. She will be expected to verify any [220] mathematical calculations in letters, such as the amounts of interest or the sums of items listed.[240]　　　　　(240)

PART 5. PROGRESS CHECKUP

LETTER PC-7

Messrs. Spain and Weeks
453 High Street
Salem, Oregon

Gentlemen

If credit buying is to continue in our business, charge accounts must be kept up to date. When a [20] credit privilege is granted, we naturally make our plans to finance our own purchases.

When a customer [40] fails to pay his account, it affects our ability to pay our accounts. Such a condition would soon cause [60] us to adopt one of two policies: Either we should have to increase our prices, or we should have to put our [80] sales on a pay-as-you-go plan. We should dislike to adopt either policy. It is, therefore, of great importance [100] to you and to us that you co-operate with us by paying your debts promptly. This is good business for both [120] of us.

As you pay your current indebtedness, we supply you with new goods. Surely, you see the value of a [140] practice such as this. Now, won't you write us a check and mail it at once? Then we can ship your next order without [160] question.

Yours very truly   (164)

PACIFIC CANNING CORPORATION

RES:GL   Credit Department

DICTATION STUDY VIII

PART 1. BASIC SKILLS

Theory Review

Directions. All the words in this theory review are used in the article that follows. Read the words until you can read them easily without the aid of the key. Then write each word at least once. Give the blend a full, rich curve, and let the ends tend to curve in.

The DEF, DEV, TIF, TIVE Blend

Key: difficult, difficulty, defends, defeat, difference, indifference, division, devices, devote, devoted, developed, development, endeavors, positive, relatively, gratifying

Word Derivatives

Key: favorite, considerate, quantities, indebtedness, disappointedly, repeatedly, undoubtedly, supposedly, unexpectedly, decidedly, good-naturedly, assuredly, preparedness

101

Directions. Read the following shorthand plate and check your reading rate. Be sure to reach your goal of at least 125 words a minute. Then make two shorthand copies of the article. Always work for accuracy and speed in writing. Go from one outline to the next without a pause. Most writing time is lost between outlines.

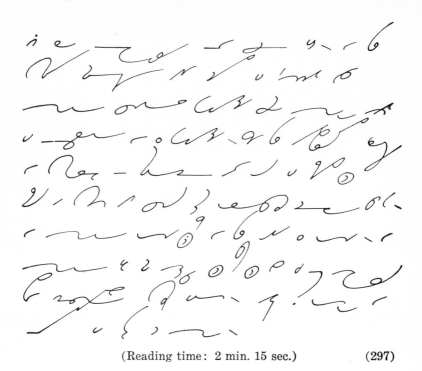

(Reading time: 2 min. 15 sec.)　　　　(297)

Punctuation Pointers

All the punctuation marks needed for the foregoing article are indicated, but only the semicolon and the comma explained in this lesson are numbered to show the pointers applied.

9. The *semicolon* is used to separate clauses of a compound sentence when no connecting word is used.

His plan worked well; he made a fortune.
He laughed heartily at the machine; it was his own invention.

10. The *comma* is used to indicate an important omission of words.

I shall go to dinner; then, to the movies.
The skilled are confident; the untrained, hesitant.

PART 2. BUSINESS INFORMATION

Directions. Always work for smoothness in your writing. Promptness in writing an outline comes from knowing your shorthand, and fluency in writing an outline comes from practicing your shorthand. Both are essential for accuracy and speed.

Vocabulary Preview

abun/dant	in/dus/try
ap/plied	in/ser/tion
be/tween the	judg/ing
book/lets	knowl/edge
cam/era	mis/cel/la/ne/ous
cat/a/logs	ob/ject
coarse	pho/to/en/grav/ing
coated	pho/to/graphed
color	pho/to/graphic
count/less	pic/tures
cov/ered	prep/a/ra/tion
cuts	qual/i/ties
de/cid/edly	re/pro/duced
de/scrip/tive	re/pro/duc/tion
dots	screen
draw/ings	sizes
es/tab/lish/ments	square inch
ex/am/i/na/tion	styles
finer	trans/fer/ring
fin/ished	type/set/ting
flood/ing	vis/its
half tone	vol/umes
hor/i/zon/tal	worker

Coarse   Course

Coarse means inferior in quality or appearance; harsh or rough; consisting of large particles.

Canvas is a coarse cloth as compared with silk.
Sand may be either coarse or fine; and so may be thread.
He had very coarse manners and shocked many of the guests.

Course means progress; progress of time; usual order of events. *Of course* means naturally.

In the course of business, many problems arise.
In the course of a year, you should expect such changes.
Events followed in due or proper course.
Of course, such action will affect our whole policy.

Printing Information

Some knowledge of printing is decidedly helpful, if not necessary, to business people today. Judging [20] from the countless catalogs, descriptive booklets, and miscellaneous advertising items flooding the [40] country, one might think that the average businessman spent a large part of his time in the printer's shop. Space does not [60] permit an extended discussion of this subject; and the fact is, the subject is so large that it could not be [80] covered in many volumes. The office worker can, however, find abundant use for some knowledge about the styles [100] and sizes of type; the kinds, qualities, and standard sizes of paper; the methods of printing pictures from both [120] drawings and photographs; and the different methods of typesetting. Much of this information can be obtained [140] by occasional visits to printing establishments.

Our correspondence in this series is concerned with one [160] phase of the printing industry—the preparation of color plates through the process of photoengraving.[180] Photoengraving itself is the art of transferring to metal plates, for printing purposes, a photograph or [200] a drawing. If the picture is to be reproduced in only one color, one plate is needed; but if the [220] picture is to be reproduced in several colors, one plate may be required for each color. The finished plates are [240] frequently called *cuts*.

Half tone is the name often applied to a photographic cut prepared for reproduction [260] by the insertion of a screen between the camera and the object, or picture, to be photographed. The screen [280] consists of a glass plate having a definite number of vertical and horizontal lines to the square inch.[300] If the cut is to be used for newspaper printing, a coarse screen, usually 60 screen or 80 screen, is [320] used. If the cut is to be used on coated paper, a finer screen, 120 screen or 133 ^{340} screen, is used. A close examination of printed pictures will show them to consist of numerous dots.^{360} These dots are the result of screening.   (366)

PART 3. BUSINESS CORRESPONDENCE

between

PUTNAM & SPILLMAN
3001 Greenvale Avenue   *and*
Detroit 6, Michigan

MISS GERTRUDE REYNOLDS
26 Boulevard
Pontiac 11, Michigan

Directions. Practice the vocabulary previews in the following two-way correspondence series and write each letter twice in shorthand. Complete all the work on one letter before proceeding to the next. Letter 40 is somewhat technical and should be read carefully. A complete understanding of the message in a letter will aid in making an intelligible transcript.

When writing the shorthand outline for "Detroit," be sure to notice that the first stroke is a *det* blend, not a *d*. Also notice that "Putnam" ends in *nam*, not *man*.

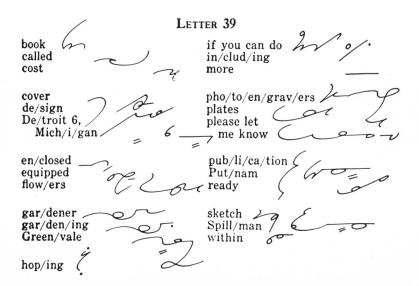

LETTER 39

book
called
cost

cover
de/sign
De/troit 6,
    Mich/i/gan

en/closed
equipped
flow/ers

gar/dener
gar/den/ing
Green/vale

hop/ing

if you can do
in/clud/ing
more

pho/to/en/grav/ers
plates
please let
me know

pub/li/ca/tion
Put/nam
ready

sketch
Spill/man
within

26 Boulevard
Pontiac 11, Michigan
June 5, 19—

Putnam & Spillman
Photoengravers
3001 Greenvale Avenue
Detroit 6, Michigan

Gentlemen

I have written for publication a book called *Flower Gardening*. I desire to make this publication [20] appeal to the home gardener through the use of an especially attractive cover. Is your company [40] equipped to make a cover design including the more common garden flowers?

If you can do this work for [60] me, please let me know how much the cost will be for the preparation of the drawing and the plates for a design [80] similar to the sketch enclosed. I shall appreciate an early answer to this letter, as I am hoping [100] to have the work completed and ready for the market within a few weeks.

Yours truly   (116)

Enc.   (Miss) Gertrude Reynolds

LETTER 40

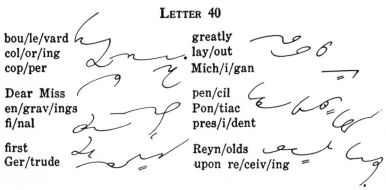

bou/le/vard	greatly
col/or/ing	lay/out
cop/per	Mich/i/gan
Dear Miss	pen/cil
en/grav/ings	Pon/tiac
fi/nal	pres/i/dent
first	Reyn/olds
Ger/trude	upon re/ceiv/ing

The outline for "Gertrude" needs careful practice, but such practice is well worth while. The use of shorthand for proper names is a sign of confidence.

June 8, 19—

PUTNAM & SPILLMAN, President

(Reading time: 1 min.)   (127)

The term "over-all size" in the foregoing letter refers to the outside dimensions of the copper plates. Note that in such a case "over-all" is written with a hyphen.

LETTER 41

best

pleases

new

pre/lim/i/nary

If you can do this work for me, please
let me know how much the cost will be for
the preparation of the drawing and the plates
for a design similar to the sketch enclosed.
I shall appreciate an early answer to this
letter, as I am hoping to have the work completed and ready for the market within a few
weeks.

Yours truly

Gertrude Reynolds

(Miss) Gertrude Reynolds

Enc.

If you can do this work for me, please
let me know how much the cost will be for
the preparation of the drawing and the plates
for a design similar to the sketch enclosed.
I shall appreciate an early answer to this
letter, as I am hoping to have the work completed and ready for the market within a few
weeks.

Yours truly

Gertrude Reynolds

(Mrs. James L. Reynolds)

Enc.

MODEL 6—SIGNATURES FOR WOMEN

Illustration A shows the type of signature that Gertrude Reynolds, a
single woman, should ordinarily use for her letters. Illustration B shows
the type of signature that Gertrude Reynolds, a married woman, should
ordinarily use for her letters. See Model 14 on page 399 for
the usual signature of a widow.

26 Boulevard
Pontiac 11, Michigan
June 10, 19—

Putnam & Spillman
Photoengravers
3001 Greenvale Avenue
Detroit 6, Michigan

Gentlemen

Enclosed is a check for $129 to cover half the cost of the drawing [20] and the plates for the cover design of my new publication on the gardening of flowers.

The idea [40] of a preliminary pencil layout pleases me greatly, as I am desirous of making this book the [60] best and most attractive job that has been done in this field.

Yours truly   (72)

Enc.   (Miss) Gertrude Reynolds

LETTER 42

as quickly as		sub/mit/ted
pos/si/ble		thank you for your
re/sults		or/der
sat/is/fied		to pro/ceed

June 12, 19—

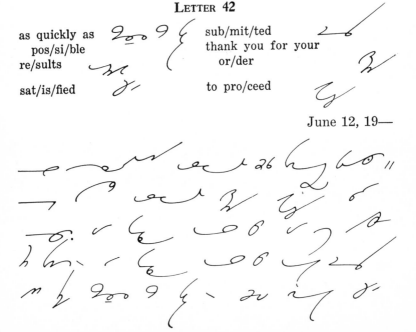

Putnam & Spillman, President
                    (Reading time: 30 sec.)   (70)

Letter 43

base
lo/ca/tion
mask

spe/cial
   de/liv/ery
tis/sue

we are mail/ing

June 16, 19—

(shorthand symbols)

Putnam & Spillman, President
                 (Reading time: 50 sec.)   (113)

Letter 44

I am sure   sat/is/fac/tory
re/turned

                              26 Boulevard
                              Pontiac 11, Michigan
                              June 18, 19—

Putnam & Spillman
Photoengravers
3001 Greenvale Avenue
Detroit 6, Michigan

Gentlemen

The pencil layout just received appears to be very satisfactory, and I am sure the [20] completed drawing will make an attractive cover.

I shall appreciate another tissue mask of the same size [40] as the plates so that I may know the name and the position of each flower.

The layout is being returned to [60] you today by special-delivery mail.

                         Yours truly   (70)

                  (Miss) Gertrude Reynolds

Letter 45

agree that this is   we shall be glad
com/ple/tion

June 23, 19—

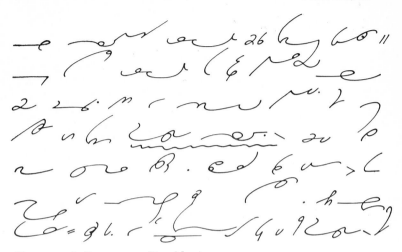

PUTNAM & SPILLMAN, President

(Reading time: 30 sec.) (68)

LETTER 46

I should like to
have
rep/re/sent

to me
work/man/ship

26 Boulevard
Pontiac 11, Michigan
June 25, 19—

Putnam & Spillman
Photoengravers
3001 Greenvale Avenue
Detroit 6, Michigan

Gentlemen

If the final plates represent the high quality of workmanship shown in the drawing, which I am [20] mailing to you today, I know I shall feel fully satisfied with my investment.

I should like to have this [40] original drawing when the plates are completed, and I hope your policy will not prevent your sending it to [60] me.

Yours truly   (63)

(Miss) Gertrude Reynolds

LETTER 47

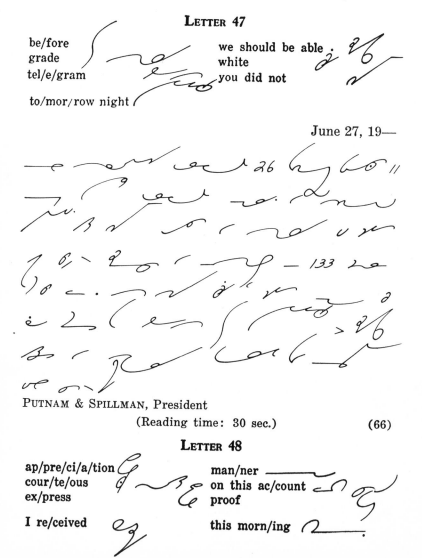

be/fore
grade
tel/e/gram
to/mor/row night

we should be able
white
you did not

June 27, 19—

PUTNAM & SPILLMAN, President

(Reading time: 30 sec.)   (66)

LETTER 48

ap/pre/ci/a/tion
cour/te/ous
ex/press

I re/ceived

man/ner
on this ac/count
proof

this morn/ing

26 Boulevard
Pontiac 11, Michigan
July 11, 19—

Putnam & Spillman
Photoengravers
3001 Greenvale Avenue
Detroit 6, Michigan

Gentlemen

I received this morning the set of three-color process engravings and the proof prepared in color [20] for the cover design of my book, *Flower Gardening.*

I am highly pleased with this work and wish to express my [40] appreciation for the courteous manner in which you have met my various requests.

Enclosed is my check [60] for $129 to cover the balance due on this account.

Yours truly   (77)

(Miss) Gertrude Reynolds

Enc.

PART 4. BUSINESS PRACTICES

This part is omitted from this dictation study because of the large number of letters in the series in Part 3.

PART 5. PROGRESS CHECKUP

LETTER PC-8

Miss Gertrude Reynolds
26 Boulevard
Pontiac 11, Michigan

Dear Miss Reynolds

We appreciate the order to go ahead with the preparation of the color plates for [20] the cover design of your book *Flower Gardening.*

We have instructed our art department to prepare a [40] pencil layout first. This layout will be submitted to you for approval. It will then be colored and submitted [60] to you again for approval before we proceed with the plates. When the plates are completed, we shall prepare a [80] color proof for you. We shall also send you a tissue mask showing the position of each flower.

When you have [100] had an opportunity to check the drawing, please indicate the grade of paper to be used for the cover [120] of the book. We can then prepare the engravings in the proper screen.

We are sure that the drawing will please you and [140] that the final preparation of the three-color process engravings will be thoroughly satisfactory.[160] It gives us much pleasure to work with you on this publication.

Yours very truly   (175)

Putnam & Spillman

President

VAF:AD

DICTATION STUDY IX

PART 1. BASIC SKILLS

Theory Review

Directions. All words in this theory review are used in the article that follows. Read the words until you can read them easily without the aid of the key. Then write each word at least once. In making the *OI* diphthong, be sure to keep the hook deep and narrow and the circle small. In the words *pile* and *child*, notice the special manner of writing the *I* diphthong.

The OI Diphthong

Key: point, avoided, boy, joy, enjoyment, to join, choice, oil, spoil, annoyances, disappointments, noises, point of view

The I Diphthong

Key: find, otherwise, worth while, derived, outside, of any kind, realize, arises, provides, ride, pile, child, open-mindedly, life

Directions. Are you watching your shorthand reading rate? Never be satisfied until you can read shorthand at a speed of at least 125 words a minute or, better still, 150 words a minute. Rapid reading aids understanding.

117

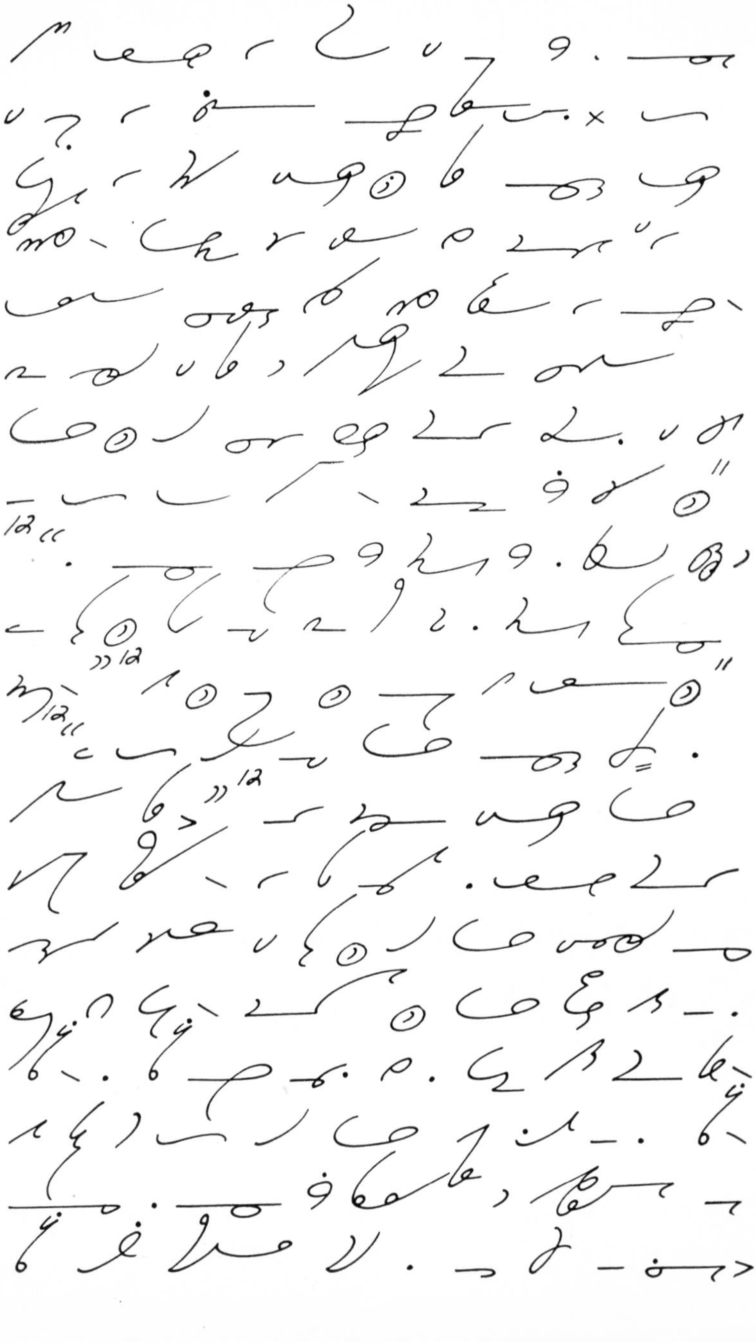

(Reading time: 2 min.)   (273)

Punctuation Pointers

All the required punctuation for the foregoing article is given, but only the punctuation marks explained in the following paragraphs are numbered to show the pointers applied.

11. The *comma* is used after an informal introduction to a quotation.

On page 2 you will find, "These prices are subject to change without notice."

Mark Twain once said, "Everybody talks about the weather, but nobody does anything about it."

We should remember, "Necessity is the mother of invention."

12. *Quotation marks* are used to indicate an exact quoting of someone's words. The capitalization in the quotation should agree with the original.

On October 16 we wired you as follows: "Not ready to order handles. Getting other prices. Writing."

"Price ceases to exist when quality is present," is an old Chinese proverb.

A man should respect his own work and should "claim for it the respect it deserves."

PART 2. BUSINESS INFORMATION

Directions. Practice the shorthand preview. Some words need less practice than others, but all should be practiced until they can be written with ease and without hesitation. Then make two shorthand copies of the article "Complaints and Adjustments."

Vocabulary Preview

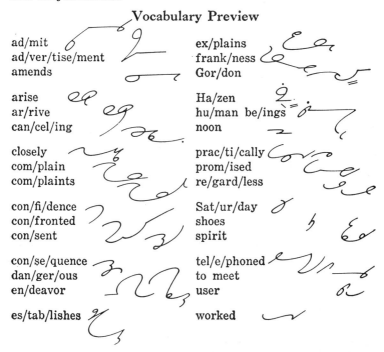

ad/mit
ad/ver/tise/ment
amends

arise
ar/rive
can/cel/ing

closely
com/plain
com/plaints

con/fi/dence
con/fronted
con/sent

con/se/quence
dan/ger/ous
en/deavor

es/tab/lishes

ex/plains
frank/ness
Gor/don

Ha/zen
hu/man be/ings
noon

prac/ti/cally
prom/ised
re/gard/less

Sat/ur/day
shoes
spirit

tel/e/phoned
to meet
user

worked

Complaints and Adjustments

Regardless of honest intention and careful attention to business, complaints arise and will continue to [20] arise as long as human beings remain human beings. In the following series we are confronted with [40] two complaints, one from a retail dealer and the other from a retail customer. Some businesses maintain that,[60] in the matter of complaints, customers are always right. These businesses feel that a satisfied customer is [80] a good advertisement. Such a policy, however, may be a dangerous one in some cases. The constant [100] attempt to meet a customer's wishes may sometimes encourage the customer to complain at every turn.[120]

Our company, the Superior Shoe Manufacturers, has one set policy for the handling of complaints: [140] We believe in a frank discussion of the situation so that we may finally arrive at a fair [160] settlement. If the fault is ours, we expect to admit it; if the fault lies with the customer, we expect him to [180] make amends. A reputation for honest dealing establishes confidence on the part of the public.

We [200] have worked closely with the Hazen Shoe Company and have given it particularly good service. As a [220] consequence its orders have shown a marked increase. On Saturday, July 12, at noon, the Hazen Company telephoned [240] about shoes promised for July 10 delivery. Our letter of July 14 explains the situation.[260] On July 16 it wrote a letter canceling the order. Our letter of the 17th was an [280] endeavor to obtain its consent to accept the shoes, which were practically ready for shipment.

The second complaint [300] arises from a misunderstanding between the Gordon Shoe Company and one of its customers. Frankness [320] and a spirit of co-operation again brought about the desired result and left a user satisfied [340] with our product.   (344)

PART 3. BUSINESS CORRESPONDENCE

between

SUPERIOR SHOE MANUFACTURERS		HAZEN SHOE COMPANY
Superior Building	*and*	1296 Springdale Avenue
Brockton 2, Massachusetts		Newark 4, New Jersey

and

MR. WILLIAM H. ANDERSON		GORDON SHOE COMPANY
121 Fourteenth Street	*and*	Congress Square
Clarion, Pennsylvania		Reading, Pennsylvania

LETTER 49

ac/cept/ance   could not be done
an/nual   fac/tory
as fast as   has been made

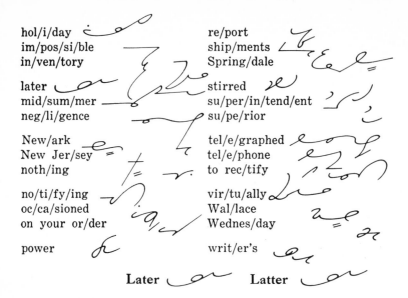

hol/i/day	re/port
im/pos/si/ble	ship/ments
in/ven/tory	Spring/dale
later	stirred
mid/sum/mer	su/per/in/tend/ent
neg/li/gence	su/pe/rior
New/ark	tel/e/graphed
New Jer/sey	tel/e/phone
noth/ing	to rec/ti/fy
no/ti/fy/ing	vir/tu/ally
oc/ca/sioned	Wal/lace
on your or/der	Wednes/day
power	writ/er's

Later   Latter

Later refers to time after a specified time. It is the comparative form of *late*.

We had dinner together; later, we went to a show.
The train arrived later than the time announced.

Latter refers to the end of a period of time; to the second of two things mentioned.

During the latter part of this month, we shall open our branch office.
The former policy is too lenient; the latter policy is too strict.

July 14, 19—

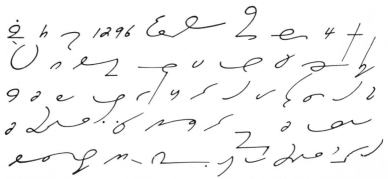

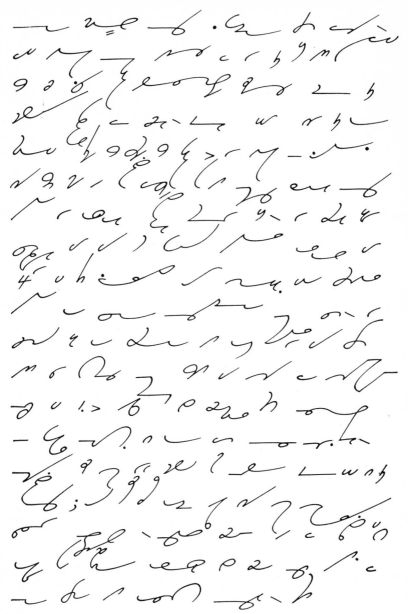

SUPERIOR SHOE MANUFACTURERS, Sales Manager
(Reading time: 2 min.)   (275)

LETTER 50

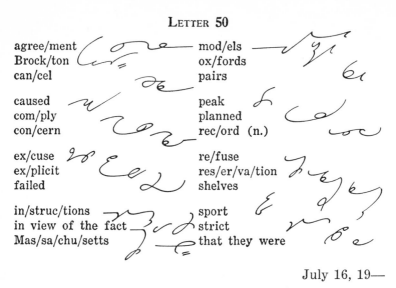

agree/ment
Brock/ton
can/cel

caused
com/ply
con/cern

ex/cuse
ex/plicit
failed

in/struc/tions
in view of the fact
Mas/sa/chu/setts

mod/els
ox/fords
pairs

peak
planned
rec/ord (n.)

re/fuse
res/er/va/tion
shelves

sport
strict
that they were

July 16, 19—

Superior Shoe Manufacturers
Superior Building
Brockton 2, Massachusetts

Gentlemen

Your letter of July 14 fully explains your position with regard to our order, but it [20] certainly does not excuse the situation. The 85 pairs of Style 2124 [40] white sport oxfords were ordered with the strict understanding that they were to be delivered by July 10. It is [60] now the 16th, and we have only two more weeks in which to dispose of our sport models.

Your failure to ship promptly [80] has caused us no little concern. We had planned and even advertised a sale of sport oxfords at [100] $5.95 a pair, and you will see from the enclosed record the ease with which we moved the shoes already on [120] our shelves. We could have sold as many more. The peak of our sale is past, however, and your shipment of our order [140] at this time would load us up with a stock that we could not sell.

Our instructions with the order were explicit; and [160] Mr. Wallace, of your factory, accepted them without reservation. In view of the fact that these shoes were [180] ordered for a definite purpose and that you failed to comply with your part of the agreement, we feel that we [200] must cancel the order and refuse the shipments.

Yours very truly (212)

HAZEN SHOE COMPANY

President

LH:AM
Enc.

LETTER 51

ac/knowl/edge		pre/paid	
dis/turbed		pret/ti/est	
earned		re/quire/ment	
ef/fi/cient		sea/son	
ev/er y/thing		suc/ceeded	
im/me/di/ate		300 per cent	
in/ter/vened		to re/lieve	
June		we hadn't	
mer/its		we have done	
of these goods		we have given you	
pock/ets		we shouldn't	
pos/si/bly		win/dow	

July 17, 19—

SUPERIOR SHOE MANUFACTURERS, Sales Manager
(Reading time: 2 min.)   (260)

LETTER 52

can be made
mu/tual
splen/did

we have de/cided
we re/gret the
you have done

July 18, 19—

Superior Shoe Manufacturers
Superior Building
Brockton 2, Massachusetts

Gentlemen

There is no question that during the past two years you have done splendid work in co-operating with [20] us. This co-operation has been of mutual advantage. Because of your prompt service in the past, however,[40] we failed to understand your delay in handling our present order.

We have decided to try your suggestion [60] of continuing our sale for another two weeks, and we shall therefore accept the sport oxfords if shipment [80] can be made immediately.

We regret the misunderstanding exceedingly, and we are hoping that the [100] results from our present sale will help us to forget it.

Yours very truly   (114)

HAZEN SHOE COMPANY

LH:AM   President

LETTER 53

An/der/son
any/where
as/cer/tain

Fri/day
I am writ/ing
man/u/fac/ture

Clar/ion
Con/gress
Flex Tred

my under/stand/ing
pro/cure
quoted

Read/ing　　　　　　　　　　Wil/liam
square　　　　　　　　　　　you may be sure
wear

July 11, 19—

SUPERIOR SHOE MANUFACTURERS, Sales Manager

(Reading time: 1 min. 10 sec.)　　　　(158)

LETTER 54

an/tic/i/pate		grades	
any/one else		in/con/ven/ience	
ap/prox/i/mately		ob/tain	
com/fort		op/er/a/tions	
de/liv/ered		re/quire/ments	
from your let/ter		re/tail/ers	

(Copy to GORDON SHOE COMPANY)

July 11, 19—

SUPERIOR SHOE MANUFACTURERS, Sales Manager
(Reading time: 1 min. 40 sec.)   (224)

LETTER 55

in ref/er/ence   thank you for your
Rear/don   your let/ter
Rob/ert

July 17, 19—

Superior Shoe Manufacturers
Superior Building
Brockton 2, Massachusetts

Attention of Mr. Robert Reardon

Gentlemen

We appreciate your letter of July 11 and the letter that you wrote to Mr. William [20] H. Anderson in reference to Flex Tred shoes.

We followed this matter up immediately and obtained [40] satisfactory results. Thank you for your co-operation.

Very truly yours   (55)

GORDON SHOE COMPANY

CNS:OW   Manager

PART 4. BUSINESS PRACTICES
Vocabulary Preview

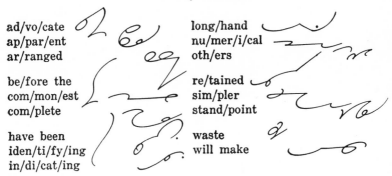

ad/vo/cate	long/hand
ap/par/ent	nu/mer/i/cal
ar/ranged	oth/ers
be/fore the	re/tained
com/mon/est	sim/pler
com/plete	stand/point
have been	waste
iden/ti/fy/ing	will make
in/di/cat/ing	

Addresses for Dictated Letters

One of the necessary evils in a business office, from a dictation standpoint, seems to be the recording [20] of addresses for dictated letters. As a result of the apparent waste of time, several methods [40] have been suggested and used by office workers.

The commonest method of recording addresses is the [60] dictated method, in which the dictator reads the full address for a letter that is to be dictated and the [80] stenographer records it in her notebook. Many writers advocate the use of longhand for the recording [100] of addresses, but the good stenographer will make every effort to record at least the simpler names and [120] addresses in shorthand. The use of shorthand for the writing of proper names and addresses has one decided [140] advantage: that of indicating the stenographer's complete confidence in her shorthand ability.

For [160] the handling of letters dictated in answer to others, the numbering method of indicating addresses [180] is an excellent substitute for the dictated method. In the numbering method the dictator numbers [200] each of the letters to be answered and the stenographer uses a similar number before the [220] recorded answer to each letter. At the end of the dictation, the original letters, arranged in numerical [240] order, are used by the stenographer as the sources of the addresses for the letters to be transcribed.[260]

A third method of indicating addresses during dictation is the use of the initials of the ²⁸⁰ person or the business addressed. These initials serve as a means of identifying the original ³⁰⁰ letter, which then becomes the source of the address. The stenographer must copy the full address from any ³²⁰ individual letter that is to be retained by the dictator or sent to another department.   (338)

PART 5. PROGRESS CHECKUP

Letter PC-9

Gordon Shoe Company
Congress Square
Reading, Pennsylvania

Gentlemen

For the past three years you have been handling Flex Tred shoes, and we are sure you have found the agency well ²⁰ worth while. We have been interested in the fact that your sales have increased 300 per cent over your first year's ⁴⁰ record. This is an excellent indication of the value of co-operation between manufacturer ⁶⁰ and merchant.

During the time you have had the Flex Tred agency in Reading, we have endeavored always to ⁸⁰ give orders from you our prompt attention, and we are confident we have succeeded. You, in turn, have been most ¹⁰⁰ reasonable in your demands, and you have shown patience in your attitude toward our attempts to meet your wishes.¹²⁰

We are mailing this letter to you now because, at the beginning of this fourth year, we want to express our ¹⁴⁰ appreciation for the pleasant relations that we are enjoying in our dealings with you. We shall continue ¹⁶⁰ to give your requests our prompt attention, and we promise you complete co-operation. We shall look forward to ¹⁸⁰ a further increase in your sales during this present year.

                    Very truly yours   (193)

                    Superior Shoe Manufacturers

RR:ET   Sales Manager

DICTATION STUDY X

PART 1. BASIC SKILLS

Brief-Form Review

Directions. The following article contains 70 different brief forms and brief-form derivatives. Many of them have been used in previous chapters, but some of them are given here for the first time. If you know your brief forms well, you will be thoroughly acquainted with approximately seven out of every ten words you meet in ordinary writing. They are therefore very important to you in your stenographic work. Read the article until you can read at the rate of at least 125 words a minute. Then make two shorthand copies, and give full attention to accuracy and speed.

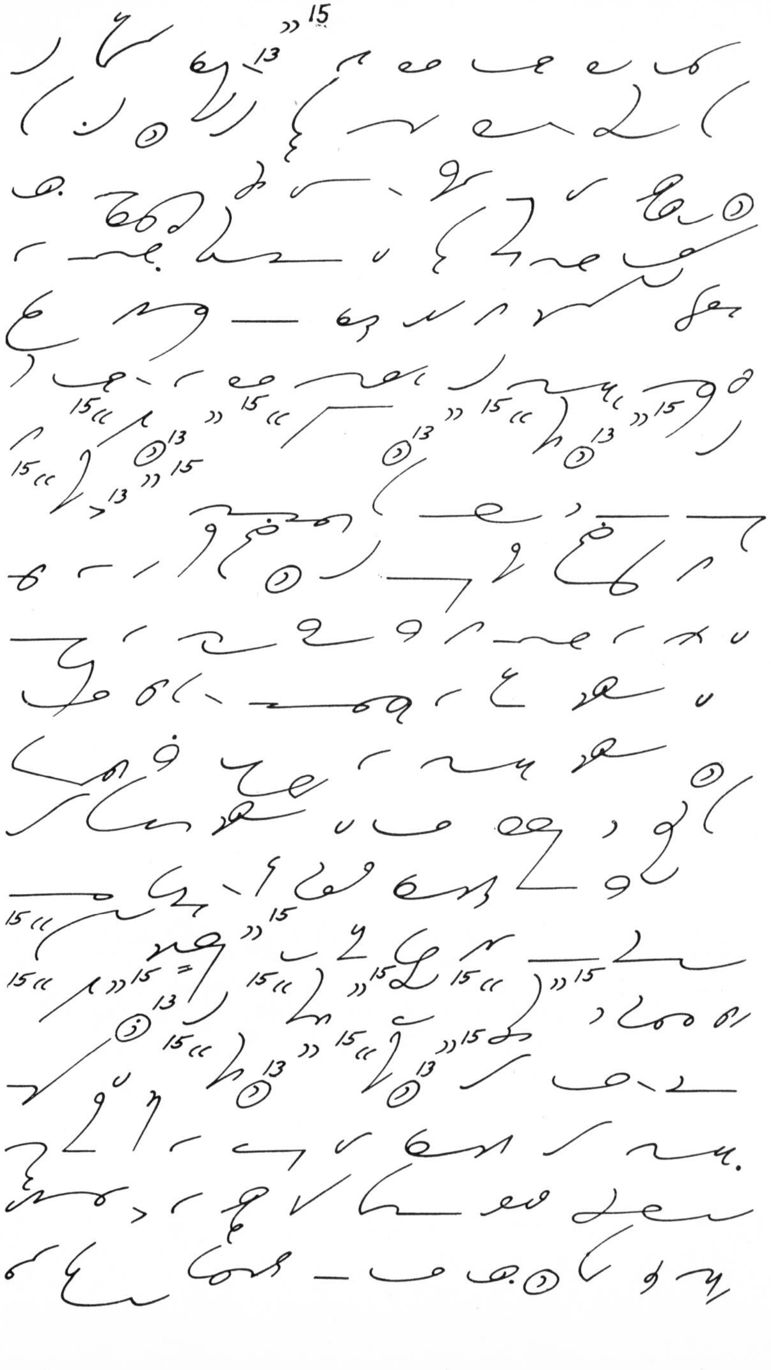

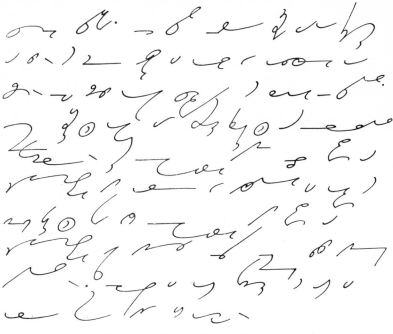

(Reading time: 3 min. 15 sec.)   (441)

Punctuation Pointers

The numbers in the foregoing article indicate the application of the following punctuation pointers. This exercise will also give you a good opportunity to review several of the pointers that have been explained in preceding dictation studies.

13. When used in combination with quotation marks, the *period* and the *comma* are always written *before* the final quotation marks. The colon and the semicolon are always written *after* the final quotation marks.

He remarked, "Enough is enough"; then he hurried from the room.
When I called him "Chief," he looked up in surprise.
Sign the letter with the firm name followed by "Sales Manager."

14. The *question mark* and the *exclamation mark* are placed inside the quotation marks if they belong to the quotation itself, and outside the quotation marks if they belong to the sentence as a whole.

He spoke to "Tiny": "Are you going?"
Did he say, "I have lived in that neighborhood for almost ten years"?
In his excitement, all he could say was "John!"
This will be the "hit of the ages"!

15. *Quotation marks* are used around words that are to be emphasized, around slang expressions, and around words that are used in some special way.

"Diphthong" is used to designate two vowel sounds combined in one syllable.

He is "behind the eight ball."

"Yours sincerely" is the proper closing for such a letter.

PART 2. BUSINESS INFORMATION

Vocabulary Preview

base/ball	meas/ur/ing	
Burns	oc/cu/py/ing	
ca/pac/ity	pool	
car/rier	pro/gresses	
de/fray	rout/ing	
di/rec/tor	San/dusky	
Eas/ton	sat/is/fac/to/rily	
five gal/lons	set/tled	
freight	shift	
Greg/ory	square feet	
higher than	stains	
hu/mor	traf/fic	
lengthy	world	

Shingles and the World Series

Well, here we are again with the Preston Stained Shingle Company. Our series is both interesting and lengthy [20]— eleven letters in all.

The Sandusky Lumber Company has written for a special price on eighteen squares [40] of shingles. (A square is 100 square feet, measuring 10 by 10.) Of course, we have one standard price and cannot [60] give one customer preference over another. When the Sandusky Lumber Company understands this, its [80] order comes through but includes a request for five gallons of green stain to be delivered without charge. This request [100] gives rise to further correspondence, but everything is finally settled satisfactorily.

As the [120] correspondence progresses, it becomes semipersonal between Mr. Frank Burns and Mr. F. E. Gregory.[140] Notice the shift from a discussion of shingles and stains to a discussion of baseball and the World Series.[160] Notice Mr. Burns's humor in the tenth letter and Mr. Gregory's reaction in the eleventh.

You [180] will find one letter dictated by Mr. Robert Easton, our traffic director. The traffic department of [200] a business is concerned with the proper routing of shipments from one point to another, the tracing of delayed [220] or lost shipments, and, frequently, the settling of claims with carriers.

When a shipment of freight fails to fill a car,[240] it is necessary for the carrier to find another shipment to help defray the expense of sending [260] the car. Consequently, the rate for such small shipments is higher than that for a shipment occupying the full [280] capacity of the car. These small shipments are known as L.C.L. (or less-than-carload) shipments; and the rate is [300] the L.C.L. rate. A car carrying such shipments is known as a pool car.   (314)

PART 3. BUSINESS CORRESPONDENCE

between

PRESTON STAINED SHINGLE COMPANY
177 National Street
Buffalo 5, New York

and

SANDUSKY LUMBER COMPANY
701 Press Building
Sandusky, Ohio

LETTER 56

com/pa/nies	please let us hear
deal/ers	from you
fig/ured	spec/i/fied
Lo/rain	talked

September 20, 19—

Preston Stained Shingle Company
177 National Street
Buffalo 5, New York

Gentlemen

We have just sold material for a job at Lorain, Ohio, which requires 18 squares of [20] 18-inch 5- to 2¼-inch green stained shingles. We have specified Preston shingles on this job and, because [40] of competition, figured them at $9 a square delivered to Lorain. Two other stained shingle companies [60] quoted this price to our Lorain manager, and their representatives talked with the owner of the house.

Our [80] manager has made it very clear to the owner that we handle only Preston shingles and will furnish no [100] other on this job. This statement, however, will hold only if you will meet the price quoted by the two other [120] dealers.

Please let us hear from you promptly.

Very truly yours   (131)

SANDUSKY LUMBER COMPANY

FEG:MM   President

LETTER 57

a hun/dred pounds	George
ad/mits	na/tion/ally
Al/len	pros/pect
ba/sis	sec/tion
cheap/ened	sit/u/ated
con/ces/sions	strictly
con/vinc/ing	to com/pete
econ/omy	to ren/der
f.o.b.	To/ledo

September 22, 19—

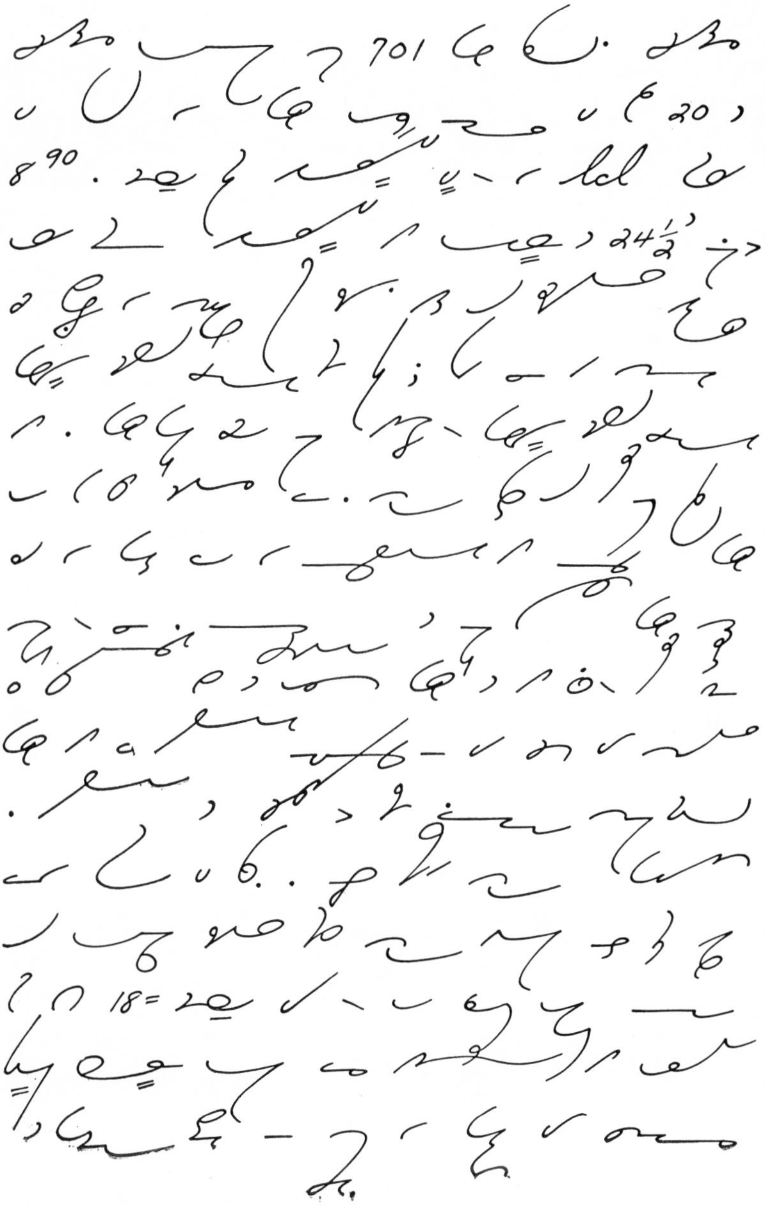

v G L . ___ ____ . __ P __

PRESTON STAINED SHINGLE COMPANY, Wm. M. Lloyd, Sales Department

(Reading time: 1 min. 45 sec.)   (239)

LETTER 58

flex/i/bil/ity
Lloyd
main/tain/ing
mis/in/ter/preted
rather than

September 24, 19—

Preston Stained Shingle Company
177 National Street
Buffalo 5, New York

Attention of Mr. Wm. M. Lloyd

Gentlemen

From your letter of the twenty-second, regarding the order for stained shingles at Lorain, it is ^{20} apparent that you have misinterpreted our letter of the twentieth.

What we meant was a cost price of ^{40} $9, f.o.b. Lorain, rather than a selling price of $9. We appreciate all you have said ^{60} regarding the quality of Preston shingles and your policy of maintaining a certain price; but we believe,^{80} under present conditions, there should be some flexibility in your selling policy.

We still feel that you ^{100} should meet a cost price of $9, f.o.b. Lorain, on the shingles referred to. If you can meet this cost price,^{120} we will use Preston shingles on the Lorain job and also on a number of others on which we are figuring ^{140} at the present time.

Yours very truly   (148)

SANDUSKY LUMBER COMPANY

FEG:MM   President

LETTER 59

apol/ogy
as low as
brands

cheer/fully
con/sist/ent
cor/rect

di/rect
fre/quent

in/clude
in/volves
Knapp

level
off/set
one of them

pool-/car (adj.)
trans/por/ta/tion

September 26, 19—

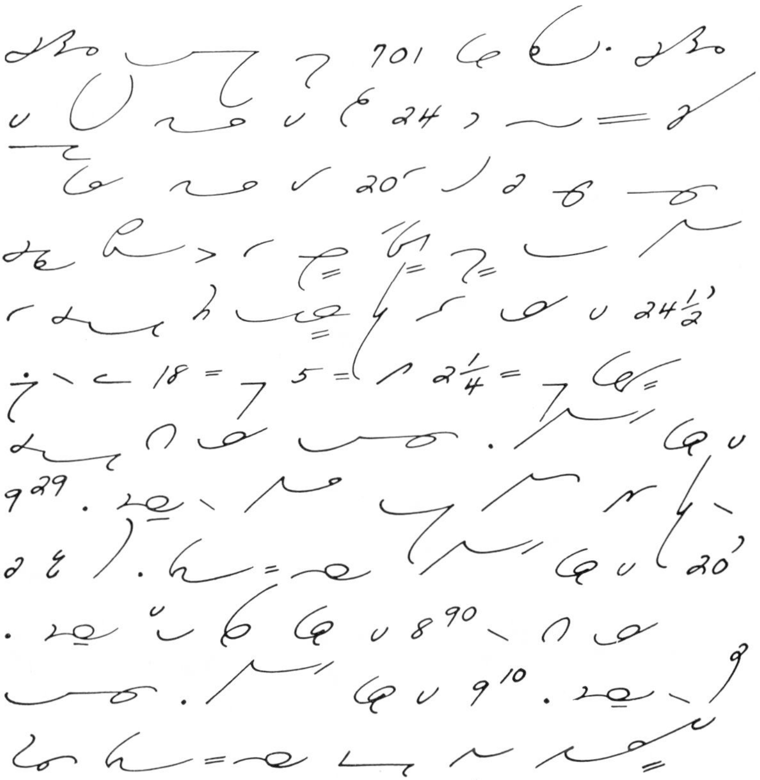

PRESTON STAINED SHINGLE COMPANY, Wm. M. Lloyd, Sales Department

(Reading time: 2 min.)   (269)

LETTER 60

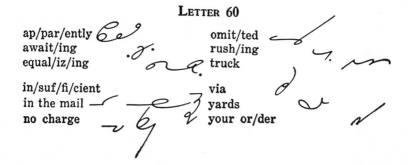

ap/par/ently	omit/ted
await/ing	rush/ing
equal/iz/ing	truck
in/suf/fi/cient	via
in the mail	yards
no charge	your or/der

September 27, 19—

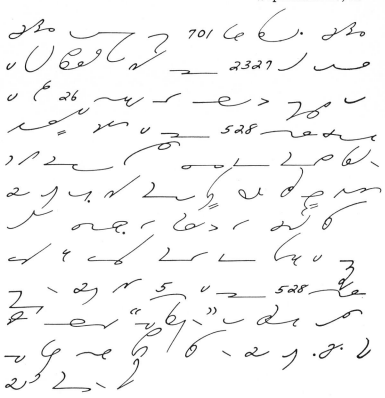

PRESTON STAINED SHINGLE COMPANY, Wm. M. Lloyd, Sales Department

(Reading time: 1 min.)   (132)

The expression "equalizing the freight" means the customer will pay on the shipment of shingles freight charges equal to those from Toledo to Lorain. Our company will pay the extra charges for the shipment from Buffalo. We do this because we are responsible for our inability to make the shipment from Toledo as we had intended.

LETTER 61

as we do not know ⟋ par/a/graph ⟋
day or two   trace

September 30, 19—

Preston Stained Shingle Company
177 National Street
Buffalo 5, New York

Gentlemen

We are entirely satisfied with the manner in which you have handled our order No.²⁰ 2327. We shall need these shingles within the next day or two and therefore ask that you trace ⁴⁰ the shipment to avoid any possible delay.

We have requested our Lorain manager to answer the ⁶⁰ last paragraph of your letter, as we do not know for what purpose this paint is intended.

Very truly yours ⁸⁰   (80)

SANDUSKY LUMBER COMPANY

FEG:MM   President

LETTER 62

ar/rived

tracer

reached

October 2, 19—

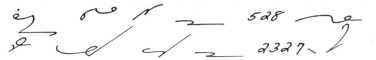

PRESTON STAINED SHINGLE COMPANY, Robert Easton, Traffic
Director
(Reading time: 40 sec.)   (88)

LETTER 63

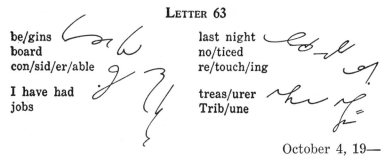

be/gins
board
con/sid/er/able

I have had
jobs

last night
no/ticed
re/touch/ing

treas/urer
Trib/une

October 4, 19—

Mr. Frank Burns, Treasurer
Preston Stained Shingle Company
177 National Street
Buffalo 5, New York

Dear Frank

I have had considerable correspondence recently about 18
squares of shingles for Lorain; [20] and I, naturally, lost in
the argument.

With this order of shingles, however, I asked for five
gallons [40] of stain to be used in retouching this job and
one or two other jobs of stained shingles. The 18-square
order [60] has been shipped and received, but for some reason or other your company refused to grant the request
for the stain [80] to be shipped without charge. Will you
please look over our correspondence with Mr. Lloyd and
do what you can to help [100] us in this matter.

Last night when I went home, I noticed that a board had
been put up in front of the Tribune Building.[120] You know
the World Series begins today.

Cordially yours   (131)

FEG:MM   F. E. Gregory

LETTER 64

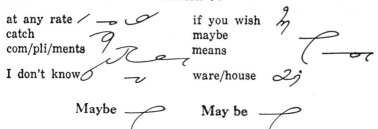

at any rate		if you wish	
catch		maybe	
com/pli/ments		means	
I don't know		ware/house	

Maybe   May be

Maybe means perhaps; it is written as one word in longhand.

Maybe we shall be able to give this matter some consideration in another week.
Maybe you can suggest a solution to this situation.
Maybe we shall get the order this week.

May be is a verb phrase; it is written as two words in longhand.

This may be the wisest step you have ever taken.
He may be right, but I doubt it.
She may be able to complete the work by that time.

October 7, 19—

Wm. M. Lloyd, Sales Department, PRESTON STAINED SHINGLE
COMPANY

(Reading time: 35 sec.)   **(83)**

LETTER 65

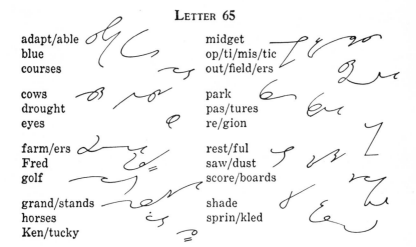

adapt/able	midget
blue	op/ti/mis/tic
courses	out/field/ers
cows	park
drought	pas/tures
eyes	re/gion
farm/ers	rest/ful
Fred	saw/dust
golf	score/boards
grand/stands	shade
horses	sprin/kled
Ken/tucky	

October 8, 19—

Frank Burns, Treasurer
        (Reading time: 1 min. 15 sec.)   (166)

Letter 66

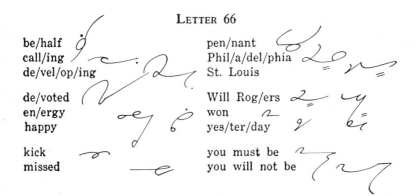

be/half		pen/nant	
call/ing		Phil/a/del/phia	
de/vel/op/ing		St. Louis	
de/voted		Will Rog/ers	
en/ergy		won	
happy		yes/ter/day	
kick		you must be	
missed		you will not be	

Missed _____ 𝑒   Mist _____ 𝑒

Missed is the past tense and the past participle of the verb *to miss.*

> He missed his train and was delayed two hours.
> She missed the old home and found it difficult to adjust herself to her new surroundings.

Mist refers to anything that dims or blurs the vision, especially a foglike atmosphere.

> The mist made driving difficult.
> The mist lifted like a veil and left his vision perfectly clear.

October 11, 19—

Mr. Frank Burns, Treasurer
Preston Stained Shingle Company
177 National Street
Buffalo 5, New York

Dear Frank

I got a great "kick" out of reading your letter of October 8. I believe you have missed your calling,[20] for surely you are developing into a second Will Rogers.

We have received the five gallons of No.[40] 528 green stain and appreciate all the time and energy you devoted in our behalf.[60] You probably thought that we had lost our usual courteous manner when we kept insisting that this stain [80] be shipped "no charge"; but we needed it—that is our only excuse.

As Philadelphia won the game yesterday,[100] you must be in a very good humor. You will not be so happy, however, when I tell you that St. Louis [120] will win the pennant. On second thought, I should say that St. Louis will win the World Series. I certainly wish you [140] and I could enjoy the games together.

Cordially yours   (150)

FEG:MM   F. E. Gregory

PART 4. BUSINESS PRACTICES

This part has been omitted from this dictation study because of the length of the letter series.

PART 5. PROGRESS CHECKUP
Letter PC-10

Preston Stained Shingle Company
177 National Street
Buffalo 5, New York

Gentlemen

For a number of years we have been buying shingles from you, and we have always found both the quality ^{20} and the service thoroughly satisfactory. The truth is that you have given most of our orders such prompt ^{40} and considerate attention that it has seldom seemed necessary to indicate the conditions under ^{60} which the shingles were to be shipped.

We appreciate the attention you have accorded our business and, for that ^{80} reason, it is difficult for us to understand why you hesitate to grant our present request for five ^{100} gallons of No. 528 green stain to be shipped without charge. This stain is requested for use on ^{120} a few jobs for which Preston shingles have been specified. It seems to us that the amount of business we have given ^{140} you should justify your granting a request of this sort.

When we have to meet competition on a job, we ^{160} sometimes figure our profit so closely as to make little allowance for any expense beyond that expected.^{180} If you can ship the stain to us free of charge, it will enable us to continue supplying Preston products ^{200} on jobs on which the profit is small.

Very truly yours　　(210)

SANDUSKY LUMBER COMPANY

FEG:MM　　　　　　President

DICTATION STUDY XI

PART 1. BASIC SKILLS

Theory Review

Directions. The blend words listed below are all used in the article that follows. Read them until you no longer need the key; then write them at least once each. In making the blend, notice that the ends tend to close in.

The JENT-JEND, PENT-PEND Blend

Key: gentle, gentleman, diligent, intelligent, pageants, sergeant, urgent, legendary, carpenter, repent, spent, cheapened, dependent, happened, impending, opened, responds, sharpened

Directions. Read the following article until you can reach your reading goal easily; then make two shorthand copies of it. Remember that speed in writing requires you to pass from one outline to another without hesitation. Accuracy in writing makes reading easy.

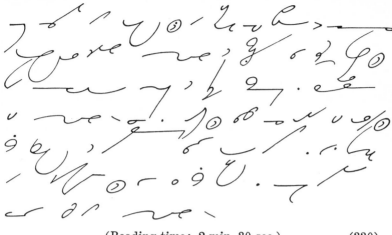

(Reading time: 2 min. 30 sec.)　　　　　　(330)

Punctuation Pointer

All medial punctuation marks required in the foregoing article have been given. Commas are not needed at points numbered 16.

16. When pairs of words or phrases appear in series, no comma is placed after the first member of the pair.

This material is available in black and white, brown and beige, and blue and rose.

". . . in all love and honor, in all duty and service, in all faith and tenderness . . ."

Greatness may exist in the financial genius and in the diligent carpenter, in the gentleman of society and in his humble servant, in the toughest sergeant and in the most timid soul.

PART 2. BUSINESS INFORMATION

Vocabulary Preview

ad/vance
af/fair
ap/pro/pri/a/tions

au/to/matic
based
by no means

com/bine
cre/ate
dealer

en/ve/lopes
ex/ten/sive
forces

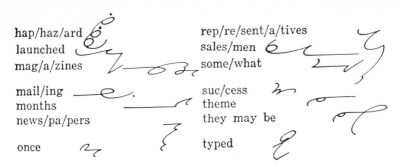

hap/haz/ard

launched

mag/a/zines

mail/ing

months

news/pa/pers

once

rep/re/sent/a/tives

sales/men

some/what

suc/cess

theme

they may be

typed

Follow-up Letters

Not all letters are written in answer to others, and not all letters are answered. In this series we have six [20] letters without a single answer. These letters are really part of an extensive advertising campaign [40] in which newspapers and magazines are used to create public demand for the goods, and letters and salesmen [60] co-operate to obtain dealer representatives.

An advertising campaign is by no means a haphazard [80] affair. It is planned in detail months in advance; and, when once launched, all forces combine to make it a complete success.[100] Some large companies make their appropriations and organize their campaigns to extend over a five-year [120] period.

If letters are to play any part in an advertising campaign, they are planned and written ahead [140] of time. The series is based on some one central theme, but each letter has its individual appeal. The method [160] of preparing the letters for mailing depends somewhat on the size of the mailing list. They may be [180] individually typed on an ordinary typewriter or on an automatic typewriter, or they may be [200] multigraphed or printed. The envelopes are usually addressed on an addressing machine. If one hundred [220] letters bring in ten inquiries and these inquiries result in one good sale, the company may well consider [240] the mail campaign a success.

Sales letters deserve all the time and attention that can be devoted to them. Both [260] the dictator and the stenographer should see that the job is well done.   (273)

PART 3. BUSINESS CORRESPONDENCE

between

GOODWIN FOUNTAIN PEN COMPANY
6824 Michigan Boulevard
Chicago 7, Illinois

and

JUDSON STATIONERY COMPANY
324 Anderson Avenue
Missoula, Montana

LETTER 67

as/sort/ment		open/ing		
broad		page		
cir/cu/lar		pen		
col/ored		plenty		
foun/tain		prin/ci/pal		
Good/win		sup/port		
guar/an/tee		town		
im/por/tant		trav/el/ing		
Mis/soula		twice		
Mon/tana		vol/ume		

October 10, 19—

GOODWIN FOUNTAIN PEN COMPANY, Sales Director

(Reading time: 2 min. 15 sec.)   (290)

GOODWIN FOUNTAIN PEN COMPANY

6824 MICHIGAN BOULEVARD • CHICAGO 7, ILLINOIS

October 10, 19--

Judson Stationery Company
324 Anderson Avenue
Missoula, Montana

Gentlemen

Our salesman who is traveling in your territory tells us that
your district is open; and, inasmuch as he will be unable to
see you at once, we are taking this method of letting you know
just what the Goodwin proposition will mean to you as a dealer:

1. You will make 22% more profit on the Goodwin pen
than on any other.

2. You will have a four-time annual stock turnover
if you are an average Goodwin dealer. One dealer in
a small town has a $3,000 annual Goodwin sales volume
on a $600 investment, and he has had it for years.

3. You will have, on the average, twice as much advertising support on Goodwin merchandise as on other
important merchandise. Goodwin page advertisements
run in the leading monthly and weekly magazines and
in more than 200 principal newspapers.

4. You will have a complete stock of quality merchandise with a broad guarantee, and plenty of merchandising helps that will start the trade coming and
keep it coming at large profits.

Your discount is 40% on an opening order of $200, and it will
remain 40% year after year if your purchases continue to
amount to $200 every year. If your annual purchases increase
to $500, your discount becomes 40-10%.

Enclosed is a colored circular showing representative numbers.
Check the assortment you desire, and return the circular to
us. We shall see that you get immediate delivery.

Very truly yours

GOODWIN FOUNTAIN PEN COMPANY

W. C. Sutherland

WCS:DL   Sales Director

Enc.

MODEL 7—MODIFIED BLOCK LETTER WITH NUMBERED PARAGRAPHS
The modified block style of letter is widely used by businesses. Numbered
paragraphs should agree with the rest of the letter in style of indention.

157

LETTER 68

ag/gres/sive
brings
Cas/per

count
down
dur/ing the past year

ex/clu/sively
for in/stance
in the past

meant
or/der blank

pains
pro/gram
pro/tects

se/lected
stores
sweep/ing

through/out the
to tie
un/e/qualed

we are pleased
Wy/o/ming

November 1, 19—

GOODWIN FOUNTAIN PEN COMPANY, Sales Director

(Reading time: 1 min. 50 sec.) (251)

LETTER 69

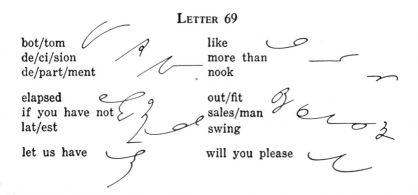

bot/tom		like	
de/ci/sion		more than	
de/part/ment		nook	
elapsed		out/fit	
if you have not		sales/man	
lat/est		swing	
let us have		will you please	

November 18, 19—

Goodwin Fountain Pen Company, Sales Director

(Reading time: 1 min. 20 sec.) (180)

LETTER 70

bona fide		iron/clad	
Christ/mas		le/git/i/mate	
climb/ing		lucky	
con/tri/bu/tions		ma/rine	
doc/u/ment		mean/while	
en/sem/ble		ob/scure	
es/tab/lish		stars	
ex/qui/site		star/tling	
glance		these will be	
in/no/va/tions		top-notch	
in/sur/ance		you'll	

December 2, 19—

GOODWIN FOUNTAIN PEN COMPANY, Sales Director
(Reading time: 1 min. 50 sec.) (246)

LETTER 71

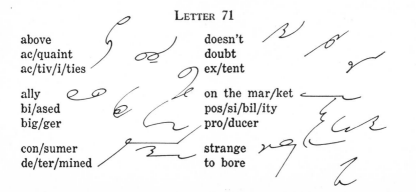

	doesn't
above	doubt
ac/quaint	ex/tent
ac/tiv/i/ties	
ally	on the mar/ket
bi/ased	pos/si/bil/ity
big/ger	pro/ducer
con/sumer	strange
de/ter/mined	to bore

December 18, 19—

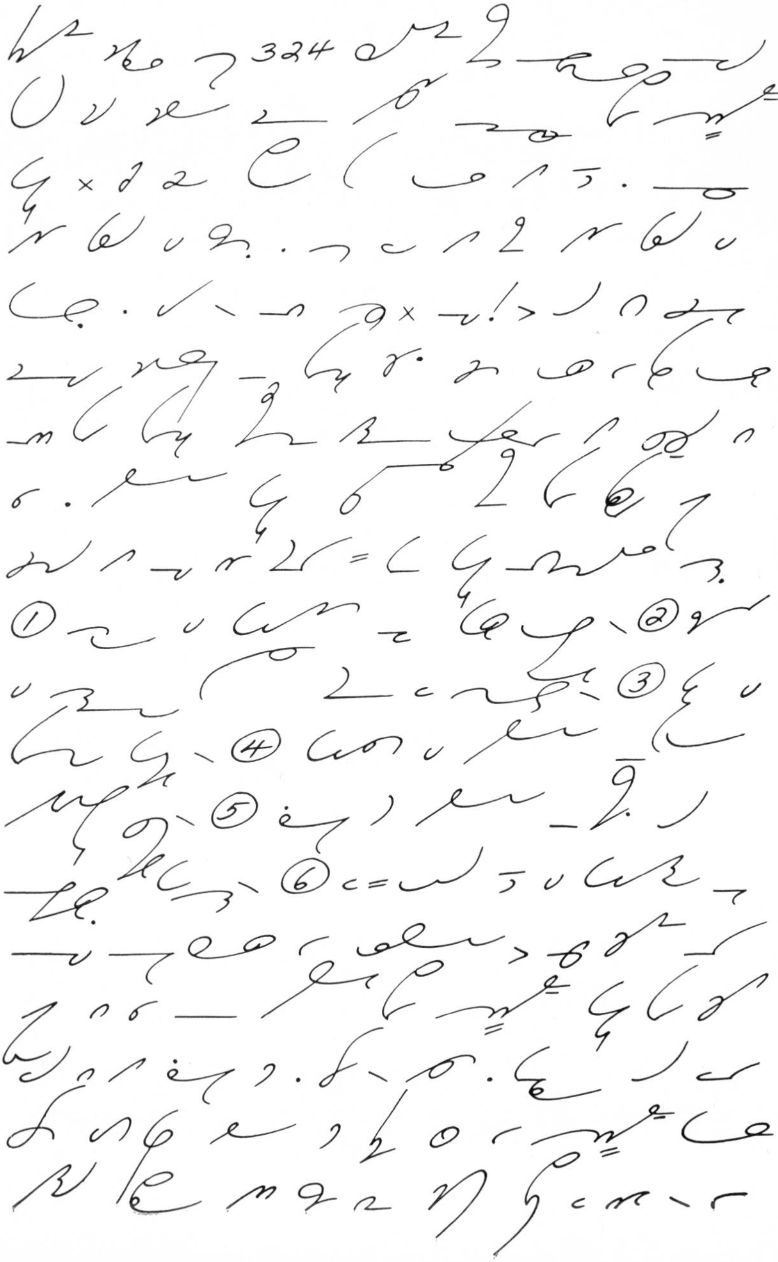

GOODWIN FOUNTAIN PEN COMPANY, Sales Director
(Reading time: 2 min.)   (259)

LETTER 72

ad/vance/ments
as/sisted
com/pet/i/tive

cre/a/tors
dis/cov/er/ing
dis/tance

dis/tinc/tive
equip/ment
fore/most

fran/chise
in/cal/cu/la/ble
in/tro/duc/ing

look/ing
pre/sented
pres/tige

pro/tec/tive
range
urge

January 10, 19—

GOODWIN FOUNTAIN PEN COMPANY, Sales Director
(Reading time: 1 min. 40 sec.)　　　(231)

PART 4. BUSINESS PRACTICES
Vocabulary Preview

ad/vis/able
an/noy/ance
at/tends

be/hind
copy/holder
cul/ti/vate

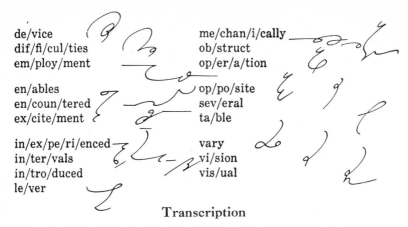

de/vice
dif/fi/cul/ties
em/ploy/ment

en/ables
en/coun/tered
ex/cite/ment

in/ex/pe/ri/enced
in/ter/vals
in/tro/duced
le/ver

me/chan/i/cally
ob/struct
op/er/a/tion

op/po/site
sev/eral
ta/ble

vary
vi/sion
vis/ual

Transcription

The first day in the business office is a very trying one for an inexperienced stenographer [20] because of the fact that a certain amount of excitement attends the obtaining of the first position. Then, too,[40] conditions in the business office vary somewhat from conditions existing in school. The student stenographer [60] will do well to cultivate systematic methods of handling her work. Such methods will carry [80] over to the business office and will help reduce the difficulties encountered in her new employment.[100]

It is advisable for the stenographer to become accustomed to transcribing with the shorthand notebook [120] placed in a definite position, the commonest of which is flat on the table at the side of the [140] typewriter opposite the carriage-return lever. This position enables the stenographer to return the carriage [160] at frequent intervals without the inconvenience or annoyance resulting from having the hand obstruct [180] the line of vision.

If the office supplies a copyholder, the stenographer will find it helpful because [200] any copyholder has a tendency to put the notebook in a more readable position.[220] Several copyholders have been introduced to indicate mechanically the particular line of notes being [240] transcribed. One such device holds the notebook in a vertical position above and behind the typewriter.[260] The operation of a lever at the front of the typewriter brings a new line of shorthand into reading [280] position. Two advantages result from the use of

Efficient transcription habits will help to reduce the excitement and the confusion that often add to the difficulties of the first days on the job.

this device: First, in case of interruption during the [300] transcription, the stenographer can return easily to the point at which the interruption occurred; second, the [320] reading line is always in the same visual position.   (328)

PART 5. PROGRESS CHECKUP

LETTER PC-11

Judson Stationery Company
324 Anderson Avenue
Missoula, Montana

Gentlemen

Some time ago we suggested that you accept our offer of the Goodwin fountain-pen franchise in [20] your territory.

We were convinced that our proposition would appeal to you, because we knew it to be the [40] best all-round proposition in the fountain-pen field. And yet we have not heard from you! For some reason, we have been [60] unable to put our message across. Won't you help us by letting us know in just what way our offer failed to [80] meet your requirements.

Goodwin fountain pens have been on the market for 16 years, and in all that time these pens have [100] retained their reputation for outstanding service to their users. Always available in attractive [120] design and color, they are in a class by themselves. There is, therefore, no important competition with other brands [140] of pens.

The Goodwin proposition offers you so many advantages that it seems to us that you should not [160] pass up this opportunity without further thought. Why not let our representative call on you to explain [180] the matter in detail? He will be in position to answer any question about the Goodwin franchise and [200] to give you the best dealer deal available in the fountain-pen business.

Very truly yours   (217)

Goodwin Fountain Pen Company

WCS:DL   Sales Director

DICTATION STUDY XII

PART 1. BASIC SKILLS

Theory Review

Directions. The letter R joins to many different letters, and each joining presents its own problem. The following words will give you practice in making some of the joinings. The special stroke for RD can be made more easily if you will start the stroke slightly downward.

Words containing R and RD

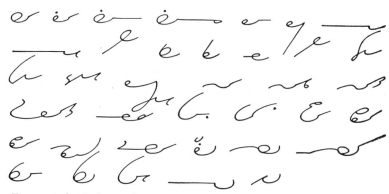

Key: art, hurt, harm, harmony, earn, urge, manner, manners, dare, share, cheer, near, dear, bitter, better, sisters, elevators, curt, curtesy (also courtesy, curtsy, and curtsey), courteous, flirtations, merit, burning, pertaining, expert, assert, exert, concerned, smart, overheard, guard, unguarded, pardon, barred, burdens, mannered, toward

Directions. Read the following article until you are sure of your reading goal; then make two shorthand copies of it. All of the words listed above are used in the article. If you know them, your work will be easier.

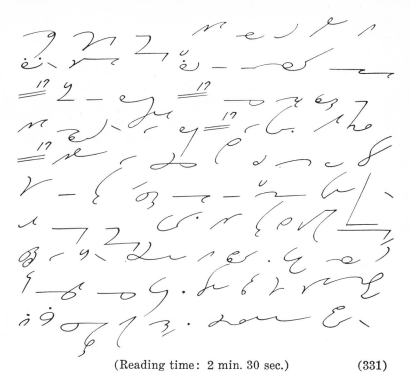

(Reading time: 2 min. 30 sec.)   (331)

Punctuation Pointer

All punctuation required in the foregoing article has been indicated, but only the punctuation explained in this study has been numbered to show the application of the pointer.

17. The *dash* is used to indicate an abrupt change in the thought of a sentence, and to emphasize a parenthetical expression.

Our series is both interesting and lengthy—eleven letters in all.

I spoke to the manager—a Mr. Jones, I believe—and told him that we must have the material by Monday.

He knows—and knows well—that we cannot use this device.

PART 2. BUSINESS INFORMATION

Directions. Practice the following vocabulary preview until you can write the words with facility. By this time you should have developed the ability to write shorthand with a clear distinction in the length of strokes and in the sizes of circles. Don't neglect this important phase of shorthand writing. After you have practiced the words, make two shorthand copies of the article "Clearinghouses."

Vocabulary Preview

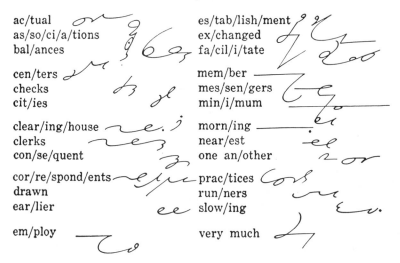

ac/tual	es/tab/lish/ment
as/so/ci/a/tions	ex/changed
bal/ances	fa/cil/i/tate
cen/ters	mem/ber
checks	mes/sen/gers
cit/ies	min/i/mum
clear/ing/house	morn/ing
clerks	near/est
con/se/quent	one an/other
cor/re/spond/ents	prac/tices
drawn	run/ners
ear/lier	slow/ing
em/ploy	very much

Clearinghouses

In earlier days, when banks received checks drawn on accounts in other banks in the same city, such checks were collected [20] through the aid of messengers, or runners, who actually took the checks to the other banks and exchanged them [40] for cash. Checks on accounts in banks in other cities were collected by mail. Such practices meant the constant shifting [60] of large sums of money and the consequent slowing up of business. Today, in the larger centers, clearinghouse [80] associations facilitate the rapid exchange of checks between banks. On the morning of every [100] banking day, clerks from all the member banks meet at a central clearinghouse and exchange checks drawn against their banks.[120] Balances are paid in cash.

In the smaller cities and towns, in which no clearinghouses exist, banks still resort to [140] runners for the exchange of checks on local banks. Checks on banks in other cities are collected through the nearest [160] clearinghouse association. Not being members of an association, the banks in such cities and towns [180] employ member banks to act as representatives. These· representatives are known as correspondents.

Clearinghouse [200] associations deal with one another in very much the same manner in which banks deal with one another.[220] The establishment of clearinghouse associations in all parts of the country has greatly increased the [240] ease with which collections can be made and has reduced the shifting of actual cash to a minimum.   (259)

PART 3. BUSINESS CORRESPONDENCE

between

CENTRAL SAVINGS BANK
619 Webster Street   *and*
Petersburg, Virginia

MR. LAWRENCE STANLEY
402 Orchard Avenue
New Rochelle, New York

LETTER 73

Her/bert
I am sorry
if you will

Pe/ters/burg
sav/ings
Stan/ley

Law/rence
New Ro/chelle
New/ton

Vir/ginia
vis/it/ing
Ward

Or/chard

Web/ster

402 Orchard Avenue
New Rochelle, New York
January 3, 19—

Central Savings Bank
619 Webster Street
Petersburg, Virginia

Attention of Mr. Herbert Ward

Gentlemen

While visiting in Petersburg for the Christmas holidays, I issued several checks that may pass [20] through your bank.

These were drawn on my account in the Newton National Bank, of New Rochelle. Unfortunately, as [40] this bank closed on December 30 for a temporary period, my checks may fail to be cleared. If you will [60] notify me immediately of any such checks, I shall take them up promptly.

I am sorry to [80] inconvenience you in this way.

Very cordially yours   (89)

Lawrence Stanley

LETTER 74

Black	harm	
com/mu/nity	has not been	
de/pos/ited	I have your let/ter	
fac/ing	pos/ses/sion	
Farmer	with re/gard	

January 5, 19—

Herbert Ward, Cashier, CENTRAL SAVINGS BANK

(Reading time: 1 min.)　　　　　　　(140)

LETTER 75

en/clos/ing
held
my/self

to cover
to/tal

402 Orchard Avenue
New Rochelle, New York
January 9, 19—

Central Savings Bank
619 Webster Street
Petersburg, Virginia

Attention of Mr. Herbert Ward

Gentlemen

I am enclosing a money order for $20 to cover the following items held [20] by you and charged against me:

Check payable to A. C. Farmer	$ 5.00
Check payable to R. W.[40] Black	10.00
Check payable to myself	5.00
Total	$20.00

I appreciate your courtesy [60] in holding these checks for me and in notifying me promptly of their failure to be cleared.

Very cordially [80] yours　　(81)

Enc., Money Order　　　　　　Lawrence Stanley

402 Orchard Avenue
New Rochelle, New York
January 9, 19--

Central Savings Bank
619 Webster Street
Petersburg, Virginia

Gentlemen

    I am enclosing a money order for $20 to
cover the following items held by you and charged
against me:

Check payable to A. C. Farmer	$ 5.00
Check payable to R. W. Black	10.00
Check payable to myself	5.00
Total	$20.00

    I appreciate your courtesy in holding these
checks for me and in notifying me promptly of
their failure to be cleared.

        Very cordially yours

        Lawrence Stanley
        Lawrence Stanley

Enclosure
  Money Order

MODEL 8—MODIFIED BLOCK LETTER WITH TABULATION
Sometimes it is desirable that the nature of enclosures be indicated at the
end of a letter. This may be done as shown in this model.

LETTER 76

con/sti/tutes	liq/ui/da/tion
de/lay	many thanks
dep/uty	no/ti/fied
draw/er's	please let us know
Fed/eral	Re/serve
filed	Rich/mond
in/formed	you will note

January 20, 19—

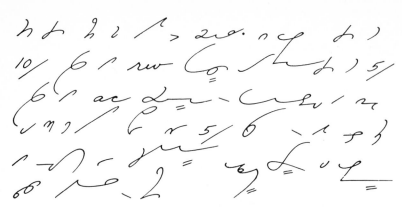

Herbert Ward, Cashier, CENTRAL SAVINGS BANK

(Reading time: 1 min. 30 sec.) (198)

LETTER 77

col/lected in ac/cord
drawee
I hope this will be

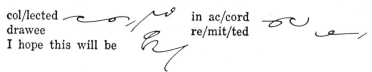

January 30, 19—

Herbert Ward, Cashier, CENTRAL SAVINGS BANK

(Reading time: 35 sec.)   (84)

LETTER 78

await
I re/gret the
prom/is/ing

re/ports
trans/ac/tion

402 Orchard Avenue
New Rochelle, New York
February 2, 19—

Mr. Herbert Ward, Cashier
Central Savings Bank
619 Webster Street
Petersburg, Virginia

Dear Herbert

My delay in answering your letters of January 20 and January 30 has [20] been occasioned by the fact that there were daily reports promising the opening of the Newton National [40] Bank, of New Rochelle. The bank is now open for the full transaction of business.

I regret the inconvenience [60] I must have caused you and thank you for your patience and courtesy. The manner in which you have taken care of my [80] checks is perfectly satisfactory to me, and I shall await your remittance of $5 to cover [100] the last item.

Very cordially yours   (107)

Lawrence Stanley

LETTER 79

add
cash/ier's
de/light

for/tune
I con/grat/u/late

on your
own
re/o/pen/ing

trag/edy

February 5, 19—

Herbert Ward, Cashier, CENTRAL SAVINGS BANK

(Reading time: 35 sec.)   (79)

PART 4. BUSINESS PRACTICES

Directions. Few experienced typists have missed the embarrassment, at some time or other, of turning the carbon paper the wrong way and thus typing the carbon copy on the back of the original. It is suggested, therefore, that you give careful attention to the content of the following article in addition to studying the shorthand. All the business practices given in this book have proved practical and are worth studying.

Practice the vocabulary preview and then make two shorthand copies of the article "Carbon Copies."

Vocabulary Preview

ap/pli/cants   pro/ce/dure
car/bon   pro/duc/ing
du/pli/cat/ing   re/al/ize

em/bar/rass/ment   re/versed
in/sert   up/ward
let/ter/head   wrong

Carbon Copies

As copies of practically all letters leaving a business office are kept in the files of the office, a [20] stenographer must be thoroughly familiar with the method of producing these copies. The carbon method [40] is the commonest duplicating method. Failure to understand the proper use of carbon paper puts the [60] stenographer at a great disadvantage, especially on her first day in the office. Applicants for a [80] position can well realize the embarrassment that might result from turning the carbon sheet the wrong way and [100] producing a reversed copy on the back of the original letter. The following procedure will [120] simplify the making of carbon copies:

1. Place the second sheet on the desk with the face upward if the sheet is [140] a letterhead.
2. Place the carbon sheet on the second sheet, with the carbon side down. Repeat this operation [160] for as many copies as are desired.
3. Place the letterhead, or the original sheet, face upward on [180] the top carbon sheet.
4. Insert the sheets into the machine as if they were one.

Carbon sheets should be changed often [200] enough to ensure good carbon copies. When not in use, the carbon sheets should be kept with the carbon side down to [220] prevent curling. The stenographer will find it worth while to sample various grades of carbon paper so that [240] she may select the grade that is best for her work.   (248)

PART 5. PROGRESS CHECKUP

LETTER PC-12

Mr. Lawrence Stanley
402 Orchard Avenue
New Rochelle, New York

Dear Lawrence

Thank you for the money order for $20 enclosed with your letter of January 9.²⁰ This money order fully covers the checks we hold in your name.

I am sorry that the closing of the bank has ⁴⁰ caused you and your community such inconvenience, and I hope that its early reopening will help to ⁶⁰ return conditions to "business as usual."

The closing of a bank does more than simply affect the savings of ⁸⁰ individuals; it often causes the public's loss of confidence in all banking houses. Such a ¹⁰⁰ situation may easily break down the credit practices of entire cities, although many of the people may ¹²⁰ never have deposited their money in the particular bank concerned. The Federal deposit insurance ¹⁴⁰ plan will help prevent future losses, as it will protect the savings in the small account.

There was a time when ¹⁶⁰ banks were used exclusively by the large corporation and by well-to-do folks, but today banks are greatly ¹⁸⁰ dependent on the average individual in the community. The greater the number of accounts, the ²⁰⁰ better the banking situation.

I hope that your present year may be filled with happiness for you, and that ²²⁰ before long your bank will once again offer complete services to the public.

Yours very cordially   (238)

Herbert Ward, Cashier

EW*   CENTRAL SAVINGS BANK

---

* When the dictator's name is typed in the signature, it is not necessary to include his initials in the identification line. The initials given here are those of the stenographer.

DICTATION STUDY XIII

PART 1. BASIC SKILLS

Brief-Form Review

Directions. The following article contains 70 different brief forms and brief-form derivatives. You should be so thoroughly familiar with your brief forms that you can write them as naturally as you do your own name—and faster. Read the article until you can read it at your goal speed—125 to 150 words a minute. Then write it twice in shorthand. Make "Speed and accuracy" your slogan.

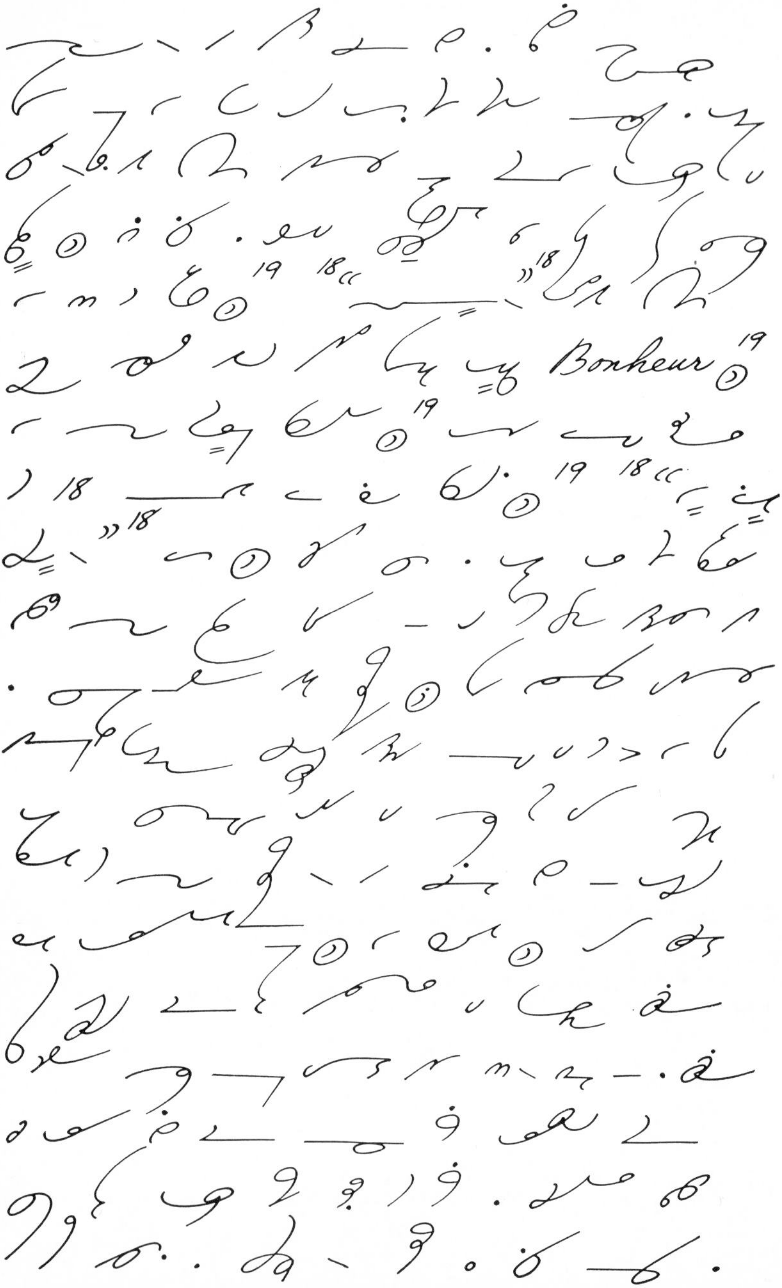
Bonheur

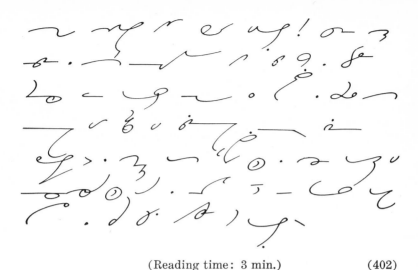

(Reading time: 3 min.)　　　　　　　(402)

Punctuation Pointers

All punctuation marks needed for the foregoing article are indicated, but numbers are used for only those marks illustrating pointers in this lesson.

18. The names of paintings, magazine articles, musical compositions, and the like are placed within quotation marks.

"Carmen" was composed by Alexandre Cesar Leopold (Georges) Bizet.

"The Horse Fair" was painted by Marie Rosalie (Rosa) Bonheur.

The subject of his talk will be "The Contribution of the Radio to Civilization."

The magazine printed his article on "The Art of Living."

19. The *comma* is used to set off words in apposition.

Mr. Frank Lewiston, our sales manager, will be in your city next week.

Our client, the Newton National Bank, has placed the matter in our hands.

Rosa Bonheur, the French artist, was noted for her animal paintings.

Miss Geraldine Banker, the best typist in our office, is leaving the first of next month.

Our receptionist, Miss Powell, has the vacation period from Monday, July 8, to Monday, July 22.

PART 2. BUSINESS INFORMATION
Vocabulary Preview

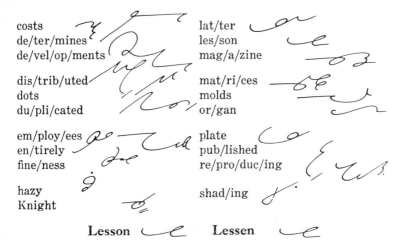

costs
de/ter/mines
de/vel/op/ments

dis/trib/uted
dots
du/pli/cated

em/ploy/ees
en/tirely
fine/ness

hazy
Knight

lat/ter
les/son
mag/a/zine

mat/ri/ces
molds
or/gan

plate
pub/lished
re/pro/duc/ing

shad/ing

Lesson   Lessen

Lesson means instruction; a thing learned or taught.

Many a lesson is learned through experience.
A student should learn a lesson so well that he derives maximum benefit from it.

Lessen means to make or become less.

Careful planning will often lessen the amount of work required for a job.
An extra support will lessen the strain on the bridge.

Printing Information

Today we give a customer a lesson in printing. The correspondent's lack of knowledge costs us just two letters [20] in this series. His idea of half tones and line cuts is rather hazy, and he apparently knows nothing [40] about screening. We wonder whether he understands the word *matrices,* which he uses in one of his letters [60] to us.

From a previous lesson we learned that a half tone is a metal plate used for reproducing a [80] photograph, on which the shading in the photograph is duplicated by means of dots made by placing a glass [100] screen between the camera and the photograph to be reproduced. We also learned that the number of lines to [120] the square inch of the screen determines the fineness of the half tone, and that coarse screens are used for newspaper work while [140] fine screens are used on better qualities of paper.

Line cuts are metal plates used for reproducing drawings. The [160] pictures, including shading, that are reproduced from such cuts are made up entirely of lines.

Because of the cost [180] of making and mailing half tones and line cuts, especially when numerous requests are received, many businesses [200] have a number of molds, or matrices, made from one cut. These matrices are then sent in answer to requests [220] for cuts. They serve a temporary purpose only. A cut is essential for continued use.

Shades of Knight is [240] a little magazine published at regular intervals by our company and distributed among our [260] employees and our customers. Such a publication is called a house organ. Many businesses use house organs [280] to create and maintain good will among their customers and to keep the latter informed of the latest [300] developments in the products of the business.   (308)

PART 3. BUSINESS CORRESPONDENCE

between

KNIGHT WINDOW SHADE COMPANY
Warren and Madison Streets
Des Moines 5, Iowa

and

BLANTON FURNITURE COMPANY
768 Hinton Street
Cedar Rapids, Iowa

Directions. Practice the vocabulary previews in this two-way series until the outlines can be written freely and easily; then make two shorthand copies of each letter. Be sure of your reading goal on the shorthand plate letters before attempting to write them. Finish all work on one letter before proceeding to the next. Most of these letters are short; but, in business, short letters are just as important as long ones and must be just as accurately written.

LETTER 80

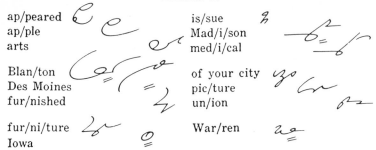

ap/peared	is/sue
ap/ple	Mad/i/son
arts	med/i/cal
Blan/ton	of your city
Des Moines	pic/ture
fur/nished	un/ion
fur/ni/ture	War/ren
Iowa	

April 25, 19—

Knight Window Shade Company
Corner Warren and Madison Streets
Des Moines 5, Iowa

Gentlemen

On the first page of a recent issue of *Shades of Knight*, there appeared a picture of the new Medical [20] Arts Building of your city. As this is a very striking advertisement for your shades, we are wondering [40] whether you have any matrices of this picture that you can send us for use in our local newspaper [60] advertising.

The No. 613 apple green shade that you furnished for the new Western Union Building [80] is most attractive. We are sending in our order today for one dozen. These will be used for display purposes.[100]

Yours very truly   (104)

BLANTON FURNITURE COMPANY

JBB:MC   Vice-President

LETTER 81

Ce/dar Rap/ids	one of the most
cut	per/mis/sion
fa/vor	pop/u/lar
Hin/ton	roll/ers

April 30, 19—

[shorthand]

KNIGHT WINDOW SHADE COMPANY, Advertising Manager

(Reading time: 30 sec.)   (72)

LETTER 82

let/ter/heads   *[shorthand]*   suit/able   *[shorthand]*

May 2, 19—

Knight Window Shade Company
Corner Warren and Madison Streets
Des Moines 5, Iowa

Gentlemen

The cut of the Medical Arts Building arrived this morn-ing in good condition. This is, however,[20] a half tone suit-able for reproduction on letterheads, in magazines, or on any other paper of [40] good quality. What we want is a line cut suitable for newspaper advertising.

We want to produce a [60] picture like the one that appeared on the first page of the March issue of *Shades of Knight*. This picture would have a strong [80] popular appeal in our local newspaper.

If you cannot supply us with a line cut, can you let us have [100] a picture from which we may have a suitable cut **made?**

Yours very truly   (113)

BLANTON FURNITURE COMPANY

JBB:MC   Vice-President

LETTER 83

au/then/tic

au/then/tic/ity

ev/i/dent

has/ten

ide/ally

prac/ti/ca/ble

proofed

suited

May 5, 19—

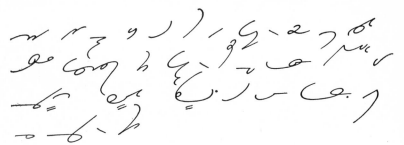

KNIGHT WINDOW SHADE COMPANY, Advertising Manager

(Reading time: 1 min. 10 sec.) (160)

LETTER 84

church

clip/ping

county

greedy

May 9, 19—

Knight Window Shade Company
Corner Warren and Madison Streets
Des Moines 5, Iowa

Gentlemen

After seeing the newspaper clipping enclosed in your letter of May 5, we are fully convinced [20] that the cut of the Medical Arts Building will serve our purpose well.

We do not want to appear greedy, but we [40] should like to have a duplicate of this cut. We could then use one for our regular newspaper advertising [60] and save the other for special advertisements appearing in church booklets and county fair programs.

We are [80] featuring Knight shades in all our current advertising.

Yours very truly (93)

BLANTON FURNITURE COMPANY

JBB:MC Vice-President

PART 4. BUSINESS PRACTICES

Vocabulary Preview

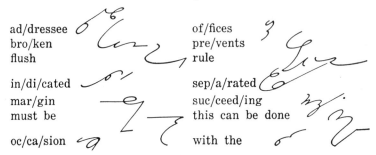

ad/dressee
bro/ken
flush

in/di/cated
mar/gin
must be

oc/ca/sion

of/fices
pre/vents
rule

sep/a/rated
suc/ceed/ing
this can be done

with the

Two-Page Letters

When a stenographer has occasion to write a letter of two or more pages, she should use a letterhead [20] for the first page and blank paper of the same size and quality for each succeeding page. This rule of correspondence [40] should not be broken. The second and succeeding pages must be marked with some form of identification.[60] This can be done easily in the following manner:

Two inches from the top of the page, at the left margin,[80] the name of the addressee is written. In the middle of the same line, the number of the page is indicated.[100] The date of the letter is then written flush with the right-hand margin in the form used on the first page. This method [120] provides full identification for both the original and the carbon copy.

In some offices [140] the carbon copy of the second page of a two-page letter is written on the back of the copy of the [160] first page. This plan saves space in the files and prevents the annoyance of having carbon copies become separated.[180]   (180)

Vocabulary Preview

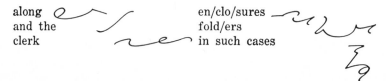

along
and the
clerk

en/clo/sures
fold/ers
in such cases

it has been	rib/bon
ob/tain/able	sig/na/ture
pre/sent/ing	slip
re/moved	this may be done

Enclosures

When several enclosures are to be sent with a letter, the stenographer is ordinarily expected [20] to get them ready and to clip them to the letter before presenting the letter for her employer's [40] signature. This is especially true when the enclosures are important papers, such as checks or notes. Sometimes,[60] however, the enclosures consist of advertising folders or other matter easily obtainable by [80] the mailing clerk. In such cases the stenographer need only indicate the nature of the enclosures. This [100] may be done in either of two ways:

First, the stenographer may pencil a list of the enclosures on a slip [120] of paper and clip this list to the letter.

Second, after the letter has been completed but before it has [140] been removed from the typewriter, she may insert a slip of paper between the ribbon and the letter and then [160] typewrite a list of the enclosures. Through this method the enclosures are listed on the carbon copy, and the [180] filing record is thus made complete. Either the carbon copy or the slip of paper may be passed along to [200] the mailing clerk.   (203)

PART 5. PROGRESS CHECKUP

LETTER PC-13

Blanton Furniture Company
768 Hinton Street
Cedar Rapids, Iowa

Gentlemen

We are happy to send you, by separate mail, a cut of the Medical Arts Building in Des Moines.[20] This cut is a half-tone engraving made with a 60-line screen, and it is ideally suited for use in [40] newspaper advertising. Half tones are better than line drawings for advertising Knight window shades, because half [60] tones give the appearance of authenticity. The Medical Arts Building is an attractive building, and the [80] enclosed photographic reproduction will add a pleasant and convincing touch to the advertisement with which [100] it is used.

The No. 613 apple green window shade, which you like so well, has been recently used [120] to equip the local Western Union Building. This new building is to be the cover feature of the March [140] issue of *Shades of Knight*, which will emphasize the beauty of No. 613.

As you know, we have always [160] devoted all our advertising for a given period to just one item. It is, therefore, a good [180] policy for you to feature the apple green shade when we can offer you strong advertising support. By placing [200] an order for a stock of this shade now, you will gain the benefits of our newspaper and magazine advertising.[220] The enclosed business reply envelope will bring your order without delay.

Very truly yours   (239)

KNIGHT WINDOW SHADE COMPANY

VAF:SH   Manager

DICTATION STUDY XIV

PART 1. BASIC SKILLS

Theory Review

Directions. Words in which two consecutive vowels are both written in shorthand do not occur too often, but they occur often enough to test the stenographer's knowledge of her shorthand theory. The following examples will help you to review this particular phase of shorthand writing.

Natural vowel sequence

Key: portfolio, radio, studio, neon, poems, poetry, poets, slowly, chaos

Special vowel combinations

Key: aviation, criteria, mania, piano, areas, create, recreation, diet, prior, science, via, quiet

Directions. After reading and writing the foregoing words until you can apply your shorthand theory without difficulty, read the following article, which contains all the words listed. Always strive to reach your reading goal; then make two shorthand copies of the article, working for speed and accuracy.

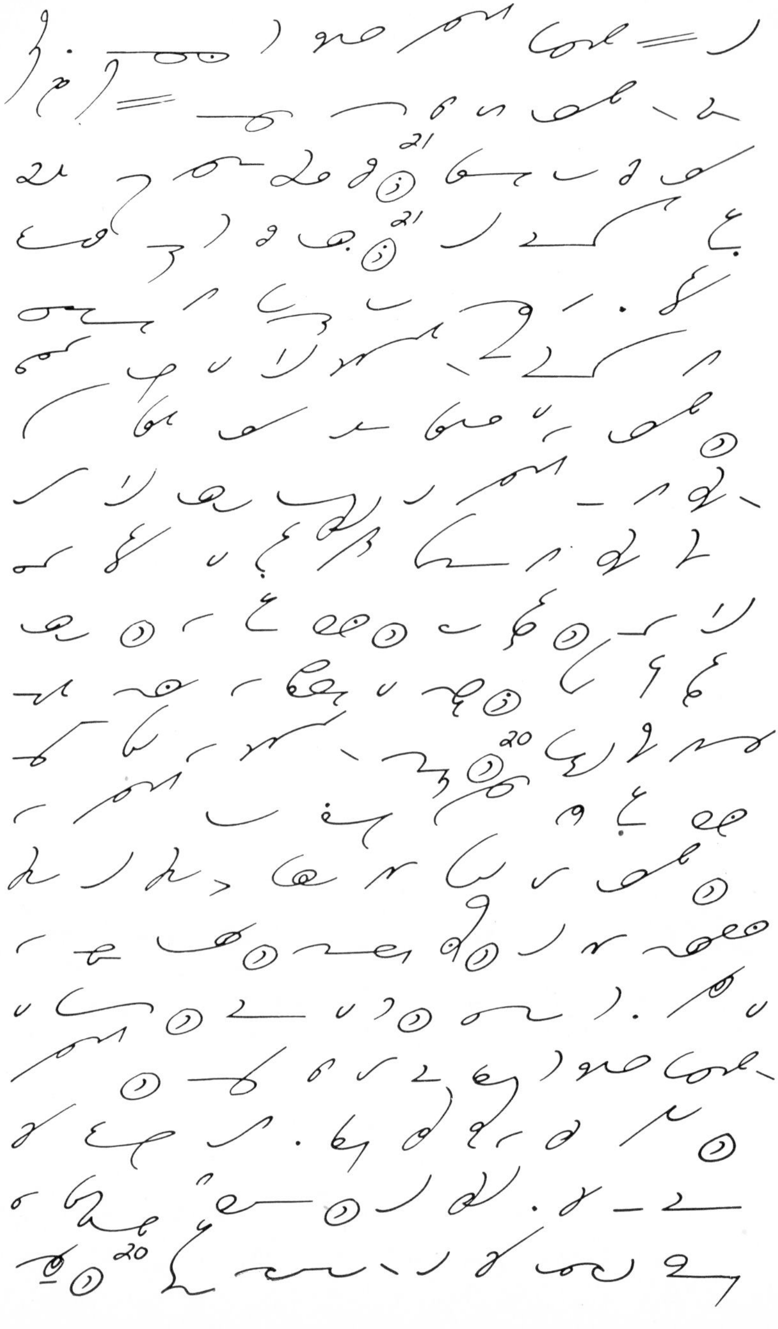

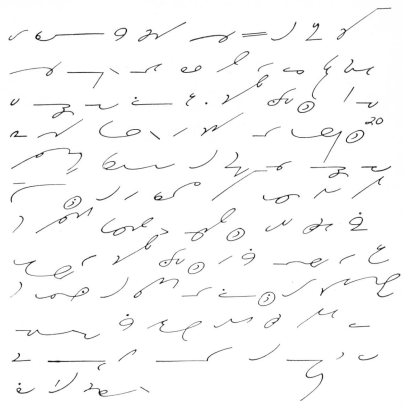

(Reading time: 2 min. 30 sec.)   (326)

Punctuation Pointers

All punctuation marks needed in the foregoing article are indicated, and the medial punctuation marks explained in this lesson are numbered to show the pointers applied.

20. A *comma* is used to separate two or more consecutive parallel adjectives modifying one or more nouns.

A long, low, open shed stood at one end of the lot. (long and low and open)

The piano was in the large, dignified parlor. (large and dignified)

This work requires conscientious, persistent effort. (conscientious and persistent)

We found a seat in a quiet, obscure corner. (quiet and obscure)

You will need a great deal of extra dictation practice. (not extra and dictation)

21. The *semicolon* is used to separate clauses arranged in series, when emphasis is desired.

These patterns represent the combined thinking of outstanding designers; they are modern in every sense of the word; and they come to you with complete and detailed instructions.

Our paints are easy to use; they outlast competing products; and their low cost will surprise you.

PART 2. BUSINESS INFORMATION

Vocabulary Preview

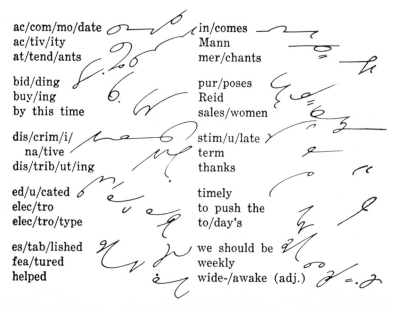

ac/com/mo/date	in/comes
ac/tiv/ity	Mann
at/tend/ants	mer/chants
bid/ding	pur/poses
buy/ing	Reid
by this time	sales/women
dis/crim/i/	stim/u/late
na/tive	term
dis/trib/ut/ing	thanks
ed/u/cated	timely
elec/tro	to push the
elec/tro/type	to/day's
es/tab/lished	we should be
fea/tured	weekly
helped	wide-/awake (adj.)

Business Co-operation

By this time we should be quite familiar with the term *cut*, but probably not with the name *electrotype* or [20] *electro*. At any rate, today's mail brings a request for a cut to be used for advertising purposes. Of [40] course, we accommodate the customer and, at the same time, put in a word of advertising for ourselves.[60]

Wide-awake businesses never miss an opportunity to push the sale of their products or to stimulate [80] activity on the part of their dealers. Art departments must be established for the preparation of attractive [100] displays, and advertising departments must co-operate in distributing these displays. Today we find [120] manufacturers bidding against one another for window space in retail stores. Many of the very [140] attractive displays in store windows bring to the merchants weekly incomes in the form of goods or cash from the [160] manufacturers of the particular articles featured.

In our correspondence with Reid & Mann, Inc.,[180] notice that each letter offers additional help in the form of advertising display. Of course, we get [200] a real return from such advertising. In fairness to all manufacturers, it is only right to say [220] that their effort to increase distribution has helped to change store attendants from order clerks to salesmen and [240] saleswomen, and has educated the public to the point of discriminative buying.

Finally, notice our [260] timely letter of November 19 — thanks to our follow-up file. Such a letter is really worth while when [280] it results in the good will expressed in the answer from Reid & Mann, Inc. Good will represents a [300] real value, and it is our policy to maintain it. It is important, therefore, that we serve our customers [320] well.   (321)

PART 3. BUSINESS CORRESPONDENCE

between

WAKEMAN SOAP COMPANY   REID & MANN, INC.
1092 State Street   *and*   628 Canal Street
Trenton 9, New Jersey   Liberty Bluff, Wisconsin

Directions. The following correspondence, like that of the preceding chapter, consists chiefly of short letters, but each letter plays its part in the series and is, therefore, important. Don't neglect your practice when work appears simple. Simple words are often words of high frequency and, consequently, require special practice for high-speed writing. Practice the previews and make two shorthand copies of each letter. Complete all work on one letter before proceeding to the next.

LETTER 85

cir/cu/lar/i/za/tion
il/lus/tra/tion
in/stalled

Mul/ti/graph
soap

State Street
Tren/ton
two weeks ago

Wake/man

August 16, 19—

Wakeman Soap Company
1092 State Street
Trenton 9, New Jersey

Gentlemen

About two weeks ago we wrote to you requesting a
Wakeman soap cut similar to illustration [20] No. 25 in the
Manufacturers Cut Book and suitable for use on a Junior
Multigraph,[40] which we have recently installed.

As we have not received the cut and have had no word
from you, we think our letter [60] may have been lost. If
you care to furnish such a cut, we shall be glad to use it
for advertising your product [80] through a circularization
campaign.

Yours truly   (89)

REID & MANN, INC.

HC:FS   Manager

LETTER 86

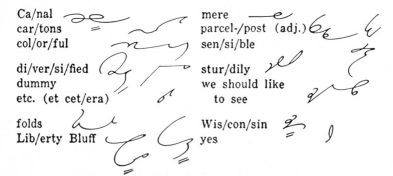

Ca/nal
car/tons
col/or/ful

di/ver/si/fied
dummy
etc. (et cet/era)

folds
Lib/erty Bluff

mere
parcel-/post (adj.)
sen/si/ble

stur/dily
we should like
to see

Wis/con/sin
yes

August 19, 19—

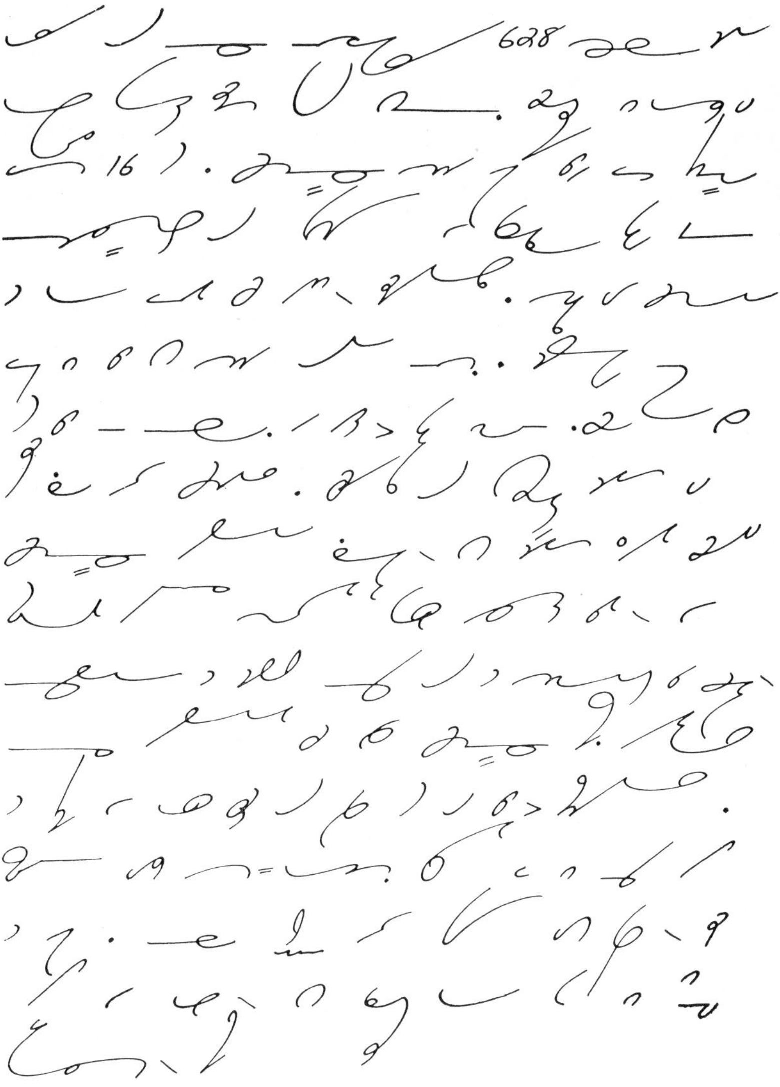

WAKEMAN SOAP COMPANY, Advertising Department

(Reading time: 1 min. 10 sec.) **(166)**

LETTER 87

de/sired
ex/pect/ing
im/pres/sion

mails
sheets
six hun/dred

August 27, 19—

Wakeman Soap Company
1092 State Street
Trenton 9, New Jersey

Gentlemen

Enclosed is a copy of the circular for which we desired the Wakeman cut. Six hundred of these [20] sheets have been distributed through the mails, and we are expecting good results.

The cut makes a very neat impression.[40] We appreciate your help.

Yours truly   (48)

REID & MANN, INC.

HC:FS   Manager
Enc.

LETTER 88

clever
com/pli/ment

of/fer/ings
type

September 3, 19—

WAKEMAN SOAP COMPANY, Advertising Department

(Reading time: 50 sec.) (116)

LETTER 89

cal/en/dar
holds
in/ci/den/tally
pro/gress/ing

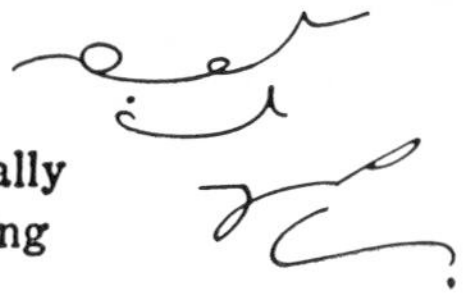

re/minds
Thanks/giv/ing
three months
ago

November 19, 19—

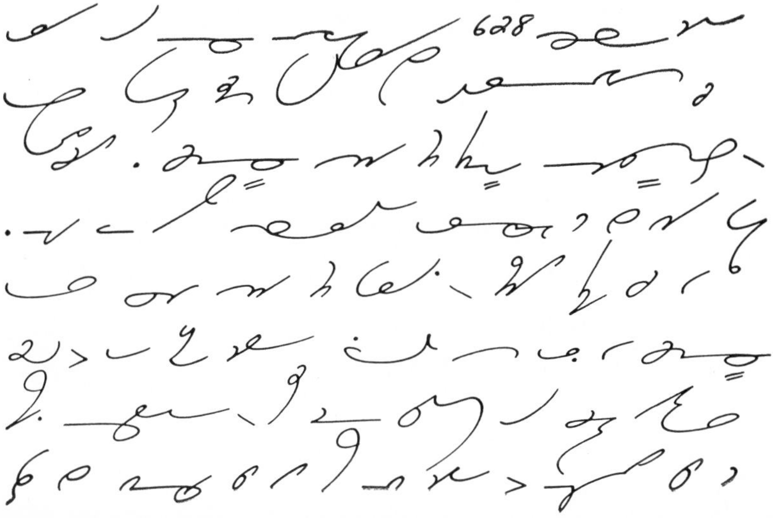

WAKEMAN SOAP COMPANY, Advertising Department

(Reading time: 1 min.)   (126)

LETTER 90

felt

lead/er/ship

try/ing

un/u/sual

December 5, 19—

Wakeman Soap Company
1092 State Street
Trenton 9, New Jersey

Gentlemen:

We appreciate the interest you took in our advertising; and as you felt it worth while to [20] follow the matter up, we are trying another special. Enclosed is our current circular.

It is rather [40] unusual for a manufacturer to show so much interest in the sales efforts of a small store. Such [60] a policy helps explain Wakeman's leadership.

Our Wakeman cut is still in good condition, and we have no [80] immediate need for a duplicate.

Yours truly   (89)

REID & MANN, INC.

HC:FS   Manager
Enc.

PART 4. BUSINESS PRACTICES

Directions. The business practices described in the various chapters are not the only ways of performing the many office duties, but they do represent desirable methods of doing your work. Are you learning to apply them? Unless your teacher instructs you to the contrary, use these methods whenever you have the opportunity. Practice the previews and then make two shorthand copies of the articles "Envelopes" and "Folding Letters."

Vocabulary Preview

be/low		pref/er/ably
care		re/cep/ta/cle
cen/ter		ste/nog/ra/pher's
clipped		taken
com/pared		to be sure
one-/half		up/per

Envelopes

The address to be typed on an envelope should be taken from the same source that was used for the inside address,[20] preferably the original letter. The envelope address and the inside address should be compared to [40] be sure that they agree.

When an address is to be typed on an envelope, the first line should be started [60] approximately one-half inch to the left of the vertical center of the envelope and one line below the [80] horizontal center. The style of address should follow that used in the letter, although either double spacing or [100] single spacing may be used. A special line in the address (such as "General Delivery," "In care of," or [120] "Attention of") may be placed in the lower left-hand corner of the envelope.

When the typing has been completed,[140] the envelope should be clipped over the upper left-hand corner of the letter and placed in a receptacle [160] on the stenographer's desk.   (166)

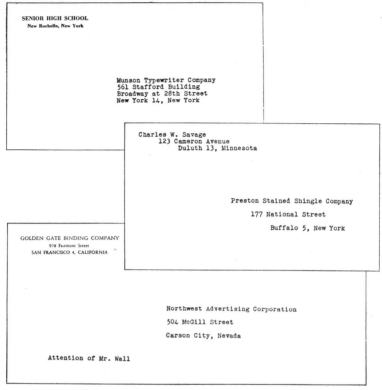

```
SENIOR HIGH SCHOOL
   New Rochelle, New York




                    Munson Typewriter Company
                    561 Stafford Building
                    Broadway at 28th Street
                    New York 14, New York


                        Charles W. Savage
                            123 Cameron Avenue
                              Duluth 13, Minnesota



                                      Preston Stained Shingle Company

                                          177 National Street

                                           Buffalo 5, New York

GOLDEN GATE BINDING COMPANY
       978 Fairmont Street
   SAN FRANCISCO 4, CALIFORNIA




                        Northwest Advertising Corporation

                        504 McGill Street

                        Carson City, Nevada

     Attention of Mr. Wall
```

MODEL 9—STYLES OF ENVELOPE ADDRESSES

An envelope address should agree with the letter address in style of
indention. A three-line envelope address is frequently double-spaced.

Vocabulary Preview

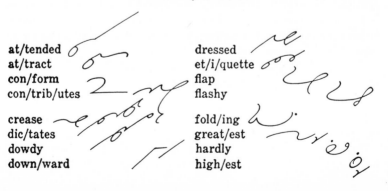

at/tended	dressed
at/tract	et/i/quette
con/form	flap
con/trib/utes	flashy
crease	fold/ing
dic/tates	great/est
dowdy	hardly
down/ward	high/est

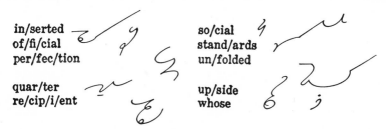

in/serted	so/cial
of/fi/cial	stand/ards
per/fec/tion	un/folded
quar/ter	up/side
re/cip/i/ent	whose

Folding Letters

If a letter is to be of the greatest value possible, every detail that contributes toward [20] perfection must be attended to. Just how much value is attached to any single detail can hardly be [40] determined, but it is safe to assume that every item has its value.

It has often been said that a [60] well-dressed man is one whose dress does not attract attention. Dress that is either flashy or dowdy is not in agreement [80] with the dictates of social etiquette. In a similar way a letter must conform to the highest standards [100] of business correspondence.

Courtesy requires a letter to be folded in a way that will cause the [120] recipient the least possible inconvenience in opening it. When a letter is unfolded, it should be [140] ready for reading; it should not be upside down. The folds should be neat and flat, and the edges even.

When folding [160] a letter for insertion into a business envelope of the usual size, fold the lower half so that [180] the bottom edge will be about one-half inch from the top edge. Next make a one-third fold from right to left, and then a [200] fold slightly less than one third from left to right. When inserting the letter into the envelope, hold the envelope [220] in your left hand, with the flap open toward the right, and the letter in your right hand, the last crease being [240] toward the left and the last fold facing you.

When a letter is folded for insertion into an official [260] envelope, the bottom third of the letter is folded toward the top and the top third is folded downward to within [280] one-quarter inch of the first crease. The letter is inserted into the envelope with the last fold against [300] the back of the envelope and with the open side toward the top of the envelope. (316)

PART 5. PROGRESS CHECKUP

Letter PC-14

Reid & Mann, Inc.
628 Canal Street
Liberty Bluff, Wisconsin

Gentlemen

You have made such good use of the electrotype which we sent you some time ago that we are taking [20] the liberty of sending you another for use on your Junior Multigraph. We were pleased to see the circular [40] that you distributed in September, and we are sure that this advertising program sold a good lot of [60] merchandise for you. Your Wakeman offerings were well arranged, and the electrotype displays made the circular [80] most attractive.

It is difficult to determine just how much selling is the result of an advertising [100] campaign, but we are convinced that there is sufficient advantage to make frequent advertising attempts justified.[120] We suggest that you circularize your customers again between Thanksgiving and Christmas.

Have you given [140] thought to the possibility of distributing a folder devoted completely to Wakeman products? If [160] you wish to try such a plan, we shall be glad to cooperate with you by making a free-goods offer that will [180] appeal to your customers. If this suggestion interests you, let us know at once and we will forward complete [200] details to you promptly.

We also suggest that in the meantime you consider further the use of some of the [220] attractive Wakeman counter displays in your store. These displays are colorful, sensible, and sturdily made. They [240] are yours for the asking.

Yours very truly   (248)

Wakeman Soap Company

ERB:CA   Manager

DICTATION STUDY XV

PART 1. BASIC SKILLS

Theory Review

Directions. Do you know when to use the adverb instead of the adjective? Try your shorthand theory on the following words. Read them until you no longer need the key; then write each word at least once.

LY Words

Key: bodi*ly*, general*ly*, individual*ly*, necessari*ly*, satisfactori*ly*, usual*ly*, rare*ly*, real*ly*

ILY-ALLY Words

Key: bus*ily*, eas*ily*, happ*ily*, heart*ily*, read*ily*, stead*ily*, materi*ally*, natur*ally*, occasion*ally*, soci*ally*, person*ally*, speci*ally*, education*ally*, financi*ally*

UALLY Words

Key: act*ually*, continu*ally*, effect*ually*, equ*ally*, grad*ually*, habit*ually*, mut*ually*, perpetu*ally*, spiritu*ally*

Directions. Proceed in the usual manner.

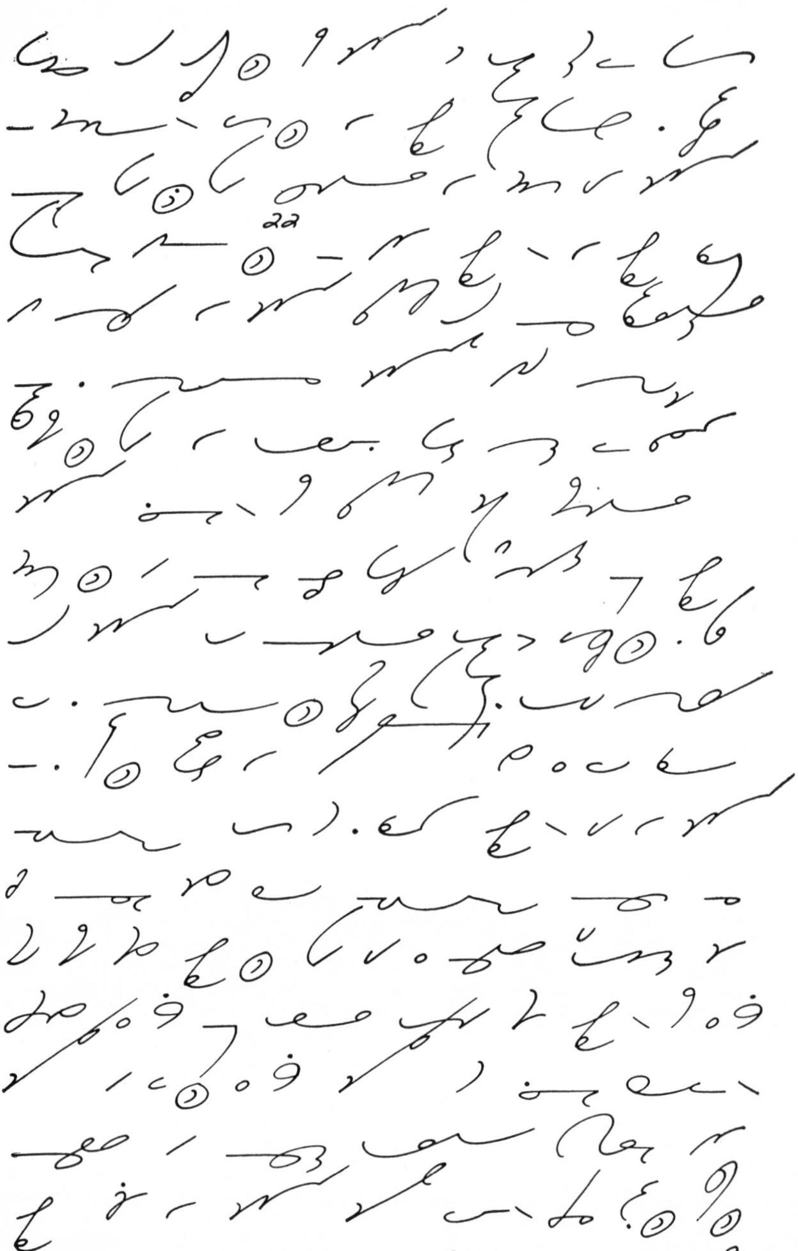

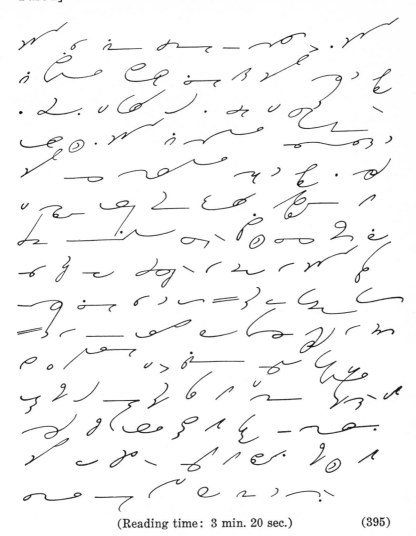

(Reading time: 3 min. 20 sec.)   (395)

Punctuation Pointer

All the punctuation marks needed in the foregoing article are given. Can you explain their use?

22. Place a *comma* between a positive statement and a negative statement in the same sentence.

Our books are bought by the school board, not by the students.

Facts, not opinions, are the things we need.

PART 2. BUSINESS INFORMATION

Vocabulary Preview

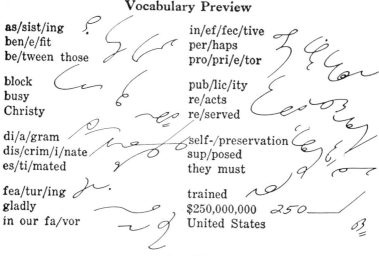

as/sist/ing
ben/e/fit
be/tween those

block
busy
Christy

di/a/gram
dis/crim/i/nate
es/ti/mated

fea/tur/ing
gladly
in our fa/vor

in/ef/fec/tive
per/haps
pro/pri/e/tor

pub/lic/ity
re/acts
re/served

self-/preservation
sup/posed
they must

trained
$250,000,000
United States

Advertising

Our advertising department is keeping busy. Today's mail brings in another request for help in a [20] publicity campaign. This time we are asked to prepare a newspaper layout featuring Christy furniture, our [40] product. As such advertising naturally reacts in our favor, we gladly offer assistance.

A complete [60] advertising layout is a diagram showing the position of cuts, the proper arrangement of [80] descriptive matter, the size of type to be used for various lines, and the distribution of the white space. The [100] advertising copy is the wording to be used in the copy block or space reserved for the descriptive material.[120]

In a large organization the advertising copy may be prepared by one person, and the [140] advertising layout may be the work of another. In a small business the full advertisement will probably [160] be prepared by the proprietor or one of his office workers, perhaps the stenographer. If all advertisements [180] were prepared by trained workers, the businesses of the United States might save much of the annual loss [200] of $250,000,000 estimated to be spent in ineffective publicity.

It is [220] not to be supposed that businesses are selfish in assisting others. They are in business for profit; and, in [240] the face of hundreds of requests for assistance, they must, for self-preservation, discriminate between those [260] requests of mutual benefit and those that mean losses. (270)

PART 3. BUSINESS CORRESPONDENCE

between

CHRISTY MANUFACTURING COMPANY   RICHARDSON & HARRISON
602 Tenth Street   *and*   387 Center Avenue
Gary, Indiana   Springfield, Missouri

LETTER 91

an/nounce/ments   sched/ule
calls   stress
de/ferred   we are plan/ning

Gary   will you please
Rich/ard/son   see

February 20, 19—

Christy Manufacturing Company
602 Tenth Street
Gary, Indiana

Gentlemen

For the month of March we are planning a special sale featuring Christy furniture. Our schedule calls [20] for an opening full-page newspaper advertisement, followed by several half-page and quarter-page displays.[40] These announcements will stress our deferred-payment plan.

Will you please see that we get a complete set of advertising [60] materials for both window and newspaper, including mats.

You have been most helpful in the preparation [80] of our sales campaigns. We have made no attempt to record the extent to which your assistance has actually [100] increased the volume of our stock turnover. We are willing, however, to give a great deal of the credit to [120] you. We appreciate your co-operation.

Yours very truly (132)

RICHARDSON & HARRISON

SN:MH   Publicity Manager

LETTER 92

cush/ions	pre/mium
in or/der to	re/vers/ible
pre/pare	Spring/field
Jac/quard	suites
Mis/souri	to con/tain
mo/hair	upon re/ceipt
pen/ciled	ve/lours

February 24, 19—

CHRISTY MANUFACTURING COMPANY, Advertising Department

(Reading time: 1 min.)   (134)

LETTER 93

an/nounced		lamp	
bridge		men/tion	
floor		space	

February 26, 19—

Christy Manufacturing Company
602 Tenth Street
Gary, Indiana

Gentlemen

The enclosed list will give you the information for the advertising layout you are preparing [20] for us.

The space for the prices on the suites should be left blank. In a copy block, however, you may mention that [40] we have two-piece suites from $79.50 up and that with each suite will be given a bridge lamp, [60] a floor lamp, or an occasional table.

Our deferred-payment plan may be announced in such a sentence as, "A [80] small down payment will deliver any suite—balance weekly or monthly, at your convenience."

Upon receipt of [100] the layout the prices will be inserted and the copy turned over to the newspaper. We shall write you about [120] the results we obtain.

Yours very truly   (129)

RICHARDSON & HARRISON

SN:MH   Publicity Manager

Enc.

LETTER 94

event

ex/cep/tion

liv/ing

room

shortly

time

Mon/day

pack/age

please be sure

to give us

to let us know

you may find

February 28, 19—

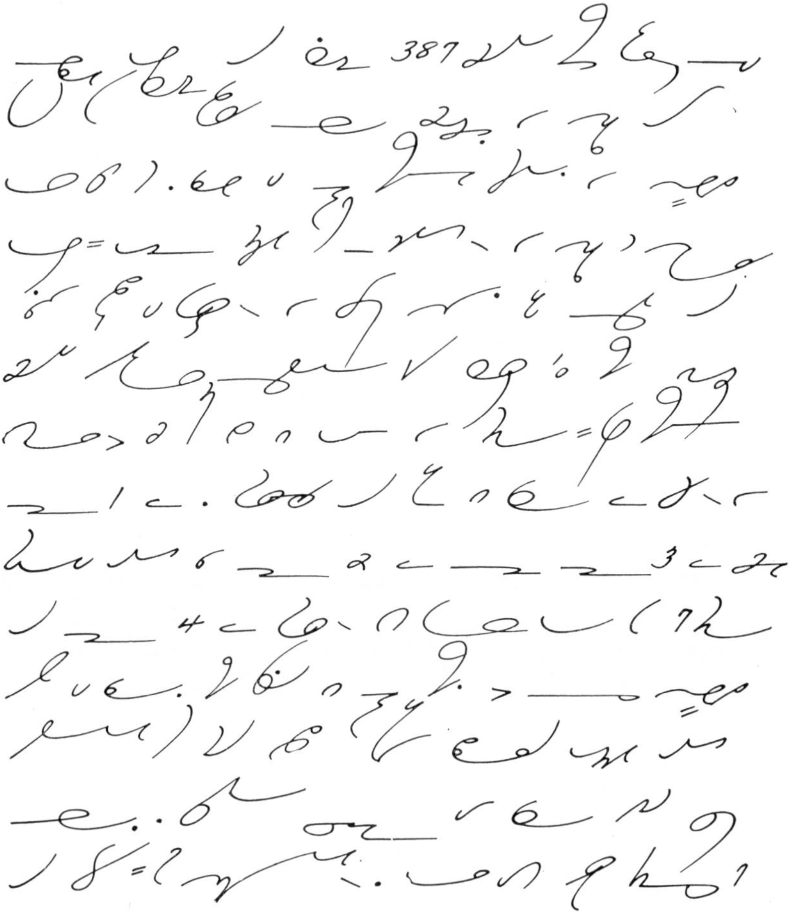

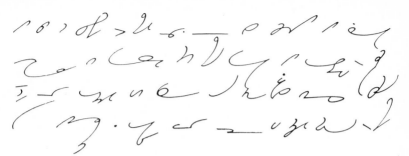

CHRISTY MANUFACTURING COMPANY, Advertising Department

(Reading time: 1 min. 30 sec.) (208)

LETTER 95

cour/ier smart/est
Dear Mrs. Smith
de/signs Thurs/day

Mrs. Wash/ing/ton
on these days

(Suggestion for a Circular Letter.
Copy to Richardson & Harrison.)

March 5, 19—

Mrs. James Smith
622 Washington Street
Springfield, Missouri

Dear Mrs. Smith

On Friday night the Springfield *Courier* will announce an unusual showing and sale of the [20] smartest new designs in Christy living-room furniture. Prices on these pieces are especially low, and [40] convenient terms have been arranged. In addition, with any suite you buy, we will give you your choice of a bridge lamp, a [60] floor lamp, or an occasional table.

Thursday and Friday have been set aside as courtesy days for our [80] regular customers. On these days, while our stock is still complete, you may select the new pieces you have wanted; and [100] you may take advantage of our special prices, special terms, and gift offer.

Be sure to drop in on either [120] Thursday or Friday to see the outstanding values in living-room furniture made by Christy.

Cordially yours   (139)

RICHARDSON & HARRISON

SN:MH   Publicity Manager

PART 4. BUSINESS PRACTICES
Vocabulary Preview

ab/sent
ac/cept/able
blot/ter

cus/tom/ary
di/rectly
ef/fi/ciently

fil/ing
  de/part/ment

from those
from which
piled

rush
sig/na/tures
tran/scrip/tion

The Finished Letter

After the transcription has been finished, the original letters should be taken to the employer's desk for [20] his signature. If the employer is ready to sign the letters, the stenographer should place them, face up, in [40] front of him. She may even be expected to stand with blotter in hand to dry the written signatures. If the [60] employer is busy at his desk, however, the letters should be placed to one side, face up. If the employer [80] is absent from his desk, the letters should be left neatly piled, face down.

In some offices it is customary [100] for the stenographer to separate letters requiring immediate signatures from those about which there [120] is no great rush. In such a case the letters to be deferred are placed to one side, and the letters

A rush letter should have the prompt attention of both stenographer and employer. Ordinarily, however, the stenographer should complete her transcription before taking the letters to her employer for signature.

requiring prompt [140] attention are placed directly in front of the employer.

Two methods of handling carbon copies are in common [160] use. In the first method the carbon copy may be left with the original letter as the letter goes [180] through the process of signature. Both are then passed on to the mailing clerk, who separates the carbon copy and [200] turns it over to the filing department. In the second method the stenographer separates the carbon [220] copy from the original and puts it in a receptacle on her desk, from which it is later collected [240] for the filing department. In the small office in which the stenographer does the mailing and the filing,[260] too, any method that will enable her to do her work efficiently is acceptable.   (277)

219

PART 5. PROGRESS CHECKUP

LETTER PC-15

Messrs. Richardson & Harrison
387 Center Avenue
Springfield, Missouri

Gentlemen

We are very happy to help you in your advertising plans for March, and we are especially [20] glad that you are expecting to feature Christy furniture. By applying your window space and your newspaper [40] space to the various suites that you are offering, you will obtain your greatest return from your advertising.[60]

We suggest a procedure of this sort: First, display the most attractive items in your windows, following the [80] plan shown in the attached drawing. Then, let us help you with suitable layouts for newspaper display during the [100] week previous to your sale. (Details about this appear later in this letter.) Finally, circularize your [120] active customers with a letter that invites them to call at your store a day or two before the sale begins.[140] Such a letter is included for your approval.

Now about your newspaper advertising: We suggest that [160] you let us plan your layouts for you. We have a complete copy and art department, and the assistance of this [180] department is at your service. Send us a list of the particular numbers you are offering in this sale;[200] let us know whether you are giving special premiums to early buyers; and tell us what terms of payment you [220] will permit. Our advertising organization will then prepare your complete newspaper campaign.

We know such [240] a campaign will work as satisfactorily for you as it has for many another Christy dealer.

Yours [260] very truly   (263)

CHRISTY MANUFACTURING COMPANY

FML:DR   Manager
Enc.

DICTATION STUDY XVI

PART 1. BASIC SKILLS

Brief-Form Review

Directions. The following article contains 80 different brief forms and brief-form derivatives. Of course, many of them have been used over and over again in preceding lessons. Do you know them? Keep your brief forms at your finger tips for instant use. They are extremely useful in building speed. Read the article until you can read it at the rate of at least 125 words a minute—better still at 150 words a minute. Then make two shorthand copies.

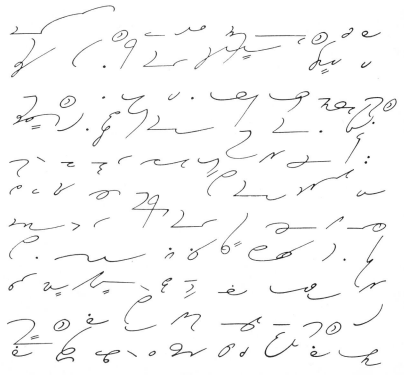

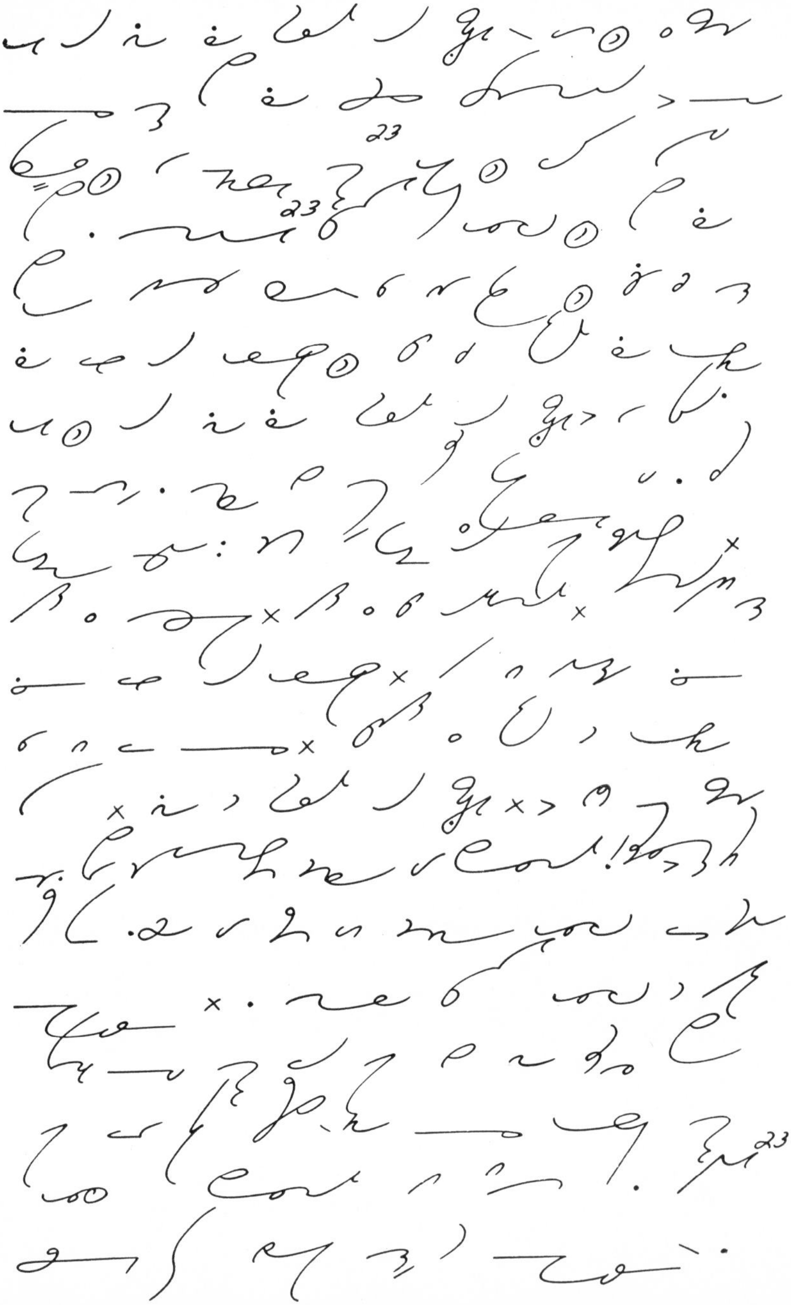

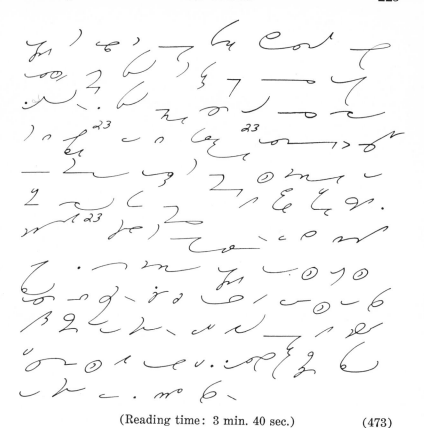

(Reading time: 3 min. 40 sec.)   (473)

Punctuation Pointer

Although all necessary punctuation is given in the fore-going article, only the words in which singular possession appears are numbered to show the application of the pointer in this lesson.

23. Add *'s* to form the singular possessive of a noun. Remember that possession belongs to whatever precedes the apostrophe.

A girl's attendance record (the attendance record of a girl)
A doctor's office (the office of a doctor)
A student's notebook (the notebook of a student)
Mr. Burns's hat (the hat belonging to Mr. Burns)
Mrs. Adams's letter (a letter from or belonging to Mrs. Adams)

PART 2. BUSINESS INFORMATION

Vocabulary Preview

ac/cepted
ac/com/pa/nied
bill of lad/ing

care/ful
claim/ant
claimed

con/cerns
con/signee
con/tains

dam/age
dam/aged
deals

de/scrib/ing
ex/cep/tions
ex/tend/ing

for/mal
in/ves/ti/ga/tion
ship/per

tech/ni/cal
throws
to this

trans/act/ing
transit

Common Carriers

The correspondence in the following series deals with the loss of goods in transit and concerns the filing or [20] placing of a claim for damage. When a common carrier has accepted a shipment of goods for transportation [40] and delivery, the law holds that carrier strictly responsible for prompt and safe delivery. There [60] are some legal exceptions to this rule, but they are too technical to be considered at this time. At any [80] rate, a damaged or a lost shipment immediately brings a claim for settlement.

A claim for damage or loss [100] should be filed promptly, and materials or information that will help in the settlement of the claim should be [120] carefully preserved. Carriers do not often settle claims on the mere request of the claimant.

Either the [140] shipper or the consignee may file the claim for loss. The shipper usually throws the responsibility on [160] the consignee, but offers any assistance needed for proper collection. The carrier, before considering [180] a claim, requires the claimant to furnish a copy of the bill of lading or the shipping receipt,[200] accompanied by a letter describing the nature of the loss and indicating the amount claimed. If the [220] amount is small and the fault appears to lie with the carrier, the claim is usually settled after nothing [240] more than a formal investigation; but, if the amount claimed is large, legal proceedings extending over [260] many months may be necessary for final settlement.

Businesses sometimes give little thought to practices [280] that help to facilitate the transaction of business. This is especially true of the small business in which [300] all transactions pass through one office. In such a business, orders and complaints may be handled by the same person. [320] As a result, an organization consisting of many departments may often receive letters containing [340] subjects to be considered by two or more departments. Such letters are a common cause of delay in [360] transacting business. It is well to remember that a careful writer will see to it that each letter contains [380] only one subject. An order and a complaint to be sent to the same company should be written as separate [400] letters, although they may be mailed in one envelope. (409)

PART 3. BUSINESS CORRESPONDENCE

between

GOODWIN & HARTLEY, INC.   WILLIAM PAMPLIN COMPANY
Ferndale Avenue   *and*   612 Watson Street
Silver Lake, Kansas   Birmingham 4, Alabama

and

MR. H. F. LOWRY, Claim Agent
American Railway Express Company
Topeka, Kansas

Letter 96

ad/vised	cat/a/log
agent	cause
as a re/sult	dahlia
box	Fern/dale
boxes	Free/mont
bulbs	frozen

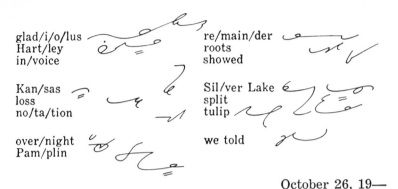

glad/i/o/lus	re/main/der
Hart/ley	roots
in/voice	showed
Kan/sas	Sil/ver Lake
loss	split
no/ta/tion	tulip
over/night	we told
Pam/plin	

October 26, 19—

Goodwin & Hartley, Inc.
Ferndale Avenue
Silver Lake, Kansas

Gentlemen

Your shipment of October 15 arrived in split delivery, the box of tulip bulbs reaching [20] us on the 22d and the box of gladiolus bulbs and dahlia roots coming in on the 25th. [40] As a result of this overnight delay, all the dahlia roots and 18 of the gladiolus bulbs were [60] frozen.

Of course, when we learned that the boxes had become separated, we told the express agent here that the [80] delay would probably cause the loss of the bulbs. Later, when the second box arrived, we showed him the condition of [100] the bulbs. He made the proper notation and advised us to place a claim. It will help us very materially [120] if you will send us a separate invoice showing the cost of these losses.

Enclosed is a check for [140] $25, for which please send us two dozen gladiolus bulbs No. 1321 and three dozen dahlia [160] roots No. 792. For the remainder of the check you may send us any assortment except the items [180] included in the Freemont catalog. We shall appreciate a copy of your most recent booklet.

Yours [200] truly   (201)

WILLIAM PAMPLIN COMPANY

JW:EB   Manager
Enc.

Letter 97

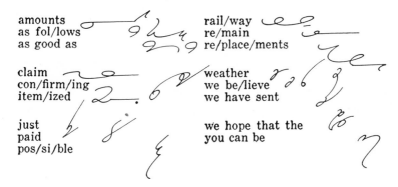

amounts
as fol/lows
as good as

claim
con/firm/ing
item/ized

just
paid
pos/si/ble

rail/way
re/main
re/place/ments

weather
we be/lieve
we have sent

we hope that the
you can be

October 27, 19—

Goodwin & Hartley, Inc.
Ferndale Avenue
Silver Lake, Kansas

Gentlemen

We have today filed a claim with the American Railway Express Company for $22,[20] itemized as follows:

3 dozen dahlia roots	$18.00
18 gladiolus bulbs	2.25 [40]
Express charges paid	1.75
Total	$22.00

With the claim we have [60] sent a copy of the original invoice. As it is just possible that the company may question the [80] amounts claimed for the cost of the replacements, will you please write the express company, confirming the prices. We [100] believe you can be of material help in getting this claim paid promptly.

We hope that the weather will remain [120] as good as it now is and that our second order will be delivered without delay.

Yours truly　　　　　(138)

WILLIAM PAMPLIN COMPANY

JW:EB　　　　　　　Manager

Letter 98

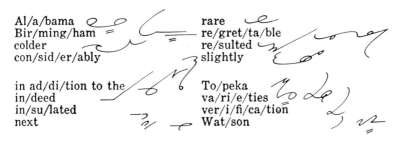

Al/a/bama		rare	
Bir/ming/ham		re/gret/ta/ble	
colder		re/sulted	
con/sid/er/ably		slightly	
in ad/di/tion to the		To/peka	
in/deed		va/ri/e/ties	
in/su/lated		ver/i/fi/ca/tion	
next		Wat/son	

October 31, 19—

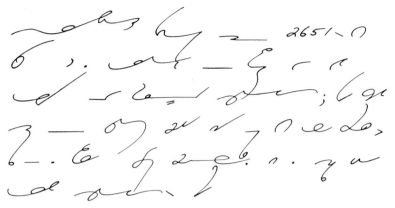

Goodwin & Hartley, Inc., President

(Reading time: 1 min. 40 sec.)   (218)

Letter 99

be/sides		one of our
con/sign/ees		saved
de/layed		to sub/mit

hours		would have been
Lowry		

October 31, 19—

Goodwin & Hartley, Inc., President

(Reading time: 50 sec.)   (111)

Letter 100

ac/com/pa/ny/ing   in this in/stance
con/sisted   show/ing
ex/act   whom

November 3, 19—

Goodwin & Hartley, Inc.
Ferndale Avenue
Silver Lake, Kansas

Gentlemen

Claim of William Pamplin Company

The thing to do in this instance is to furnish your customer [20] with an exact copy of the original express receipt showing just what the shipment consisted of; and [40] then, in a letter accompanying the receipt, to give any other information requested by the [60] consignee.

The William Pamplin Company should send the receipt and the letter to the agent through whom the claim [80] was presented.

Yours truly   (85)

American Railway Express Company

HFL:DS   Claim Agent

PART 4. BUSINESS PRACTICES

Vocabulary Preview

costly
dan/ger
eas/ier

meth/ods
oc/cur

platen
re/write
smudg/ing

thin
ty/po/graph/i/cal

Correction of Typographical Errors

The correction of errors is extremely costly; but, as errors do occur even in the best of offices,[20] it is essential that the stenographer be thoroughly familiar with efficient methods of correcting [40] typographical ones. The first tendency, after an error has been made, is to rewrite the paper; but [60] rewriting means the waste of materials as well as the loss of time. A careful correction frequently saves [80] a typewritten page.

If the error is to be corrected while the papers are in the typewriter—and this is [100] the easier method—the stenographer should insert a thin card or a sheet of paper between each carbon[120] sheet and the letterhead or the carbon copy, to avoid smudging. The error should be erased from the [140] original and then from each carbon copy in turn. As it is erased from each sheet, the card or the piece of paper [160] should be removed. This procedure avoids the danger of leaving a card or a piece of paper between sheets and [180] thus producing a blank spot on a carbon copy. When the erasing has been completed, the correct word or [200] letter is typed.

The typist will keep her typewriter clear of pieces of eraser if, before erasing, she [220] turns the line in which the error occurs to the top of the platen and then moves the carriage to one side of the [240] machine. This procedure will bring the error into such a position that the pieces of eraser will remain [260] on the top of the platen or drop to the table, instead of falling into the working parts of the [280] typewriter.　　　(281)

Vocabulary Preview

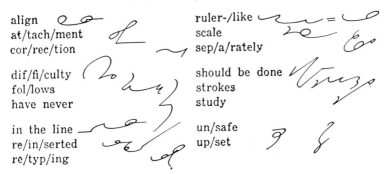

align
at/tach/ment
cor/rec/tion

dif/fi/culty
fol/lows
have never

in the line
re/in/serted
re/typ/ing

ruler-/like
scale
sep/a/rately

should be done
strokes
study

un/safe
up/set

Correction of Typographical Errors (Concluded)

If an error is discovered after the papers have been re-moved from the typewriter, the erasing should be [20] done before the sheets are reinserted. Each sheet should be corrected separately because it is unsafe to [40] attempt the correction of several sheets at once.

Many students and office workers have difficulty in [60] returning to the correct writing position a paper that has been removed from the typewriter and then [80] reinserted. This difficulty is caused by the fact that they probably have never taken the trouble to study [100] their machines carefully. Every typewriter is equipped with a black scale, or ruler-like attachment, at [120] the front of the platen. This device is helpful in determining whether the paper is straight or not. It also [140] contains a number of white lines to show the position of the letters in the line of writing.

A study [160] of the individual letters typed on a machine will show that *i* and *l* consist of straight vertical strokes [180] that appear in the middle of the space devoted to the letter. After having reinserted a sheet into [200] the typewriter, the stenographer should turn to the line of writing in which a correction is to be made [220] and should align an *i* or an *l* in that line with a white line on the platen scale. In this way she will bring the [240] sheet into the proper writing position for the retyping of any letter in the line. The period [260] may be used in a similar way for determining the proper writing position.

The correction of errors [280] on carbon copies follows the same plan. The stenographer need not be upset by the appearance of a [300] page on which all the words have been typed by means of carbon paper except that in which a correction has been made.[320]   (320)

PART 5. PROGRESS CHECKUP

LETTER PC-16

Goodwin & Hartley, Inc.
Ferndale Avenue
Silver Lake, Kansas

Gentlemen

On October 11 we placed with you an order for a number of items selected from [20] the Freemont catalog. Your shipment was made on October 15 and should have reached us within a day or two.[40]

The two boxes making up the shipment were lost in transit, and one of the boxes was delayed three days after [60] the other box was received. Meanwhile, the weather turned considerably colder. As a result, when the second [80] box arrived, we found all the dahlia roots and many of the gladiolus bulbs frozen. We showed the box to the [100] express agent here. He made the proper notation and advised us to place a claim for the loss. This we did. We [120] felt convinced that, in spite of the weather, there would have been no loss if the boxes could have come straight through without delay.[140]

The American Railway Express Company now asks that we get from you a statement verifying the [160] amount claimed. Will you, therefore, send us either a letter or a separate invoice showing our losses itemized [180] as follows:

3 dozen dahlia roots	$18.00	
18 gladiolus bulbs	2.25	[200]
Express charges paid	1.75	
Total	$22.00	

We are confident that you can ²²⁰ assist us in getting this claim settled promptly, and we shall appreciate anything you may do in our behalf.²⁴⁰

The enclosed check is intended to cover a replacement of the merchandise lost. Will you please be sure to ²⁶⁰ make the new shipment in a box that is properly insulated so that there will be no doubt about its ²⁸⁰ arriving in good condition. We certainly don't want to take any chance with the new shipment, and we cannot at ³⁰⁰ the present time count on the weather.

Thank you for your generous co-operation.

Yours truly   (317)

WILLIAM PAMPLIN COMPANY

JW:EB   Manager
Enc.

DICTATION STUDY XVII

PART 1. BASIC SKILLS

Theory Review

Directions. All of the following past tense words are used in the article in this lesson. Read them until you can read without the aid of the key. Then write each word at least once. The disjoined *t* is always written with an upward stroke. The joined past tense is expressed by a *t* or a *d* according to sound. The *ld* is made by raising the end of the *l*. In making this stroke, drop the *l* slightly before beginning the upstroke. Notice the word *yielded*, which has an *ld stroke* followed by an extra *d*. The *rd* in *measured* and *appeared* is written more easily by starting slightly downward.

The Past Tense

Key: mattered, returned, resembled, used, walked, expressed, worked, placed, fixed, asked, finished, convinced, passed, watched, kept, produced, blocked, acquainted, wanted, discouraged, advised, disappointed, studied, carried, removed, associated, admitted, hesitated, needed, lifted, adapted, started, permitted

235

The LD and the RD Strokes

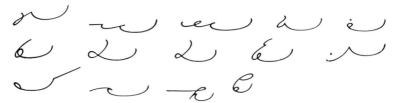

Key: settled, unrolled, rerolled, sold, held, piled, failed, filled, spoiled, handled, yielded, called, measured, appeared

Directions. Read the following article until you can easily read at your goal rate—125 to 150 words a minute. A satisfactory reading time is indicated at the end of the article. Make two copies in shorthand. If you have practiced the foregoing words, both the reading and the writing should be easy for you.

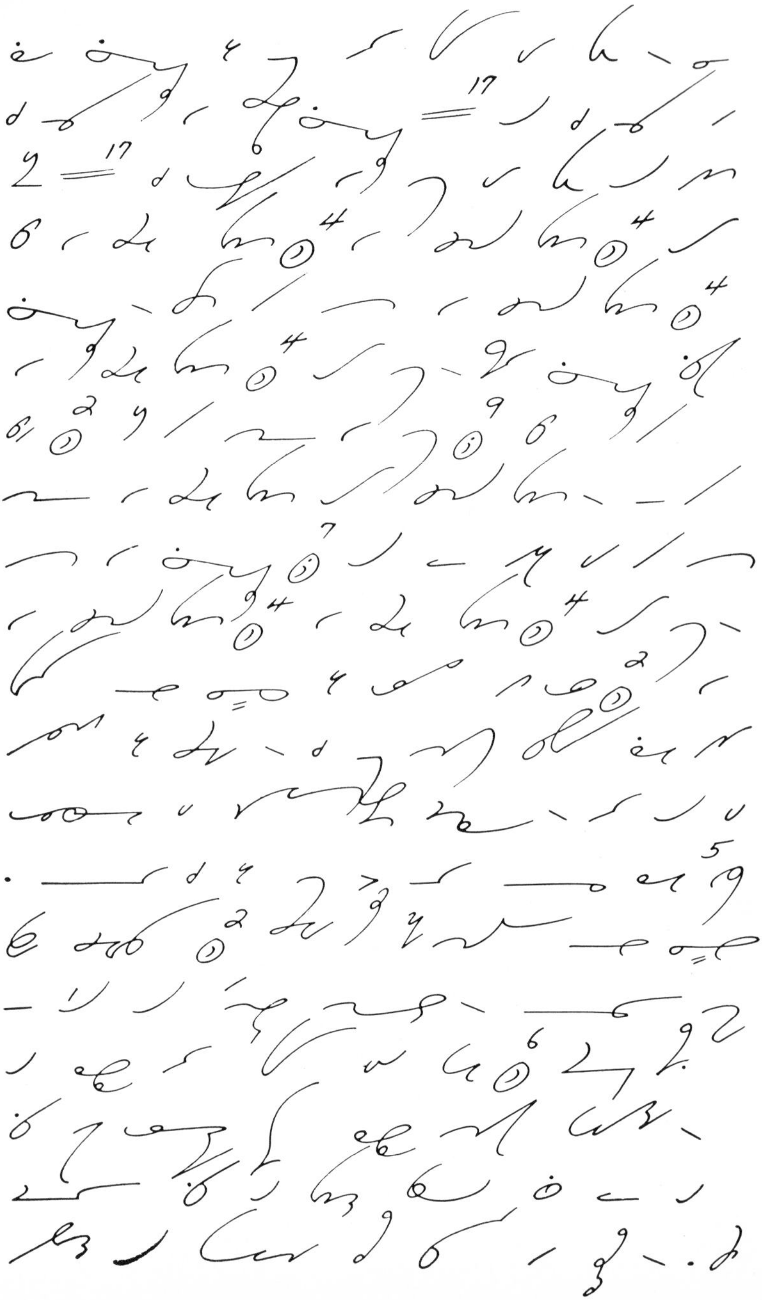

(Reading time: 4 min.)   (518)

No new punctuation pointer is given in this lesson; however, thirty-six medial punctuation situations have been used to illustrate nine of the pointers previously presented. Each of these situations is numbered to show the pointer applied. Use this opportunity to refresh your memory.

PART 2. BUSINESS INFORMATION

Vocabulary Preview

ar/gue

Chil/dress

clean/li/ness

dec/la/ra/tion

ed/u/ca/tion

ed/u/ca/tional

ed/u/ca/tional
  de/part/ments

fac/to/ries

fla/vors

in/creas/ingly

in/gre/di/ents

in/stances

in/tel/li/gent

mak/ers

man/u/fac/tur/ing

me/di/ums

mixed

mu/seum

no longer

out/fits

proc/esses

re/al/i/za/tion

sci/en/tific

some of this

stages

tests

work/men

Educational Departments

Manufacturers and merchants are finding it increasingly difficult to sell to the public on the mere [20] declaration of quality. The various educational mediums are keeping people informed of [40] the developments in business methods and manufacturing processes. The result is a market of more [60] intelligent buyers.

Business organizations are playing their part, too, in this general scheme of education.[80] Food manufacturers no longer argue only the excellent flavors of their foods, but put special [100] stress on the cleanliness of their factories and the care with which the ingredients are selected, mixed, and preserved.[120] Makers of other materials argue the skill of their workmen, the reliability of their [140] scientific departments, and the advantages of their particular method of manufacture over some [160] other. The educational departments of such companies print numerous folders and booklets telling of [180] the various tests and processes through which a product goes before it is ready for use.

These educational [200] departments, often quite separate from the advertising departments, co-operate with schools by furnishing [220] authentic literature describing methods of manufacture, and in some instances by supplying [240] display outfits showing products at the several stages of manufacture. Some of this educational [260] effort is probably the result of campaigns to force truth in advertising; but much of it is prompted by [280] the realization that an intelligent buyer is the best customer.

In the following series of [300] letters, the materials sent to the Childress Art Museum come from our educational department, even [320] though the transaction is handled by our advertising manager.   (333)

PART 3. BUSINESS CORRESPONDENCE

between

KARIM RUG MANUFACTURERS		CHILDRESS ART MUSEUM
1628 Broad Street	*and*	107 Allegheny Avenue
Brooklyn 13, New York		Charleston 5, West Virginia

LETTER 101

Brook/lyn		loom	
car/pets		Marks	
chil/dren		mod/ern	
cork		mod/ern/is/tic	
cov/er/ings		ori/en/tal	
de/signed		prim/i/tive	
for/eign		rug	
grate/ful		sec/re/tary	
John		sup/ple/men/tary	
Ka/rim		tile	
li/no/leum		to let us have	

January 23, 19—

Karim Rug Manufacturers
1628 Broad Street
Brooklyn 13, New York

Gentlemen

The annual exhibit of the Childress Art Museum, beginning on March 4, will include floor [20] coverings of primitive peoples, oriental rugs, rugs of foreign countries, carpets of modern design, and [40] floor coverings of cork, linoleum, and tile. Supplementary material will show how the floor coverings [60] are made.

Because of the museum's educational work for children, we are especially interested [80] in obtaining a Jacquard loom. Are you willing to let us have one for the exhibit?

We should like also [100] to show some of your modernistic rugs like the one designed by John Marks. We shall be grateful for any assistance [120] you can render us.

Yours truly (126)

CHILDRESS ART MUSEUM

CHL:EM Secretary

LETTER 102

Al/le/gheny		hooked	
anal/y/sis		Lan/dry	
Charles/ton		West Vir/ginia	
con/ceived		you will find	

January 28, 19—

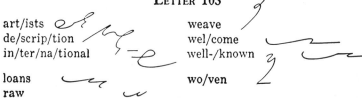

KARIM RUG MANUFACTURERS, Advertising Manager

(Reading time: 30 sec.)   (75)

LETTER 103

art/ists		weave	
de/scrip/tion		wel/come	
in/ter/na/tional		well-/known	
loans		wo/ven	
raw			

February 2, 19—

Karim Rug Manufacturers
1628 Broad Street
Brooklyn 13, New York

Gentlemen

We appreciate your willingness to let us use the modernistic rug designed by John Marks. The [20] rug analysis, too, will be a welcome addition to our exhibit. Can you tell us about the type of [40] loom on which the John Marks rug was woven? May we have also a description of its weave and the raw materials [60] of which it is made? The name of your company will, of course, be mentioned in the descriptive card accompanying [80] your loans.

Have you any other rugs by well-known artists that you are willing to exhibit? Is the John [100] Marks rug the one that is at present being shown in connection with the International Exhibit?

Thank you [120] for your co-operation.

Yours truly   (127)

CHILDRESS ART MUSEUM

CHL:EM   Secretary

LETTER 104

any other	pat/tern
che/nille	spe/cially
com/pa/ra/ble	sum/mary
ex/hibit	that will be
ex/hi/bi/tion	we re/gret
pam/phlets	yarn

February 7, 19—

KARIM RUG MANUFACTURERS, Advertising Manager

(Reading time: 1 min.) (138)

LETTER 105

as soon as	of/fered
pos/si/ble	should like to have
in/stall/ing	tell us
	to lend

February 14, 19—

Karim Rug Manufacturers
1628 Broad Street
Brooklyn 13, New York

Gentlemen

Will you tell us when we may expect the delivery of the John Marks rug and the rug analysis,[20] which you offered to lend the museum. We are installing the exhibit now and, therefore, should like to have [40] them as soon as possible.

Yours truly   (47)

CHILDRESS ART MUSEUM

CHL:EM   Secretary

LETTER 106

anx/i/ety   caus/ing
apol/o/gize   you may be able ⸴·

February 19, 19—

KARIM RUG MANUFACTURERS, Advertising Manager

(Reading time: 25 sec.)   (59)

PART 4. BUSINESS PRACTICES

Vocabulary Preview

al/ter/nate   omis/sion
back/space   partly
de/pressed   pre/ced/ing

in this man/ner   re/lease
mar   slide
move/ment   spoil/ing

Insertion of Extra Letters

When a letter has been omitted from the middle of a word, it is possible to insert that letter without [20] spoiling the appearance of the page. To make such a correction, the stenographer should erase the entire [40] word and then bring the paper into position for writing the first letter of the word. By the use of the paper [60] release, the stenographer should slide the paper half a space to the right and type the word to be inserted.[80] Moving the paper in this manner permits the stenographer to insert the omitted letter in a space [100] taken partly from the full space preceding the word and partly from the full space following the word. The reduction [120] of the amount of space before and after the word does not mar the appearance of the page.

The use of the [140] backspace key gives an alternate method of inserting an extra letter in a word. In this method the [160] stenographer must control the movement of the carriage by holding the backspace key slightly depressed during the striking [180] of each letter. This method permits the insertion of two or three letters in fairly long words. A little [200] practice in making corrections of this sort will often save the stenographer much retyping of material.[220]

When a letter has been omitted from the beginning or the end of a word, it is not necessary [240] to erase the word. Through the use of the backspace key, the omitted letter can be inserted in the proper [260] place by using only part of the space at the beginning or the end of the word in which the omission occurs.[280]   (280)

PART 5. PROGRESS CHECKUP

Letter PC-17

Karim Rug Manufacturers
1628 Broad Street
Brooklyn 13, New York

Gentlemen

On March 4 the Childress Art Museum will start its annual exhibit. This exhibit will run [20] for a period of six

INSERTION OF EXTRA LETTERS

When a letter has been omitted from the middle of a word, it is possible to insert that letter without spoiling the appearance of the page. To make such a correction, the stenographer should erase the entire word and then bring the paper into position for writing the first letter of the word. By the use of the paper release, the stenographer should slide the paper half a space to the right and type the word to be inserted. Moving the paper in this manner permits the stenographer to insert the omitted letter in a space taken partly from the full space preceding the word and partly from the full space following the word. The reduction of the amount of space before and after the word does not mar the appearance of the page.

The use of the backspace key gives an alternate method of inserting an extra letter in a word. In this method the stenographer must control the movement of the carriage by holding the backspace key slightly depressed during the striking of each letter. This method permits the insertion of two or three letters in fairly long words. A little practice in making corrections of this sort will often save the stenographer much retyping of material.

When a letter has been omitted from the beginning or the end of a word, it is not necessary to erase the word. Through the use of the backspace key, the omitted letter can be inserted in the proper place by using only part of the space at the beginning or the end of the word in which the omission occurs.

MODEL 10—INSERTION OF EXTRA LETTERS

This article includes a correction of each of the types described. See "middle" in the first line of the first paragraph for an example of the type of correction described in that paragraph. Likewise, note "stenographer" in the last line of the second paragraph, "beginning" in the first line of the last paragraph, and "end" in the second line of that paragraph.

weeks and will feature different types of hand-made and machine-made floor coverings. We [40] are especially desirous to display the work of primitive peoples, rugs of various foreign countries,[60] oriental rugs, and carpets of modern design. We also wish to include floor coverings of linoleum,[80] cork, and tile.

Undoubtedly, you can supply us with materials that will be of value in this exhibit.[100] Perhaps you can let us have some raw materials and some rugs in process of manufacture showing present [120]-day methods. If you can let us have an old loom as well as models of new types of machines, you will add a [140] great deal to the display.

We are planning to arrange the exhibition material in a manner that will [160] show the art of rug manufacture, calling attention to the success of the factory system, which brings [180] quality rugs within the financial range of persons of average means.

Any materials you may lend us [200] will be on display with a card bearing your name. Supplementary descriptive booklets will be distributed [220] in multigraphed or printed form to be sure that persons visiting the exhibit will have a complete description [240] of the display. In these supplementary booklets we shall acknowledge our indebtedness to those who help [260] to make the affair a success.

May we request your assistance in this matter. We are confident that your [280] co-operation will greatly stimulate the educational interest that we are trying to encourage [300] in this part of the country. Use the enclosed sheets to let us know how much help we may expect.

Very truly yours [320]   (320)

CHILDRESS ART MUSEUM

CHL:EM   Secretary
Enc.

DICTATION STUDY XVIII

PART 1. BASIC SKILLS

Theory Review

Directions. The following words are all used in the article in this lesson. Read them until you can read them easily without the aid of the key; then write each word at least once in shorthand. In practicing the words with disjoined prefixes, learn to pass promptly from the prefix to the next stroke of the word. By careful attention to your practice you will soon learn where to place the prefix so that your hand will have the shortest possible move from the prefix to the next stroke.

TR Words

Key: centered, concentrated, contract, contrary, controls, contribute, controversy, contrivance, construction, constrains, construed, instructions, instrument, restrict, restricted, retribution, destroyed, distribution, detracts, detrimental, extraordinary, extravagant, extremely, external, *electri*cal, *inter*esting, *inter*ests, *inter*nal, *inter*national, *inter*view, *intro*duce, *intri*gue, *enter*tain, *enter*prise

Directions. The following article contains all the foregoing words. If you have practiced the words properly, the reading and the writing of the article should be easy for you. Read the article until you can read it at your goal rate; then make two shorthand copies of it.

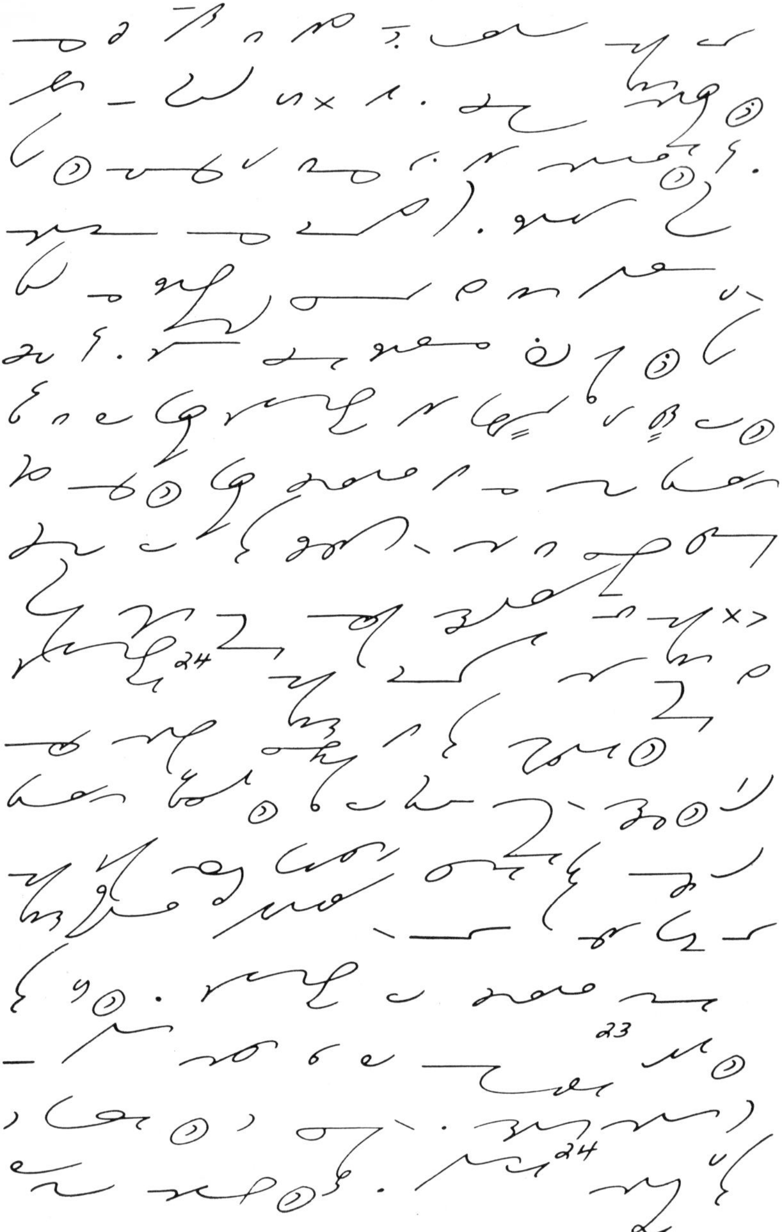

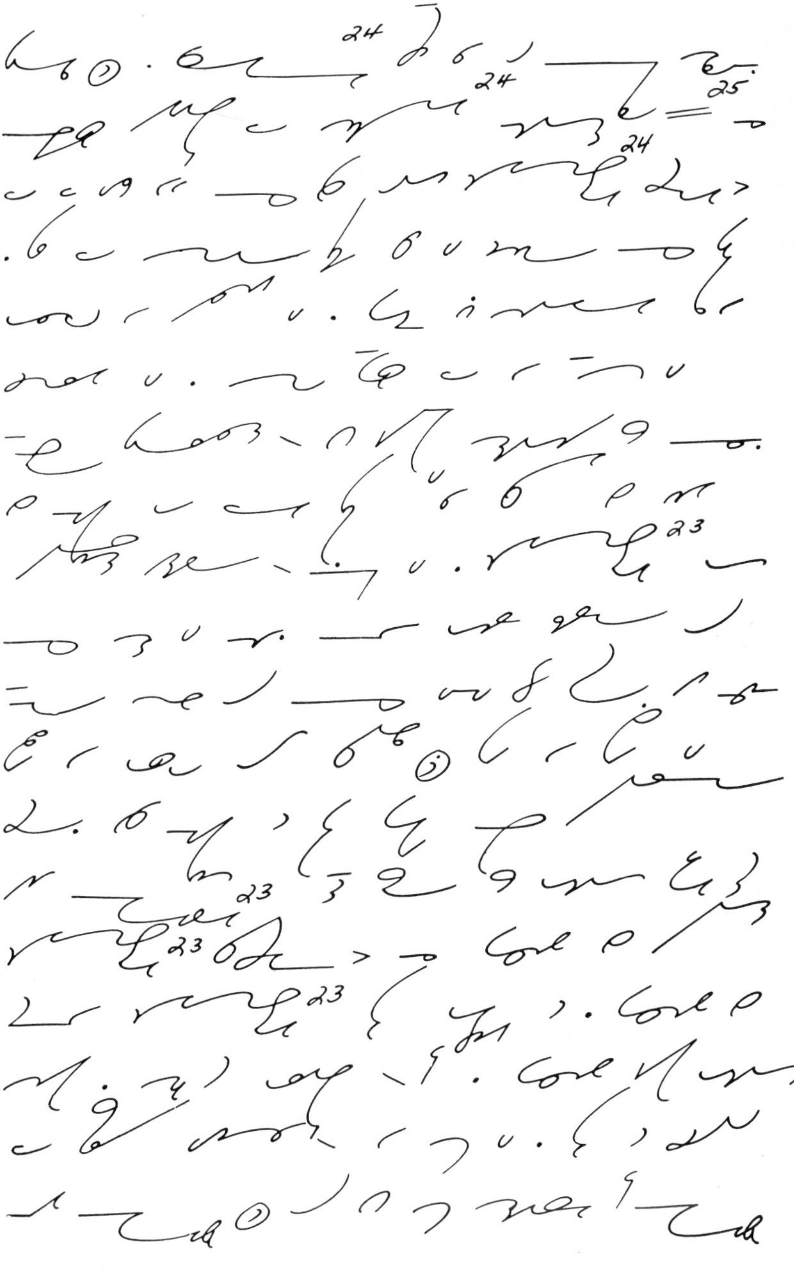

(Reading time: 4 min.)   (511)

Punctuation Pointers

All medial punctuation needed in the foregoing article is shown, but numbers are used only for the pointers explained in this lesson and for Pointer 23 of the preceding lesson. Can you spell the possessive words numbered 23 and 24?

24. Plural possession is expressed by adding an apostrophe to words ending in *s*, and by adding an apostrophe and *s* to all other words.

Plural	*Singular*
stenographers' notebooks	a stenographer's notebooks
employers' offices	an employer's office
a directors' controversy	a director's objection
customers' instructions	a customer's order
a salesmen's interview	the salesman's territory
children's books	a child's book

25. A *dash* precedes a statement that summarizes expressions in series.

A careless attitude, repeated tardiness, irregular attendance —these things spell inefficiency.

Desks, machines, books, cabinets—all were moved on the same day.

She is prompt in reporting to the office; she can assume responsibility; she is loyal to a trust—these are qualities that we value.

PART 2. BUSINESS INFORMATION
Vocabulary Preview

al/most

Amer/i/ca's

any/body

breed/ing

by re/turn mail

Clem/ens

Con/nect/i/cut

cu/ri/os/ity

de/vices

di/vulge

Hart/ford

I don't like

I don't want

I had

joker

mail/bags

prac/ti/cal

prog/ress (n.)

re/ported

star/tle

stopped

to see

tons

Twain

un/in/i/ti/ated

va/ri/ety

Typewriters

On March 19, 1875, Mark Twain wrote from Hartford, Connecticut, as follows:

"Gentlemen: [20]

Please do not use my name in any way. Please do not even divulge the fact that I own a machine. I have [40] entirely stopped using the Type-Writer, for the reason that I never could write a letter with it to anybody [60] without receiving a request by return mail that I would not only describe the machine but state what progress [80] I had made in the use of it, etc., etc. I don't like to write letters, and so I don't [100] want people to know that I own this curiosity-breeding little joker.

Yours truly,

Saml. L. Clemens" [120]

Mark Twain lived to see this "curiosity-breeding little joker" become a machine of practical value.[140] In business it has increased the field of correspondence to so great an extent that the figures almost startle [160] the uninitiated.

One of America's large department stores is reported to receive approximately [180] ten thousand letters in its daily mail. Another large organization is credited with four [200] tons of daily incoming mail. And there are hundreds of other businesses, the correspondence of which can be [220] handled only through the use of a great variety of time-saving machines and devices.

The following [240] correspondence is typical of many letters that help fill the mailbags of big companies. They have no [260] particular value to the company in question, but each must be answered with courtesy. One company writes,[280] "It is our standard policy to answer, or at least to acknowledge, every letter on the date of its [300] receipt."

(301)

PART 3. BUSINESS CORRESPONDENCE

between

WILSON KOOL KOLA COMPANY		MR. EDWIN R. TAYLOR
1622 South Adams Street	*and*	945 St. Andrews Street
Raleigh, North Carolina		Yonkers 11, New York

and

MR. JOHN S. SAVAGE
132 Westover Avenue
Charleston 8, West Virginia

LETTER 107

drink	Ra/leigh
Ed/win	re/fresh/ment
equal	St. An/drews
Grand Cen/tral	South Adams
I have been	stock/holder
Kool Kola	Tay/lor
main/tained	ter/mi/nal
New York City	that there is
North Car/o/lina	Wil/son
op/er/at/ing	Yon/kers

945 St. Andrews Street
Yonkers 11, New York
July 15, 19—

Wilson Kool Kola Company
1622 South Adams Street
Raleigh, North Carolina

Gentlemen

For ten years I have been a stockholder of your company, and for an equal period of time [20] I have found refreshment and pleasure in the use of Kool Kola. I have often wondered how a drink of this [40] quality could be sold for five cents. I have been especially interested in the fact that dealers have maintained [60] this price even in the face of increasing operating costs.

Realizing the advertising value of [80] the five-cent price, I want you to know that there is in the Grand Central Terminal of New York City a dealer [100] who charges ten cents for a drink of Kool Kola.

Very truly yours (112)

Edwin R. Taylor

LETTER 108

ar/bi/trar/ily	ounce
as/sist/ant	pro/hib/i/tive
ball	pro/por/tions
car/bon/ated	rail/road
cir/cuses	rent
de/light/ful	sirup
dol/lars	sta/tions
ex/ec/u/tive	to charge
fac/tor	vi/tal
ice	wa/ter

July 21, 19—

(shorthand outlines)

WILSON KOOL KOLA COMPANY, Executive Assistant
(Reading time: 1 min. 40 sec.)   (220)

LETTER 109

mar/ket/ing   slight
proved   tested
ranks   West/o/ver

132 Westover Avenue
Charleston 8, West Virginia
July 19, 19—

Wilson Kool Kola Company
1622 South Adams Street
Raleigh, North Carolina

Gentlemen

I am not now and have never been connected with the sirup-drink business. I have, however, a [20] formula that has been tested and proved practicable.

Would you consider marketing my product? The cost of [40] the materials is so slight that a five-cent drink would produce a good profit, and the flavor will certainly [60] put this drink in the ranks of a best seller.

May I have an opportunity of talking my proposition [80] over with you?

Yours very truly   (86)

John S. Savage

LETTER 110

de/vel/op/ment   served
en/er/gies   sound
ev/i/denced   to pro/mote
for more than

July 22, 19—

Wᴵʟꜱᴏɴ Kᴏᴏʟ Kᴏʟᴀ Cᴏᴍᴘᴀɴʏ, Executive Assistant
(Reading time: 40 sec.)   (94)

PART 4. BUSINESS PRACTICES
Vocabulary Preview

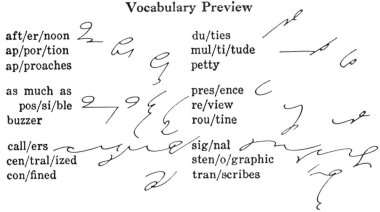

aft/er/noon
ap/por/tion
ap/proaches

as much as
   pos/si/ble
buzzer

call/ers
cen/tral/ized
con/fined

du/ties
mul/ti/tude
petty

pres/ence
re/view
rou/tine

sig/nal
sten/o/graphic
tran/scribes

The Stenographer

Stenographic duties vary greatly according to the nature of the office in which the stenographer [20] is employed. If the stenographer happens to be the only office worker in her particular office,[40] she will be expected to handle the correspondence and the filing, answer the telephone, meet callers, and [60] attend to a multitude of petty jobs and details too numerous to mention. Such a position requires [80] a broad knowledge of business in general, the ability to work in the presence of interruptions, and [100] the ability to handle matters in the absence of the employer.

Bigger businesses frequently [120] organize a stenographic department and have a chief stenographer in charge of that department. In businesses [140] of this sort the stenographer's position more nearly approaches the routine in which she takes dictation [160] and transcribes her letters. Her desk is probably situated in a general office, and she takes dictation [180] at a signal from a buzzer. In some cases her dictation duties are confined to the writing of [200] material for definite persons in the organization. In other cases she may be required to take [220] dictation from anyone connected with the business.

It is the duty of the chief stenographer to [240] apportion the work among the members of her department, to review this work before it is submitted to her [260] employers, and to assume general responsibility for the operation of her department.

There [280] is a tendency on the part of businesses to centralize the stenographic work as much as possible.[300] One company that has offices in various parts of a big city has so centralized its stenographic [320] department that all dictation is given over telephones. Neither dictators nor stenographers have [340] to move from their desks. In the afternoon a special messenger distributes the letters to the particular [360] dictators concerned.   (364)

Vocabulary Preview

care/ful at/ten/tion		rem/edy
ef/fect		rib/bons
in/vested		sal/a/ries
rec/om/mend/ ing		suf/fer
		thereby

Economical Use of Carbon Paper

Leaks and losses in the business office may sometimes become so great as to have a material effect on [20] the cost

Ewing Galloway

This central stenographic office employs twelve stenographers, four transcribing machine operators, four statistical clerks, and one supervisor. Notice the variety of equipment. The executive offices are to the rear.

of operation, and may thereby cause salaries to suffer. By careful attention to typewriter [40] ribbons, carbon papers, and similar office materials, the efficient stenographer can do much toward [60] reducing such waste.

As the average business letter is less than ten lines in length, only a small part of [80] a carbon sheet is actually used. This means that a great part of the money really invested in carbon [100] paper is spent for material that is not put to service. The stenographer can remedy such a [120] situation by recommending the buying of thirteen-inch carbon paper instead of eleven-inch carbon [140] paper. The cost is practically the same. By using first one end of the carbon paper and then the other [160] end, the stenographer can get almost double wear from this particular item,

A sheet of medium [180]-weight carbon paper will ordinarily give eight to ten copies before it should be changed. With medium-weight [200] carbon papers and office stationery of ordinary weight, four or five clear copies can be made at one [220] time on the average typewriter.

Usually, the carbon papers for the first and second copies get more [240] wear than the carbon papers for the third, fourth, or fifth copies. It is advisable, therefore, to change the order [260] of the carbon papers for each new carbon pack. A sheet of carbon paper that is used for a first carbon [280] copy in one carbon pack should be used for the last copy in the next carbon pack. A similar change of order [300] should be applied to all carbon papers in the pack. This practice will ensure the quality of each carbon [320] copy and will prevent the overuse of any one carbon sheet.

The stenographer should use new carbon paper [340] as often as necessary to produce clear copies. Quality should not be sacrificed for economy.[360]   (360)

PART 5. PROGRESS CHECKUP

Letter PC-18

The Taylor Corporation
945 Westover Avenue
Yonkers 9, New York

Gentlemen

A number of complaints have been received from time to time about the fact that you are charging ten cents [20] for a drink of Kool Kola. It is not the policy of this company to force particular retail [40] practices on its dealers, and this letter should not be considered an attempt in that direction. We want to call [60] to your attention, however, the following pertinent thoughts:

For over forty years this company has [80] devoted all its energies to the development of its one product, Kool Kola. The power of this policy [100] is evidenced by the fact that more than nine million Kool Kolas are sold every day for public refreshment.

Year [120] after year, the Wilson Kool Kola Company refuses opportunities to manufacture different [140] types of soft drinks. We are confident that we can serve your own and our interest best by using our advertising [160] appropriations in one definite direction. The volume of business you offer us each year shows that [180] you recognize the value of this attitude.

In a further attempt to be of service to you, we have put [200] our prices at a level that will enable you to serve a standard six-ounce drink for only five cents and still [220] realize a fair profit on the sale. By always serving a combination of one ounce of sirup and five [240] ounces of carbonated water for five cents, you enjoy the benefits of a national demand that has [260] been established through extensive advertising and standard practices. Any change of proportions or price causes [280] you to sacrifice some of the value to be obtained through co-operating in our national campaign.[300]

We should be happy to have you give this question some thought in establishing your own local policy with [320] reference to the sale of Kool Kola. If there is any way in which we have failed to be of the greatest possible [340] assistance to you, please let us know promptly.

Very cordially yours   (353)

WILSON KOOL KOLA COMPANY

ALS:GP   Executive Assistant

DICTATION STUDY XIX

PART 1. BASIC SKILLS
Brief-Form Review

Directions. The following article contains 95 brief forms and brief-form derivatives. Most of them you have met many times before. All of them you will meet many times during your stenographic career. You will need to know them well. Read the article until you can read it easily and then write it twice in shorthand.

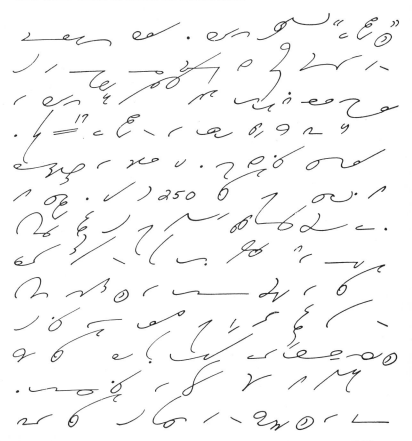

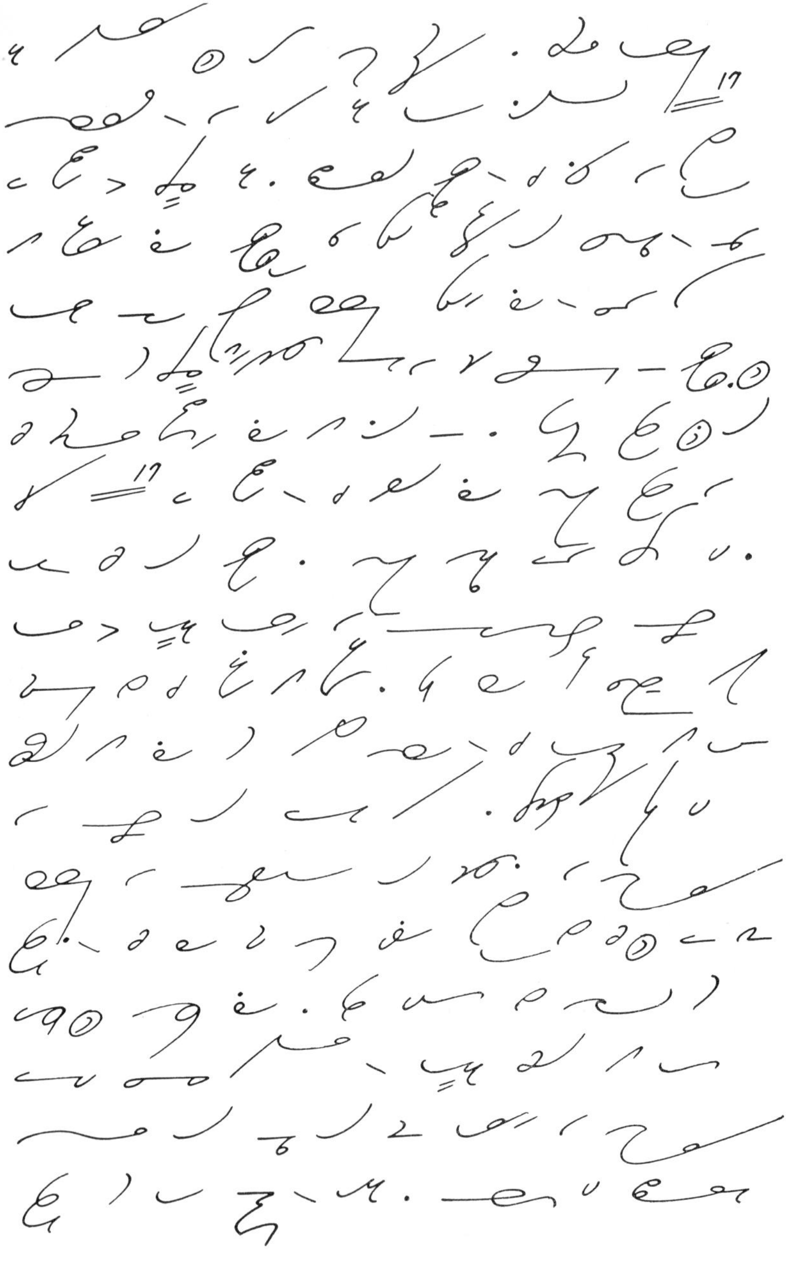

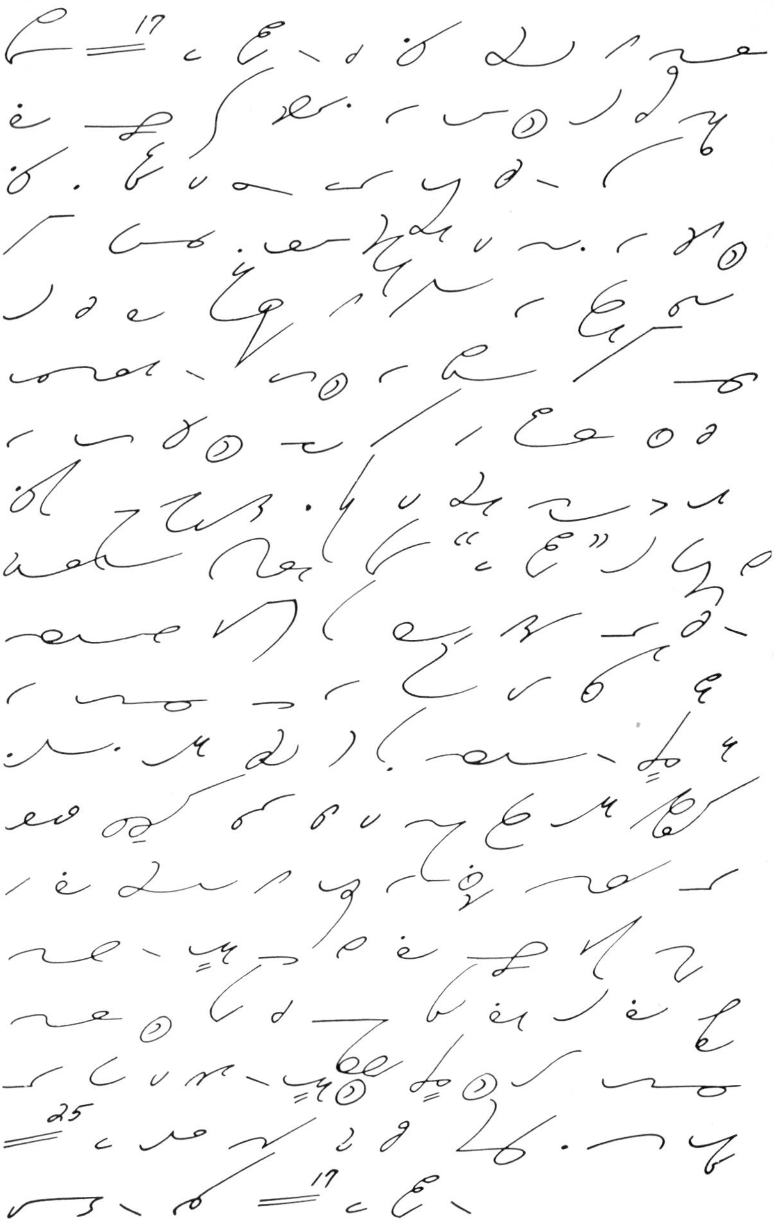

(Reading time: 4 min.) (528)

No new punctuation pointers are given in this lesson. All needed punctuation marks have been inserted in the foregoing article, and the numbers 17 and 25 have been used to indicate the pointers applying to the dash.

PART 2. BUSINESS INFORMATION
Vocabulary Preview

added	in/creases
af/fects	list price
ap/pli/ca/tions	mar/ket price
chain	ne/ces/sity
com/mer/cial	nor/mal
de/cep/tive	ob/vi/ates
de/duc/tion	quan/tity
de/ducts	re/print/ing
dif/fers	suc/cess/fully
dis/tin/guished	sur/pris/ingly
el/e/ment	to take ad/van/
fluc/tu/a/tions	tage
high enough	var/y/ing
in ad/di/tion	

List price   **Price list**

List price refers to the catalog price of an article, the price before any discounts are taken.

We allow a discount of 25 per cent from the list price given on page 14.
The list price is subject to change without notice.

Price list refers to a list of prices on many articles.

A copy of our latest price list is enclosed.
Our price list will give prices and instructions for ordering.

Discounts

In preceding letters we have frequently met the word *discount* in at least three of its applications: bank discount,[20] trade discount, and cash discount. These discounts are distinguished, one from the other, by their nature.

Bank discount is [40] an amount that a bank deducts from a note on which money is borrowed. The discount is really the interest [60] for the period from the date of deduction to that of maturity. As can be seen, the element [80] of time greatly affects the amount of the discount. In this respect bank discount differs from commercial discount.[100] In passing, we should add that bank discount differs from interest in that discount is payable at the beginning [120] of a period and interest is payable at the end of a period.

Trade discount is a [140] deduction or a series of deductions from the list price of goods. Such a discount may be offered to encourage [160] quantity buying, in which case the amount of the discount increases as the size of the order increases; [180] or it may be offered to adjust the list price of goods to the current market price. The list prices printed in [200] catalogs are usually high enough to cover normal market fluctuations, and varying discounts [220] are used to bring the prices down to the market level. This plan obviates the necessity for frequently [240] reprinting expensive catalogs.

Trade discounts are sometimes surprisingly deceptive. For instance, the chain discounts [260] of 40-20-10-5, while adding to 75, are really equivalent to [280] 58.96 per cent. Chain trade discounts are never added together, but must be figured separately.[300]

Cash discount is a deduction from the amount of the invoice, in consideration of the prompt payment [320] of the invoice. Many business concerns make it a practice to take advantage of cash discounts. They consider [340] this a good business policy and claim that it enables them to meet price competition successfully. Such [360] a discount may be offered in addition to trade discounts. It appears on an invoice as part of the credit [380] terms. It may be expressed, for instance, as "2/10, n/30," meaning 2 per cent discount for payment within ten [400] days, the full amount being due in thirty days.   (409)

PART 3. BUSINESS CORRESPONDENCE

between

VIRGINIA HARDWARE COMPANY   FLUDPRUF STOVE COMPANY
589 Melville Street   *and*   7110 North Avenue
Roanoke 2, Virginia   Baltimore 7, Maryland

LETTER 111

Bal/ti/more	Har/ris
date	Mel/ville
dis/trib/u/tor	move
Flud/pruf	on or be/fore
for/mer	over
gas/o/line	Ro/a/noke
hard/ware	stoves

February 28, 19—

Virginia Hardware Company
589 Melville Street
Roanoke 2, Virginia

Gentlemen

When Mr. Harris recently discussed with you the question of your handling our Fludpruf gasoline [20] stoves, he mentioned some equipment still held by our former distributor, the Richmond Hardware Company. It is [40] our impression that you expressed a willingness to take over this equipment on May 1.

The Richmond [60] distributor is now asking us to move its stock at once. Naturally, we do not want to go to the expense of [80] having these stoves returned to Baltimore. If you will take them in stock now, we shall pay the transportation charges, [100] date our invoice May 1, and give you the opportunity of selling a large part of this equipment before [120] any payment actually becomes due. We are convinced that this offer alone should be especially [140] attractive to you; but, in addition, we are willing to grant a discount privilege of 2 per cent for payment [160] on or before May 10.

May we hear from you at once?

Very truly yours   (173)

FLUDPRUF STOVE COMPANY

DM:V   Manager

LETTER 112

among them

dem/on/stra/tion

dis/cour/ag/ing

en/thu/si/as/tic

hasty

hes/i/tancy

jus/tice

next few weeks

North Av/e/nue

op/posed

pos/si/bil/i/ties

prom/ises

store/rooms

to any kind

to re/vive

March 3, 19—

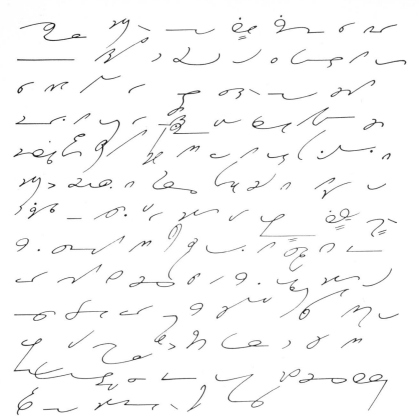

VIRGINIA HARDWARE COMPANY, President

(Reading time: 1 min. 50 sec.) (248)

LETTER 113

ab/so/lutely	de/lighted
ad/ver/tis/ers	dis/ap/point/ment
aroused	in/dif/fer/ent
burn/ers	in/spired
can't	ob/jec/tion/able
Daw/son	op/po/si/tion

March 5, 19—

Virginia Hardware Company
589 Melville Street
Roanoke 2, Virginia

Gentlemen

Your salesmen must have experienced keen disappointment on meeting the opposition that merchants [20] naturally
show toward gasoline stoves. We don't blame them. But it
is well to keep in mind that this opposition [40] inspired the
building of the Fludpruf gasoline stove—the stove that
absolutely prevents flooding, the one [60] objectionable feature of other gasoline burners.

When you consider the fact that you and your salesmen
were [80] decidedly indifferent toward our product before our
demonstration, and that this demonstration aroused [100] a
strong enthusiasm, can't you see the possibilities of selling
your customers in the same way? And [120] remember, too,
that when you once really sell to a man who was opposed
to the product, he becomes one of [140] your best advertisers.

We feel confident that your sales force will be in an
entirely different frame of mind [160] after Mr. Harris has
worked with them. He has just covered the field for the
Dawson Company, of Washington; [180] and Mr. Dawson is
delighted with the results already obtained.

We are so sure of your own satisfaction [200] with Fludpruf that we are asking the Richmond Hardware Company
to ship you its stock the first of next week. Payment [220] for
this stock may be made at your own convenience.

Very truly yours   (232)

FLUDPRUF STOVE COMPANY

DM:V   Manager

LETTER 114

as a mat/ter
car/load

com/pete
cook/ing

less than		seems to be	
over/come		sur/prised	
re/mit/tances		un/der/stand/ing	

March 15, 19—

[shorthand outlines]

VIRGINIA HARDWARE COMPANY, President

(Reading time: 1 min. 15 sec.)   (168)

Letter 115

April   *e*   ker/o/sene
con/ver/sa/tion   out/lin/ing

March 18, 19—

Virginia Hardware Company
589 Melville Street
Roanoke 2, Virginia

Gentlemen

Mr. Harris has just written us a letter outlining his conversation with you with regard [20] to the Fludpruf gasoline stove. He feels that we should comply with your request for May 1 dating on all the stoves,[40] as it is quite evident that you are temporarily overstocked.

You will note that our invoice for the Richmond [60] shipment is dated May 1 and has a discount privilege of 2 per cent for payment on or before May [80] 10. On that portion of your order No. 3320 which covers gasoline stoves amounting [100] to $2,559, we are granting the same extension of time. The remainder [120] of the invoice, however, which covers kerosene cook stoves, is to continue on the April 1 dating with [140] a discount privilege of 2 per cent for payment on or before April 10.

We are glad to help you in this [160] way, as we want you to be thoroughly satisfied with the agency for the Fludpruf gasoline stove.

Very [180] truly yours   (182)

FLUDPRUF STOVE COMPANY

DM:V   Manager

Letter 116

book/keep/ing   con/ven/iently
de/part/ment   over/due

June 3, 19—

Virginia Hardware Company
589 Melville Street
Roanoke 2, Virginia

Gentlemen

Our bookkeeping department has called to our attention your account, which is indicated on the [20] enclosed statement.

The first item, amounting to $673.47, covers [40] a shipment of kerosene cook stoves on which the invoice date was April 1, and the terms were 2 per cent, April [60] 10. As this amount is now two months overdue, we hope you can conveniently make settlement.

The next two items [80] cover two shipments of Fludpruf gasoline stoves, one from our Baltimore factory and one from the Richmond [100] Hardware Company. The invoices on these shipments were dated May 1, and the terms were 2 per cent, May 10. Won't [120] you let us have a check for at least one of these items?

How is the Fludpruf selling now? We are sure that your [140] salesmen are beginning to realize that Fludpruf stoves will do all that we promise. Prospective customers can be [160] convinced of this, too.

Very truly yours   (167)

FLUDPRUF STOVE COMPANY

DM:V   Manager
Enc.

LETTER 117

con/cen/trated
gen/er/ally
have been able

mis/un/der/stood
re/mained

re/mit
to rest
un/touched

very lit/tle
we took

June 7, 19—

[shorthand text]

VIRGINIA HARDWARE COMPANY, President
(Reading time: 1 min. 10 sec.)   (161)

LETTER 118

col/lect/ing	*[shorthand]*	ex/pe/ri/ence	*[shorthand]*
com/pet/i/tor	*[shorthand]*	hap/pen	
ex/clu/sive	*[shorthand]*	in your	*[shorthand]*

it has be/come		reap	
pi/o/neer		rights	
prof/it/able		some time	
re/act		we shall be	

June 14, 19—

Virginia Hardware Company
589 Melville Street
Roanoke 2, Virginia

Gentlemen

Suppose we let the question of the Fludpruf gasoline stove rest until September 1. In the meantime [20] we shall be collecting data that may be of material help to you in your fall campaign.

Has it not [40] been your experience that any new worthwhile thing takes some time to become established? And even after it [60] has become established, it does not always bring a big sale because some competitor may reap the benefit [80] of the hard work done by the pioneer.

This, however, cannot happen in your case. You have exclusive rights in [100] your territory. Every single effort you put forth will react to your own favor. You may meet some [120] difficulties at first, but Fludpruf and your salesmen can produce profitable results.

Very truly yours   (139)

FLUDPRUF STOVE COMPANY

DM:V   Manager

PART 4. BUSINESS PRACTICES

Vocabulary Preview

af/fect/ing		grip/ping	
as/sem/bled		pull	
gen/u/ine		sep/a/ra/tion	

whole   ᒼ⁀   with this   ♫

Separation of Carbon Sheets from Letter Sheets

The use of the thirteen-inch carbon paper proves a genuine help in the separation of carbon sheets and [20] letter paper, especially when a number of copies have been prepared at one time.

When a new package of [40] carbon paper is opened, the stenographer should cut the upper left-hand corner and the lower right-hand corner [60] diagonally from the carbon sheets. A whole package may be cut at once.

When standard letter stationery [80] is assembled with this long carbon paper, the ends of the carbon sheets will extend about two inches below [100] the ends of the stationery. After the typing has been completed, the stenographer may easily [120] separate the sheets by gripping the stationery at the upper left-hand corner and the carbon papers at [140] the bottom. A slight pull will bring the carbon sheets entirely clear of the typed copies. The cutting of the two corners [160] of the carbon sheets permits turning either end of the carbon paper toward the top without affecting [180] the separation of the pages after typing.   (189)

PART 5. PROGRESS CHECKUP

LETTER PC-19

Fludpruf Stove Company
7110 North Avenue
Baltimore 7, Maryland

Gentlemen

We take exception to the attitude expressed in your letter of June 3 with regard to our [20] indebtedness in the amount of $3,232.47.

When we [40] agreed to take over the agency for Fludpruf stoves, we also agreed to accept a shipment of the stoves from [60] the Richmond Hardware Company; but we informed you at that time that we were very doubtful about our ability [80] to market the stoves without a long and enthusiastic campaign in this territory.

You promised [100] us that we might make payments on account at our own convenience. As a matter of record, you dated your invoice [120] May 1 and offered terms of 2 per cent, May 10; but it was our understanding that there would be no obligation [140] to settle on either May 1 or May 10.

It has been our policy to take advantage of a discount [160] when possible, and we should certainly do so in this instance were it not for the fact that we have been [180] unable to dispose of any of the stoves. We cannot settle for the Richmond stock or continue the agency [200] unless we can count on the complete support and co-operation of your office.

We do agree with you [220] that a few satisfied buyers of Fludpruf stoves in this section would materially encourage sales, but to [240] get those satisfied buyers is more of a job than we had expected. Of course, our men are inexperienced [260] in handling this type of product and will need training in selling stoves; but we can help them very little. You will [280] have to furnish us with all possible assistance until our sales actually show that we no longer need [300] your help.

Please instruct your bookkeeping department not to send us any further requests for payment until we [320] sell some of the stoves. We are sure that we both wish to be convinced that this agency has possibilities of [340] success and should therefore be continued. With your co-operation, we should be able to sell Fludpruf stoves as [360] well as any other agency in the country.

Yours very truly   (373)

VIRGINIA HARDWARE COMPANY

RA:JP   President

DICTATION STUDY XX

PART 1. BASIC SKILLS

Theory Review

Directions. All of the following words are used in the article in this lesson. Read them until you can read them easily and then write each word at least once in shorthand. When writing words that have two or more separated strokes, learn to pass from one stroke to another promptly and directly. It is hesitation that causes loss of speed.

Joined and disjoined suffixes expressing NITY, CITY (SITY), RITY, LITY

Key: vicinity, community, sanity, dignity, capacity, curiosity, generosity, scarcity, ma*jority*, autho*rity*, since*rity*, matu*rity*, secu*rity*, re*ality*, pen*ality*, fac*ulty*, fac*ility*, ut*ility*, fide*lity*, possib*ility*, responsib*ilities*, ab*ility*, adaptab*ility*, advisab*ility*

Directions. Read the following article until you can read it easily at your goal rate; then write it twice in shorthand. If you have practiced the foregoing words, the reading and writing should be easy for you, as all the words are used in the article.

279

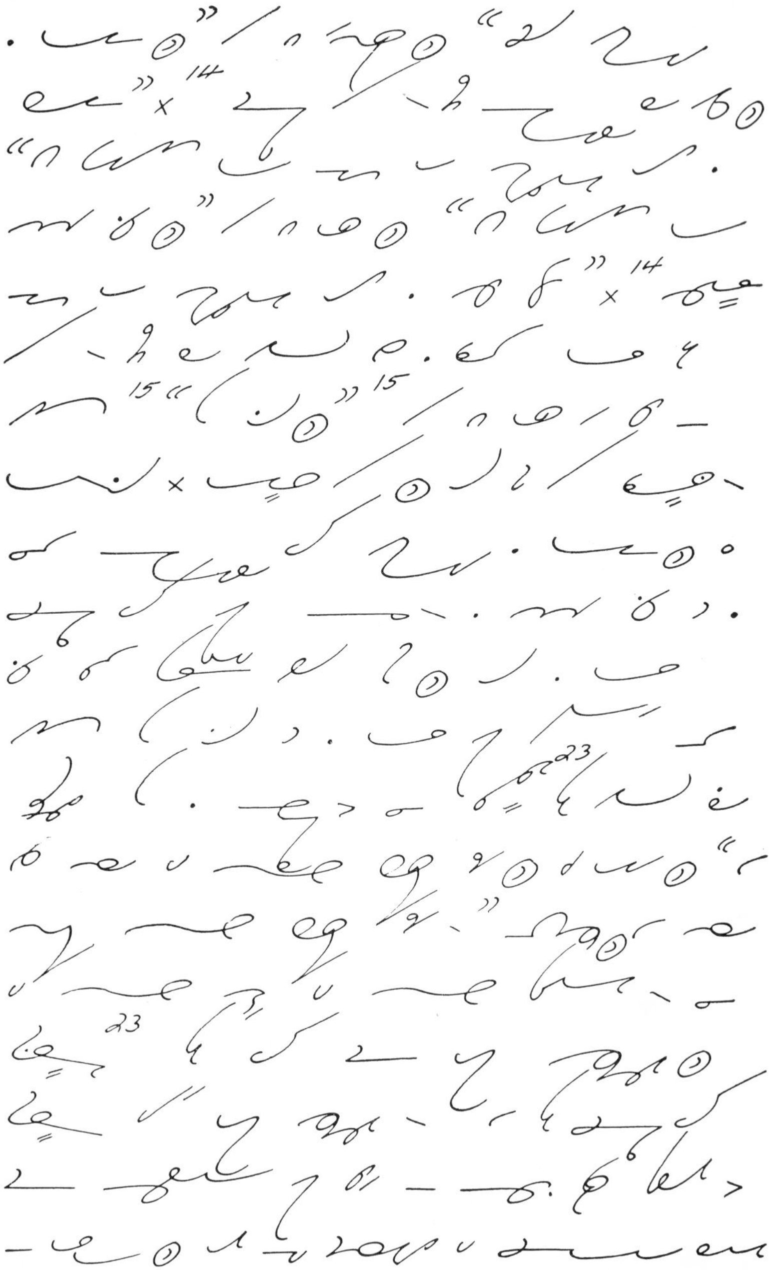

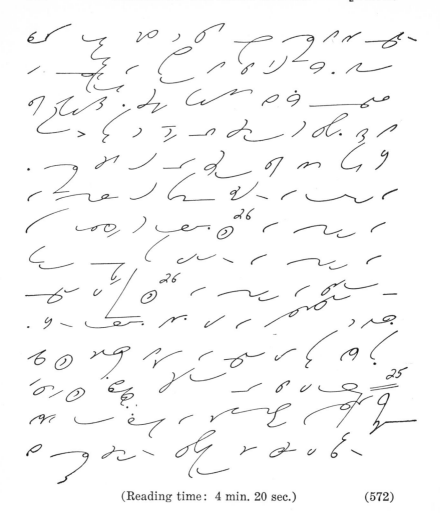

(Reading time: 4 min. 20 sec.)   (572)

Punctuation Pointers

In the foregoing article, all necessary medial punctuation is given. The less common punctuation pointers, including the pointers in this lesson, are indicated by the numbers appearing in the article.

26. A *comma* is often used between interrelated expressions.

The more one has, the more he wants.
The more impatient he becomes, the more difficult his work seems.

27. When the conjunction is repeated between the items of a series, the comma is usually omitted.

Successful stenographic work requires job curiosity and sincerity of effort and generosity of time.

The circulars were tested in Chicago and Denver and San Francisco.

PART 2. BUSINESS INFORMATION

Vocabulary Preview

adopted	man/u/als
de/rived	mov/able
dic/tion/a/ries	pam/phlet
Eng/lish	phase
ex/actly	printer
fas/tened	proof/read/ers
foun/da/tion	proof/read/ing
gal/ley	prove
gave	re/al/ized
Gu/ten/berg	re/set/ting
in/ac/cu/ra/cies	trans/ferred
in the world	trial
in/tro/duces	un/der/tak/ing

Proofreading

When Gutenberg, in 1443, gave to the world his idea of using movable type in [20] printing, he probably little realized that he was building the foundation of an industry that would some [40] day affect practically every other industry in the world. Much has already been written about [60] the value to be derived from a knowledge of some of the practices in printing. This article introduces [80] one more phase of the subject—proofreading.

When type is set up for printing, it is usually fastened in [100] a tray known as a galley. If this type were transferred to the press before a proof had been taken, numerous [120] errors might be found. The correction of the errors would be a rather expensive undertaking. Consequently,[140] it is customary to take an impression of the galley of type before the material goes to press.[160] This impression, or trial sheet, is taken for the purpose of examination or correction and is called [180] a galley proof, or proof sheet. Any errors due to the work of the printer are corrected free of charge, but [200] errors resulting from inaccuracies in the original copy are corrected at the expense of the [220] customer.

The proof sheets should be read very carefully, and the desired corrections should be indicated [240] clearly. To facilitate the easy indication of changes to be made, printers and proofreaders have [260] adopted a number of arbitrary signs that can be interpreted exactly. These signs, called proofreaders' marks, are [280] usually listed in dictionaries, typewriting manuals, and business English books. Such lists may also [300] be obtained from printers' shops.

If the material to be printed is important, it may be necessary [320] to correct several proofs before the changes satisfy the writer. If the material is to be [340] put in pamphlet or book form, a reprint may be desired from time to time. A resetting of type would prove very [360] costly, and keeping the type set up and out of use for long periods of time would also be expensive. Hence,[380] it is customary in such cases to mold plates from the type. These plates are kept on hand for reprinting, but the [400] type is distributed for use in setting up other material.   (413)

PART 3. BUSINESS CORRESPONDENCE

between

PUTNAM & SPILLMAN
Photoengravers
3001 Greenvale Avenue
Detroit 6, Michigan

and

WESTERN PUBLISHERS, INC.
125 University Avenue
Ann Arbor, Michigan

LETTER 119

ar/rang/ing	if you will
bev/eled	let us know
edges	inch
for your con/	mar/gins
ven/ience	neg/a/tive
group	pub/lish/ers

March 11, 19—

Putnam & Spillman
Photoengravers
3001 Greenvale Avenue
Detroit 6, Michigan

Gentlemen

We are again in need of approximately two hundred small cuts. For your convenience we shall group [20] the photographs on cards if you will let us know the size of negative you expect to use. In arranging the [40] pictures, we shall leave margins of $\frac{1}{4}$ of an inch to $\frac{5}{16}$ of an inch for separation and beveled [60] edges.

Yours very truly   (65)

WESTERN PUBLISHERS, INC.

EO:AB   Advertising Manager

LETTER 120

Ann Ar/bor	**uni/ver/sity**
it will have	**with us**
mount/ings	

March 14, 19—

P<small>UTNAM</small> & S<small>PILLMAN</small>, President

(Reading time: 40 sec.)   (87)

L<small>ETTER</small> 121

com/pe/tent
if you think   sug/ges/tions

March 23, 19—

P<small>UTNAM</small> & S<small>PILLMAN</small>, President

(Reading time: 25 sec.)   (55)

LETTER 122

es/ti/mate	to be made
how soon	we are send/ing
sized	you

March 25, 19—

Putnam & Spillman
Photoengravers
3001 Greenvale Avenue
Detroit 6, Michigan

Gentlemen

We are sending you 198 photographs from which full-sized cuts are to be made. Will you [20] please give us an estimate of the cost of this work.

After the order is placed, how soon can delivery be [40] made?

Yours very truly   (44)

WESTERN PUBLISHERS, INC.

EO:AB   Advertising Manager

LETTER 123

all	mak/ing
by you	will be

March 28, 19—

PUTNAM & SPILLMAN, President

(Reading time: 30 sec.)   (73)

LETTER 124

au/thor/ized
back/ground
con/trast

elec/tric
model
quo/ta/tion

re/fer
strengthen
train

trol/ley
wall

March 30, 19—

Putnam & Spillman
Photoengravers
3001 Greenvale Avenue
Detroit 6, Michigan

Gentlemen

While your quotation of March 28 is higher than we had expected it to be, you are [20] authorized to go ahead with the preparation of the cuts.

Can you strengthen the photograph No. 40, or [40] maybe show a little more contrast against the background of wall and table? There are two photographs No. 40; [60] but we refer to the small model of the first trolley car, not to the electric train.

Yours very truly [80]   (80)

WESTERN PUBLISHERS, INC.

EO:AB   Advertising Manager

LETTER 125

full
of the
pho/to/graph

that the
we are
we can

April 2, 19—

[shorthand]

PUTNAM & SPILLMAN, President
(Reading time: 45 sec.)   (104)

LETTER 126

ex/am/in/ing
ex/cept
freck/les

re/mov/ing
we find

April 21, 19—

Putnam & Spillman
Photoengravers
3001 Greenvale Avenue
Detroit 6, Michigan

Gentlemen

The package of cuts came in this morning. On examining the proofs, we find them all good except the [20] one enclosed. Can you improve this cut by removing the "freckles"?

Yours very truly   (35)
WESTERN PUBLISHERS, INC.

EO:AB   Advertising Manager
Enc.

LETTER 127

elim/i/nate	re/fin/ish/ing	
freck/led	re/pho/to/graph	
prom/i/nently	re/touch	
re-etching	spots	

April 24, 19—

PUTNAM & SPILLMAN, President

(Reading time: 1 min.)   (128)

LETTER 128

please mail ⎯⎯⎯ we are re/turn/ing ⎯⎯⎯
re/moval

April 28, 19—

Putnam & Spillman
Photoengravers
3001 Greenvale Avenue
Detroit 6, Michigan

Gentlemen

We are returning to you the cut for the removal of the "freckles" by re-etching and refinishing,[20] as you suggested in your letter of April 24.

Please mail to us the photograph and the proof.[40]

Yours very truly   (44)

WESTERN PUBLISHERS, INC.

EO:AB   Advertising Manager

PART 4. BUSINESS PRACTICES

This part is omitted from this dictation study.

PART 5. PROGRESS CHECKUP

LETTER PC-20

Western Publishers, Inc.
125 University Avenue
Ann Arbor, Michigan

Gentlemen

We shall be glad to prepare the half-tone engravings for the 198 photographs that[20] we received from you this morning. In making these half tones, we prepare group mountings according to size; but it is[40] necessary also to consider the tone value of each photograph. This means that we sort the pictures in[60] groups on the basis of their contrasting shades. This sorting of pictures enables us to produce half tones of [80] superior quality.

Occasionally, in a lot of pictures such as yours, we find dull or freckled photographs [100] that call for special treatment. In such cases, we usually rephotograph the pictures; strengthen the shades [120] in the developing and printing process; touch out the freckled spots, if any; and then produce a half tone from [140] which all the faulty spots of the original photograph have been completely removed. This process is a little [160] more expensive, but it will produce quality half tones that you can use with pleasure and satisfaction.

The [180] group mountings will somewhat offset the cost of this special process through savings in the number of photographic [200] plates. Understand, of course, that the group mountings are a manufacturing device only, and we will furnish you [220] an individual cut for each picture. After the group half tones are completed, the individual cuts [240] are separated and finished with beveled edges.

We have not given your photographs a detailed examination,[260] but we can quote you an estimate of $617 for half tones to be finished square [280] and without line. This estimate does not include the cost of any special attention to be given to faulty [300] photographs, but the additional cost for such work should not be over $50. In another day [320] or two we should be able to quote you an accurate amount that will cover the complete cost of half tones such [340] as you will want to use in your publication.

It is a pleasure to serve you, and we shall do everything we [360] can to maintain the happy relations that have marked our associations in the past. Let us have an immediate [380] letter telling us to proceed with the work, and we will give your order prompt attention. The cuts should then [400] be in your possession by April 30.

Very truly yours   (412)

Putnam & Spillman

VAF:AD   President

DICTATION STUDY XXI

PART 1. BASIC SKILLS

Theory Review

Directions. By this time, you probably have reached a shorthand speed at which you may become careless about word endings. In the following exercise there are many words ending in *s*, and in at least twenty situations it is impossible to recognize the need of the *s* from context alone. You can see, therefore, that you must indicate the *s* in your shorthand; otherwise, you might have as many as twenty errors in your work.

Proceed in the usual manner.

Expressing the S

Key: gives, degrees, characters, indicates, provokes, uses, persons, differs, rivals, results, changes, suggests, definitions, divisions, explanations, pronunciations, reputations, knows, Mrs., years, expresses, controls, plurals, exasperates, comedians, means, claims, synonyms, antonyms, elements, king's, languages, aggravates, parts, shades, words, contains, patterns, irritates, meanings, spellings, places, tenses, vexes, listeners, performers, Webster's, readers

Directions. All the foregoing words are used in the following article. Read the article until you can easily reach your reading-rate goal. A satisfactory reading time is given at the end of the article. Make two shorthand copies—one for accuracy, and one for fluency.

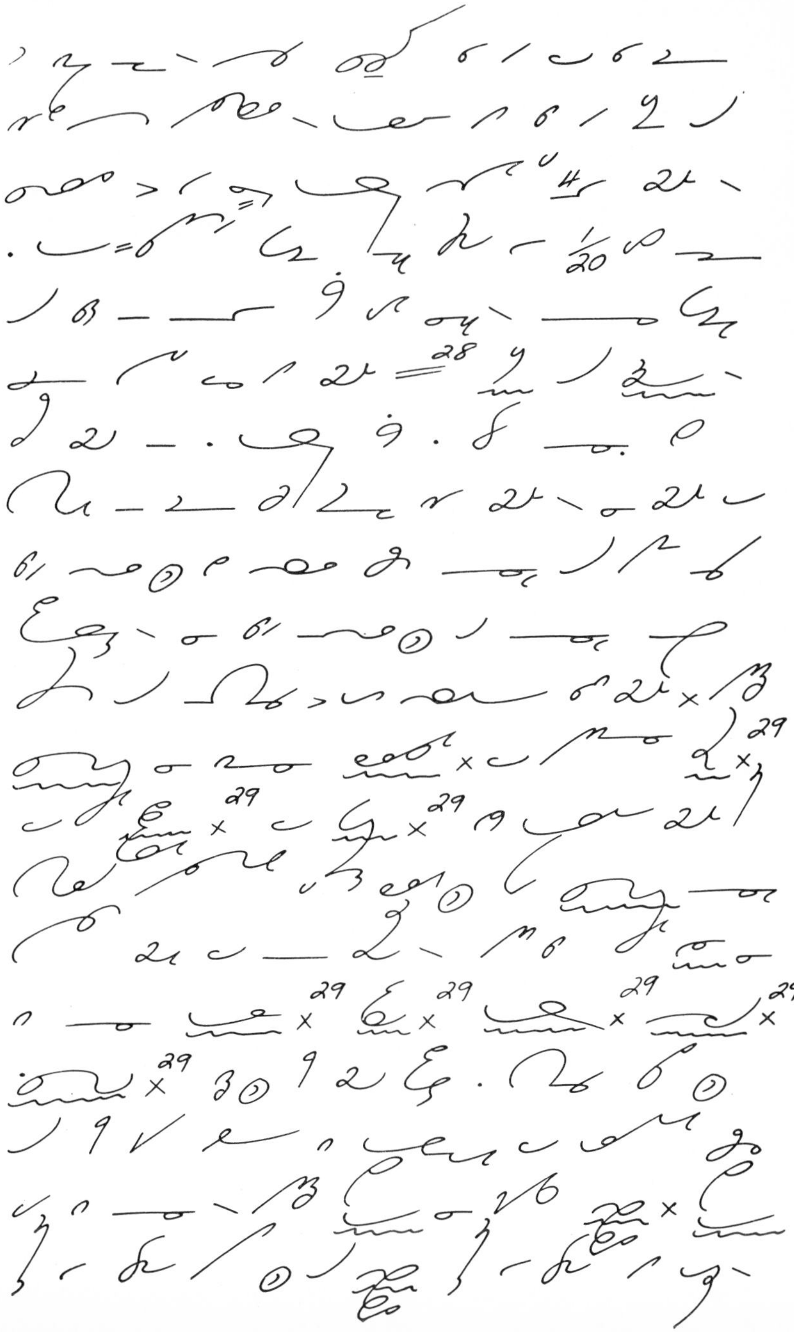

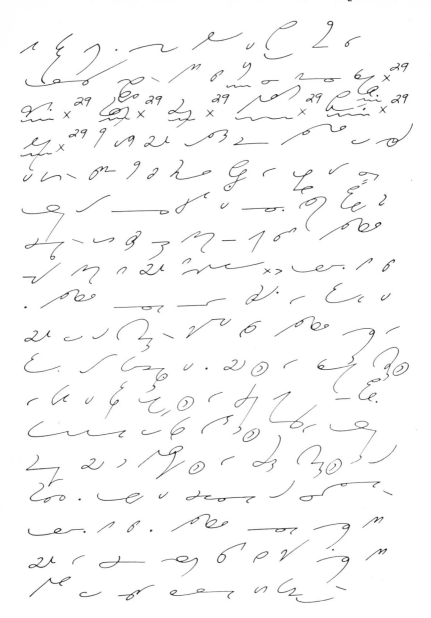

(Reading time: 4 min. 40 sec.) (600)

Punctuation Pointers

All punctuation needed in the foregoing article is given, but numbers are used to indicate only the punctuation pointers explained in this study.

28. A *dash* is used in certain types of apposition, especially when emphasis is desired.

Some persons know only two words—*awful* and *swell.*
They have national reputations—the results of great contributions to science.
Our salesmen—Mr. Hall, Mr. Munt, and Mr. Roberts—will be at the convention.

29. A *question mark* is used after each of several questions appearing in the same sentence. Note that such questions are not capitalized unless they begin with proper nouns or proper adjectives.

Do you like swimming? fishing? boating?
Do you mean *vexes? exasperates? provokes?*
What would you do? say? expect?
What happened to Donald? Frank? the other boys?

PART 2. BUSINESS INFORMATION

Vocabulary Preview

ac/com/plishes
ad/just/ment
al/low

an/noy/ing
builder
car/ries

cloud
con/sid/er/ate
di/rect/ness

ear/nest
ex/er/cise
ex/pla/na/tion

ex/pres/sions
force/ful
he wants

in/form/a/tive
lan/guage

life/less
mean/ing/less
mis/tak/ing

oc/cur/rence
re/sist/ance
sen/tences

sim/pli/fies
sin/cere
sin/cer/ity

sleep
so many
some/one

tact
un/dis/turbed
un/told

we hope that this
wis/dom

Adjustment for an Error

"We expect to pay for errors made in our organization." That is the policy of our house, and it certainly [20] simplifies the handling of complaints. Someone has said that collections and complaints offer greater opportunities [40] for the exercise of tact than can be found in any other field of business correspondence. Be [60] that as it may, our manager has shown excellent ability in the adjustment of the following complaint. [80]

There is no mistaking our customer's attitude in the sentence, "This is an annoying occurrence." He [100] wants satisfaction, and he wants it quickly. The opening paragraph of our letter of October 6 shows [120] our earnest desire to satisfy. We believe in action first, explanation later. The wisdom of this [140] policy is shown in the change in the customer's attitude, as indicated in his letter of October [160] 12. Frankness and sincerity gradually break down his resistance until, on October 22, the [180] customer writes, "We hope that this estimate will be satisfactory to you." By November 1 the customer [200] deems us "both considerate and generous." The job is then done.

"We expect to pay for errors made in our [220] organization." This is a good business policy, and it keeps good customers.

Letter writing offers untold [240] possibilities as a business builder. It is regrettable that so many letter writers allow [260] these opportunities to sleep undisturbed. They fill their correspondence with meaningless expressions and lifeless [280] sentences; they cloud their thoughts with such expressions as "acknowledge receipt," "beg to remain," and "are glad to say"; and [300] they treat their letters as necessary evils in the course of business.

Notice the directness of the following [320] letters. Each opening is forceful and informative; each closing, sincere and effective. Each letter carries [340] its message in simple, clear language that accomplishes its purpose and creates good will. The writers of these [360] letters have shown a definite understanding of the reasons for which letters are written.   (376)

PART 3. BUSINESS CORRESPONDENCE

between

GRIFFIN FURNITURE COMPANY		THE REVEREND F. P. YOUNG
Brown and Richards Streets	*and*	Waverly Methodist Church
Grand Rapids 6, Michigan		Mamaroneck, New York

LETTER 129

ar/rival		pas/tor
Brown		Rich/ards
chairs		tap/es/try
Grand Rap/ids		three
Grif/fin		Wa/verly
Meth/od/ist		wooden

October 1, 19—

Griffin Furniture Company
Corner Brown and Richards Streets
Grand Rapids 6, Michigan

Gentlemen

Our church check for $59.22 to cover your invoice of September 23 [20] has been awaiting the arrival of the chairs.

Yesterday a shipment of chairs came in. These surely cannot,[40] however, be the ones we ordered. There are only ten chairs in the lot—three in green velours, five in tapestry,[60] and two with wooden seats.

Our order called for twelve No. 417 chairs with No. 21 brown [80] seat and back.

This is an annoying occurrence. We ask you to take any action necessary to settle [100] this matter promptly. We need the chairs we ordered.

Yours truly   (111)

WAVERLY METHODIST CHURCH

FPY:AD   Pastor

LETTER 130

er/ror	~~	re/im/burse	~~
Ma/mar/o/neck	~~	rev/er/end	~~
mis/take	~~	un/nec/es/sary	~~
of this kind	~~	Young	~~

October 6, 19—

GRIFFIN FURNITURE COMPANY, Manager

(Reading time: 50 sec.) (123)

LETTER 131

con/fu/sion   to which

October 12, 19—

Griffin Furniture Company
Corner Brown and Richards Streets
Grand Rapids 6, Michigan

Gentlemen

The eleven chairs to which you refer in your letter of October 6 were received this afternoon.[20] We are enclosing our check in payment of your invoice of September 23. This payment, of course, includes [40] the sample chair No. 317.

Before returning the chairs received in the former shipment,[60] we should like to have your quotation on the full lot in order to preclude further confusion and delay.

Yours [80] truly   (81)

WAVERLY METHODIST CHURCH

FPY:AD   Pastor
Enc.

LETTER 132

dis/pleased   **Ok/la/homa**
ev/ery   **pack/ing**
in/curred   **what/ever**

October 15, 19—

GRIFFIN FURNITURE COMPANY, Manager

(Reading time: 1 min. 35 sec.)   (214)

LETTER 133

as we have		price list	
lesser		rep/re/sented	
of your let/ter		re/tain	

October 22, 19—

Griffin Furniture Company
Corner Brown and Richards Streets
Grand Rapids 6, Michigan

Gentlemen

After considering the offer made in the **third paragraph** of your letter of October 15,[20] we believe the lesser evil is for us to retain the chairs in question rather than to return them. We[40] are therefore enclosing our check for $50.35 in payment.

As we have no price list, the[60] amount represented in the check is an estimate based on the cost of our original order. We hope[80] that this estimate will be satisfactory to you.

Yours truly   (92)

WAVERLY METHODIST CHURCH

FPY:AD   Pastor
Enc.

LETTER 134

al/to/gether	over/pays
con/tri/bu/tion	voucher
ev/i/dence	we hope you will

Altogether   All together

Altogether means wholly, thoroughly, on the whole.
   You were altogether right in the decision you made on the question.
   He was altogether too generous in giving all the credit to others.

All together means in one place or group, assembled.
   The family were all together for the first time in five years.
   If the materials were all together, our job would be easier.

October 25, 19—

GRIFFIN FURNITURE COMPANY, Manager

(Reading time: 50 sec.)   (113)

LETTER 135

ap/pre/ci/ated
at/trib/utes (v.)
gen/er/os/ity

grate/fully
lib/eral

on our part
over/pay/ment
re/fund

un/in/ten/tional
you were

November 1, 19—

Griffin Furniture Company
Corner Brown and Richards Streets
Grand Rapids 6, Michigan

Gentlemen

Your letter of October 25 attributes too **much generosity**
to us because of [20] our overpayment of $4.09. This liberal
spirit, we can assure you, was quite unintentional [40] **on our
part.**

In turn, you were both considerate and generous in the refund check of $15, which [60] was so promptly sent. Your action in this matter is gratefully appreciated, especially since such [80] experiences here are few—very few.

Very cordially yours　　　(91)

WAVERLY METHODIST CHURCH

FPY:AD　　　　　　　Pastor

PART 4.　BUSINESS PRACTICES

Vocabulary Preview

avoided	pres/sure
ditch	pre/vented
edge	re/leased
into the	ruled
mul/ti/ple	thick

Preparation of Multiple Copies

In the preparation of a number of carbon copies at one time, some difficulty may be experienced [20] by the failure of the typewriter to receive the papers easily and by the tendency of the papers,[40] when once in the machine, to slip. This condition is especially troublesome when the typist is using [60] paper with ruled lines, in which case the writing on the carbon copies often crosses the lines or appears too far [80] above the lines. These troubles may be avoided, in the first instance, by the use of the paper release when the [100] papers are inserted and, in the second instance, by the use of a "ditch."

The paper release releases the [120] pressure of the feed rollers on the platen and permits the easy insertion of a group of papers. When fifteen [140] or twenty copies are to be made, it may be necessary to leave the paper release in the released [160] position.

A "ditch" is a folded sheet of paper that is placed over the edge of a group of papers to be [180] inserted in the typewriter. The papers thus held together by the ditch are inserted into the machine [200] far enough so that the ditch can be removed at the front of the platen. In this way the papers are prevented [220] from slipping while being inserted into the machine. If the group is not too thick, a good substitute for the [240] ditch is an ordinary envelope, the flap of which serves as a fold for the papers.

An alternate method [260] of arranging materials for multiple copies—and one that is very popular in some offices [280] —consists of inserting the typewriting papers into the machine about an inch and then inserting the [300] carbon sheets between the typewriting papers. This method has the advantage of causing the carbon sheets to extend [320] beyond the ends of the typewriting sheets as then the pages may be easily separated after the work [340] is typed. This method, however, does not permit writing near the upper edge. The typist should be careful to see [360] that the carbon sheets are turned in the proper direction.   (370)

PART 5. PROGRESS CHECKUP

Letter PC-21

The Reverend F. P. Young, Pastor
Waverly Methodist Church
Mamaroneck, New York

Reverend Sir

The manner in which we have thus far handled your order must be a source of genuine annoyance [20] to you. It is hard to realize that so many mistakes could be made in filling one order for chairs. We [40] could very easily say that the difficulty was due to new and inexperienced help. Such a statement,[60] however, would not be of any value to you, but it would be exceedingly unfair to the many workers [80] who are helping us to keep Griffin furniture at the highest level of quality. Really, our records [100] do not indicate just where or how the mistakes occurred, but we are doing everything possible to [120] correct them and to supply you with the chairs you ordered and expected.

Your original order was for twelve [140] No. 417 chairs with No. 21 brown seats and backs. Through a confusion of orders, we [160] shipped you fourteen No. 417 chairs with velours seats and backs. We also sent you one sample chair No. [180] 317 with velours seat, five chairs with tapestry seats, and two chairs with wooden seats. Ten of these chairs [200] were not ordered by you.

In an effort to correct this confusion without too much inconvenience or annoyance [220] to you, we are happy to give you your choice of either of the following suggestions:

First, you may return [240] the extra chairs to us with the understanding that we will reimburse you for any expense incurred in [260] handling the shipment, including packing. We should prefer that you do this. Second, you may keep the extra chairs and [280] send us a check for $84.22 to close the account. This amount would include [300] $59.22 to cover the original order and an arbitrary amount of [320] $25 for the extra chairs. The list price of these extra chairs is $46.26,[340] but we shall gladly contribute the difference of $21.26 to the good work that [360] you are doing.

We do not wish you to be under any pressure in making your decision. These two suggestions [380] are being made only with the thought of helping you to avoid further concern in trying to close the matter.[400] Errors of this kind are always expensive, and, of course, we should prefer to avoid them; nevertheless, your [420] satisfaction is our first responsibility, and we expect to pay for errors we make.

Very cordially [440] yours   (441)

GRIFFIN FURNITURE COMPANY

HEF:CP   Manager

DICTATION STUDY XXII

PART 1. BASIC SKILLS

Brief-Form Review

Directions. There are 96 different brief forms and brief-form derivatives in the following article. Many of these words have been used in previous studies many times. Remember: Brief forms are common words and must be known well if they are to be of most help in building speed in writing. Ease of reading also depends upon accuracy in the use of brief forms. Read the following article until you can easily reach your reading rate. Then make two copies of the article in shorthand.

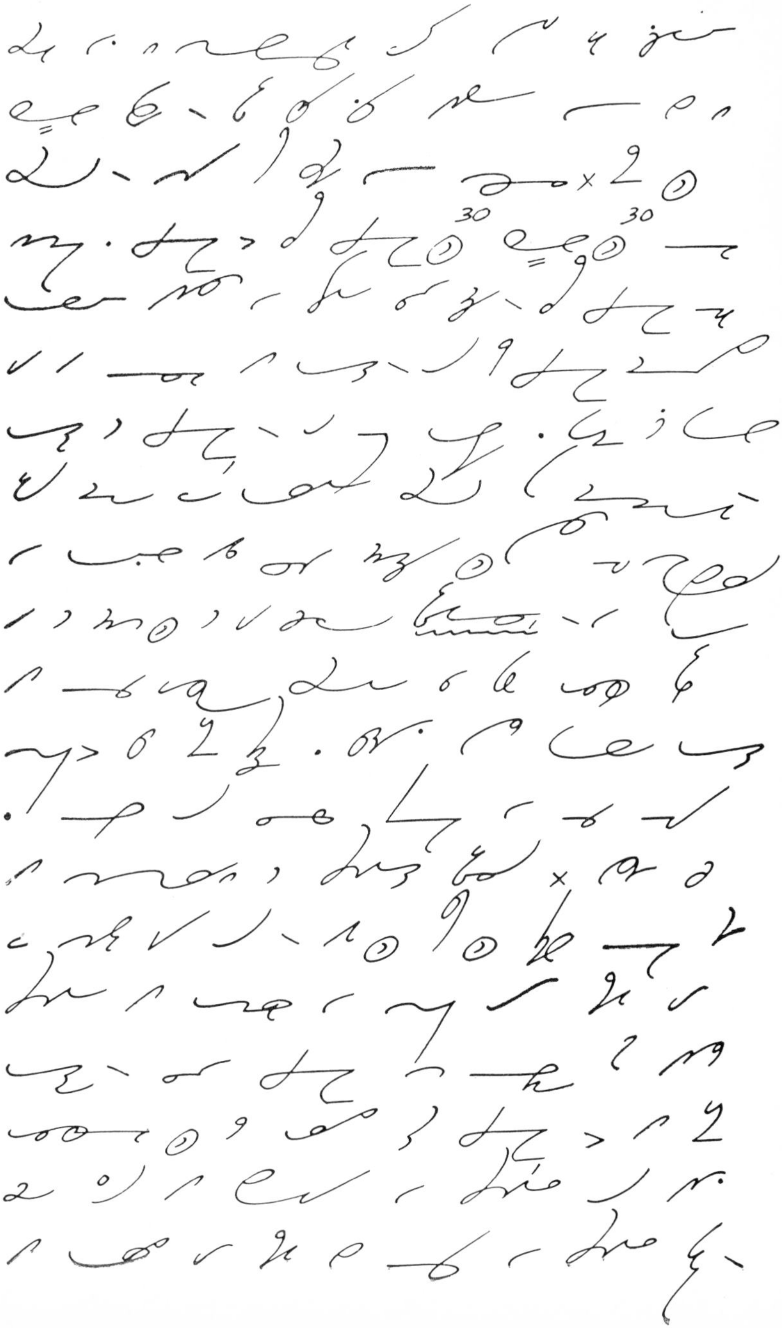

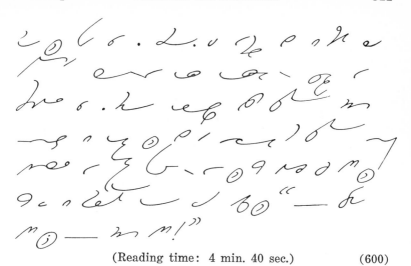

(Reading time: 4 min. 40 sec.) (600)

Punctuation Pointer

All punctuation needed in the foregoing article is given, but only the punctuation explained in this lesson is numbered.

30. Words used in direct address are separated from the rest of the sentence by *commas*.

I do not understand, Mr. Brooks, how this plan can benefit our company.

Mr. Chairman, this matter should be given preferred consideration.

I suggest that you, Mr. President, appoint the committee.

David, we are counting on you to head the campaign.

PART 2. BUSINESS INFORMATION

Vocabulary Preview

charge		night let/ter	
con/firm		quot/ing	
con/fir/ma/tion		tel/e/grams	
con/firmed		tel/e/graph	
day let/ter		tel/e/graphic	
even		trans/mit/ted	
mailed		trip/li/cate	
mes/sages		wise	

Telegraphic Service

Telegraphic service plays so great a part in the transaction of modern business that the stenographer must [20] understand the method of handling telegrams. As telegraphic messages are usually dictated,[40] it becomes the duty of the stenographer to arrange these messages for delivery to a telegraph [60] office.

Telegrams are prepared in duplicate or triplicate, one copy being sent to the telegraph [80] office, a second copy placed on file, and a third copy sometimes mailed to the addressee as a confirmation.[100] Instead of using a third copy, many business houses confirm a telegram by quoting the message [120] in a letter. Not all messages are confirmed, but it is wise to confirm those messages containing important [140] information. When a telegraphic message is quoted in a letter, the message should be set up in [160] its own paragraph; its lines should be single-spaced, even though the letter may be double-spaced; and its margins, both [180] left and right, should be wider than those of the rest of the letter.

The fast telegram, the day letter, and the night [200] letter represent three common types of telegraphic services. The rate depends on the type of service and [220] the number of words in the message. The charge for a fast telegram is based on a minimum of ten words; that [240] for a day letter, on a minimum of fifty words; and that for a night letter, on a minimum of [260] twenty-five words. The letters represent what is known as deferred service because they are transmitted at times when [280] telegraph offices are not busy sending fast telegrams.   (291)

PART 3. BUSINESS CORRESPONDENCE
between

Anderson Scout Axe Company		Clinton Handle Company
600 Madison Avenue	*and*	467 Railroad Avenue
Binghamton, New York		Clinton, Tennessee

Letter 136

axe   Bing/ham/ton

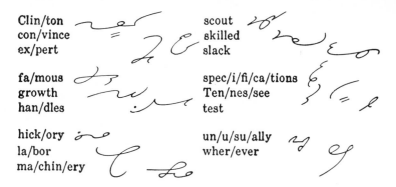

Clin/ton	scout
con/vince	skilled
ex/pert	slack
fa/mous	spec/i/fi/ca/tions
growth	Ten/nes/see
han/dles	test
hick/ory	un/u/su/ally
la/bor	wher/ever
ma/chin/ery	

November 8, 19—

Anderson Scout Axe Company
600 Madison Avenue
Binghamton, New York

Gentlemen

Down here in Clinton, Tennessee, in the very heart of the hickory district, is a handle mill [20] in which skilled labor and modern machinery turn out a product that is as good as the best and better than [40] the rest. Quality materials and expert workmanship have made Clinton handles famous wherever the axe [60] is used.

Slack season makes prices unusually attractive. Why not send us your inquiries or specifications,[80] and let us convince you that even quality handles may be had at reasonable cost? We use only [100] second growth or test-grade hickory.

Yours very truly   (111)

CLINTON HANDLE COMPANY

JLW:MS   Sales Department

LETTER 137

com/bined	shrink/age
mois/ture	spec/ify
pur/chas/ing	wood

November 17, 19—

ANDERSON SCOUT AXE COMPANY, Purhasing Agent

(Reading time: 40 sec.)   (91)

LETTER 138

an/tic/i/pates   pol/ished
belts   pride
it is un/der/stood   will/ingly

November 24, 19—

Anderson Scout Axe Company
600 Madison Avenue
Binghamton, New York

Gentlemen

We can furnish you 1,000 dozen scout-axe handles, simi-lar to your sample, at 60 cents [20] a dozen f.o.b. Clinton. Of course, it is understood that 25% of these handles will be grade [40] SAW and SBW combined, the remaining 75% to be grade SBR.[60] It is further understood that the entire lot must contain no more than 10% moisture when the wood is [80] turned.

If this quotation appeals to you, we shall willingly make up several handles for your approval.

Our [100] price anticipates the use of some excellent dry stock that was cut more than a year ago when the sap was down.[120] This hickory, finished coarse and polished over two belts, will produce handles that you may well use with pride.

Yours [140] very truly   (142)

CLINTON HANDLE COMPANY

JLW :MS   Sales Department

LETTER 139

(Night Letter)

wire *ᒑ*

CLINTON TENN DEC 11

ANDERSON SCOUT AXE CO

600 MADISON AVE BINGHAMTON NY

REGARDING QUOTATION TWENTY FOURTH SCOUT HANDLE WIRE DECISION OUR EXPENSE   (14)

CLINTON HANDLE CO

LETTER 140

(Fast Telegram)

other *ᴡ*

BINGHAMTON, N.Y., DEC. 12

[shorthand symbols]

ANDERSON SCOUT AXE CO.

(Reading time: 5 sec.)   (12)

LETTER 141

in an/swer to your — *[shorthand]*

December 12, 19—

[shorthand outlines]

ANDERSON SCOUT AXE COMPANY, Purhasing Agent

(Reading time: 30 sec.)   (65)

LETTER 142

(Fast Telegram)

fifty cents *[shorthand]*   **one thou/sand** *[shorthand]*

CLINTON TENN DEC 15

ANDERSON SCOUT AXE CO
600 MADISON AVE BINGHAMTON NY

REDUCE SCOUT HANDLE TO FIFTY CENTS DOZEN
ONE THOUSAND DOZEN WIRE   (12)

CLINTON HANDLE CO

CLASS OF SERVICE DESIRED	
DOMESTIC	CABLE
TELEGRAM	ORDINARY
DAY LETTER	URGENT RATE
SERIAL	DEFERRED
NIGHT LETTER X	NIGHT LETTER

Patrons should check class of service desired; otherwise the message will be transmitted as a telegram or ordinary cablegram.

WESTERN UNION

A. N. WILLIAMS
PRESIDENT

1206

CHECK
ACCOUNTING INFORMATION
TIME FILED

Send the following telegram, subject to the terms on back hereof, which are hereby agreed to

CLINTON, TENN., DEC. 11, 19

ANDERSON SCOUT AXE CO.

600 MADISON AVE., BINGHAMTON, N. Y.

REGARDING QUOTATION TWENTY-FOURTH SCOUT HANDLE WIRE

DECISION OUR EXPENSE.

CLINTON HANDLE CO.

CLASS OF SERVICE

This is a full-rate Telegram or Cablegram unless its deferred character is indicated by a suitable symbol above or preceding the address.

WESTERN UNION

JOSEPH L. EGAN
PRESIDENT

1201

SYMBOLS
DL = Day Letter
NL = Night Letter
LC = Deferred Cable
NLT = Cable Night Letter
Ship Radiogram

The filing time shown in the date line on telegrams and day letters is STANDARD TIME at point of origin. Time of receipt is STANDARD TIME at point of destination

ZH22 10 NL XU=CLINTON TENN 11

19 DEC 11 AM 10 45

ANDERSON SCOUT AXE CO=

600 MADISON AVE BINGHAMTON NY=

REGARDING QUOTATION TWENTY FOURTH SCOUT HANDLE WIRE DECISION

OUR EXPENSE=

CLINTON HANDLE CO.

THE COMPANY WILL APPRECIATE SUGGESTIONS FROM ITS PATRONS CONCERNING ITS SERVICE

MODEL 11—TELEGRAMS

The first illustration shows the telegram as it is delivered to the telegraph company; note that the typed information is double spaced. The second illustration shows the same telegram as it is delivered by the telegraph company.

LETTER 143

(Fast Telegram)

one hun/dred   /   **re/tel**

BINGHAMTON, N.Y., DEC. 15

ANDERSON SCOUT AXE CO.

(Reading time: 10 sec.)   (23)

LETTER 144

ac/cu/rately   some weeks
fash/ioned   ago
gauged   Tues/day

December 20, 19—

Anderson Scout Axe Company
600 Madison Avenue
Binghamton, New York

Gentlemen

We are sending you by parcel post today several scout-axe handles fashioned after the sample [20] you sent us some weeks ago.

Your sample has been gauged on a gauging machine, but there is no such machine in our [40] factory. We are, however, turning and belting the handles accurately.

Your order will be shipped on Tuesday,[60] December 23.

Yours very truly   (69)

CLINTON HANDLE COMPANY

JLW:MS   Sales Department

LETTER 145

as/sur/ance
badly
culled

meas/ure/ments
poor
that it is

in/spected
knots
meas/ured

to re/ject
var/i/a/tion
you will be able

January 23, 19—

(shorthand symbols)

ANDERSON SCOUT AXE COMPANY, Purhasing Agent
(Reading time: 1 min. 20 sec.)   (176)

LETTER 146

apol/o/gies   *(shorthand)*   small/est   *(shorthand)*
di/men/sions   tem/plates
pat/terns   *(shorthand)*   we as/sure you   *(shorthand)*

re/gret   *(shorthand)*

January 26, 19—

Anderson Scout Axe Company
600 Madison Avenue
Binghamton, New York

Gentlemen

You want satisfaction, not apologies; therefore, we assure you that the next shipment of handles [20] will meet your requirements satisfactorily. Of course, we regret the variations in the last lot.

Enclosed [40] is a sketch drawn from templates used in making patterns. This sketch shows dimensions on inch centers taken from the sample [60] you sent us. To preclude any further chance of error, please check this drawing to see whether the shape and the [80] size are correct. Then return the sketch with your order for 1,000 dozen handles, and let us show you that we [100] can satisfy you to the smallest detail.

We are happy to serve you.

Yours very truly   (116)

CLINTON HANDLE COMPANY

JLW:MS   Sales Department

Enc.

LETTER 147

blue/print	per/mit/ted
in or/der that	there may be
max/i/mum	tol/er/ances
per/mis/si/ble	

February 10, 19—

ANDERSON SCOUT AXE COMPANY, Purchasing Agent

(Reading time: 45 sec.)   (107)

LETTER 148

by ex/press	started
de/pends	

February 23, 19—

Anderson Scout Axe Company
600 Madison Avenue
Binghamton, New York

Gentlemen

As you requested in your letter of the tenth, we are shipping to you by express today two dozen [20] sample axe handles made from new patterns according to your blueprint and specifications.

Let us know at [40] once whether these samples are correct. Prompt delivery depends upon our getting started on this order [60] without delay.

Yours very truly   (66)

CLINTON HANDLE COMPANY

JLW:MS   Sales Department

LETTER 149

(Day Letter)

will be made

BINGHAMTON, N.Y., FEB. 27

ANDERSON SCOUT AXE CO.

(Reading time: 10 sec.)   (28)

LETTER 150

fore/man   on re/ceipt   to work

February 28, 19—

Anderson Scout Axe Company
600 Madison Avenue
Binghamton, New York

Gentlemen

Immediately on receipt of your day letter, we started to work on your order for 1,000 [20] dozen scout-axe handles. Every possible effort is being made to get the first lot of 250 [40] dozen to you promptly. Our foreman says that they should be ready for shipment by March 5.

The rest of the [60] order will be in your plant by April 1.

Yours very truly　　　(71)

CLINTON HANDLE COMPANY

JLW:MS　　　Sales Department

PART 4. BUSINESS PRACTICES

This part has been omitted from this dictation study.

PART 5. PROGRESS CHECKUP

Letter PC-22

Clinton Handle Company
467 Railroad Avenue
Clinton, Tennessee

Gentlemen

The price of 50 cents a dozen for scout-axe handles is thoroughly satisfactory. We shall [20] willingly place our order for 1,000 dozen with your company if you can convince us that you can make [40] handles that will comply with our specifications. On November 17 we mailed you a sample handle [60] to serve as a pattern. This handle has been measured very carefully inch by inch from the eye end to the grip [80] end. You may, therefore, follow the measurements as closely as your equipment will permit. The enclosed sheet shows the [100] tolerances that we can allow, and you will see that the permissible variation is rather small.

If [120] you accept this job, we must insist that 25 per cent of the handles be grade SAW and [140] SBW combined and that the remaining 75 per cent be grade SBR. It is absolutely [160] necessary that the wood contain not more than 10 per cent moisture when turned, as no allowance is made for [180] shrinkage. The wood should be a good grade of hickory, and the finished handles should be polished over two belts.

Our [200] specifications are very exact, and we therefore hesitate to encourage you in trying to handle [220] the order unless you are confident that you can compete against mills with gauging machines and extensive [240] automatic equipment.

We produce a high-grade axe, and it is important that our handles be free of knots and [260] splits. Suppose we let you make up a trial order of 100 dozen handles. We shall then inspect these handles [280] for quality and check them with our own blueprint to see how accurately you can meet our measurements. If these [300] handles prove satisfactory, we will telegraph you our permission to proceed with the larger order.

If [320] we order 1,000 dozen handles from you, can you give us some idea of when the handles might be [340] ready? It is not essential that we have the handles before the first of March, but it will be of considerable [360] help to us in planning if we may know approximately the time when delivery can be made. We [380] understand that the Christmas season might affect the handling of our order, but that will make little difference to [400] us. We are not expecting to use these handles for our Christmas business, but we shall use them at the opening [420] of our summer sport season. Our spring calendar, therefore, depends on our being informed of the probable date [440] of delivery.

Yours very truly   (447)

ANDERSON SCOUT AXE COMPANY

REF:LD   Purchasing Agent

Enc.

DICTATION STUDY XXIII

PART 1. BASIC SKILLS

Theory Review

Directions. This study gives further practice in the writing of words containing R. Some RD words are included, and there are several outlines from which the R is omitted. Read the words until you read easily at the goal rate without the aid of the key; then write each word at least once in shorthand.

More R and RD Words

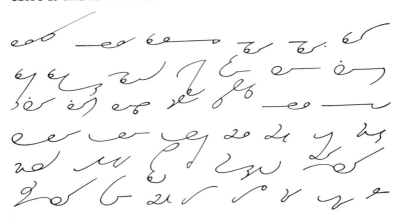

Key: irritated, merit, ceremony, insert, inserting, certain, surges, surplus, concerned, danger, spurn, arm, harmful, heart, hurtful, earnestly, stir, I dare say, merely, manner, alert, learn, largely, worry, first, revert, sources, warrant, endorsed, absurd, flustered, guarded, safeguarded, burden, words, ordinary, ordinarily, sort, resort, turn

Directions. All the theory words included in this study are used in the following article. Read the article until you can reach your reading goal. Write the article twice in shorthand.

[shorthand symbols]

(Reading time: 4 min. 40 sec.)　　　　(600)

No new punctuation pointer is given in this lesson. Many of the pointers given in previous lessons, however, are reviewed in the foregoing article, and all necessary punctuation marks are shown.

PART 2.　BUSINESS INFORMATION

Vocabulary Preview

ac/counts	*[shorthand]*	drawer	*[shorthand]*
briefly	*[shorthand]*	ef/fec/tive/ness	*[shorthand]*
col/lec/tions	*[shorthand]*	im/pair	*[shorthand]*

owes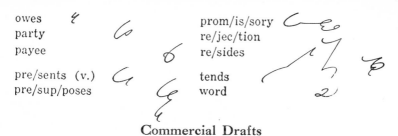
party
payee

pre/sents (v.)
pre/sup/poses

prom/is/sory
re/jec/tion
re/sides

tends
word

Commercial Drafts

In a previous lesson the value and the service of collection agencies were discussed briefly. In the [20] collection of difficult accounts, the collection agency represents not the only recourse preceding [40] legal steps. Many businesses make regular use of the draft as a means of assisting in collections.

A [60] draft is a written order drawn by one party and directing a second party to pay a certain sum of [80] money to a third. The first party is called the drawer; the second, the drawee; and the third, the payee. The drawer [100] and the payee may be one party; that is, the drawer may make the draft payable to himself. A draft [120] naturally presupposes that the drawee owes the drawer money.

The method of handling a draft is as [140] follows: The draft, after having been properly made out, is sent to a local bank for collection. This bank, in turn,[160] sends the draft to a correspondent bank in the city in which the drawee resides or does business. The correspondent [180] bank presents the draft to the drawee for acceptance or rejection. The drawee indicates his willingness [200] to pay the draft by writing across the face of the draft the word *Accepted,* the date of acceptance, and his [220] signature.

An accepted draft has the force of a promissory note. When the draft is paid, the original [240] bank is notified and the amount is credited to the account of the payee. A small fee is usually [260] charged for such collection.

If the drawee refuses to accept the draft, the paper is returned to the [280] original bank with a notice of rejection. The rejection of a draft, without sufficient reason, tends to [300] impair bank credit. This fact accounts for the effectiveness of the draft as a collection medium.　　　(319)

PART 3. BUSINESS CORRESPONDENCE
between

COASTAL CO-OPERATIVE FRUIT GROWERS
2701 Redwood Avenue
San Francisco 4, California

and

HANFORD WHOLESALE GROCERS
Morris and Tremont Streets
Salt Lake City 2, Utah

and

WEST COAST COLLECTION AGENCY
1410 Atwater Building
San Francisco 3, California

LETTER 151

and let us hear	grow/ers
from you	Han/ford
coastal	in/ves/ti/gate
co-operative	Red/wood
cre/den/tials	San Fran/cisco,
fruit	Cal/i/for/nia
gro/cers	whole/sale

September 26, 19—

Coastal Co-operative Fruit Growers
2701 Redwood Avenue
San Francisco 4, California

Gentlemen

We were surprised to receive your letter of September 24, requesting a check on our account.[20]

Some time ago we gave a check for $65 to a representative of a collection agency [40] who presented credentials to show that you had requested his company to collect that amount from [60] us.

Please investigate the matter and let us hear from you again.

Yours truly   (74)

HANFORD WHOLESALE GROCERS

BWS:JF   Manager
Enc.

LETTER 152

brought

cease

Dan/iels

few days

in your city

it was not

just as soon as

Mor/ris

Salt Lake City

should have been

some/where

this was done

to my at/ten/tion

Tre/mont

true

Utah

with/draw

September 28, 19—

[shorthand symbols]

Robert Daniels, President, COASTAL CO-OPERATIVE FRUIT GROWERS

(Reading time: 1 min.) (129)

LETTER 153

At/wa/ter	*[shorthand]*	from this	*[shorthand]*
claim	*[shorthand]*	we in/fer	*[shorthand]*
coast	*[shorthand]*	west	*[shorthand]*

September 28, 19—

[shorthand symbols]

COASTAL CO-OPERATIVE FRUIT GROWERS, President

(Reading time: 45 sec.) (102)

LETTER 154

re/fer/ring to   we did
  your let/ter

September 29, 19—

Coastal Co-operative Fruit Growers
2701 Redwood Avenue
San Francisco 4, California

Gentlemen

Referring to your letter of September 28, we did receive the check for $65 [20] from the Hanford Wholesale Grocers, of Salt Lake City.

In settlement we are enclosing our check for [40] $32.50, the balance of $32.50 being retained as our fee for the [60] handling of this account.

We are sorry to have caused you embarrassment in dealing with your customers.

Very [80] truly yours   (82)
WEST COAST COLLECTION AGENCY

JHH:EB   Manager
Enc.

LETTER 155

de/duct/ing   in this case
fee

September 30, 19—

1410

32 50 =

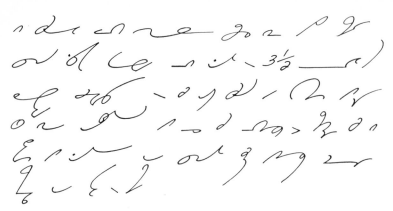

Coastal Co-operative Fruit Growers, President

(Reading time: 45 sec.)   (96)

Letter 156

in/con/ven/ienced   these mat/ters

in the fu/ture   watched

October 2, 19—

Coastal Co-operative Fruit Growers
2701 Redwood Avenue
San Francisco 4, California

Gentlemen

    We admit our error in deducting a fee for the collection of $65 from the [20] Hanford Wholesale Grocers, of Salt Lake City, and therefore enclose our second check for $32.50 [40] to complete the payment of this account.

    In the future these matters will be watched very carefully. Our [60] correspondents will be instructed promptly so that neither you nor your customers will be inconvenienced.

Yours [80] very truly   (82)

West Coast Collection Agency

JHH:EB   Manager
Enc.

LETTER 157

ev/i/dently

October 4, 19—

COASTAL CO-OPERATIVE FRUIT GROWERS, President
(Reading time: 40 sec.)　　　(84)

PART 4. BUSINESS PRACTICES
Vocabulary Preview

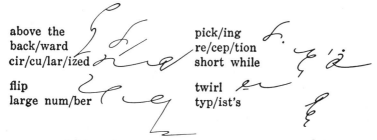

above the
back/ward
cir/cu/lar/ized

flip
large num/ber

pick/ing
re/cep/tion
short while

twirl
typ/ist's

Addressing Envelopes for Circular Letters

In the business office, it is customary to address an envelope for a letter immediately [20] after the completion of the letter. There are occasions, however, when it is desirable to address [40] a large number of envelopes at one time. For instance, when a mailing list is to be circularized, it is [60] essential to address many envelopes in a short while. Any device that will tend to increase the typist's [80] efficiency in handling this job is well worth consideration.

When an addressing machine is not to be [100] used, a large number of envelopes may be addressed rapidly as follows:

Fold a sheet of ordinary letter [120] paper in half and insert it into the typewriter with the folded edge first, allowing about one inch [140] of the paper to extend above the writing position. Then insert an envelope between the front of the [160] platen and the folded edge of the paper; give the platen a backward turn, which will cause the envelope to come [180] immediately into the writing position; address the envelope; and then flip it out of the typewriter [200] by a twirl of the platen knob. The same flip will bring the paper back into position for the reception [220] of the next envelope.

This method will enable a good typist to address at least one hundred and twenty [240] envelopes an hour. A wire filing basket placed behind the typewriter will catch the finished envelopes and thus [260] save the trouble of picking them up.   (266)

<h2 style="text-align:center">Vocabulary Preview</h2>

ad/di/tion			bound	
bind			of such	

<h3 style="text-align:center">Insertion of Bound Papers into the Typewriter</h3>

Sometimes, especially in businesses such as those that require the typing of legal papers or specifications,[20] the stenographer has occasion to bind papers at the top. The method described in the article [40] on addressing envelopes for circular letters will enable the stenographer to insert readily [60] into the typewriter any page of such a bound group that requires a correction or an addition. Although[80] this problem may not occur too frequently in most business offices, it is wise to know how to handle it,[100]   (100)

PART 5. PROGRESS CHECKUP

Letter PC-23

Coastal Co-operative Fruit Growers
2701 Redwood Avenue
San Francisco 4, California

Gentlemen

A study of our records for the past several months shows that you have not permitted us the [20] privilege of serving you since last October. At that time, we had the very unfortunate experience of [40] collecting an account for you and failing to remit promptly. This experience was costly to you, but it [60] was even more costly to us if it means we failed to hold a good client. We certainly hope that is not the [80] case in this instance.

Recently, one of our representatives was instructed to call on Mr. Robert [100] Daniels, the president of your company; but Mr. Daniels was apparently not available then. We are, [120] therefore, writing this letter for the purpose of again calling your attention to our service.

As you know, our [140] organization is one of the most complete collection agencies in the United States. We maintain [160] offices in all the important cities of this country, and we have correspondents in every other community [180] where there is telegraph, telephone, or mail service. You can see, therefore, that we can, for all practical [200] purposes, call on every merchant who could possibly be a customer of yours. Ordinarily, [220] we could have an agent working on your claim in a matter of one or two days. Our organization can support [240] your claim, if necessary, by legal proceedings. Thus, if there is any chance at all for the collection [260] of difficult accounts, we have the means for promising success.

Our collection costs, we are sure you will agree, [280] are reasonable. They are based on the date of the record and the amount concerned. There is a maximum fee [300] equal to half the amount collected, but most of our costs are below this. A reference to your files will prove [320] to you that your collection costs with us have seldom reached our maximum fee.

You are interested in a [340] national market for your products; consequently, your customers cannot always be easily reached by your [360] representatives. This means that you must investigate very carefully the financial standing of prospective [380] credit accounts or take the chance of substantial losses. It may sometimes happen also that sources of information [400] as to the value of an account do not furnish complete and accurate data. Thus, even though an [420] attempt is made to avoid unnecessary losses, some accounts prove to be a collection problem. That is [440] the time when our collection agency can be of most assistance to you.

Why not check through your records and let [460] us have a list of accounts that are three or more months old. We want to convince you that our service can be efficient.[480] We, of course, regret your previous experience with us; but we are confident that, if offered another [500] opportunity, we can prove that this experience was unusual rather than typical of our [520] regular service. May we hear from you soon?

Very truly yours   (531)

WEST COAST COLLECTION AGENCY

JHH:EB   Manager

DICTATION STUDY XXIV

PART 1. BASIC SKILLS

Theory Review

Directions. The following words are all used in the article in this study. Read the words until you can read each one easily without the key; then write each word at least once. Give special attention to any outline that you cannot write smoothly.

The Superlative EST

Key: greatest, newest, silliest, fanciest, prettiest, easiest, highest, strongest, smallest, poorest, simplest, brightest, nearest, biggest, sharpest, scarcest, closest, severest, meanest, keenest, smartest, fastest, oldest, hardest

Directions. The following article contains all the foregoing words. If you have practiced the words properly, you should be able to read them easily when you meet them in the article. Read the article until you can reach your reading goal. Write the article twice in shorthand. Keep in mind that you should pass from one outline to another without hesitation.

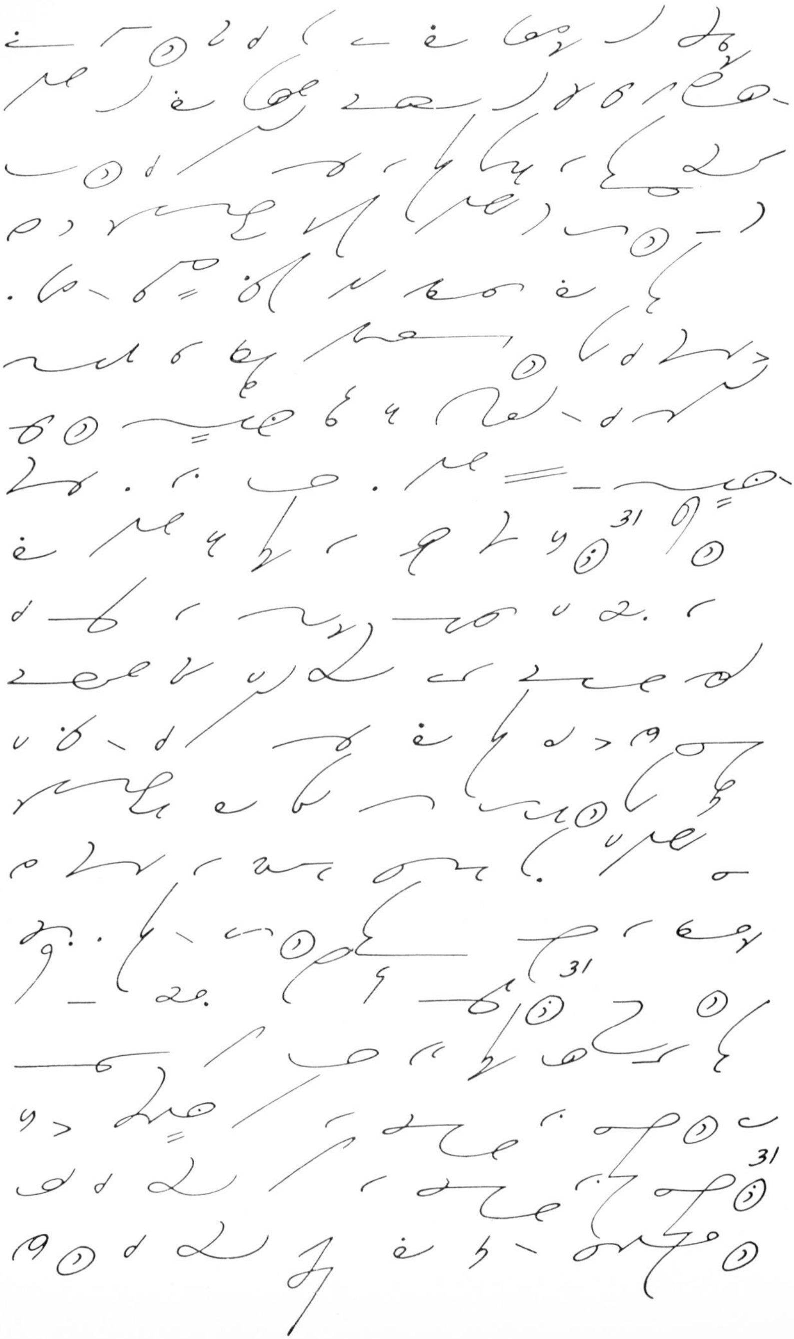

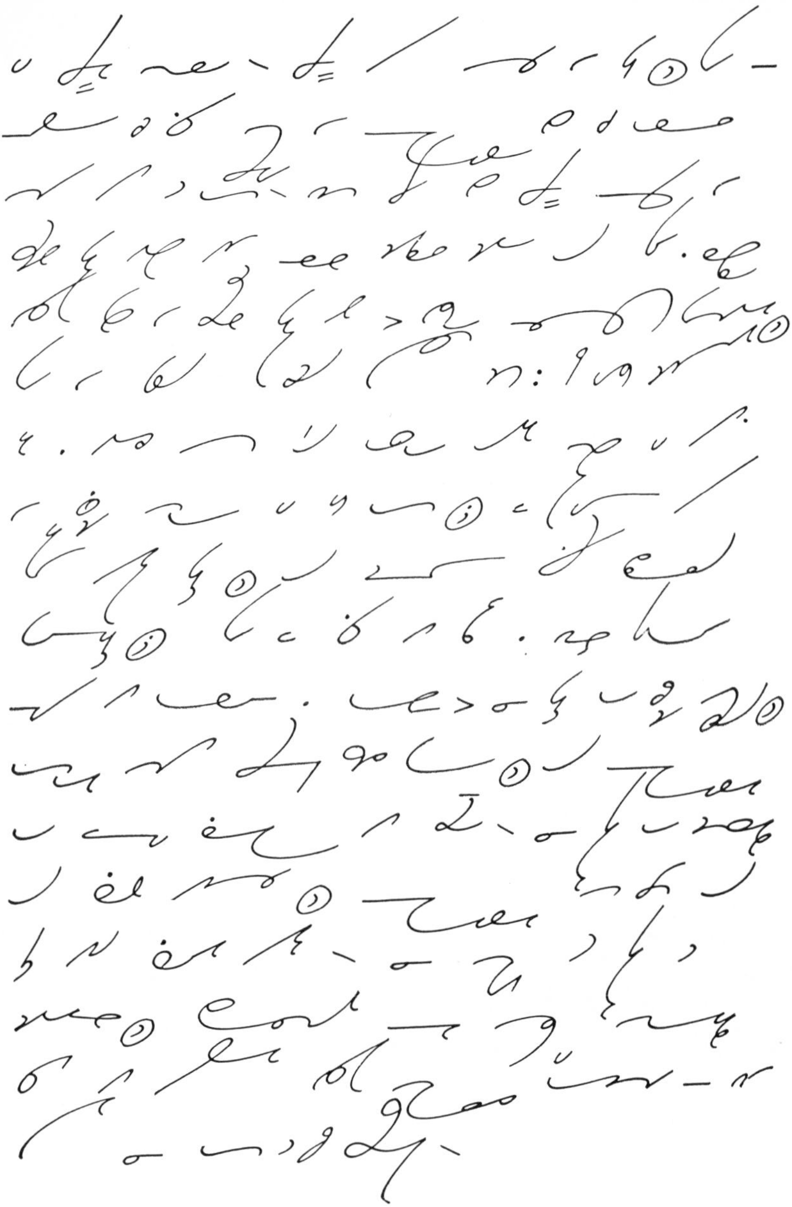

(Reading time: 4 min. 40 sec.) (600)

Punctuation Pointer

31. When such words as *namely, for instance, that is,* and *for example* introduce a series of items, an explanation, or an illustration; and when such words as *accordingly, consequently, nevertheless, otherwise,* and *moreover* connect two independent clauses, a *semicolon* usually precedes these words and a *comma* usually follows them.

We were particularly successful with three kinds of vegetables; namely, beets, carrots, and lettuce.

The attendance at the meetings was excellent; for instance, only one member was absent at the final session.

She failed to do one thing; that is, she failed to change her shoes.

We should not worry about such matters; nevertheless, we do want things properly arranged.

He must have missed his train; otherwise, he would have been here long ago.

PART 2. BUSINESS INFORMATION

Vocabulary Preview

ad/ja/cent	ob/jec/tion
an/tag/o/nized	old-fashioned
bed/lam	pho/tog/ra/pher
bor/rowed	pho/tog/ra/phy
Chi/cago	pneu/matic
com/pos/ite	po/lice/man's
crit/i/cism	pro/fes/sional
fin/gers	quiet
for/tu/nately	rec/og/niz/able
girls	riv/eter
hurt	se/ri/ously
in/ad/vert/ently	showed
in/su/la/tion	shut
lay/man	stu/dio
lively	stuff/ing
Lou/i/si/ana	va/lid/ity
mas/ter/piece	wares
news/boy's	weak/ened
noise/less	when/ever
noises	whis/tle

Handling a Complaint

The effects of advertising are far-reaching and sometimes surprising, as in the case of the present series [20] of letters. These letters show that the advertising of a soap business in Chicago may seriously [40] affect a wood products business in Louisiana.

Some time ago a rather interesting situation [60] developed when a manufacturer of noise insulation employed a photographer to prepare an [80] illustration to accompany advertising copy. The picture showed an executive at his desk, stuffing [100] his fingers into his ears in a vain attempt to shut out the multitude of noises that fill a business office [120] in a busy city. Through a masterpiece of composite photography, the various noises were shown [140] to be arising from a pneumatic riveter, a policeman's whistle, a newsboy's effort to sell his wares,[160] a lively discussion in an adjacent office, and the rattle of typewriter keys. Inadvertently, the [180] photographer pictured a noiseless typewriter. Of course, the typewriter company objected. The answer to [200] the objection proved a masterpiece in avoiding trouble:

"We appreciate your calling attention to our [220] advertisement, and we realize the validity of your criticism. Fortunately, the typewriter is [240] not recognizable by the layman.

"When this photograph was to be taken, we simply borrowed a typewriter [260] from one of the girls in the office. There was no question of choice because only noiseless typewriters are used [280] in the office. It will hurt our photographer's professional pride to know that he overlooked a detail that [300] weakened the force of the illustration and antagonized you.

"We are passing your letter along to the [320] commercial studio and asking it to make a point of featuring noiseless typewriters in quiet scenes only.[340] Whenever another bedlam illustration comes our way, we shall beg or borrow a noisy old-fashioned make [360] because we will not buy one."

(365)

PART 3. BUSINESS CORRESPONDENCE

between

WOODSON SOAP COMPANY
1645 Michigan Avenue
Chicago 6, Illinois

and

SOUTHERN WOOD PRODUCTS COMPANY
129 East Pine Street
Lafayette, Louisiana

LETTER 158

at/tracted
brooms
cast

in/stru/ments
mops
ob/so/lete

Chi/cago 6,
Il/li/nois
clean/ing
de/tec/tive

re/flec/tion
south/ern
spe/cial
at/ten/tion

dust/ers
il/lus/trated

Wood/son

August 1, 19—

Woodson Soap Company
1645 Michigan Avenue
Chicago 6, Illinois

Gentlemen

The drawing used in connection with your advertisement in the *Illustrated Detective Magazine* [20] has attracted our special attention. We are manufacturers of handles for brooms, mops, and dusters; and [40] this picture seems to suggest that these cleaning instruments are now obsolete and are no longer recommended [60] by you.

Is it your idea in advertising to cast reflection on the broom, mop, and duster? Is it your [80] intention to attempt to hurt another business in order to improve your own business?

We should like to have [100] a copy of the booklet offered in the advertisement.

Yours very truly   (114)

SOUTHERN WOOD PRODUCTS COMPANY

HBN:CR   President

LETTER 159

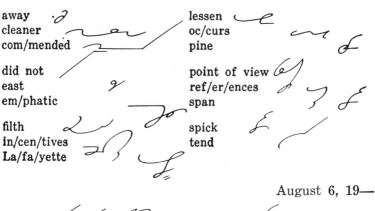

away	lessen
cleaner	oc/curs
com/mended	pine
did not	point of view
east	ref/er/ences
em/phatic	span
filth	spick
in/cen/tives	tend
La/fa/yette	

August 6, 19—

WOODSON SOAP COMPANY, Publicity Director

(Reading time: 1 min. 45 sec.) (223)

LETTER 160

ap/prove
be/lief
clean/ers
con/cluded

heart/ily
hor/ror
if we can be
im/ple/ments

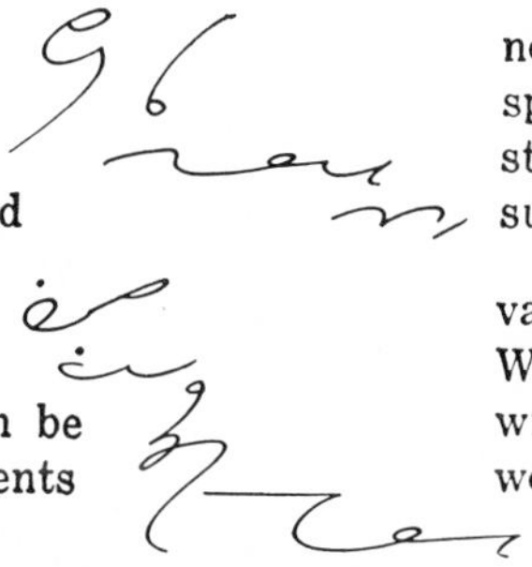

no one
spread/ing
stand
sup/plant/ing

vac/uum
Walker
wished
woman

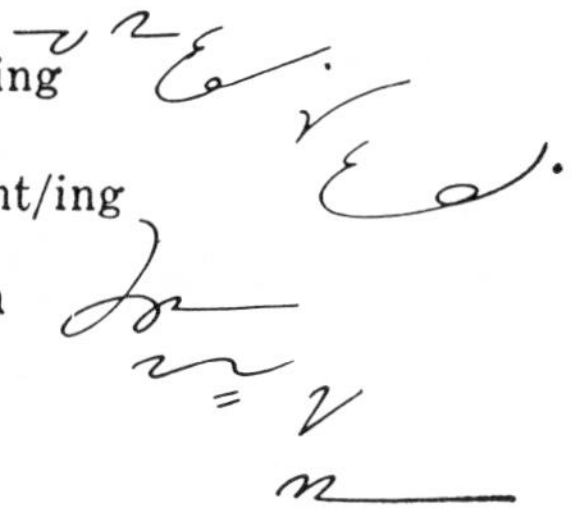

August 9, 19—

Woodson Soap Company
1645 Michigan Avenue
Chicago 6, Illinois

Attention of Mr. Walker, Publicity Director

Gentlemen

We want to compliment you on the booklet enclosed in your letter of August 6. It is a fine ²⁰ piece of work, and we agree with you in the belief that its distribution will be helpful to any ⁴⁰ manufacturer of cleaning devices.

The first glance at your advertisement left the impression that no one should use ⁶⁰ a broom, brush, or mop for cleaning purposes. It seemed that the woman in the illustration was looking with horror ⁸⁰ at these implements. We concluded that you wished to advertise vacuum cleaners as supplanting the things ¹⁰⁰ in which we are most interested.

We are glad of this opportunity to become familiar with your program,¹²⁰ and we heartily approve of it. If we can be of any assistance in spreading this information ¹⁴⁰ for the good of the cause, we stand at your service.

Yours truly   (151)

SOUTHERN WOOD PRODUCTS COMPANY

HBN:CR   President

LETTER 161

ac/knowl/edg/ing   com/mu/ni/cate
com/ment   va/ca/tion

August 13, 19—

Secretary to Mr. Walker

(Reading time: 40 sec.)   (83)

PART 4. BUSINESS PRACTICES

Vocabulary Preview

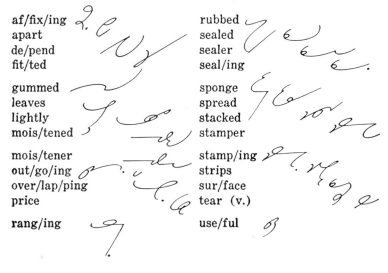

af/fix/ing
apart
de/pend
fit/ted

gummed
leaves
lightly
mois/tened

mois/tener
out/go/ing
over/lap/ping
price

rang/ing

rubbed
sealed
sealer
seal/ing

sponge
spread
stacked
stamper

stamp/ing
strips
sur/face
tear (v.)

use/ful

Sealing and Stamping Envelopes by Hand Methods

Numerous devices have been put on the market to facilitate the handling of outgoing mail. Sealing [20] and stamping machines will be discussed in the next lesson. Many small offices and some large offices, however,⁴⁰ consider these machines too expensive for their needs. They consequently depend on hand methods for the sealing ⁶⁰ and stamping of their letters.

In offices in which the daily outgoing mail amounts to only a few ⁸⁰ letters, a hand sealer will be found very useful. One type of hand sealer consists of a tube filled with water ¹⁰⁰ and fitted at the open end with a piece of sponge or felt. When rubbed lightly over the flap of an envelope,¹²⁰ such a sealer leaves sufficient moisture on the gummed surface to serve the purpose of sealing. A device of this ¹⁴⁰ kind may be bought for a price ranging from ten cents to fifty cents.

When a number of envelopes are to be sealed ¹⁶⁰ quickly, the stenographer will find the following plan both efficient and easy:

Pick up about ten envelopes ¹⁸⁰ at a time and arrange them with the flaps all turned one way. Now, insert one envelope under the flap of ²⁰⁰ another; then, insert a third envelope under the flap of the second. Continue this procedure until the ²²⁰ envelopes are stacked with overlapping flaps. Open the flaps and spread the envelopes, address side down, in a row ²⁴⁰ on a desk or a table and in such a position that the gummed surface of each flap extends beyond the edge ²⁶⁰ of the flap below it. A ruler may be used to hold the flaps in position, and a wet sponge will serve the purpose ²⁸⁰ of a moistener. All the envelopes should be moistened at the same time, but each should be sealed separately.³⁰⁰

To facilitate stamping, it will be found advisable to buy the stamps in sheets and to tear the stamps apart ³²⁰ in strips. There is also available a small and inexpensive hand stamper that serves the double purpose of ³⁴⁰ moistening the stamp and affixing it to the envelope.

The stenographer should keep always on the lookout ³⁶⁰ for new methods of doing the routine work of the office. Many good office practices have been given their ³⁸⁰ start by stenographers with interest and understanding.   (391)

PART 5. PROGRESS CHECKUP

Letter PC-24

Mr. Frederick Walker, Publicity Director
Woodson Soap Company
1645 Michigan Avenue
Chicago 6, Illinois

Dear Mr. Walker

We recently filed an objection to an illustration accompanying your advertisement [20] in the *Illustrated Detective Magazine*. At that time you were so very courteous that we are [40] now taking the liberty of writing for information about advertising practices.

For many years [60] you have been advertising regularly in the principal newspapers and leading monthly magazines. Your [80] layout has included various types of displays and varying amounts of space. Your experience, therefore,[100] has been extensive.

We are planning to increase our field of advertising, and our agent is trying to [120] interest us in modernizing our styles of publicity. We have always had commercial artists prepare picture [140] illustrations. Our material has been kept on the highest level, as we felt that our product should make [160] a serious appeal. We have noticed, however, that a great many advertisers use picture strips instead [180] of the more formal displays, and we greatly desire to ascertain what the results of this kind of advertising [200] really are.

If we adopt this type of illustration, it will mean a definite shift from the policy [220] we have been following for more than twenty years. For that reason, we want to consider the matter seriously.[240] It is true that recent study has shown that the illustrated strips are the most popular form of [260] literature, and this may apply also to advertising. There may be a very profitable advertising [280] field in this sort of display.

You have had considerable experience in the use of less formal [300] advertising, and we should like to know what your

reaction is. Are you planning to continue the use of drawings [320] in your own advertising? Is there a definite improvement in public attitude as a result of this [340] kind of
display? Any opinions you can give us in this connection
will be accepted seriously and [360] will be greatly appreciated.

We are also considering the use of commercial photog-
raphy as [380] a substitute for art work in our advertising.
Please bear in mind this possibility when you answer this [400]
letter.

It seems reasonable that a combination of the two types
of advertising may be very effective.[420] We are decidedly
interested in the possibilities to be found in the use of a [440]
photographic illustration. Aside from giving the appearance of being definitely authentic, the [460] photograph may
offer a great variety of possibilities. The picture may present a serious [480] situation, or it may be based on humor.
This type of advertising may make it possible to appeal to [500]
persons of many different social levels.

An immediate answer is not requested, but we should [520]
appreciate a letter from you after you have had time to
give our problem a little thought.

Yours truly   (540)

SOUTHERN WOOD PRODUCTS COMPANY

HBN:CR   President

DICTATION STUDY XXV

PART 1. BASIC SKILLS

Brief-Form Review

Directions. The following article contains 88 different brief forms and brief-form derivatives. Read the article until you can read easily at your reading rate of at least 125 words a minute. Make two copies of the article in shorthand.

[Shorthand outlines]

(Reading time: 4 min. 40 sec.)   (600)

No new pointer is given in this lesson, but all punctuation marks needed in the foregoing article are shown.

PART 2. BUSINESS INFORMATION
Vocabulary Preview

af/fix	me/ter
af/fix/ers	min/ute (n.)
as they are	mois/ten/ing
ca/pa/ble	must have
con/tracted	op/er/ated
con/trolled	per/tain
driven	plat/form
eco/nom/i/cally	post of/fice
18,000	quan/ti/ties
ejected	rolls
gov/ern/ment	short time
locked	thick/nesses

Minute (n.)   Minute (adj.)

Minute (noun) refers to time.

This job can be completed in a minute or two.
This machine will produce 100 copies a minute.

Minute (adj.) means very small, trifling.

She gave close attention to minute details.

Envelope Sealing and Stamping Machines

There are machines that will do efficiently and economically almost every routine job of the [20] modern business office. The following form letters pertain to one of these machines.

Envelope sealers may be [40] bought in many styles and sizes, and as either hand-driven or power machines. They are equipped to handle [60] envelopes of varying thicknesses and shapes. The stacked envelopes, containing the letters, are placed on the machine [80] platform; the machine is operated at practically any desired speed; and the sealed envelopes are [100] ejected into a receptacle, again neatly stacked. As the sealing and stamping of envelopes is a [120] last-minute job, these machines must have a capacity for handling vol-

The mailing machine pictured here is similar to the type of machine discussed in this dictation study. The sorting rack, the mail table, and the postal scales are indications of a well-ordered mail room.

ume work with great speed. The sealer discussed in [140] our correspondence will seal 18,000 envelopes in an hour.

Mechanical stamping machines are of two [160] types: those that actually affix stamps to envelopes, and those that print a government mailing permit on [180] envelopes. Stamp affixers are usually hand-operated machines that contain rolls of stamps and some means of [200] moistening the stamps.

The use of the permit machine, better known as a meter machine, is controlled by the [220] United States Post Office Department. When installed in a business office, the machine is given a permit [240] number and is locked by the Government representative in such a manner that it will print only the number [260] of mailing permits actually paid for. A meter keeps count of the permits as they are printed. At frequent [280] intervals additional permits must be con-tracted for. Such a machine is capable of handling large [300] quantities of mail in an exceedingly short time.

Without the assistance of sealing and stamping machines, business [320] concerns would find it practically impossible to carry through big circularizing campaigns.   (338)

PART 3. BUSINESS CORRESPONDENCE
between

EFFICIENCY MACHINE COMPANY
1201 Copley Square
Boston 2, Massachusetts

and

McCLURG DRY GOODS COMPANY
1919 Congress Street
Portland 3, Maine

LETTER 162

ac/knowl/edg/ment	grav/ity
an/noy/ances	haste
cap/il/lary	Maine
de/pend/ably	many
desk	Mc/Clurg
du/ra/ble	ne/ces/si/ties
econ/o/mies	Port/land
ef/fi/ciency	pos/i/tively
elim/i/nates	pos/tal card
folder	suc/tion
for/merly	trou/bles
400,000	wicks
goods	widely

October 15, 19—

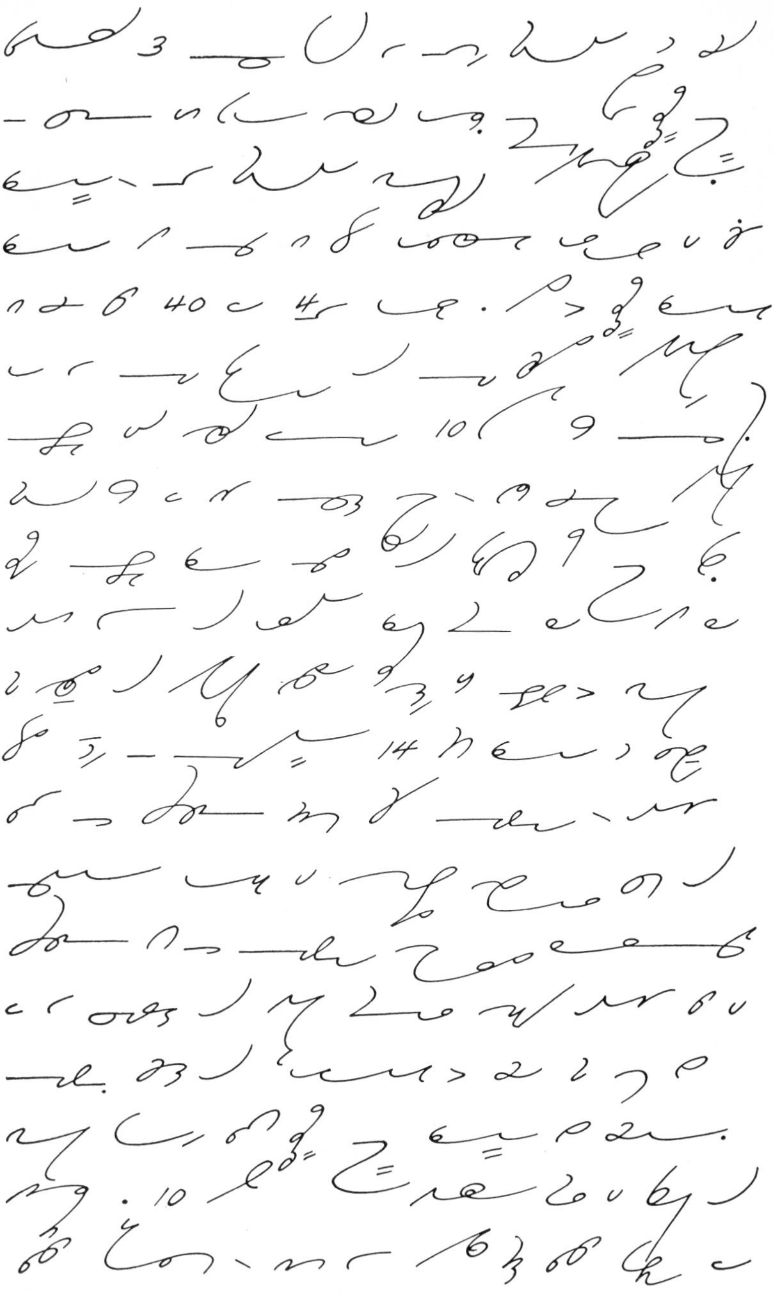

E<small>FFICIENCY</small> M<small>ACHINE</small> C<small>OMPANY</small>, Sales Manager

(Reading time: 2 min. 10 sec.)   (278)

LETTER 163

af/fixer		fa/cil/ity	
course		in/vi/ta/tion	
de/scribes		schemes	
dis/tinct		tackle	
drudg/ery		un/der/take	
en/cour/age/ment		vim	
en/tail		years ago	

October 29, 19—

EFFICIENCY MACHINE COMPANY, Sales Manager

(Reading time: 1 min. 40 sec.)   (211)

LETTER 164

dis/a/gree/able		tried	
in/ef/fi/ciency		un/a/void/able	
likes		un/pro/duc/tive	
se/lec/tion		wel/fare	
smooth			

November 12, 19—

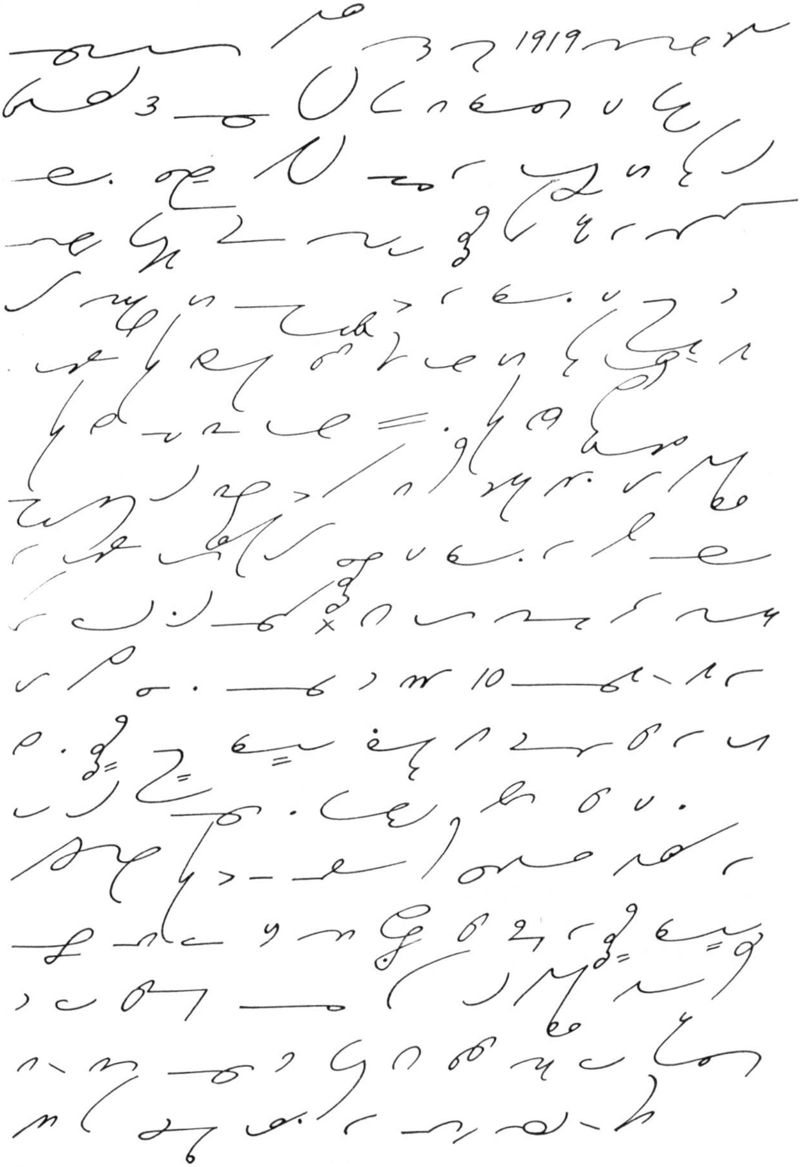

Efficiency Machine Company, Sales Manager

(Reading time: 1 min. 30 sec.) (201)

LETTER 165

any/one		in or/der to be sure
as lit/tle as		in/stal/la/tion
cor/dial		re/quire
fa/cil/i/ties		wor/thy

Anyone   Any one

Anyone, written as one word, means any person, anybody.

Do you know anyone who may be interested in a position with this company?

Give the report to anyone in the main office.

Any one, written as two words, refers to one selected without question of choice.

Any one of the stenographers could have done this work.
Any one of the books will be satisfactory for our purposes.
You may use any one of the typewriters.

November 26, 19—

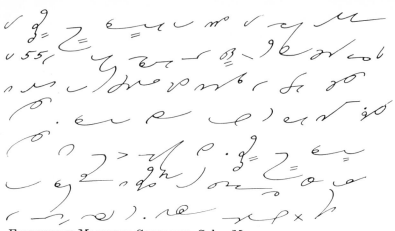

EFFICIENCY MACHINE COMPANY, Sales Manager

(Reading time: 1 min. 45 sec.)   (221)

LETTER 166

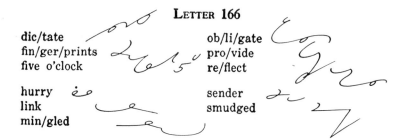

dic/tate
fin/ger/prints
five o'clock

hurry
link
min/gled

ob/li/gate
pro/vide
re/flect

sender
smudged

December 3, 19—

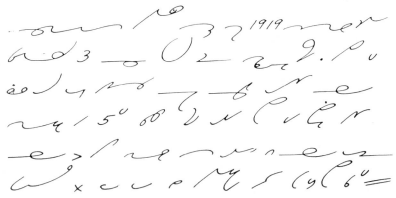

EFFICIENCY MACHINE COMPANY, Sales Manager

(Reading time: 1 min. 20 sec.)   (174)

LETTER 167

| cent | | over/look | |
| gainer | | uni/formly | |

Model 12, page 367, shows an attractive arrangement of the following letter. The stenographer is frequently expected to use her own ideas with reference to letter display.

December 17, 19—

(shorthand outlines)

EFFICIENCY MACHINE COMPANY, Sales Manager

(Reading time: 1 min. 30 sec.) (196)

Efficiency Machine Company

1201 COPLEY SQUARE • BOSTON 2, MASSACHUSETTS

December 17, 19--

McClurg Dry Goods Company
1919 Congress Street
Portland 3, Maine

Gentlemen

    Fifty-five thousand business houses in the United States
are convinced that Efficiency Envelope Sealers

        eliminate the drudgery and routine work of sealing
        letters by hand;

        seal every envelope neatly, uniformly, and posi-
        tively, at the rate of from 9,000 to 18,000 an
        hour;

        save time, space, and confusion in the handling of
        mail.

    You, too, can become convinced of these facts by merely
agreeing to try a machine in your own office. We shall send
one to you by prepaid transportation. If it makes good, you
will be the gainer; if it does not, merely return the machine
to us, transportation charges collect. You will then have the
satisfaction of knowing that you did not overlook an opportunity to save money.

    This trial will not obligate you in any way or cost you
a cent. It will have all the advantages of allowing you to
see for yourself, without pressure or hurry, just how much
money, time, and drudgery an Efficiency Envelope Sealer will
save you.

    The enclosed card will do the trick.

               Very truly yours

               EFFICIENCY MACHINE COMPANY

               Charles Dackett

CD:6   Sales Manager

Enc.

**MODEL 12—MODIFIED BLOCK LETTER SHOWING AN ATTRACTIVE
DISPLAY OF MATERIAL**

The appearance of a letter helps to govern the attention given to it by
the reader. A well-written letter deserves the best possible dress.

PART 4. BUSINESS PRACTICES

Vocabulary Preview

ac/com/plished
bring/ing
faint

life
pro/long/ing
put/ting

forced
ham/mer/ing
in/di/ca/tor

re/verse
spool

Prolonging the Life of Typewriter Ribbons

When a ribbon has been used for some time on a type-writer and the writing begins to get faint from the con-stant [20] use of the top edge, the typist should adjust the ribbon so that the lower part can be used. Instead of bringing [40] the lower part into use through moving the ribbon indicator to the red position, the typist should remove [60] the ribbon from the machine and reverse it, bringing to the top the edge that was formerly at the bottom.[80] This plan, of course, applies only to ribbons of one color. On some machines this reversing can best be accomplished [100] by putting the left-hand spool in the right position and the right-hand spool in the left position.

When the part [120] of the ribbon now in use becomes faint, a return to the original position will give additional [140] life to the ribbon because the typist will be able to use the ink that has been forced into the lower part [160] of the ribbon by the constant hammering of the type.

It is wise to reverse the ribbon at least once a week,[180] whether such reversing is apparently needed or not.

This is an economy step, but the office worker [200] should bear in mind that she should not practice economy at the expense of quality. Many companies [220] feel that quality letters tend to build good will and also have strong advertis-ing value. These companies would [240] prefer to buy ribbons more often than to sacrifice the quality of their letters.

•

(256)

PART 5. PROGRESS CHECKUP

Letter PC-25

McClurg Dry Goods Company
1919 Congress Street
Portland 3, Maine

Gentlemen

This letter is written in answer to your request for further and more detailed information about [20] sealing and stamping machines. This company makes three types of machines to meet the mailing requirements of a [40] business office. We are very happy to furnish the following descriptions in addition to the material [60] presented in our catalog of office equipment:

For the small office, mailing daily from forty [80] or fifty to five or six hundred letters, we recommend Model 6 Sealer, a hand-operated sealing [100] machine, and our Junior Stamp Affixer. This office equipment is fairly inexpensive, yet efficient and [120] durable.

The Model 6 Sealer has an estimated capacity of one hundred letters. The letters [140] are simply stacked on the machine platform. They move quietly through the machine at the rate of twenty to thirty [160] a minute—the speed depends on the wishes of the mailing clerk. The letters are sealed neatly, uniformly, and [180] positively and are ejected into a receptacle where the envelopes are easily available [200] for stamping. Model 6 is so arranged that it will accommodate letters of varying thicknesses and [220] sizes.

The Junior Stamp Affixer is a small, convenient device that will actually affix stamps to [240] your letters with a minimum of work and at the rate of forty to fifty a minute. This machine accommodates [260] five hundred stamps that may be bought in rolls at any post office. Each stamp is moistened mechanically just [280] before it is placed on the envelope.

Both the hand-operated sealer and the Junior Stamp Affixer are [300] illustrated on page 28 of the catalog that is being mailed to you in a separate envelope.[320] These two devices are small enough to be used on a side table and to be put away when not in use.[340]

Our Model 14 Sealer and Stamper is the machine for the office with a volume of outgoing mail. This [360] electric machine will seal and stamp from nine thousand to eighteen thousand envelopes an hour. As with Model 6 [380] Sealer, the envelopes are stacked on the machine platform; but with this equipment the envelopes are sealed and stamped [400] in one operation and with little attention on the part of the mail clerk. We are sure you understand that [420] this machine does not actually affix a stamp to the envelope, but rather it prints a mailing permit [440] when authorized by the United States Post Office Department.

With your permission, we shall be glad to send a [460] representative to your office to suggest the machines that will best do your work. These machines will then be placed [480] in your office for a trial period without cost or obligation to you. If, after the trial, the [500] machines have not measured up to our promises, they may be returned to us. We will pay the expense. Why not give [520] us this opportunity to convince you that we can serve you to your profit. The attached card, filled in and mailed [540] promptly, should arrive at our desk without delay and will bring our representative to your office within a [560] week. He will help you without pressure or haste.

Very truly yours   (572)

EFFICIENCY MACHINE COMPANY

CD:6   Sales Manager
Enc.

DICTATION STUDY XXVI

PART 1. BASIC SKILLS

Theory Review

Directions. The following words are all used in the dictation material of this lesson. Read the words until the key is no longer needed. Write each word at least once.

OGRAPH, EGRAPH, and GRAM

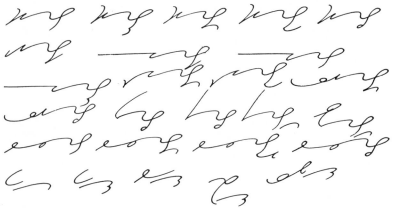

Key: photo*graph*, photo*graphs*, photo*graphic*, photo*grapher*, photog-raphy, auto*graphed*, mimeo*graphed*, mono*graph*, mono*graphs*, steno-*graphic*, steno*grapher*, litho*graphic*, litho*graphy*, bio*graphy*, geog-raphy, geo*graphical*, typo*graphical*, tele*graph*, tele*graphic*, tel-e*graphers*, tele*graphy*, pro*gram*, pro*grams*, tele*grams*, cable*grams*, radio*grams*.

Directions. Read the following letters until you can read easily, and then make two copies in shorthand.

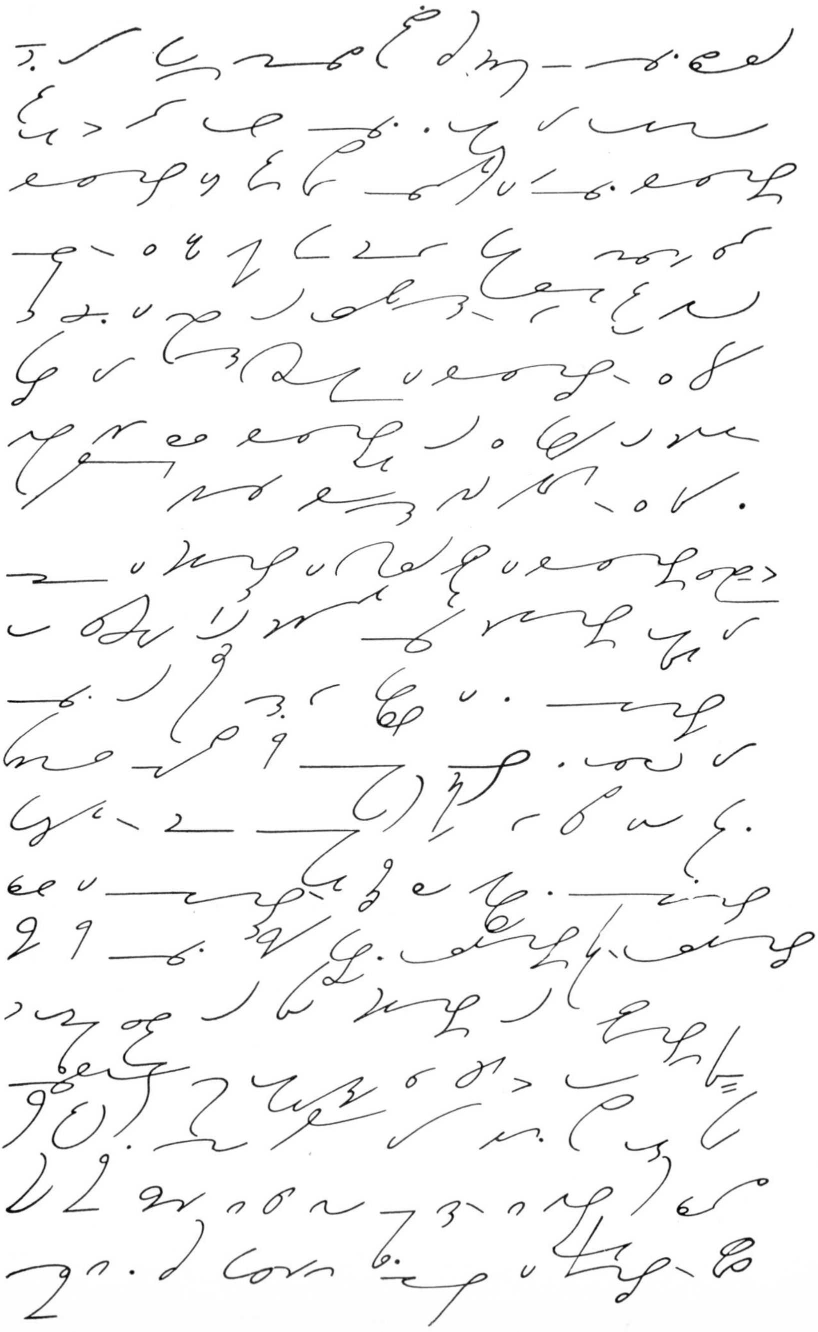

(Reading time: 4 min. 40 sec.)   (600)

No new punctuation pointer is given in this lesson, and medial punctuation marks are not indicated in the foregoing letters.

PART 2. BUSINESS INFORMATION

Vocabulary Preview

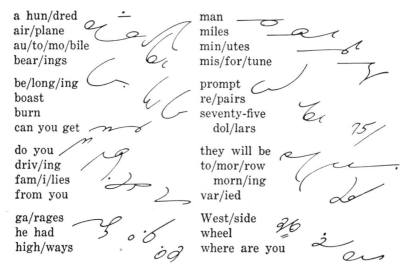

a hun/dred	man
air/plane	miles
au/to/mo/bile	min/utes
bear/ings	mis/for/tune
be/long/ing	prompt
boast	re/pairs
burn	seventy-five
can you get	dol/lars
do you	they will be
driv/ing	to/mor/row
fam/i/lies	morn/ing
from you	var/ied
ga/rages	West/side
he had	wheel
high/ways	where are you

Service

On one occasion the owner of an automobile belonging to America's "four hundred" in automobile [20] families was driving his car through central Ohio when he had the misfortune to burn out the bearings [40] of the right front wheel. In those particular days small-town garages could not boast of the varied stock now [60] available anywhere on the main highways; so, after several vain attempts to have the repairs attended [80] to, the car-owner called the General Service Company by long-distance.

"How soon can you get a set of front-wheel [100] bearings to me?" asked the owner.

"Where are you now?" came back over the line.

"I am at Westside, Ohio, with [120] no immediate chance of getting away."

"Well, we can have a set of bearings in your possession within an [140] hour," was the prompt reply.

"Man, do you realize that I am a hundred miles from you?" asked the surprised owner.

"Yes," [160] was the answer; "but we have an airplane ready to rush the bearings to you. It can leave within three minutes."

"How [180] much will that cost?"

"The cost, including the bearings, will be seventy-five dollars."

"How soon can you get the bearings [200] to me by special delivery?"

"They will be in your hands by tomorrow morning. We can mail them at once."

"Well,[220] that will do. Send the bearings by special delivery. Your company certainly gives service."

" 'Service' is our [240] middle name."   (242)

PART 3. BUSINESS CORRESPONDENCE

between

WHEELER SLIDING DOOR COMPANY   MR. BERNARD L. ROBINSON
1416 West 34th Street   *and*   141 Monument Avenue
Memphis 3, Tennessee   New Bern, North Carolina

and

WHEELER SLIDING DOOR COMPANY
8706 Laurel Street
Raleigh, North Carolina

Directions. In the preceding dictation studies, all dictation was given at a timed pace and with a rhythmic smoothness that is essential in building speed. Actual office dictation, however, is frequently not so smooth or rhythmic, and many dictators pause during their dictation in order to clarify their thinking and to construct meaningful sentences.

Your teacher may wish to dictate the following letters in uneven, untimed style somewhat similar to office dictation; consequently, Letters 168, 171, and 174 are so arranged as to give you some idea of the type of dictation to expect. The complete letter for No. 168 is given to show what it should look like when prepared for mailing. You will note that some punctuation marks have been dictated in these letters. Some employers feel that it is necessary to dictate punctuation unless they have full confidence in the ability of the stenographer to handle this phase of the work. You will practice the vocabulary previews and all the letters as instructed in previous dictation studies. It is suggested that you read aloud Letters 168, 171, and 174 to hear how they would sound if you were the dictator.

Letters 169, 170, 172, and 173 are given in shorthand plates as they might appear in your own notebook. Your teacher may decide to dictate them also in office style.

LETTER 168

at the		New Bern	
Ber/nard		pleased	
buf/fer		Rob/in/son	
con/crete		signs	
con/tact		split/ting	
de/scent		strip	
I should like		that could be	
to know		that might be	
I thought		used	
Mem/phis,		Wheeler	
Ten/nes/see		you might have	
mon/u/ment			

At the end of the following letter you will find directions pertaining to the method of handling this letter in the business office. Record these directions in shorthand unless your instructor instructs you otherwise.

October 21, 19—

Miss Cameron, take a letter to the Wheeler Sliding Door Company, 1416 West 34th Street, Memphis 3, Tennessee (pause) Gentlemen I am writing this letter to let you know (pause) that I am well pleased (pause) with the sliding door I had installed last May paragraph

At the same time (pause) I should like to know whether you have any attachment (pause) that might be used as a buffer (pause) when the door is closed (pause) period I notice signs of splitting at the base of the door comma (pause) because of the contact of the door (pause) with the concrete floor in descent (pause) paragraph

I thought you might have some sort of metal strip (pause) that could be fastened to the edge of the door (pause) to prevent further splitting (pause) Very truly yours

Set that letter up on blank paper. Be sure to type my home address at the top of the letter (141 Monument Avenue, New Bern, North Carolina). Type only my name * after the closing. No carbon copy is necessary.

* Bernard L. Robinson

This is how the finished letter should appear:

141 Monument Avenue
New Bern, North Carolina
October 21, 19—

Wheeler Sliding Door Company
1416 West 34th Street
Memphis 3, Tennessee

Gentlemen

I am writing this letter to let you know that I am well pleased with the sliding door I had installed [20] last May.

At the same time I should like to know whether you have any attachment that might be used as a buffer [40] when the door is closed. I notice signs of splitting at the base of the door, because of the contact of the door with [60] the concrete floor in descent.

I thought you might have some sort of metal strip that could be fastened to the edge of the [80] door to prevent further splitting.

Very truly yours   (89)

Bernard L. Robinson

LETTER 169

con/struc/tion	re/fer/ring
rec/om/men/	so/licit
da/tions	su/per/vi/sion

October 24, 19—

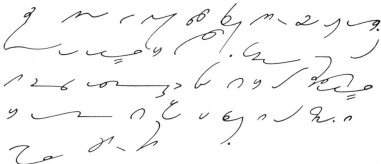

WHEELER SLIDING DOOR COMPANY, Manager

(Reading time: 1 min. 15 sec.)   (161)

LETTER 170

Em/ory ⎯⎯ (⎯   we are en/clos/
self-explanatory ⎯   ing   ⎯⎯.

WHEELER SLIDING DOOR COMPANY

October 24, 19—

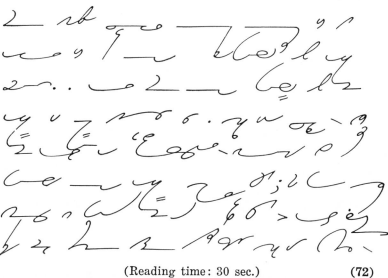

(Reading time: 30 sec.)   (72)

WHEELER SLIDING DOOR COMPANY

October 24, 19--

FROM   R. B. Emory, Manager, Memphis Office
TO   Raleigh Office
SUBJECT   **Mr. Bernard L. Robinson**

We are enclosing a letter from Mr. Bernard L. Robinson, of New Bern, together with a copy of our answer. These letters are self-explanatory. You will note that we have promised Mr. Robinson complete satisfaction; so please give this matter your prompt and special attention.

Let us hear from you just as soon as you have come to some decision as to the cause of the difficulty.

RBEmory:BK

Enc.

FOR INTERPLANT USE ONLY

MODEL 13—INTERPLANT LETTER
This style of letter is used chiefly for communication between
representatives of the same company.

LETTER 171

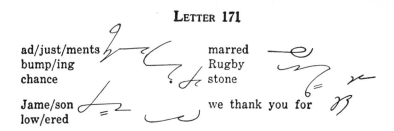

ad/just/ments
bump/ing
chance

Jame/son
low/ered

marred
Rugby
stone

we thank you for

The simplest way to indicate that this letter is to be arranged as an interplant, or interoffice, letter is to use the longhand abbreviation "Int." immediately preceding the dictation. If you are numbering your letters, "Int." should be written on the line to the right of the letter number.

To distinguish "ensure" from "insure," simply write a small "e" above the shorthand outline for "ensure." This is necessary only when the employer indicates a particular spelling to be used.

October 31, 19—

Take an interplant letter to Mr. R. B. Emory, Memphis Office, Subject Mr. Bernard L. Robinson (pause) Following the request in your letter of October 24 (pause) comma (pause) we sent Mr. Jameson to New Bern period (pause) He found that some slight adjustments were necessary (pause) to ensure (pause) spell that with an e (pause) to ensure the proper working of the door installed for Mr. Robinson period The bottom rail was not split comma (pause) but the wood was slightly marred (pause) by a stone or some similar object period (pause) paragraph

Mr. Jameson made some spring adjustments (pause) to prevent the door from bumping when it is lowered comma (pause) and everything is now in good working condition period Mr. Robinson seems well pleased paragraph

We thank you for giving us a chance (pause) to correct the trouble

Dictated by J. G. Rugby, Raleigh Office   (103)

Letter 172

ex/pres/sion   *(shorthand)*   we are writ/ing *(shorthand)*
highly   *(shorthand)*   we thank you
opin/ion   *(shorthand)*   for your *(shorthand)*

to tell him   *(shorthand)*   you have made *(shorthand)*

WHEELER SLIDING DOOR COMPANY

November 3, 19—

(shorthand outline)

(Reading time: 30 sec.)   **(66)**

Letter 173

ad/justed   *(shorthand)*   de/fec/tive *(shorthand)*
cared   *(shorthand)*   in/spect
com/pli/ance   *(shorthand)*   per/fect *(shorthand)*

November 3, 19—

(shorthand outline)

WHEELER SLIDING DOOR COMPANY, Manager
(Reading time: 50 sec.) (107)

LETTER 174

I have never
in an/swer to
your let/ter

such
to give your

November 6, 19—

Miss Cameron, a letter to Wheeler Sliding Door Company, 1416 West 34th Street, Memphis 3, Tennessee (pause) Gentlemen (pause) In answer to your letter of November 3 comma may I say that I have never received (pause) such (pause) courteous and prompt attention (pause) as your Raleigh office rendered me (pause) paragraph

I certainly appreciate your interest (pause) and earnest desire to give your customers satisfaction Very truly yours

Set that letter up on blank paper. Be sure to type my home address at the top of the letter (141 Monument Avenue, New Bern, North Carolina). Type only my name * after the closing. No carbon copy is necessary. (54)

* Bernard L. Robinson

PART 4. BUSINESS PRACTICES

This part is omitted from this dictation study.

PART 5. PROGRESS CHECKUP

LETTER PC-26

Mr. Charles A. Long
16 Young Avenue
New Bern, North Carolina

Dear Mr. Long

Mr. Bernard L. Robinson, 141 Monument Avenue, New Bern, North Carolina,[20] has granted us the privilege of using his name in writing to you with regard to Wheeler sliding doors [40] for home garages. We installed a door for Mr. Robinson last May, and he has been so well satisfied and [60] so greatly pleased with the installation that he took the trouble of writing to us. Mr. Robinson, in a [80] recent letter, expressed himself as follows:

"I am writing this letter to let you know that I am well pleased with [100] the sliding door I had installed last May."

In another letter, written after we had sent a representative [120] to inspect his sliding door, Mr. Robinson wrote:

"I have never received such courteous and prompt attention [140] as your Raleigh office rendered me.

"I certainly appreciate your interest and earnest desire to [160] give your customers satisfaction."

There you have our story—a product that is equal to, if not better than,[180] any competing product; a company that definitely stands behind its product and also considers [200] that customer's satisfaction is the first essential of good service.

Of course, you have not indicated that [220] you are planning to modernize your automobile housing facilities. We do assume, however, that you [240] are interested in knowing about the latest developments in doors for home garages.

We are sending [260] you, therefore, some of the most recent literature.

As illustrated in the pamphlets that are being sent to [280] you, Wheeler sliding doors operate on a principle entirely different from that of the ordinary [300] swinging door. By means of carefully balanced levers, the Wheeler sliding door can be moved upward with a minimum [320] of energy; in fact, so little energy is required that children can actually open the door [340] to the full extent.

It doesn't require any great exercise of the powers of thought to understand that the [360] principle of the Wheeler sliding door prevents possible blocking of the door. An object that might easily [380] obstruct the ordinary swinging door in opening cannot possibly affect the easy operation [400] of the Wheeler sliding door.

It is not our desire to bring any pressure to bear in attempting to sell you [420] the idea of a Wheeler sliding door installation. We should, of course, like to have the opportunity [440] of sending a representative to see you. Such a representative will gladly give an estimate of [460] the cost of installing a Wheeler sliding door and will cheerfully help you select the best type and size of door [480] to meet your requirements. You will be interested in the surprisingly small cost of a complete job.

The [500] Wheeler sliding door is not a new idea; it is no longer in the trial stage. Thousands of satisfied [520] customers have proved that the Wheeler door really passes every test. Early installations were expensive,[540] but prices have been lowered until the Wheeler sliding door is today within the reach of anyone owning [560] an automobile that is worthy of good housing. In addition to its strong practical value, a Wheeler [580] sliding door carries a certain pride of possession with every job that we release.

Very sincerely yours   (600)

WHEELER SLIDING DOOR COMPANY

RBE:BK   Manager

DICTATION STUDY XXVII

PART 1. BASIC SKILLS

Theory Review

Directions. All the following theory words are used in the article in this part. Read the words until you can read them easily without the aid of the key. Then write each word at least once. Speed in writing is dependent upon moving promptly from one outline to the next, whether the outlines are separate words or parts of the same word.

STIC Words

Key: artistic, elastic, scholastic, drastic, plastic, domestic, optimistic, modernistic, characteristic, realistic, majestic, enthusiastic, enthusiastically, statistical.

TIC Words

Key: systematic, dramatic, emphatic, athletics, critics, critical, theoretical, automatically, energetically, mathematical.

ULATE Words

Key: regu*lated*, specu*lation*, stimu*lated*, accumu*lated*, congratu*late*, manip*ulate*, stip*ulation*, tab*ulated*, calc*ulations*.

Directions. Proceed in the usual manner.

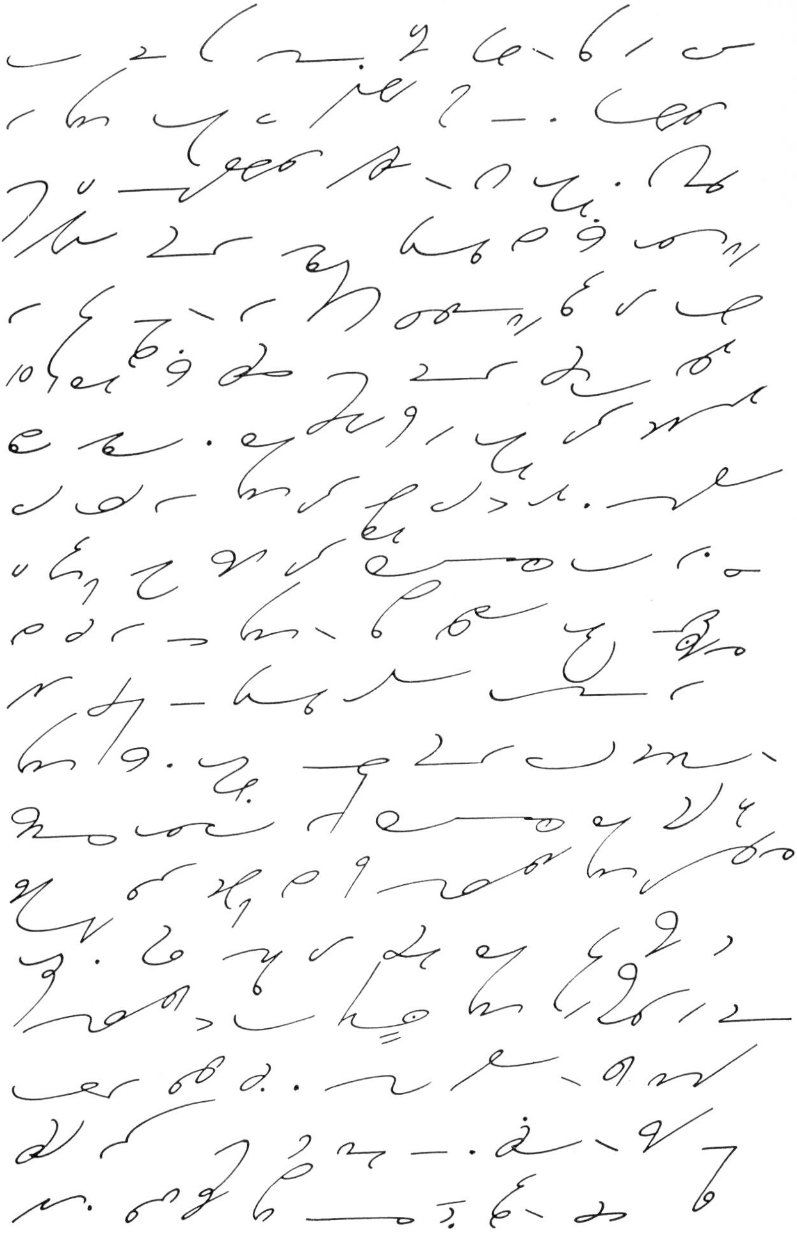

(Reading time: 4 min. 40 sec.) (600)

PART 2. BUSINESS INFORMATION

Vocabulary Preview

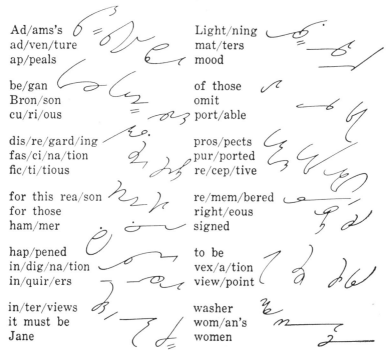

Ad/ams's	Light/ning
ad/ven/ture	mat/ters
ap/peals	mood
be/gan	of those
Bron/son	omit
cu/ri/ous	port/able
dis/re/gard/ing	pros/pects
fas/ci/na/tion	pur/ported
fic/ti/tious	re/cep/tive
for this rea/son	re/mem/bered
for those	right/eous
ham/mer	signed
hap/pened	to be
in/dig/na/tion	vex/a/tion
in/quir/ers	view/point
in/ter/views	washer
it must be	wom/an's
Jane	women

National Advertising

Here is a situation that fully deserves all the vexation expressed in Mrs. Adams's letter of [20] September 17.

As a result of national advertising, every mail brings in a number of [40] requests for further information about our product. We treat all these requests in the same way; that is, we answer [60] them with a series of form letters and then turn over to local representatives the names of those [80] inquirers who show continued interest. These form letters are purported to be signed by Miss Jane Bronson. It matters [100] not whether Miss Bronson is a real or a fictitious person. Her name is valuable because it [120] seems to give a woman's viewpoint to our correspondence with women.

On August 24 the morning mail brought [140] in a request from an inquirer who happened to be interested in price only. Unfortunately, our [160] form letters omit any reference to price because we prefer to have this subject handled by our [180] representatives during personal interviews. Thus, disregarding Mrs. Adams's question of price, we began [200] a series of appeals to her interest and continued our campaign until Mrs. Adams, in righteous [220] indignation, sent us a letter that brought our sales department to quick action.

Our sales manager, Mr. Brown, was [240] quite equal to the occasion. By a series of personal letters, he talked Mrs. Adams into a [260] receptive mood and then began to hammer at her objections to the price. And the truth is, Mrs. Adams [280] really did buy a portable Lightning washer through our district agent.

This discussion is intended as no [300] particular criticism of form letters. The fact is that form letters make it possible for us to answer [320] promptly the thousands of inquiries from persons, many of whom are not now, and probably never will be, really [340] interested in buying. Form letters help us to separate the curious inquirers from the [360] interested prospects. It must be remembered, however, that form letters cannot meet every situation of [380] business correspondence. For this reason the business letter will never become completely routine, but will [400] always hold a fascination for those who look for adventure between its lines.

(414)

PART 3. BUSINESS CORRESPONDENCE
between

LIGHTNING WASHER COMPANY		MRS. ELIZABETH ADAMS
922 Clarke Street	*and*	555 Union Street
Guthrie, Oklahoma		Pearsall, Texas

Directions. The letters of this dictation study may be used to give you further practice in office-style dictation. In addition to pauses, actual business dictation is sometimes marked by changes to be made in matter already dictated.

The stenographer must learn to make such changes without interfering too much with the dictator's line of thought. There are several ways in which changes may be indicated in the shorthand notes, but one of the best and simplest is as follows:

When a change is dictated, make three slanting strokes (///) to show a break in the dictation. For speed in writing, these strokes may be connected as shown in the following letters. Record the exact and complete instructions of the dictator; and, when possible, make three additional slanting strokes to mark the end of the change. The marks indicating corrections should be so clearly made that they can be easily noticed. During transcription, in order to avoid the necessity of rewriting your letters, you should refer to the corrections before attempting to type. At this time it may be advisable also to make additional notations in your shorthand to assist you in avoiding typing errors. This editing of the notes is especially desirable in a letter in which many changes have been indicated.

It is important to be sure that you understand just what changes your employer wants made. If there is any doubt in your mind, you should ask your employer for further instructions. Record his instructions—don't trust to memory.

In the following series, Letters 175, 176, and 177 are arranged so as to show what the stenographer's notes should look like; and Letter 178 is arranged to show how it might have been dictated. Your teacher may decide also to dictate Letters 179, 180, and 181 in office style.

Practice the vocabulary previews and the letters as previously instructed.

Letter 175

Ad/ams	clothes
baby	dainty
chif/fon	dem/on/strate

Eliz/a/beth

gen/tly

hose

lin/ge/rie

op/er/ate

Pear/sall

silk

switch

Texas

to carry

whirls

won/der/ful

wringer

your in/quiry

August 24, 19—

Jane Bronson, Home Department, LIGHTNING WASHER COMPANY
(Reading time: 1 min. 20 sec.)   (170)

LETTER 176

con/tent
haven't
I'm
mar/vel/ous

that's
they're
wash/ing
you've seen

Notice the special "Strike out" symbol used in the third line of the following letter. This symbol indicates a cancellation of dictated material. It is not necessary to use the correction strokes and the "Strike out" symbol at the same time.

August 31, 19—

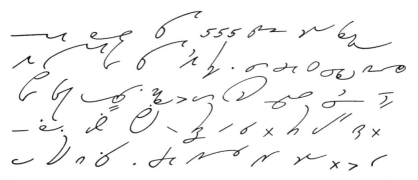

[Shorthand outlines]

Jane Bronson, Home Department, Lightning Washer Company
(Reading time: 1 min. 20 sec.)   (174)

Letter 177

ap/pealed	next day or so
au/thor/i/ties	oth/er/wise
en/dors/ing	wouldn't
ex/plain	you'd like to know
in/sist/ent	

Sometimes corrections or changes in dictation are made without a signal to the stenographer, and sometimes corrections are not clearly indicated. In such cases, the stenographer must use her judgment in deciding whether to ask the dictator for further information or to attempt to handle the matter for herself. Two typical situations appear in the second paragraph of this letter.

September 14, 19—

Jane Bronson, Home Department, LIGHTNING WASHER COMPANY

(Reading time: 1 min. 35 sec.) (204)

LETTER 178

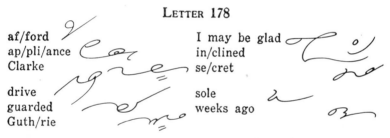

af/ford	I may be glad
ap/pli/ance	in/clined
Clarke	se/cret
drive	sole
guarded	weeks ago
Guth/rie	

Sometimes when a simple deletion is indicated, it may seem wiser actually to cross out the word or words to be omitted. The stenographer must decide for herself what she will do in a case of this kind. The method suggested here, however—that is, to record the full instructions—will usually save the employer's time. Many employers complain that their stenographers spend too much time during dictation in trying to find the point at which notes are to be corrected, especially when the turning of pages is necessary.

To distinguish "Clarke" from "Clark," simply place a small "e" over the shorthand outline for the former word. This is necessary only when the dictator indicates the spelling to be used.

September 17, 19—

Miss Brown, take a letter to Lightning Washer Company,
922 Clarke (pause) spell that with an e (pause) Street,
Guthrie, Oklahoma Gentlemen (pause) My letter written
to you about three weeks ago (pause) was for the purpose
(pause) sole purpose of asking the price of the Lightning
washer comma (pause) but you seem inclined to keep the
price a secret (pause) I do not (pause) change that to
I certainly do not intend to drive about (pause) strike out
about (pause) fourteen miles and take a half day off
(pause) from a busy office to see (pause) to look at something I may not (pause) I probably cannot afford to buy
paragraph

If you can (pause) strike out (pause) If you see fit to
divulge the closely guarded secret of price comma (pause)
I may be glad to investigate this appliance Yours very
truly

Set this letter up on blank paper. Be sure to include my
home address (555 Union Street, Pearsall, Texas) at the
top and type my signature* at the end. No carbon is necessary, and you may omit the initials.   (84)

* Mrs. Elizabeth Adams

LETTER 179

ceases	lei/sure	
Chal/mers	per/son/al/ity	
Chi/nese	prov/erb	
crit/i/cisms	Ranger	
ex/ist	San An/to/nio	
feel/ings	wanted	

September 19, 19—

555 Union Street
Pearsall, Texas
September 17, 19--

Lightning Washer Company
922 Clarke Street
Guthrie, Oklahoma

Gentlemen

My letter written to you about three weeks
ago was for the sole purpose of asking the
price of the Lightning washer, but you seem
inclined to keep the price a secret. I
certainly do not intend to drive fourteen
miles and take a half day off from a busy
office to look at something I probably cannot afford to buy.

If you see fit to divulge the closely
guarded secret of price, I may be glad to
investigate this appliance.

Yours very truly

Elizabeth Adams

(Mrs.) Elizabeth Adams

MODEL 14—SIGNATURE FOR A WIDOW

This letter shows the usual signature of a woman widowed by death **or**
divorce. For other signatures of women, see Model 6 on page 109.

Sales Manager, LIGHTNING WASHER COMPANY

(Reading time: 1 min. 30 sec.)   (185)

LETTER 180

con/sid/er/a/tion		ir/ri/tat/ing	
gar/dens		Mon/i/tor	
I did not		re/call	
I re/gret		sev/eral weeks	

555 Union Street
Pearsall, Texas
September 21, 19—

Lightning Washer Company
922 Clarke Street
Guthrie, Oklahoma

Attention of Mr. Herbert Brown

Gentlemen

I have your very courteous letter of the nineteenth **and** thank you for giving me the information [20] I have been trying to get for several weeks.

I do not recall just where I saw your advertisement, but [40] it was probably in *Better Homes and Gardens* or in the *Monitor*. I did not need any further information [60] to convince me that the Lightning would be a very useful article for a busy woman. The price [80] was the one consideration. I can assure you that it was decidedly irritating to receive three [100] letters, each of which omitted the one thing I had written to find out.

I regret that the price of the portable [120] Lightning washer makes it impossible for me to get one at this time, as the washer is not a [140] necessity for me. It does look, however, like a piece of equipment that I might find extremely convenient.

Yours [160] very truly (163)

(Mrs.) Elizabeth Adams

LETTER 181

cap/tured	ex/pend/i/tures	
cen/sure	jour/neyed	
cher/ish	jus/tify	
es/ti/mates	kind enough	
eve/ning	lim/its	
ev/ery/one	more and more	

over/step/ping		six months	
owned		to lis/ten	
pe/cul/iarly		to spend	
pes/ter/ing		vol/un/tar/ily	

September 23, 19—

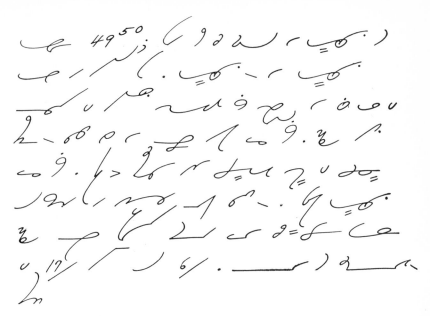

Sales Manager, Lightning Washer Company

(Reading time: 2 min. 20 sec.)　　　　　(293)

PART 4. BUSINESS PRACTICES

Part 4 is omitted from this dictation study.

PART 5. PROGRESS CHECKUP

Letter PC-27

Mrs. Elizabeth Adams
555 Union Street
Pearsall, Texas

Dear Mrs. Adams

We are taking the liberty of writing to you again in reference to the portable [20] Lightning washer. Before making your decision that the Lightning is too expensive a machine for you to [40] buy and to own, won't you grant us the courtesy of reading this letter carefully. It will cost you only ^{60} several minutes of time, and it may save you hours of unpleasant work.

First, the Lightning is a washing machine of ^{80} superior merit. Second, it is a portable machine that conforms to all standards of convenience without ^{100} sacrificing any of the advantages of washing machines. Third, the Lightning is a drying machine ^{120} that does away with the necessity of a wringer. It is well to bear in mind these points when considering ^{140} your investment: You buy a washer, a drying machine, and a portable convenience all in one.

As a ^{160} washing machine, the Lightning does a thorough job, but it is really the drying feature that makes the Lightning ^{180} especially different from other machines. The Lightning whirls the clothes dry and thus saves the wear and tear resulting ^{200} from the use of a wringer.

Hundreds of letters on hand tell us of the happiness and contentment that the ^{220} portable Lightning has brought to American families. But why not let a letter tell its own story? Mrs.^{240} J. A. Newton, of San Antonio, writes:

"We bought our portable Lightning washer last Christmas, and it has been ^{260} in almost daily use since that time. I am sure that it saves me at least two extra hours for leisure on each wash ^{280} day. My washing now is so little trouble that I don't allow the clothes to pile up. As a result, I no longer ^{300} know what is meant by blue Monday. My children are so much interested in the washer that they frequently ^{320} ask permission to do the washing. We feel that we owe you our thanks for the Lightning."

The letter from Mrs. Newton ^{340} is no exception. Women from every section of the country write us similar messages day after ^{360} day.

This wonderful little machine sells for only $49.50. It can be bought on our ^{380} deferred-payment plan for as little as $17 down and $6 a month for six months. You are not ^{400} required, however, to buy a machine in order to see for yourself how satisfactorily it will serve ^{420} you. If you will drop us a card, we will instruct the Chalmers Company, 1220 Ranger Street, San Antonio,[440] to send you one of these fine machines on approval. You may examine it and try it without pressure [460] or haste. We are willing to make such an offer because we are sure the machine will convince you that you should own [480] it.

We have such confidence in the Lightning that we sincerely believe that you should not be without one. All [500] manufacturers probably feel this way about their products, but we are willing to let you decide by free [520] trial whether or not we are right. After you have tried the Lightning at your leisure for several weeks, you may let [540] us know your decision.

If you decide against the Lightning, just notify us and we will take the machine away [560] without cost to you. If you decide that you do want to keep it, you may select your own plan of payment. Isn't [580] such a proposition fair enough? Won't you tell us to send you a Lightning at once.

Very cordially yours   (600)

LIGHTNING WASHER COMPANY

HB:EE   Sales Manager

DICTATION STUDY XXVIII

PART 1. BASIC SKILLS

Brief-Form Review

Directions. The following article contains 116 different brief forms and brief-form derivatives. Most of them you have met many times before. All of them are common words. In this and previous brief-form reviews, every brief form in your shorthand system has been used over and over again. Read the following letter until you can read easily at your goal rate—125 or more words a minute—and then make two copies in shorthand.

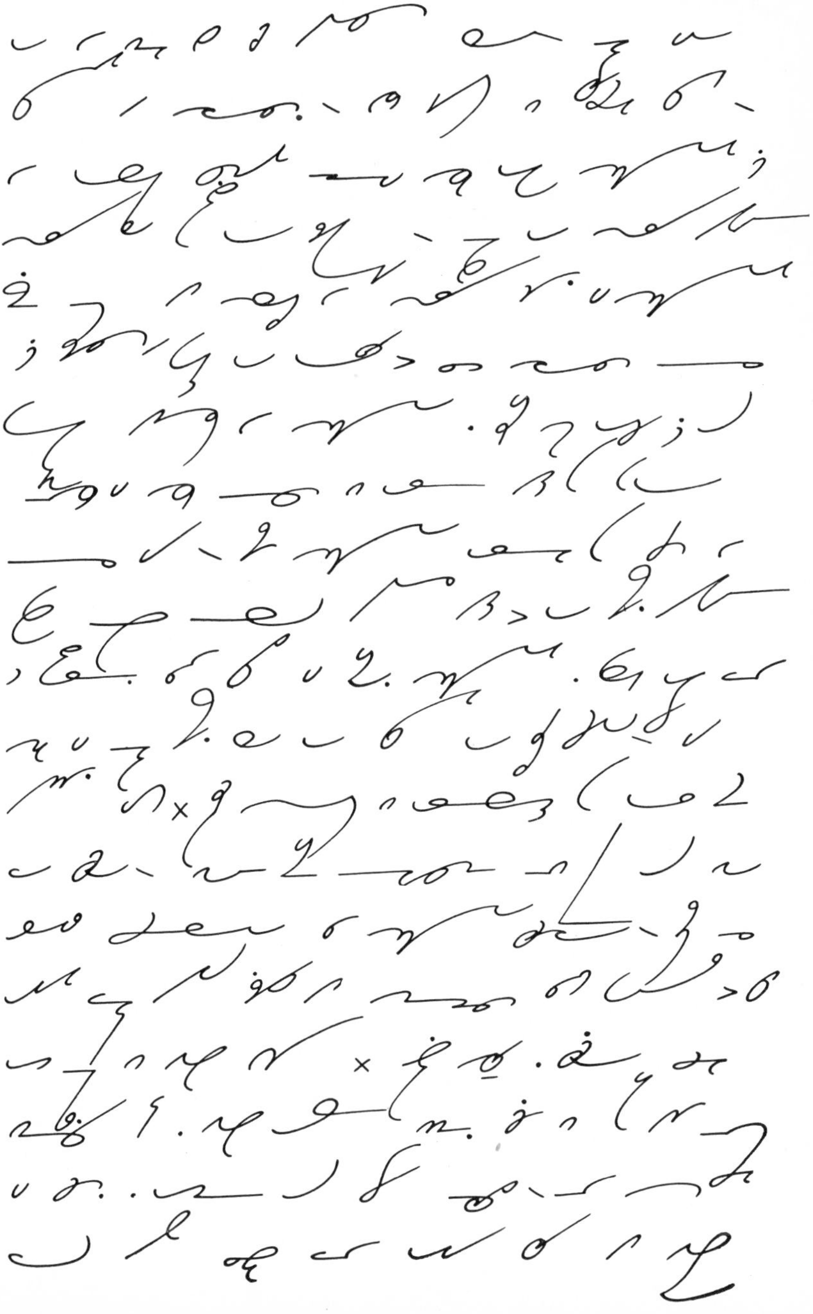

(Reading time: 4 min. 40 sec.)   **(600)**

PART 2. BUSINESS INFORMATION

Vocabulary Preview

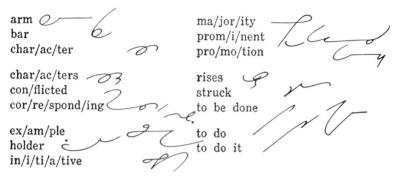

arm	ma/jor/ity
bar	prom/i/nent
char/ac/ter	pro/mo/tion
char/ac/ters	rises
con/flicted	struck
cor/re/spond/ing	to be done
ex/am/ple	to do
holder	to do it
in/i/ti/a/tive	

Type Bar vs. Type Wheel

The principle of the type bar and the principle of the type wheel have conflicted since the manufacture of [20] the first practical typewriter in 1867.

The type bar consists of a metal arm at [40] one end of which is the type block bearing the type letter or character. When a key is struck, the corresponding [60] arm rises to the printing point and causes the type letter or character to print its impression through the ribbon.[80] This principle is used in the majority of typewriters.

The type wheel consists of a circular holder [100] of type plates containing the type letters and characters. When a key is struck, the type wheel whirls and brings the proper [120] letter or character into printing position. This principle is used successfully on a prominent [140] present-day typewriter. Its special advantage is in the ease with which the style of type may be changed.

The type-wheel [160] typewriter is the subject of the following correspondence. This series of letters is an excellent [180] example of the service that a stenographer may render her company. This particular stenographer,[200] designated as "JT," arranged the entire transaction, from the time when she first interested her [220] employers in a new machine to the time when this new machine was installed and working efficiently.

Interest [240] in and enthusiasm for her work are two valuable qualities the stenographer should carry with her [260] when she enters the business field. They will be decided helps in the development of initiative—the [280] ability to do a thing that needs to be done, at the proper time and without being told to do it.[300] Initiative is a strong factor in determining promotion.   (312)

PART 3. BUSINESS CORRESPONDENCE

between

OGDEN TYPEWRITER COMPANY	MUIR MANUFACTURING COMPANY
1481 Lexington Avenue *and*	555 Westminster Street
New York 15, New York	Brantford, Ontario
	CANADA

Directions. The letters in this part are arranged for timed dictation for speed building. Practice the words in the vocabulary previews, read the shorthand plates, and write each letter twice in shorthand. Complete all the work on one letter before proceeding to the next letter.

LETTER 182

Ca/na/dian
con/den/sa/tion
con/densed

Har/ring/ton
Lex/ing/ton
Muir

New York 15,
    New York

ob/vi/ously
Og/den
par/tic/u/larly

please send us
rec/om/men/
    da/tion

sta/tis/ti/cal

August 28, 19—

Ogden Typewriter Company
1481 Lexington Avenue
New York 15, New York

Gentlemen

A recent demonstration of the Ogden typewriter in the Cleveland office of the Harrington [20] Company has interested us in the possibilities of using this typewriter in our industry,[40] particularly from the viewpoint of condensation of statistical data.

The Harrington Company [60] gave us your address with the recommendation that we get in touch with you for further information. Obviously,[80] if we consider the purchase of an Ogden, we must know what kind of service we may expect. Have you [100] a Canadian representative or an office in Buffalo or some other point near here?

We are [120] interested in the eighteen-pitch feature. Is it possible to make a carbon copy with this condensed type? Please [140] send us any literature that may prove helpful to us.

Yours very truly   (154)

Muir Manufacturing Company

CSS:JT   Manager

Letter 183

as soon as		on/ion/skin	
Brant/ford		On/tario	
Can/ada		pa/tron/age	
ex/pan/sion		price/less	
gothic		To/ronto	
head/quar/ters		we are in po/ si/tion	
leg/ible		we have not yet	
midst		West/min/ster	
min/i/a/ture			

September 2, 19—

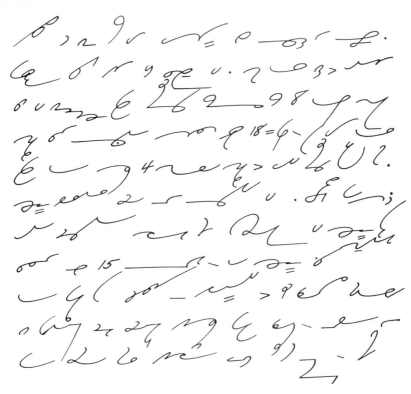

OGDEN TYPEWRITER COMPANY, Sales Director

(Reading time: 1 min. 20 sec.)   (176)

"Onionskin" is a strong, thin paper that is used for multiple carbon copies. It is available in several colors.

LETTER 184

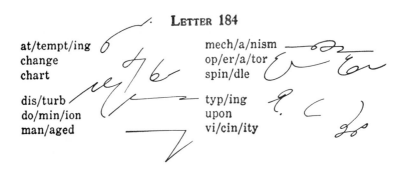

at/tempt/ing	mech/a/nism
change	op/er/a/tor
chart	spin/dle
dis/turb	typ/ing
do/min/ion	upon
man/aged	vi/cin/ity

September **6, 19—**

Ogden Typewriter Company
1481 Lexington Avenue
New York 15, New York

Gentlemen

Since receiving the literature about the Ogden type-writer, we have borrowed a machine from [20] the Dominion Bank in Toronto. This was installed for trial this morning.

Upon attempting to change the type [40] plates of the Ogden, the operator, not being familiar with the mechanism of the machine, managed to [60] disturb the spindle on which the plates are adjusted. This now seems to be in position for typing, but is locked [80] in such a manner that we can do nothing with it.

Will you please let us know whether there is in this vicinity [100] someone who can put this machine in good condition for us. You might send us a chart of the mechanism and [120] operation of the Ogden.

Yours very truly   (129)

MUIR MANUFACTURING COMPANY

CSS:JT   Manager

LETTER 185

an/vil		shut/tle	
bent		slot	
idle		straight/ened	
in/struc/tion		to any one of the	
knob		web	
shield		yoke	

September 8, 19—

OGDEN TYPEWRITER COMPANY, Sales Director

(Reading time: 1 min. 20 sec.)   **(169)**

LETTER 186

(Fast Telegram)

bank

key/board

scarcely

se/rial

BRANTFORD ONT SEPT **11**

OGDEN TYPEWRITER CO

1481 LEXINGTON AVE NEW YORK NY

WIRE LAID DOWN PRICE AT BRANTFORD AFTER ALL DISCOUNTS FOR A TWENTY INCH OGDEN. MUST BE EQUIPPED FOR TWO COLOR [20] RIBBON. STATE ALLOWANCE FOR NINE INCH SERIAL NUMBER 400775 SCARCELY [40] USED. HAVE YOU FOUR BANK KEYBOARD? IF SO, QUOTE SEPARATE PRICE.

MUIR MANUFACTURING CO (50)

LETTER 187

(Fast Telegram)

cash

key/boards

one hun/dred

dol/lars

pre/pay

NEW YORK, N.Y., SEPT. **11**

OGDEN TYPEWRITER CO.

(Reading time: 20 sec.)   (44)

MUIR MANUFACTURING COMPANY

555 WESTMINSTER STREET
BRANTFORD, ONTARIO, CANADA

September 18, 19--

Ogden Typewriter Company
1481 Lexington Avenue
New York 15, New York

Gentlemen

Enclosed is our purchase order in confirmation of our letter of September 12.

We agree with you that Model W appears most nearly to meet our requirements. In our accounting department we are confined exclusively to twelve-pitch, or elite, type on our present typewriters. The Ogden is being ordered for writing up statistical data in which condensation is the important factor. We therefore need twelve-pitch type to match our present work and sixteen-pitch type for condensation.

Of course, for setting up headings, the ten-pitch, or pica, type is likely to be of more value to us than the fourteen-pitch. On glancing over the type chart, however, we find that the smaller types are supplied only in combinations of twelve, fourteen, and sixteen. We particularly want the ten-pitch type.

In looking over type styles, we selected miniature roman. Your type chart does not indicate, however, that this style can be used in sixteen-pitch, although the sample typed statement in miniature roman does measure sixteen letters to the inch.

With these ideas in mind, you may send us a set of type that will include the miniature gothic, the miniature and the small roman, and the miniature italic. Be sure to match all types in figures. You may also match the various miniature types in capitals suitable for headings. In other words, we want types matched for both the heading and the body of our statements. We have gone into some detail in order to help you decide which model is best adapted to our requirements.

While we have asked for a thirty-day trial because of our inexperience with this machine, we shall certainly give you an opportunity to investigate any difficulties we may have. We should also appreciate a visit from your demonstrator whenever

---

MODEL 15—FIRST PAGE OF A TWO-PAGE LETTER

The bottom margin of the first page of a two-page letter should be as wide as the side margins.

he is near Brantford, as we are desirous of obtaining the best possible results.

The idea of sending a typist to your New York school seems impracticable just at present, but we should like to have a set of lessons for use in our office.

The Ogden No. 400775, which we were using, has been returned to the Dominion Bank in Toronto and consequently will not be turned in for credit.

Yours very truly

MUIR MANUFACTURING COMPANY

Clarence S. Strong

Manager

CSS:JT

Enc.

MODEL 16—SECOND PAGE OF A TWO-PAGE LETTER

The second page of a two-page letter should be written on blank paper that matches in size, quality, and color the paper used for the first page.

LETTER 188

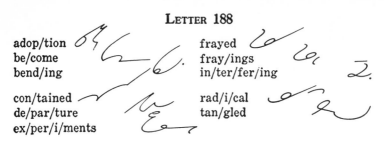

adop/tion
be/come
bend/ing

con/tained
de/par/ture
ex/per/i/ments

frayed
fray/ings
in/ter/fer/ing

rad/i/cal
tan/gled

September 11, 19—

Ogden Typewriter Company
1481 Lexington Avenue
New York 15, New York

Gentlemen

Thank you for the descriptive booklet and the information contained in your letter of September [20] 8. The ribbon shield arrived yesterday.

The trouble mentioned in our letter of the sixth was caused by a frayed ribbon.[40] The frayings had become tangled in the ribbon shield and were bending the shield, which in turn was interfering [60] with the movement of the shuttle.

We have been giving the Ogden a thorough trial in our work; and, although the [80] operator has had no previous experience with the machine, the results have been very satisfactory.[100] Our experiments convince us that we should get better results with a twenty-inch machine. We asked for [120] and received your quotation on this size today.

The adoption of an Ogden would represent a somewhat [140] radical departure from our standards, but the matter is receiving consideration. We shall write you just as [160] soon as we come to a decision.

Yours very truly   (170)

MUIR MANUFACTURING COMPANY

CSS:JT   Manager

LETTER 189

as/sum/ing ⌢   it is pos/si/ble
de/ter/mine   op/tion
ex/pec/ta/tions   re/tain/ing

if you will   trade
  send us   week or two

September 12, 19—

Ogden Typewriter Company
1481 Lexington Avenue
New York 15, New York

Gentlemen

Since writing you yesterday, we have decided to purchase a twenty-inch model Ogden on the [20] terms quoted in your telegram of September 11, which are as follows:

"Price twenty-inch including ten [40] types two hundred sixty. Two per cent cash only discount. Not permitted prepay duty. Allow one hundred dollars [60] number 400775. No four-bank keyboards."

It is possible that we [80] may take advantage of your offer to accept for credit the No. 400775 [100] typewriter that we now have in this office and that we have the option of buying. We have not, however,[120] decided whether we can use this additional machine. In the event of our retaining it in [140] a supplementary capacity, can it be fitted with a two-color ribbon? We presume the trade-in [160] offer will hold good for a week or two, that is, until we can determine the possibilities of the use [180] of this extra machine.

You, of course, appreciate that we are assuming a certain responsibility [200] in ordering this machine from New York with the knowledge that you have no service office within reasonable [220] distance. We hope therefore that you will give us a month in which to prove the machine from an operating standpoint,[240] and will allow us full price if it fails to meet our expectations.

If you will send us a sample type-face sheet,[260] we shall select the type suited to our purposes and then notify you with regard to the typewriter now [280] in our office.

Yours very truly   (286)

Muir Manufacturing Company

CSS:JT   Manager

LETTER 190

an/a/lyze	mas/ters
clos/est	out/set
con/tin/u/ously	over/haul
del/e/gate	packed
dem/on/stra/tor	pica
elite	pre/pared
em/i/nently	school
ex/chang/ing	spec/i/men
given	starts
gov/erned	stip/u/la/tion
guar/an/tees	suc/cess/ful
head/ings	things
in/struct/ing	to im/press
learn/ing	typ/ists
les/sons	

September 16, 19—

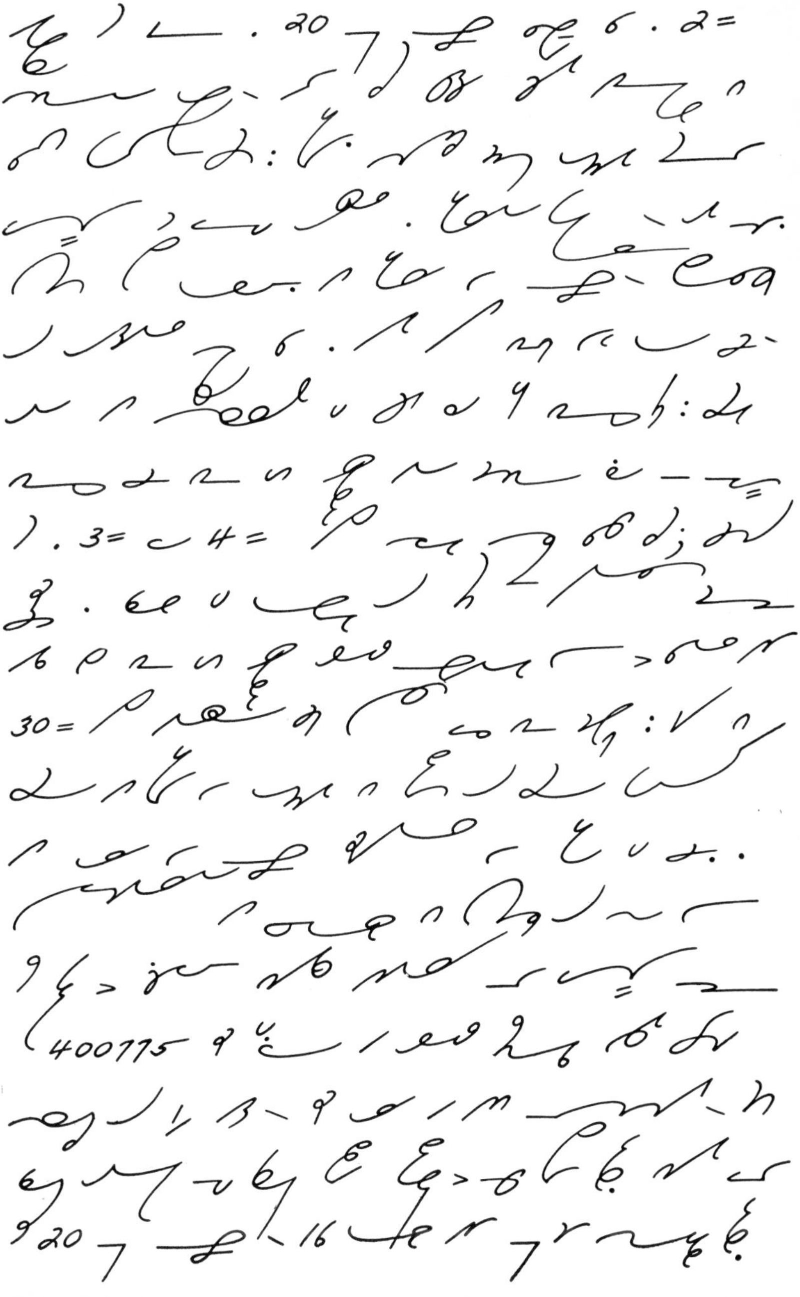

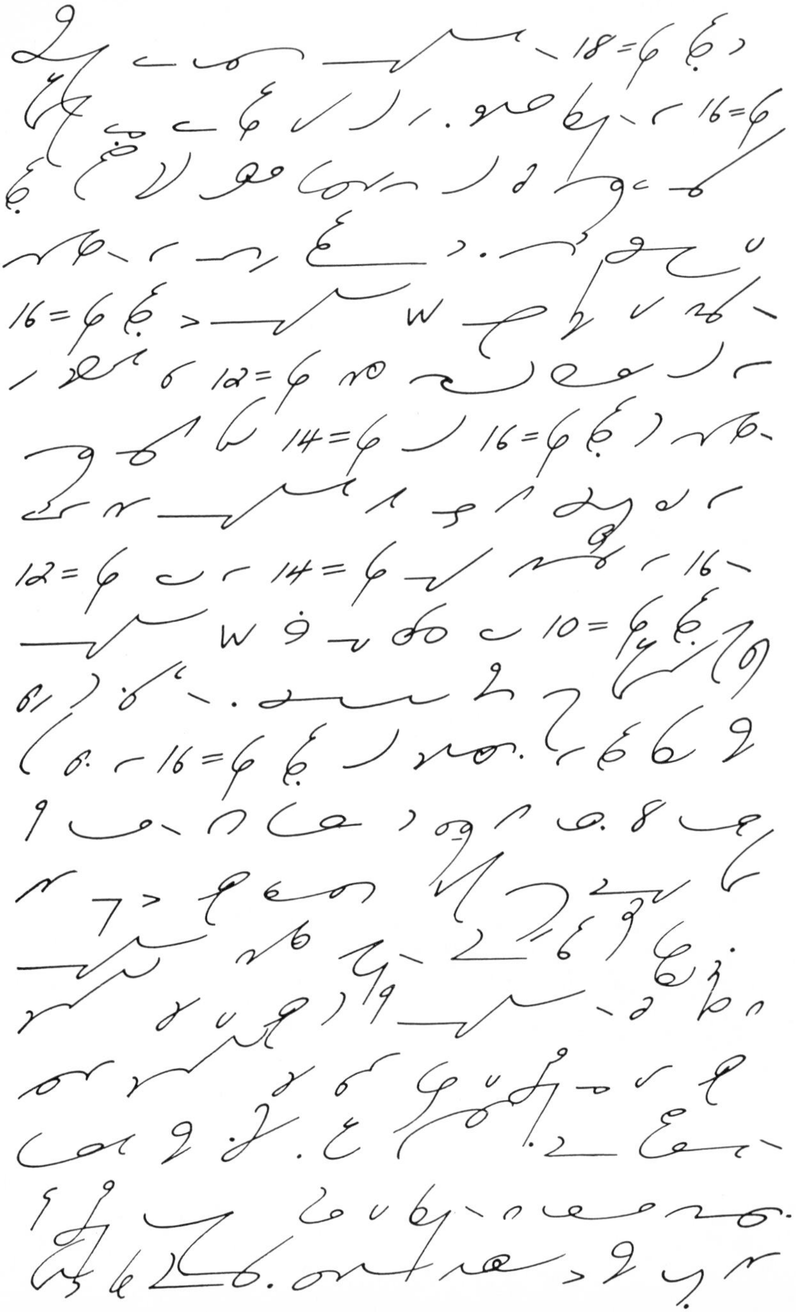

Ogden Typewriter Company, Sales Director

(Reading time: 4 min. 20 sec.)   (553)

Letter 191

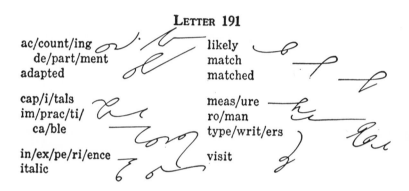

ac/count/ing	likely
de/part/ment	match
adapted	matched
cap/i/tals	meas/ure
im/prac/ti/	ro/man
ca/ble	type/writ/ers
in/ex/pe/ri/ence	visit
italic	

September 18, 19—

Ogden Typewriter Company
1481 Lexington Avenue
New York 15, New York

Gentlemen

Enclosed is our purchase order in confirmation of our letter of September 12.

We agree [20] with you that Model W appears most nearly to meet our requirements. In our accounting department we [40] are confined exclusively to twelve-pitch, or elite, type on our present typewriters. The Ogden is being ordered [60] for writing up statistical data in which condensation is the important factor. We therefore need [80] twelve-pitch type to match our present work and sixteen-pitch type for condensation.

Of course, for setting up headings, the [100] ten-pitch, or pica, type is likely to be of more value to us than the fourteen-pitch. On glancing over the [120] type chart, however, we find that the smaller types are supplied only in combinations of twelve, fourteen, and sixteen.[140] We particularly want the ten-pitch type.

In looking over type styles, we selected miniature roman.[160] Your type chart does not indicate, however, that this style can be used in sixteen-pitch, although the sample typed [180] statement in miniature roman does measure sixteen letters to the inch.

With these ideas in mind, you may [200] send us a set of type that will include the miniature gothic, the miniature and the small roman, and [220] the miniature italic. Be sure to match all types in figures. You may also match the various miniature [240] types in capitals suitable for headings. In other words, we want types matched for both the heading and the [260] body of our statements. We have gone into some detail in order to help you decide which model is best [280] adapted to our requirements.

While we asked for a thirty-day trial because of our inexperience with this [300] machine, we shall certainly give you an opportunity to investigate any difficulties we may [320] have. We should also appreciate a visit from your demonstrator whenever he is near Brantford, as we [340] are desirous of obtaining the best possible results.

The idea of sending a typist to your New [360] York school seems impracticable just at present, but we should like to have a set of lessons for use in our office.[380]

The Ogden No. 400775, which we were using, has been returned [400] to the Dominion Bank in Toronto and consequently will not be turned in for credit.

Yours very truly   (420)

MUIR MANUFACTURING COMPANY

CSS:JT   Manager
Enc.

LETTER 192

ac/cu/mu/lated
ben/e/fi/cial
ben/e/fi/ci/ary

busi/ness world
ea/ger
ex/traor/di/nary

gained

grat/i/fy/ing
lim/i/ta/tions
pos/sessed

re/mark/able
ut/most
vice-president

we may be able

September 20, 19—

OGDEN TYPEWRITER COMPANY, Vice-President

(Reading time: 1 min. 30 sec.)   (198)

LETTER 193

back/ing

mas/tery

sten/cils

we en/close

September 27, 19—

OGDEN TYPEWRITER COMPANY, Sales Director

(Reading time: 55 sec.)   (121)

LETTER 194

able *C*   par/cel *ℰ*

October 3, 19—

Ogden Typewriter Company
1481 Lexington Avenue
New York 15, New York

Gentlemen

We have today received and installed Ogden typewriter No. 491777.[20] We also received a parcel containing backing sheets for stencils.

The Ogden [40] was received in good order, with one exception. We found that the roll release lever had been assembled so that [60] it lay behind the carriage release lever. We were able to remedy this defect, however, and to make [80] the position of the part conform to that shown in the chart you sent us. The machine now seems to be perfectly [100] satisfactory.

After experimenting with the type plates supplied with the machine, we shall inform you if [120] any changes are desirable.

Yours very truly   (130)

MUIR MANUFACTURING COMPANY

CSS:JT   Manager

LETTER 195

beau/ti/ful
con/vey
maiden

prob/lems
re/frain

re/spects
so/lu/tion
we have your let/ter

worn

October 8, 19—

OGDEN TYPEWRITER COMPANY, Sales Director

(Reading time: 40 sec.)   **(91)**

LETTER 196

ac/com/plish		fi/nal/ity	
ap/ro/pos		ne/go/ti/a/tions	
as far as		un/der/took	

October 10, 19—

Ogden Typewriter Company
1481 Lexington Avenue
New York 15, New York

Gentlemen

Your reference to "JT" is quite apropos. "JT" not only set up the typewriter from a [20] mechanical standpoint, but undertook all the negotiations with you. She wrote all the letters and brought the [40] transaction to a finality.

Your impressions are correct when you say the Ogden is in the right hands.[60] "JT" is enthusiastic about the machine and is obtaining good results. She is putting the Ogden on [80] the map as far as this company is concerned.

The enclosed sheet will give you an idea of what we are [100] trying to accomplish by the use of our Ogden.

Yours very truly   (112)

Muir Manufacturing Company

CSS:JT   Manager
Enc.

Letter 197

breath

October 17, 19—

Ogden Typewriter Company, Sales Director

(Reading time: 45 sec.)   (106)

LETTER 198

con/struc/tive
crowded

inked
us/ers

November 10, 19—

OGDEN TYPEWRITER COMPANY, Sales Director

(Reading time: 1 min. 10 sec.)   (150)

PART 4. BUSINESS PRACTICES

Part 4 is omitted from this dictation study.

PART 5. PROGRESS CHECKUP

Letter PC-28

Muir Manufacturing Company
555 Westminster Street
Brantford, Ontario
CANADA

Gentlemen

The Ogden typewriter, about which you asked in your recent letter, has three outstanding features:

1.[20] The type can be changed in a matter of seconds—we mean just that. The type letters appear on a metal plate that [40] can be put on or removed from the machine by merely pressing a release key. There are available over [60] 300 such type plates, offering a wide variety of type styles that will answer the requirements of [80] every modern language.

The machine holds two type plates at the same time, and the typist can change from one to the [100] other in a moment. She may be using the miniature roman type for a given job; in a split second,[120] she can shift to the miniature italic in order to make some word or words more emphatic; and then in [140] another moment, she may once again return easily to the miniature roman. It is as simple [160] as that.

2. The Ogden is ideal for the condensation of statistical data. All models of the [180] Ogden offer flexibility in horizontal and vertical spacing. Model L is a very [200] popular machine that permits the use of 10-pitch, 12-pitch, and 16-pitch spacing. Model W comes equipped [220] with 12-pitch, 14-pitch, and 16-pitch spacing. Both models offer vertical spacing of 3, 3⅜,[240] 4½, 6, and 9 lines to the inch. When condensation is extremely important, it is possible,[260] by using 16-pitch spacing and 9 lines to the inch, to print 144 letters, figures, or [280] characters to the square inch of paper

space. This is almost 2½ times the material that the [300] ordinary pica typewriter can provide. On a quantity basis, the consequent saving in paper costs is [320] startling.

3. The new Ogden will mechanically justify the right margin of a page of typing; that is,[340] the machine will end all typewritten lines at a given point, thus providing a right margin similar to that [360] found in printed booklets. This means that a job to be printed by the offset method can be prepared, in a large [380] measure, in your own office. The Ogden is thus an important piece of office equipment in any industry [400] in which printing jobs are numerous. Of course, the Ogden is equally helpful with all duplicating [420] processes in use in the business office.

As you can see, the Ogden typewriter is really not a typewriter [440] at all. It doesn't attempt to compete with the ordinary business typewriter. It has all the features [460] of a typewriter and can be used as such whenever the occasion demands; but the Ogden rises above [480] the typewriter in offering the features mentioned. If you need only a typewriter, the Ogden is not the [500] machine you should buy. In such a case, we recommend that you buy any of the standard typewriters now [520] available. But if you need a machine that will do your typing and at the same time serve a dozen other purposes,[540] then you can't afford to be without an Ogden.

We should like to send a demonstrator to your office to [560] show you how the Ogden can be applied to your needs. This demonstrator could remain with you for a full day and [580] actually do your work. The demonstration would cost you nothing. What do you say?

> Very cordially yours [600]   (600)
>
> OGDEN TYPEWRITER COMPANY

RH:MF   Sales Director

DICTATION STUDY XXIX

PART 1. BASIC SKILLS

Theory Review

Directions. Experience has shown that shorthand writers, when put under the pressure of rapid dictation, invariably discard long and involved phrases and use only the simple, common, well-known phrases. Read the following outlines until you can read easily without the key. Then write each outline at least once.

NOT Phrases

Key: was not, it was not, there was not, that there was not, there wasn't, it is not.

Common Two-word Phrases

Key: of the, of course, it is, at the, in the, that the, was the, by the, to the, among the, so many, so much, too much, as much, with us, for us, we have, you have, I have, I told, I believe, about which, about this, through this, more than, less than, I had, had been, would have, to be, to say, to produce, to provide, to have, to do, any other, among those, were not, in our, has given, we are, we must, we give, I know, from you, next year, careful consideration, with him, any time, next time.

Other Common Phrases

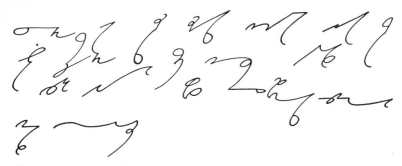

Key: I am sure, to be sure, we shall be able, we should be able, you could not be, it would be, I shall be, it has been, I have said, as you have, you gave me, during the past, that it was, at all times, I hope that, we hope you will be able, anyone else, one of the best, glad to receive.

Directions. Proceed in the usual manner.

(Reading time: 4 min. 40 sec.)   **(600)**

PART 2. BUSINESS INFORMATION

Vocabulary Preview

ap/points	few months
as/sets	great enough
auc/tion	in full
au/thor/ity	in/def/i/nite
bank/rupt	in/sol/vency
bank/ruptcy	liq/ui/date
claims	pro/por/tion/ate
con/duct	re/cov/ery
con/verted	re/sources
cov/ers	sev/eral years
cred/i/tors	state
de/clared	trus/tee
dis/posal	un/cer/tainty
dol/lar	
few cents	

Bankruptcy

Bankruptcy, or insolvency, is the state of being unable to meet the claims of creditors. When a business [20] has been legally declared bankrupt, the court appoints an individual or a corporation to act [40] as trustee, with authority to conduct the business for the benefit of the creditors or to liquidate [60] the debts by realizing the assets and paying to each creditor his proportionate part. It is not [80] often that the amount realized from the assets is great enough to pay the debts in full; sometimes it covers [100] only a few cents on each dollar of indebtedness.

The period of liquidation may extend over [120] a few months or several years, depending upon the patience of the creditors and upon the ease with which [140] the various assets can be converted into cash. When the creditors become insistent on early [160] settlement, the trustee may put up the assets for public auction. Such a sale usually results in a loss [180] greater than that which would result from a more careful disposal of the resources. When full recovery seems [200] doubtful, however, many creditors prefer to take a loss and close an account on their books rather than to [220] face the uncertainty of settlement at some indefinite future time. It is not customary to pay [240] interest on debts in bankruptcy, but creditors are entitled to such interest and sometimes insist on [260] its payment.

Although the following set of correspondence consists of only eight letters, it extends over [280] a period of more than one and one-half years. It represents, by no means, the only correspondence concerned [300] with the settlement of the accounts of the Smith Automobile Supply Company; rather, it is typical [320] of the letters that passed between the trustee and each of the creditors of this bankrupt business.

(337)

PART 3. BUSINESS CORRESPONDENCE

between

THE UNION TRUST COMPANY		J. L. WINDLAY, INC.
618 Sycamore Street	*and*	1321 Broad Street
Petersburg, Virginia		Richmond 3, Virginia

Directions. The following letters are so arranged as to give you further practice in taking office-style dictation. Letters 199, 200, and 202 show how they may have been dictated; and Letters 201 and 203 are shown as the stenographer may have recorded them. Practice the vocabulary previews and the letters as previously instructed.

Your teacher may decide also to dictate Letters 204, 205, and 206 in office style. It is suggested that you read aloud Letters 199, 200, and 202 to hear how they would sound if you were the dictator.

LETTER 199

law
sworn
Syc/a/more

trust
Wind/lay

January 19, 19—

The Union Trust Company, 618 Sycamore Street, Petersburg, Virginia Gentlemen (pause) As requested in your (pause) strike out (pause) As you requested in your letter of January 16 (pause) make that 17 comma we are enclosing the itemized statement comma (pause) properly signed and sworn to comma as required (pause) change to that is required by law period (pause) This statement shows (pause) make that represents the full amount of the account (pause) make that our account against the Smith Automobile Supply Company of your city paragraph

We shall appreciate a prompt (pause) an early settlement of this account Yours truly   (67)

Dictated by President of J. L. Windlay, Inc.

LETTER 200

against the   self-addressed
know/ing   we should like

July 14, 19—

The Union Trust Company, 618 Sycamore Street, Petersburg, Virginia Gentlemen (pause) Will you refer (pause) strike out (pause) Will you please refer to our statement of January 19 comma showing a claim of $20.25 against the Smith Automobile Supply Company period (pause) We should like to close this account on our books (pause) and shall appreciate it (pause) make that appreciate knowing when we may expect settlement paragraph

An envelope (pause) strike out (pause) For your convenience we are enclosing a self-addressed comma stamped envelope Yours very truly   (68)

Dictated by President of J. L. Windlay, Inc.

LETTER 201

have not been   of/fi/cer
hearty   pa/tient

July 16, 19—

(Reading time: 35 sec.)   (81)

LETTER 202

as it is   **this claim**
if pos/si/ble   **with you**

November 22, 19—

The Union Trust Company, 618 Sycamore Street, Petersburg, Virginia Gentlemen (pause) Will you please let us know when (pause) let us know comma if possible comma when we may expect settlement of our claim for $20.25 (pause) strike out reference to amount (pause) against the Smith Automobile Supply Company paragraph (pause)

This claim was filed with you on last January 19 semicolon (pause) and comma as it is getting near the end of

the year comma we should like to know (pause) change
that to we should like to clear this item from our books
Yours very truly   (56)

Dictated by President of J. L. Windlay, Inc.

LETTER 203

died	of his	
es/tate	prin/ci/pally	
farm	prop/erty	
in the hope that	real es/tate	

November 24, 19—

THE UNION TRUST COMPANY, Trust Officer

(Reading time: 1 min. 15 sec.)   (166)

LETTER 204

as to

early re/ply

in/volved

long time

un/rea/son/ably

with/hold/ing

May 25, 19—

The Union Trust Company
618 Sycamore Street
Petersburg, Virginia

Gentlemen

Since November 24 of last year, we have heard nothing from you with regard to our account against [20] the Smith Automobile Supply Company. It therefore appears to us that you are withholding payment an [40] unreasonably long time. It is true that the amount involved is small; but, in view of the fact that the claim is [60] about two years old, we should like to close our records or, at least, to have information as to when we may expect [80] settlement.

We shall appreciate an early reply.

Yours very truly   (94)

J. L. WINDLAY, INC.

JLW:MP   President

Letter 205

ac/quainted	good deal
ad/van/ta/geous	in/sol/vent
as much as	need/lessly
as there are	$35,000

May 27, 19—

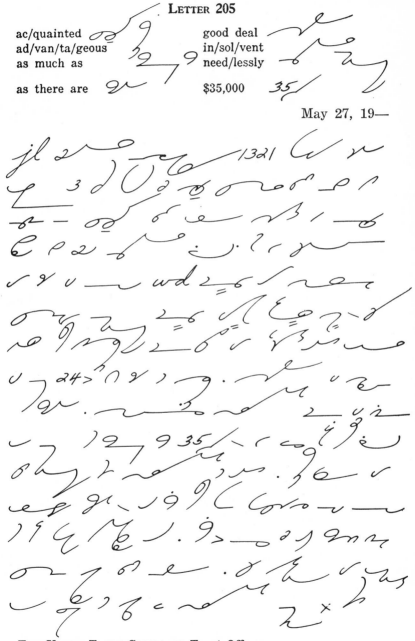

THE UNION TRUST COMPANY, Trust Officer

(Reading time: 1 min. 20 sec.)   (174)

LETTER 206

for the time

for/tu/nate

ow/ing

sign

September 21, 19—

THE UNION TRUST COMPANY, Trust Officer

(Reading time: 50 sec.)　　　　　(112)

PART 4. BUSINESS PRACTICES

Vocabulary Preview

ap/pli/ances

ar/range/ment

bands

books

caught

chair

com/part/ment

count/ers

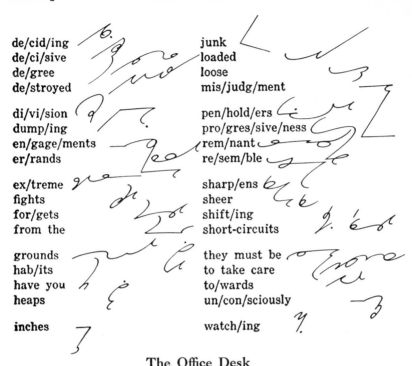

de/cid/ing	junk
de/ci/sive	loaded
de/gree	loose
de/stroyed	mis/judg/ment
di/vi/sion	pen/hold/ers
dump/ing	pro/gres/sive/ness
en/gage/ments	rem/nant
er/rands	re/sem/ble
ex/treme	sharp/ens
fights	sheer
for/gets	shift/ing
from the	short-circuits
grounds	they must be
hab/its	to take care
have you	to/wards
heaps	un/con/sciously
inches	watch/ing

The Office Desk

(Selected from *The Office Desk and Surroundings*, published by
The B. F. Goodrich Company, of Akron, Ohio.)

Have you ever caught yourself unconsciously taking the measure of a businessman from the degree of [20] progressiveness he shows in his working habits? At one extreme is the man who covers up his important papers,[40] forgets his engagements, runs his own errands, sharpens his pencils, and fights down his interruptions by sheer force. For [60] another, these things seem to take care of themselves. He sits free and easy, working carefully, watching, deciding, and [80] doing things of importance.

The desks of many businessmen resemble junk heaps or remnant counters. They are the [100] dumping grounds for every kind of commercial material. Nothing has a place, and the owner of the desk [120] can find nothing he wants. In place of holding the things needed in a day's routine, these desks are loaded with material [140] that should be filed, sent to where it could be put to use, or destroyed. The result is confusion, and confusion [160] about a desk short-circuits effective, decisive thinking and often causes misjudgment and costly mistakes.[180]

Only papers, folders, and other material regularly needed at the time should be on the working [200] surface of the desk. Only papers and appliances regularly needed in the day's work should be in [220] the desk. In the front of the center drawer, a small compartment should be set off by a division board. Here pen [240] points, clips, and rubber bands should be placed, preferably in small containers. Penholders, pencils, erasers, and a [260] ruler can be placed loose in this compartment. With this arrangement it is possible to keep the drawer in the [280] center of the desk open about two inches all the time; and, without reaching or without shifting the chair or [300] your position, you can have the necessary supplies ready for use. It is not recommended that you keep [320] personal matter in your desk; but, in case you do, place it towards the back of this drawer. Large flat record books [340] should also be kept in the back of this drawer if they must be kept in the desk.   (354)

PART 5. PROGRESS CHECKUP

LETTER PC-29

Mr. J. L. Windlay
618 Broad Street
Petersburg, Virginia

Dear Mr. Windlay

Thank you for your request for information regarding our office desks. We are glad to give [20] you this information.

For the business office, our latest model, BA-165, is the last word in [40] desk construction for the stenographer. This model, made entirely of metal, is available in colors [60] that will match, or be in harmony with, your office color scheme.

The typewriter is fitted into the left side [80] of the desk. In this way, there is no interfering with the working surface of the desk. This surface, measuring [100] 30 x 60 inches, will provide sufficient space for file folders, price catalogs, and other material [120] that a stenographer would ordinarily use in her daily work.

The drawer space is especially [140] convenient. The daily supply of stationery is kept in the right middle drawer. Just above this is [160] another drawer that holds two desk file receptacles. Rather than sacrifice any of the working surface [180] of the desk, we have placed in this drawer the two letter receptacles that should be a part of the equipment [200] of every desk. These are easily removed from the drawer and can be used either in the drawer or on the [220] desk, according to the preference of the stenographer.

The bottom drawer of the desk contains a basket [240] for used paper. This, too, can be easily removed whenever necessary. Your stenographer will be pleased [260] with the attractive arrangement of the drawer, which really adds a great deal to the convenience of the desk.[280]

The center drawer of the desk is, in all its measurements, larger than the center drawer of the average [300] office desk. It will easily accommodate personal items or office material of considerable [320] size.

A utility slide on either side of the desk completes the equipment of the desk. In some [340] respects, you might believe that this desk is not so very different from other desks; but once you have had a chance to [360] see the convenience of its new features, you will agree, I am sure, that it is a marvelous improvement [380] over old models. And we have not even mentioned the beauty of design or the expert workmanship that will make [400] this desk a piece of property that you can own with pride. Best of all, the desk sells for only $135.[420]

Now for the really good news:

For the office in your home, there is HA-165, a [440] junior model that is complete in every detail and differs from Model BA-165 only in [460] size. This model is made for the limited space of a small room and yet has a working surface measuring [480] 26 x 48 inches. The drawer space has been cut down as much as possible without affecting the [500] practical value of the desk. We have kept constantly aware of the necessity of building a desk that [520] will serve its owner in a thoroughly practical manner. This desk sells for only $95.

We have [540] a display room situated at the corner of Lafayette Avenue and Lexington Street in Richmond. There [560] you will be able to see these fine desks and also many other types of office furniture. Our salesmen will [580] be eager to help you select the furniture that will best satisfy your requirements.

Yours very truly [600]   (600)

THE UNION OFFICE SUPPLY COMPANY

SC:KL   Sales Manager

DICTATION STUDY XXX

PART 1. BASIC SKILLS

Theory Review

Directions. All the following theory words are used in the letter in this part. Read them until you can do so without the aid of the key; then write them at least once each in shorthand. Remember to pass promptly from one part of an outline to the next part. Note that *hood* and *ward*, as individual words, are written in full. *Award* and *toward* also have full outlines.

HOOD, WARD Suffix

Key: hood, neighbor*hood*, boy*hood*, likeli*hood*, man*hood*, brother*hood*, *ward*, a*ward*ed, to*ward*, up*ward*, straightfor*ward*, out*ward*, in*ward*, on*ward*, down*ward*, re*ward*ed.

SUPER, SUPRE, SUPPOR Prefix

Key: *super*b, *super*ior, *super*ficial, *super*vision, *super*fluous, *super*visor, *super*lative, *supre*me, *suppre*ss, *suppor*ting, *suppor*ts.

Directions. All the foregoing words appear in the following letter. If you have practiced the words carefully, you should know them when you meet them. Read the letter until you can reach your reading goal. Then make two shorthand copies of the letter.

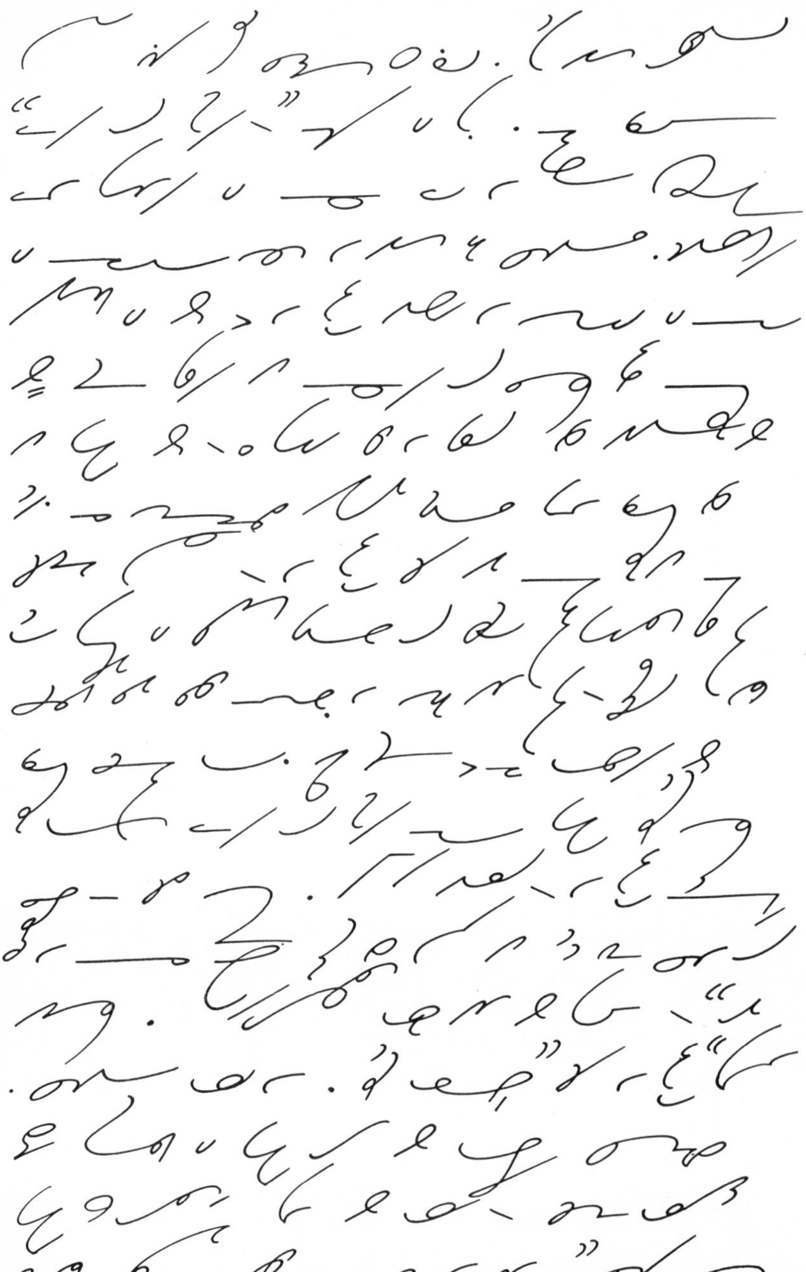

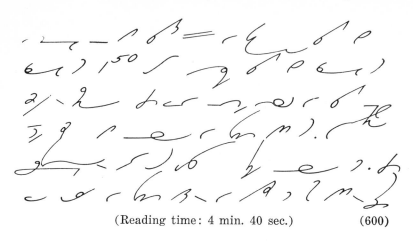

(Reading time: 4 min. 40 sec.)   (600)

PART 2. BUSINESS INFORMATION

Vocabulary Preview

ac/cept/ances
be/sieged
bills
bind/ing

it is given
lack/ing
re/newal
re/newed

debtor
dif/fer/ences
fun/da/men/tally

there are
ways

Commercial Paper

There are several ways of paying invoices or bills, or at least of satisfying the creditors [20] temporarily. Of course, the most satisfactory way of settling a debt is through the use of cash or a check; but,[40] lacking this, the besieged debtor may resort to notes, drafts, or trade acceptances. Fundamentally, these commercial [60] papers are similar in that they are mere substitutes for money; but there are decided differences [80] in their uses.

A promissory note is a promise to pay a certain sum of money at a definite [100] future time. It is given by the debtor to the creditor and carries with it legal responsibility.[120] A note is accepted in temporary payment of a debt, but it may be renewed on its date of [140] maturity. Collateral may be required to secure the payment of the note.

A time draft is a request to [160] pay a certain sum of money at the end of a definite period of time. It is drawn by the creditor [180] against the debtor and may be payable to the creditor himself or to a third party. The draft carries [200] no legal responsibility until it has been accepted by the debtor; then it becomes in nature [220] like a note.

A trade acceptance is a time draft drawn at the time of a sale to a credit customer. It [240] arises from the sale of goods and carries definite legal responsibility. It is drawn by the [260] creditor against the debtor, but it must be accepted by the debtor in order that it may become legally [280] binding. A trade acceptance is not used to pay a balance on an open account; but it is issued, at [300] the actual time of a sale of goods, in settlement of the amount incurred in the sale. The obligation [320] represented by a trade acceptance may be renewed at maturity, but the renewal should be in the [340] form of a promissory note and not in the form of a trade acceptance.   (354)

PART 3. BUSINESS CORRESPONDENCE
between

JAMES CLOCK COMPANY   ADAMS DEPARTMENT STORE
101 Tenth Street   *and*   110 Franklin Street
La Salle, Illinois   Louisville 2, Kentucky

Directions. The following letters are so arranged as to give you further practice in taking office-style dictation. Letters 207 and 209 are shown as the stenographer may have recorded them, and Letters 208 and 210 are shown as they may have been dictated. Proceed in the usual way.

LETTER 207

clock
Frank/lin
Lou/is/ville,
  Ken/tucky

prior
re/minder
to re/mind you

May 10, 19—

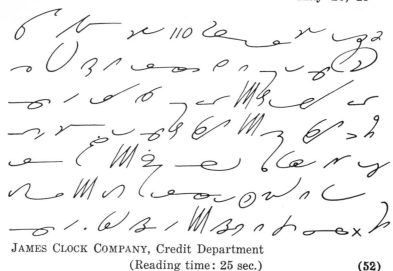

JAMES CLOCK COMPANY, Credit Department
(Reading time: 25 sec.) **(52)**

LETTER 208

crop		in/dul/gence	
for/get		La Salle	
Il/li/nois		plus	

When special instructions (look up spelling, check with bookkeeper, get folder from file, etc.) are given during dictation, the stenographer will be very wise to record them—at least, in short form. There is no value, however, in recording "just a moment—let me see—yes" if the stenographer can identify such words as the employer's "talking to himself."

May 17, 19—

James Clock Company, 101 Tenth Street spell out tenth La Salle, Illinois (pause) you had better look up the spelling of that town (pause) Gentlemen Enclosed is our trade acceptance for (pause) just a moment—let me see—yes (pause) for $388.08 to cover your statement of May 10 plus 6 per cent interest (pause) you had better get the bookkeeper to check those figures paragraph

We regret that this method of payment (pause) is necessary (pause) comma but our collections (pause) strike out our (pause) but collections have been very poor indeed (pause) Crop conditions are improving however (pause) you'd better insert commas there (pause) and indicate an excellent business for this fall (pause) paragraph

We thank (pause) strike out (pause) We shall not forget (pause) your kind indulgence Yours truly   (72)

Dictated by Manager of Adams Department Store

LETTER 209

billed

hand/i/cap

in/stance

in/voices

ma/ture

obliged

time/pieces

were

May 29, 19--

JAMES CLOCK COMPANY, Credit Department
(Reading time: 1 min. 20 sec.)   **(171)**

LETTER 210

com/ing   to give you
share   we shall be able

"Get that letter out promptly" means "transcribe ahead of other work." A longhand RUSH should be written at the beginning of the letter when this instruction is given.

June 5, 19—

James Clock Company, 101 Tenth Street, La Salle (pause) I think that is a capital S. You'd better look it up (pause) Illinois Gentlemen (pause) We are enclosing the check you request (pause) the check requested in your letter of May 29 period (pause) paragraph

We realize fully the fairness of your policy (pause) make that your collection policy and regret that business situations (pause) that business conditions prevented our sending (pause) strike out sending (pause) making this payment more promptly period (pause) If present improvements continue (pause) comma we shall soon (pause) strike out soon (pause) we shall be able to give you a good share (pause) of our business during the (pause) coming months paragraph

Will you have your salesman (pause) change that to your representative call on us when he is (pause) when he is (pause) in this vicinity Yours truly (pause) get that letter out promptly please (81)

Dictated by Manager of Adams Department Store

PART 4. BUSINESS PRACTICES

Vocabulary Preview

bur/ied	per/tain/ing
cans	stand/ard/ized
di/rec/tory	stor/age
in other words —	text/books
paste	·tick/ler
pend/ing	tow/els

The Office Desk
(Continued)

The right-hand top drawer is perhaps the most used. The things needed most frequently in the day's work— rubber stamps, ink [20] pads, paste, etc.—should therefore be kept in this drawer. Of course, if these things are used constantly all day, they [40] should be put on the top of the desk. In other words, the tools in constant use should be arranged for the greatest [60] convenience consistent with the highest degree of efficiency.

The upper left-hand drawer is preferably [80] used for blanks, forms, and other supplies that are in daily use. If a small tickler file or other daily reminder [100] is used, it should be placed in this drawer.

The lower right-hand drawer is usually a file drawer that [120] contains only material pending completion or pertaining to the department. This file space should not be [140] a storage place for general folders, but should be used for reference information, reports, correspondence,[160] follow-up data, and work in process.

In the back of this drawer, cleaning and dusting cloths, oil cans, typewriter [180] tools, and towels can be stored. They are then never buried and are easily available when wanted.

The two [200] lower left-hand drawers are most convenient for keeping those things that are not used constantly but are often needed [220] in the day's routine. Textbooks and reference books, sales manuals, and the telephone directory should be [240] placed in these two drawers.

On the top of most business desks are two highly important kinds of equipment, the [260] telephone and the mail trays. A pad should always be near at hand so that notations regarding messages received [280] over the telephone can be made. It is usually unnecessary to have more than two trays on any [300] desk. The "in" tray should be on the left side of the desk and the "out" tray on the right side. Material may then [320] be passed from one tray to the other in the standardized direction, that is, from left to right.   (336)

PART 5. PROGRESS CHECKUP

LETTER PC-30

To Our District Agencies

Many requests have been received from time to time with regard to our collection [20] policy.

We do not wish to encourage the use of credit privileges; neither do we take any steps to [40] investigate credit reliability. We have no plan for deferred-payment buying. Charge accounts,[60] nevertheless, may be opened for any prospective customer who is acceptable to the agency.[80] Ordinarily, the central office doesn't question the regular monthly accounts of our agencies. It is not [100] the acceptance or rejection of charge-account applications with which we are concerned. As long as accounts are [120] kept in good standing by regular and prompt payment, our office doesn't enter into the picture. When an [140] account becomes past due, we are compelled, in order to protect both the agency and ourselves, to take over the [160] collection.

Our prices are based on the cash sale of our merchandise, and no discount is offered for either cash [180] payment or quantity buying. Our agencies are authorized, however, to approve credit up to the 10th [200] of the next month following the date of purchase. This is not to be considered an invitation to use to [220] excess the credit courtesy, and all overdue accounts are automatically considered delinquent [240] accounts. On the 10th of every month, therefore, we expect our agencies to send us a list of all unpaid [260] accounts. Until individual accounts have been settled in full, each agency must refuse further credit to [280] names on its list.

The practices in operation in our office are not intended to embarrass either [300] our agencies or their customers. As a result, three collection letters are mailed at intervals of fifteen [320] days. The first letter is simply a reminder that the bill has not been settled. This letter takes into [340] consideration the fact that the customer's check may be in the mail when our letter is written.

The second [360] letter is written to appeal to the customer's belief in honest dealing and to suggest a possible [380] refusal of future credit privileges. This letter is mailed to the customer one month after the due date [400] of his bill. Consequently, if the customer is planning to settle his account voluntarily, there is [420] sufficient time for him to make payment.

The third letter names definite time limits for the payment of accounts,[440] and the customers are notified that their accounts will be turned over to a collection agency if [460] payment is not made by the date specified.

Our collection policy and our attitude toward credit accounts [480] may seem extreme to some agencies, but we should like to call attention to the following:

Our national [500] reputation has been established upon a financial policy that enables us to give the public the [520] highest quality merchandise at the lowest possible price. You can meet your customers with confidence in [540] the product you sell, because you know that such a product cannot be bought at any better price. If we are to [560] continue our high standards of quality and service, we must insist on the full co-operation of the [580] agencies. In turn, we offer the maximum of advertising and sales assistance.

Very cordially yours [600]   (600)

JAMES CLOCK COMPANY

EJ:ID   Accounting Department

DICTATION STUDY XXXI

PART 1. BASIC SKILLS

Brief-Form Review

Directions. The following letter contains 88 different brief forms and brief-form derivatives. In this letter the brief forms are repeated many times and represent at least 50 per cent of the words. You can therefore see the need of knowing your brief forms well. Unless you can write them instantly and read them easily, they are of no value to you. Give your brief forms careful attention. Read the letter until you can read easily at your reading rate of at least 125 words a minute. Then make two shorthand copies of the letter.

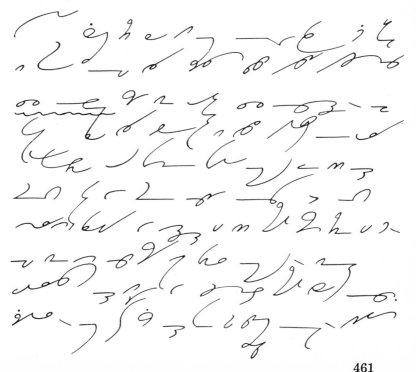

(Reading time: 4 min. 40 sec.)   (600)

PART 2. BUSINESS INFORMATION

Vocabulary Preview

ac/quaint/ances		month's	
ap/proach		op/er/a/tors	
av/e/nues		per/cent/age	
bu/reaus		place/ment	
clas/si/fied		qual/i/fi/ca/tions	
con/tacts		reg/is/ter/ing	
dis/il/lu/sion/ ment		reg/is/tra/tion	
fam/ily		sal/ary	
		scores	
friend		search	
if this		seek/ing	
in these days		stood	
in/dus/trial		strain	

Employment Agencies

When a stenographer is fully prepared to do satisfactory office work, there are several avenues [20] open in the search for work. Probably the best means of obtaining employment is through some friend or some friend's [40] friend. Among the many acquaintances of the average family, there is frequently one who has an [60] opening for a stenographer, or one who knows of an opening in the office of someone else. If this means [80] of approach fails, the stenographer still has recourse to other methods of finding work.

Classified newspaper [100] advertisements require prompt action because in these days of keen competition it is not unusual to [120] find scores of applicants for a single position. Another very satisfactory means of getting a [140] position is through the school itself. Many schools maintain actual placement departments and, through business contacts,[160] obtain employment for numbers of their students. Then again, the manufacturers of various types of office [180] machines have well-organized employment bureaus and assist machine operators in finding suitable [200] work. In most cases the services of such manufacturers are offered without charge, but the passing of some [220] sort of test is one of the qualifications for registration.

If the patience of the one seeking a [240] position has stood the strain of disappointment and disillusionment, there is yet a wide avenue open.[260] Professional employment agencies are responsible for the placement of a large number of office workers; [280] in some instances they practically control the office employment of certain industrial companies.[300] The addresses of some of the agencies can be obtained at the school office or from the classified section [320] of the telephone directory. These agencies frequently require applicants to take tests before registering.[340] Some employment agencies charge registration fees and, in addition, collect a certain percentage [360] of the first month's salary; others are satisfied with the percentage only.   (374)

PART 3. BUSINESS CORRESPONDENCE

between

MUNSON TYPEWRITER COMPANY
561 Stafford Building   *and*
Broadway at 28th Street
New York 14, New York

MR. WALTER B. BROWER
Senior High School
New Rochelle, New York

and

MR. ALBERT JOHNSON, President
Johnson Business College
Sedalia, Missouri

Directions. The letters in this part are arranged for timed dictation for speed building. Practice the words in the vocabulary previews, read the shorthand plates, and write each letter twice in shorthand. Complete all the work on one letter before proceeding to the next letter.

ap/pear/ing
Broad/way
Brower

classes
class/room
ex/am/ples

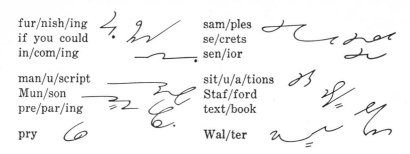

fur/nish/ing	sam/ples
if you could	se/crets
in/com/ing	sen/ior
man/u/script	sit/u/a/tions
Mun/son	Staf/ford
pre/par/ing	text/book
pry	Wal/ter

Senior High School
New Rochelle, New York
November 6, 19—

Munson Typewriter Company
561 Stafford Building
Broadway at 28th Street
New York 14, New York

Gentlemen

I am preparing for publication a manuscript of dictation material to be used [20] in office training classes, and I am seeking your aid in getting samples of actual business letters.

I [40] do not wish to pry into any business secrets, but I should like to get examples of real business [60] situations as shown in incoming letters and answers. It would be especially helpful if you could let me [80] have some correspondence pertaining to a situation in which several letters were required to close the [100] matter. Of course, all names appearing in the letters will be changed.

Your co-operation in furnishing this [120] material will help bring into the classroom letters of a more practical nature than those found in the average [140] textbook. May I count on you?

Yours very truly   (149)

Walter B. Brower

LETTER 212

them   ⌐   we hope you can   [shorthand]

November 8, 19—

[shorthand outline]

MUNSON TYPEWRITER COMPANY, School Department

(Reading time: 25 sec.)   (62)

LETTER 213

Al/bert   [shorthand]   John/son   [shorthand]
col/lege   Se/da/lia   [shorthand]
in any other   [shorthand]   there will be   [shorthand]

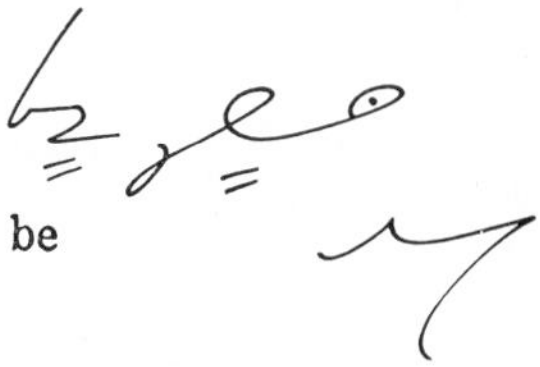

November 9, 19—

[shorthand outline]

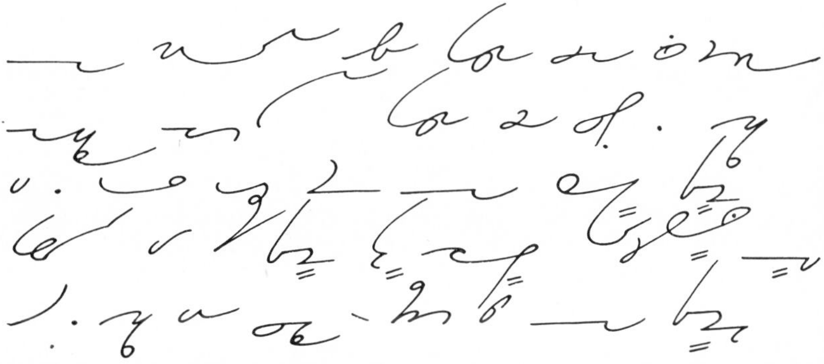

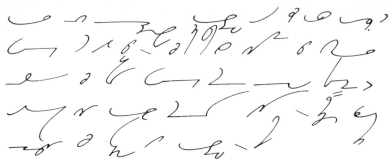

MUNSON TYPEWRITER COMPANY, School Department
(Reading time: 45 sec.)   (103)

LETTER 214

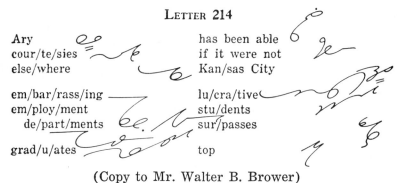

Ary		has been able
cour/te/sies		if it were not
else/where		Kan/sas City
em/bar/rass/ing		lu/cra/tive
em/ploy/ment		stu/dents
de/part/ments		sur/passes
grad/u/ates		top

(Copy to Mr. Walter B. Brower)

November 7, 19—

Mr. Frederick Reynolds
Munson Typewriter Company
561 Stafford Building
Broadway at 28th Street
New York 14, New York

Dear Mr. Reynolds

For some time we have intended writing to you to express our sincere appreciation [20] of the courtesies that have been shown us through your employment departments in various cities. With the employment [40] situation as it is now, we realize more than ever what their co-operation and assistance [60] mean. We are in the Kansas City territory and naturally expect a little more help here than is [80] expected elsewhere. If it were not for this service, we should be in a very embarrassing position.[100]

Recently many of our students have been going to Chicago, where you have another wonderful organization.[120] Miss Ary, of the employment department, has shown particular interest in our graduates and [140] has been able to place many of them in lucrative positions. The fact that we are not in the Chicago [160] territory seems to make no difference in Miss Ary's attitude toward our applicants.

We feel that the [180] Munson typewriter stands at the top of the list, but we are also convinced that Munson employment service [200] surpasses the machine.

Very cordially yours   (208)

JOHNSON BUSINESS COLLEGE

President

AJ:FM

LETTER 215

as/so/ci/ates
gen/u/inely
of/fi/cials

proud
rep/re/sen/ta/tion
vi/tally

November 9, 19—

MUNSON TYPEWRITER COMPANY, School Department
(Reading time: 1 min. 30 sec.)   (192)

LETTER 216

non/tech/   thank you for
  ni/cal   your let/ters

Senior High School
New Rochelle, New York
November 11, 19—

Munson Typewriter Company
561 Stafford Building
Broadway at 28th Street
New York 14, New York

Attention of Mr. Reynolds

Gentlemen

Thank you for your letters of November 8 and November 9.

The letter from Mr. Albert Johnson [20] is the type of non-technical business letter that I am desirous of getting. Of course, I am especially [40] interested in letters arranged in series; however, I should like the privilege of using Mr.[60] Johnson's letter in my manuscript.

Please consider me at your service when I, too, may be of help.

Yours [80] very truly   (82)

Walter B. Brower

LETTER 217

if you do not 〽

November 13, 19—

MUNSON TYPEWRITER COMPANY, School Department
(Reading time: 45 sec.)   (105)

LETTER 218

in any way   we had not

of our let/ter

November 17, 19—

Mr. Frederick Reynolds
Munson Typewriter Company
561 Stafford Building
Broadway at 28th Street
New York 14, New York

Dear Mr. Reynolds

We had not thought our letter to you was outstanding in any way, but we did want to express [20] our appreciation of the benefits received from the various representatives of youɪ company. [40]

You have full permission to dispose of our letter of November 7 as you see fit. We shall be glad [60] if it can be of some use to you or to Mr. Brower.

Very cordially yours   **(75)**

JOHNSON BUSINESS COLLEGE

AJ:FM   President

LETTER 219

rein   you may have

to have you

November 20, 19—

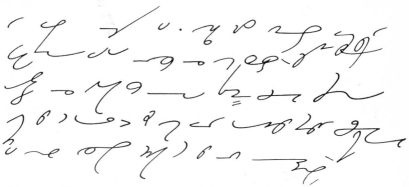

MUNSON TYPEWRITER COMPANY, School Department

(Reading time: 45 sec.)　　　　　**(104)**

PART 4. BUSINESS PRACTICES

Vocabulary Preview

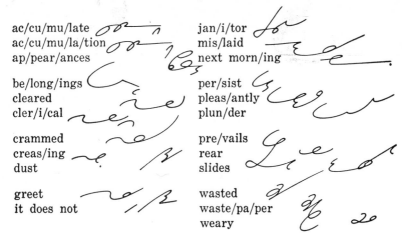

ac/cu/mu/late
ac/cu/mu/la/tion
ap/pear/ances

be/long/ings
cleared
cler/i/cal

crammed
creas/ing
dust

greet
it does not

jan/i/tor
mis/laid
next morn/ing

per/sist
pleas/antly
plun/der

pre/vails
rear
slides

wasted
waste/pa/per
weary

The Office Desk
(Continued)

While this arrangement of materials may have very little bearing on the stenographer's desk, similar [20] efficiency can be gained there through the systematic use of the desk space.

Orderly arrangement of materials is the first step toward efficient work. In this desk, the top drawer contains letter file trays; the bottom drawer, a wastepaper basket. Carbon paper and personal effects are kept in the center drawer. The typewriter is on the left side of the desk.

In many desks, the top drawer is [40] used for the supply of stationery. Letter sheets and copy sheets should be placed in the front slides, and telegraph [60] blanks and smaller papers should be put in the rear slides. Long and short envelopes should be kept in the front compartments.[80] The stenographic notebook and pencils, when not in use, may be kept in the rear compartment of the top drawer.[100]

Carbon papers are then kept in the forward section of the second drawer and should be laid flat in folders or [120] boxes to prevent creasing. The rear section of this drawer may be used for personal belongings.

The forward [140] section of the lowest drawer should contain reference books needed in the stenographer's work. The rear section [160] is a good place for typewriter tools.

On leaving the office at night, the stenographer should leave the top of her [180] desk clear of everything except the telephone and the desk trays. Effective janitor service is necessary [200] in an office building, and the clerical force must co-operate by placing articles where they will [220] not accumulate dust or create confusion. If the stenographer's desk is cleared at night, the office will greet [240] her more pleasantly the next morning.

An office is not a place for an accumulation of everything.[260] It is not a place where papers are lost, data are mislaid, records are buried, and every nook and corner [280] is crammed with plunder; where it does not matter whether one hits or misses the wastepaper basket; where a part of [300] each day is wasted in weary search for needed matter; where confusion prevails not only in appearances [320] but also in plans and methods. Those who persist in contributing to such conditions do not deserve a place [340] in a real office.　　　　　　　　　　　　　　　　　　(344)

PART 5. PROGRESS CHECKUP

It is essential that a stenographer learn to write unpracticed material from dictation. No doubt, you have been given some experience in this type of shorthand writing. In order to give you additional experience of this kind, your teacher may wish to dictate Progress Checkup letters that you have not practiced. For this reason, Part 5 has been omitted from most of the remaining dictation studies in this book. You will find, however, a Progress Checkup in Part 5 of Dictation Study XXXV and Dictation Study XL.

DICTATION STUDY XXXII

PART 1. BASIC SKILLS

Theory Review

Directions. Dictation in which a great many numbers appear is not easy to take. Words, omitted in recording dictation, can sometimes be supplied from the context of the sentence; but numbers cannot be supplied in this way. It is, therefore, necessary for the stenographer to listen very carefully when numbers are given and to be sure that they are recorded correctly. For some of the very common expressions containing numbers, there are short forms, as in $25 listed below. Less common expressions and expressions in which confusion may arise are better written in full. Read each of the expressions listed below and then write them at least once each. All are used in the letter that follows.

Expressions Containing Numbers

Key: 4-engine, 56 passengers, 50 planes, 5 miles, 80 miles, 300 miles, 1,700 miles, 115 feet, 100 feet, 30,000 feet, 6,000 pounds, 79,000 pounds, 2,000 horsepower, $20, $25, $500,000, $25,000,000, 50 per cent, 5.5 gallons, 8 a.m., 8 p.m.

Directions. All the foregoing expressions are used in the following shorthand plate. Read the plate until you can read at your goal rate. Then make two shorthand copies of the plate.

476

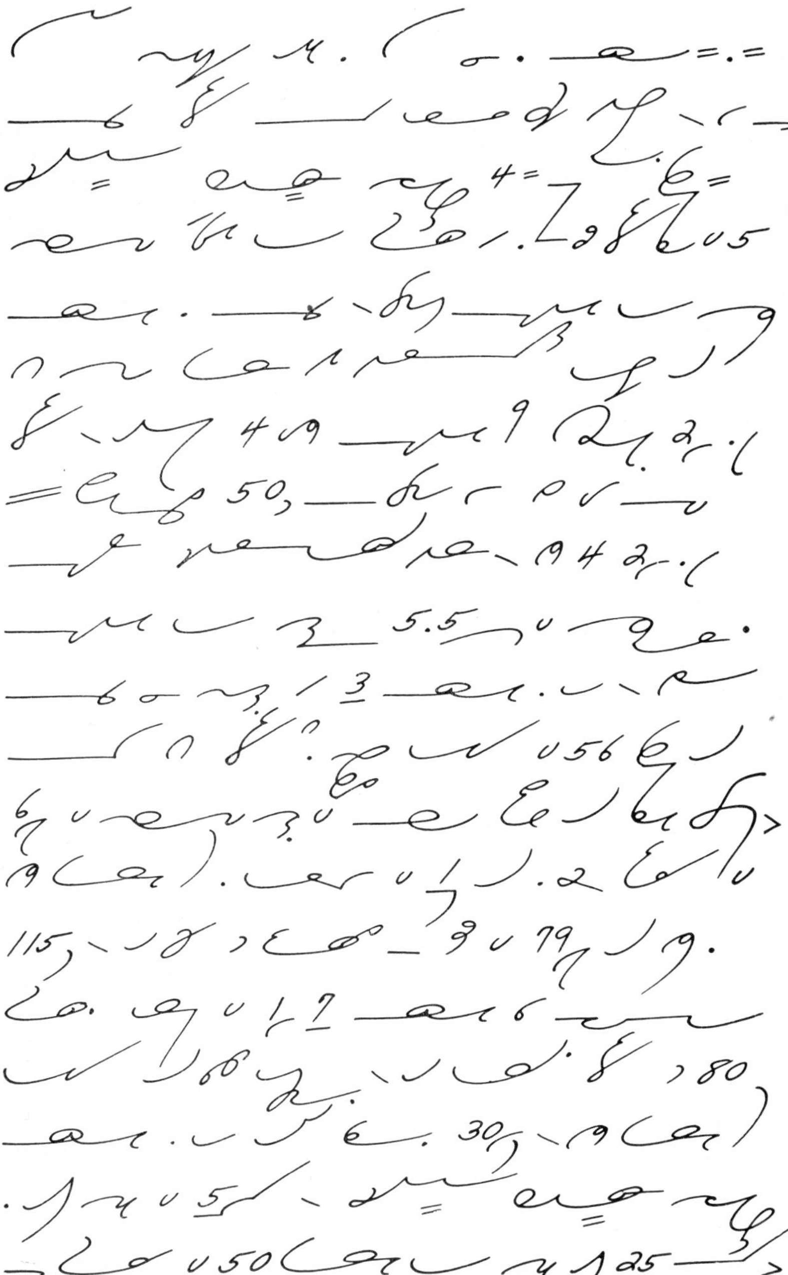

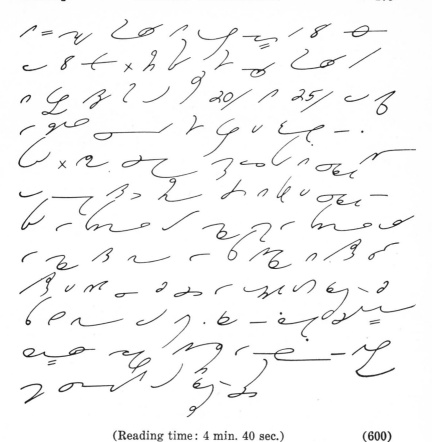

(Reading time: 4 min. 40 sec.)   (600)

PART 2. BUSINESS INFORMATION

Vocabulary Preview

aboard		brief	
abroad		buf/fet	
acted		bus	
alert		com/fort/able	
bag/gage		com/par/i/son	
boat		con/ducted	

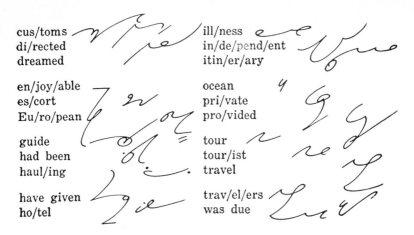

cus/toms	ill/ness
di/rected	in/de/pend/ent
dreamed	itin/er/ary
en/joy/able	ocean
es/cort	pri/vate
Eu/ro/pean	pro/vided
guide	tour
had been	tour/ist
haul/ing	travel
have given	trav/el/ers
ho/tel	was due

Travel Agencies

The increasing amount of travel and the increasing number of travelers have given rise to the establishment [20] of numerous agencies that tend to simplify the problems of travel and to make the traveler's [40] trip more enjoyable. These travel bureaus, or tour agencies, are maintained by most transportation lines, including [60] bus, railroad, boat, and airplane. Independent agencies are to be found in express companies, banks, and private [80] business offices.

These various travel agencies charge a fee very small in comparison with the [100] services they render. On a definitely planned tour, either in this country or abroad, they look after the [120] needs of the tourist from the time he starts on his trip until he returns to the starting point. Their schedule sometimes [140] includes services little dreamed of.

For instance, the plans for a certain trip included the services of a [160] man to assist with the packing of the baggage; the hauling of the baggage to the boat; and the serving of a [180] buffet meal to the friends of the traveler on the afternoon of the departure of the boat. During the trip [200] across the ocean, a representative of the bureau was constantly on the alert with offers of [220] assistance. When the boat reached the European port, a guide came aboard, made all arrangements for the handling of the [240] baggage,

and conducted the tourist to a hotel where comfortable reservations had already been made.²⁶⁰ In and near this particular city, the guide acted as personal escort to places of
interest, arranged ²⁸⁰ for medical treatment during a brief
illness, and finally started the traveler and his baggage
on ³⁰⁰ the way to the next point of the itinerary. For five
months the trip was thus supervised and directed. Even ³²⁰
the tipping had been provided for in the original arrangements with the agency.

On his return ³⁴⁰ the traveler was conducted rapidly
through the customs routine, and his baggage was delivered promptly to ³⁶⁰ his home. To top it all, the bureau
presented the returned traveler with a check for $80 and
explained ³⁸⁰ that the refund was due to the reduction of
rates during the trip.   (393)

PART 3. BUSINESS CORRESPONDENCE

between

AMERICAN TOURS CORPORATION   MR. ROLAND CABLE, **Principal**
8944 Market Street   *and* Bentley Senior High School
Philadelphia 6, Pennsylvania   Grantwood, New Jersey

and

MR. H. L. PEARSON, Senior Class **Adviser**
Bentley Senior High School
Grantwood, New Jersey

Directions. The following correspondence will give you
further practice in office-style dictation. From time to time,
a dictator may decide to dictate insertions to be made in
previously dictated sentences or paragraphs. If an insertion is short and if there is sufficient time for the stenographer to find the point at which the insertion is to be made,
the material may be written between the lines of shorthand
and the point may be indicated by a caret, in the same
manner that an insertion in longhand is made. This is especially true when the employer says, "Now, read the first
sentence of the letter. All right. You had better insert
graduating just before classes. Now, where was I?"

In most cases, however, it will save the employer's time and make the stenographer's job easier if she will treat short insertions like corrections by taking down the instructions completely and marking them clearly. The careful editing of the notes can be done at the typewriter before the transcription of the notes. Unless otherwise instructed, use this second plan for the letters in this dictation study.

Letters 220 and 222 will show how they may have been recorded by the stenographer; and Letters 221 and 223 will show how they may have been dictated. Your teacher may decide to dictate the remaining letters in this part in office style.

LETTER 220

ap/prox/i/mate		grad/u/at/ing	
Bent/ley		Grant/wood	
bul/le/tin		res/er/va/tions	
Ca/ble		Ro/land	
for this		this year	

February 20, 19—

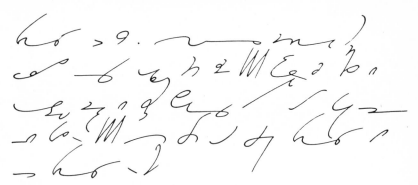

AMERICAN TOURS CORPORATION, Resident Manager

(Reading time: 35 sec.)   (83)

LETTER 221

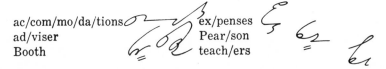

ac/com/mo/da/tions   ex/penses
ad/viser   Pear/son
Booth   teach/ers

February 26, 19—

American Tours Corporation, 8944 Market Street, Philadelphia 6, Pennsylvania Gentlemen (pause) make that attention of Mr. Albert L. Booth (pause) I am answering your letter of February 20 with reference to the senior-class trip to Washington (pause) make that Mr. Cable has asked me to answer your letter paragraph

We are planning to make the trip in April period (pause) no, comma (pause) leaving this school on the twentieth and returning on the twenty-fourth (pause) insert the morning of the twentieth (pause) There will be about thirty-five in the party comma including teachers in charge paragraph (pause)

Will you please send us full particulars about expenses accommodations and methods of transportation Very truly yours (pause) back there about accommodations, you had better insert accommodations in Washington.   (90)

Dictated by H. L. Pearson, Senior Class Adviser

LETTER 222

ar/range/ments
Field/ing
lec/turer

namely

per/son
sight-seeing
steamer

Strat/ford

March 2, 19—

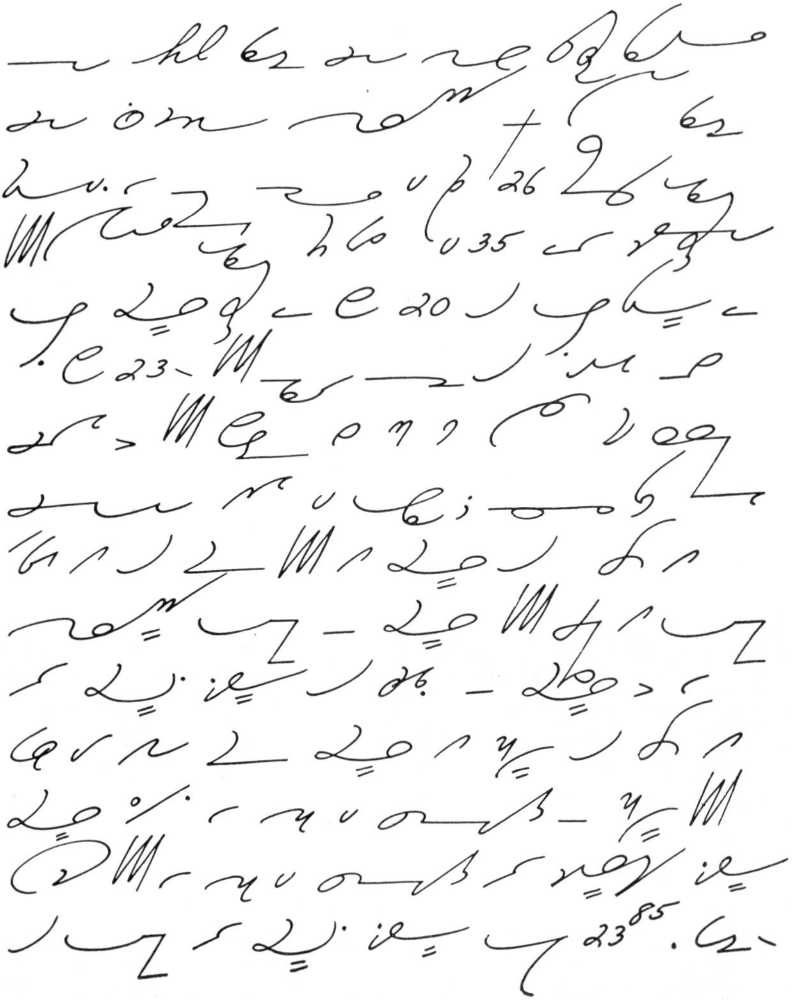

ALBERT L. BOOTH, Resident Manager

(Reading time: 1 min. 45 sec.) (229)

LETTER 223

com/fort/ably	thank you for
give me	your let/ter
seated	trans/port

March 4, 19—

American Tours Corporation, 8944 Market Street, Philadelphia 6, Pennsylvania Attention of Mr. Albert L. Booth Gentlemen (pause) Thank you for your letter of March 2 paragraph

Please make hotel reservations for our party in Washington (pause) The members of last year's group seemed highly pleased with the accommodations there paragraph (pause)

Can you give me the seating capacity of the bus that is to take (pause) make that transport us to and from Philadelphia (pause) In other words comma (pause) will all the members of our party be comfortably seated (pause) This same point comes up in connection with (pause) by the way, in that first sentence about reservations, make that reservations for our party at the Stratford Hotel in Washington (pause) Now, let's see (pause) Where was I (pause) Oh yes This same point comes up in connection with the sight-seeing tour of Washington Very truly yours   (88)

Dictated by H. L. Pearson, Senior Class Adviser

LETTER 224

am/ple   de/tails

March 7, 19—

AMERICAN TOURS CORPORATION, Albert L. Booth, Resident Manager

(Reading time: 35 sec.)   (86)

LETTER 225

ad/mis/sion   tick/ets
the/a/ter

April 4, 19—

American Tours Corporation
8944 Market Street
Philadelphia 6, Pennsylvania

Attention of Mr. Albert L. Booth

Gentlemen

For the evening of April 22, the night usually free on your tour, we are planning [20] a theater party. Can you obtain tickets for us in order that we may be seated together?

If [40] possible let me know ahead of time just what is available. If no good shows are playing in Washington on [60] the twenty-second, perhaps a visit to the Fox Theater would be enjoyable. Please quote admission prices [80] in your letter.

I suppose I shall receive full particulars of the trip within the next few days.

Very [100] truly yours   (102)

H. L. Pearson

HLP:MS   Senior Class Adviser

LETTER 226

a.m.	**fac/ulty**
an/nounce/ment	re/serv/ing
as/sign	room/ing
at/trac/tions	state/room

April 9, 19—

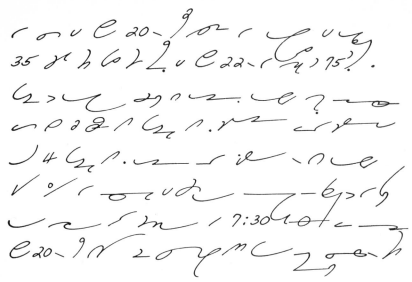

AMERICAN TOURS CORPORATION, Albert L. Booth, Resident Manager

(Reading time: 1 min.)   (131)

LETTER 227

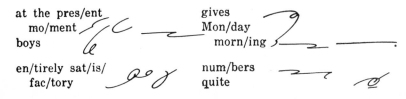

at the pres/ent mo/ment	gives Mon/day morn/ing
boys	
en/tirely sat/is/ fac/tory	num/bers quite

April 14, 19—

American Tours Corporation
8944 Market Street
Philadelphia 6, Pennsylvania

Attention of Mr. Albert L. Booth

Gentlemen

Your theater selection for April 22 is entirely satisfactory.

The enclosed [20] rooming list gives the names of three teachers, sixteen boys, and fourteen girls, or a total of thirty-three persons. Our [40] original estimate included thirty-five persons; so please note the change in numbers.

As far as I can [60] tell at the present moment, the arrangements you have made for us are very acceptable. My **rec**ords are not [80] quite clear, however, about the transportation from the boat in Baltimore to our hotel in Washington.

We [100] **shall expect the bus on Monday morning at 7:30.**

Very truly yours   (114)

H. L. Pearson
Senior Class Adviser

Enc.

LETTER 228

ar/rives	plainly	
coaches	se/curely	
con/veyed	tax/i/cabs	
de/pot	un/der sep/a/	
in/ter/ur/ban	rate cover	
motor	Wal/nut	

April 16, 19—

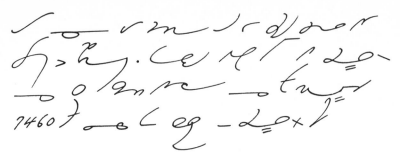

ALBERT L. BOOTH, Resident Manager

(Reading time: 50 sec.)　　　　　**(115)**

PART 4. BUSINESS PRACTICES

Vocabulary Preview

ac/com/plish/ment	ham/pered
achieves	in or/der to be
a mil/lion ·	in/ter/of/fice
au/to/mat/i/cally	must be done
de/part/men/tal	re/tard
dis/ci/pline	smoth/ered
dis/or/derly	sur/round/ings
earthly	they must have
econ/o/miz/ing	think/ing
ef/fort	tools
ex/e/cu/tion	util/ized
ex/pend/i/ture	weak/nesses

The Office Desk
(Concluded)

Efficient businessmen of today endeavor to produce the greatest amount of work with the least expenditure [20] of effort. They realize that, in order to be efficient, they must have their office desks and working tools [40] arranged in such a manner that they can be utilized to the best advantage.

All weaknesses that retard the [60] flow of office routine should be overcome. Interoffice and departmental detail must be done automatically [80] through a simple system. Effective thinking is smothered and the efficient execution of duties [100] is hampered by disorderly office surroundings.

It is difficult to make any set of rules for placing [120] desk material properly. The man at his particular desk should know better than anyone else what [140] things he needs the most and where they can be obtained quickly and easily. Desk efficiency is not a fad, but [160] it is a real factor in success for all businessmen.

The man who achieves the greatest success is the man [180] who uses to the best advantage sixty full minutes in every hour. Time-economizing is more [200] important than money-economizing. The right use of time is the price of every earthly accomplishment.[220] Businessmen can borrow a million in money; but they cannot beg, borrow, steal, or create a minute. The businessman [240] should do everything possible to accomplish the most in the least time. Desk materials should be [260] arranged so that all things are near at hand and in a place where they are readily available. Desk efficiency [280] involves discipline.   (284)

PART 5. PROGRESS CHECKUP

See page 475.

DICTATION STUDY XXXIII

PART 1. BASIC SKILLS

Theory Review

Directions. The letter in this part will give further practice in the writing of numbers. Notice how the numbers in the following exercise are broken into their parts; for example, 4,200 is written in shorthand as 4 thousand 2 hundred. This method of writing reduces the chance of error. Read each of the expressions listed below; then write each at least once in shorthand.

Expressions Containing Numbers

Key: May 15, 1918; April 17, 1926; 8 years; 25 years; 20 acres; 800 acres; 25 miles; 360 landings; 500 landings; 3½ minutes; 1,000 times; 1,000 airports; 3,000 airports; 1,500 airports; $110,000; $20,000,000; $100,000,000; $2,000,000,000; 2,500 feet; 5,500 feet; 5,800 passengers; 90 per cent; 12 cents; 5 cents; 5,000,000; 20,000,000; 2,501,074,036.

Directions. All the foregoing expressions are used in the following shorthand plate. Read the plate until you can easily reach your reading goal. Then make two shorthand copies of the plate.

492

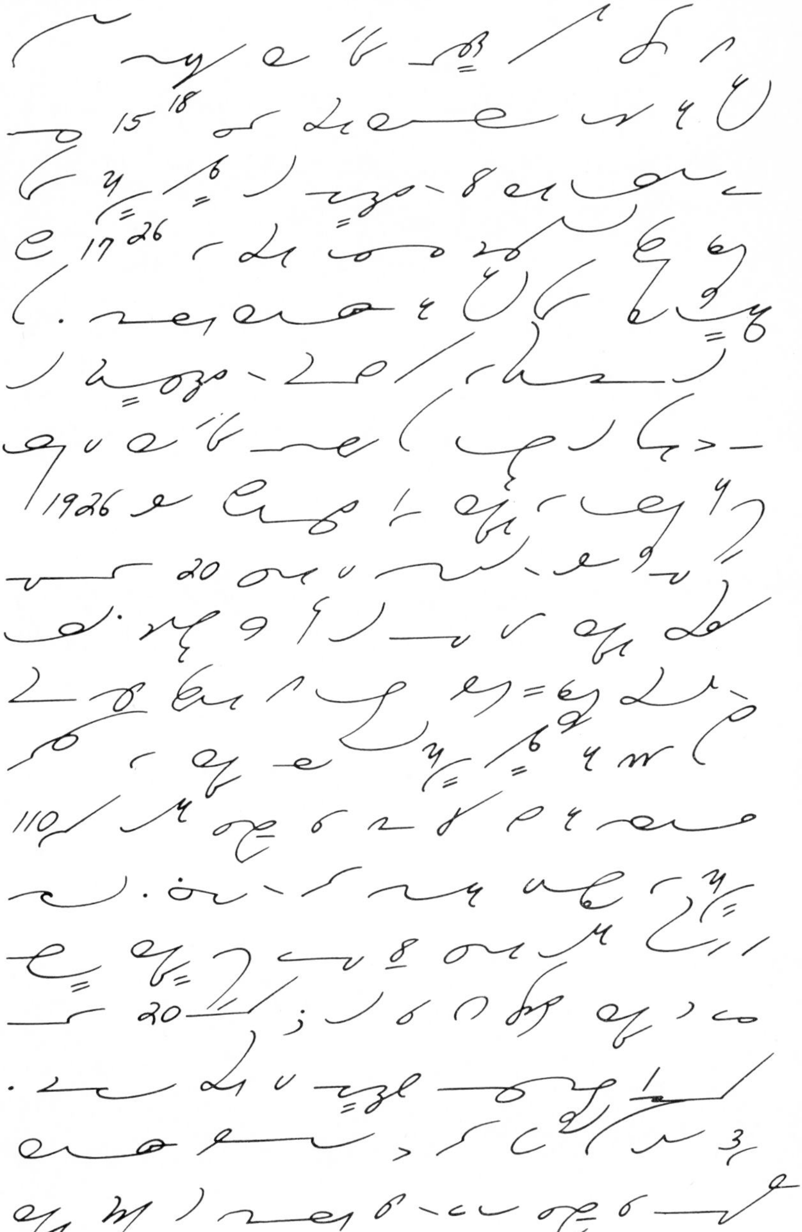

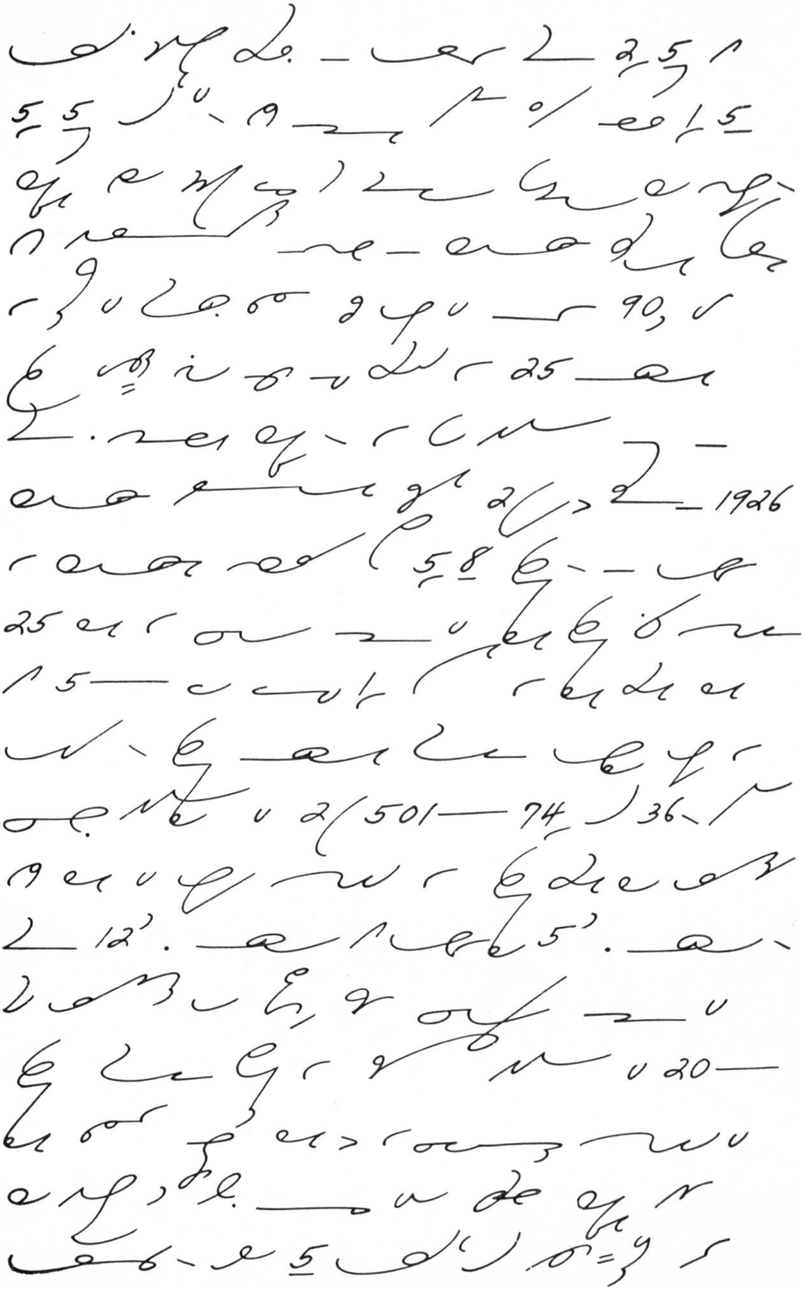

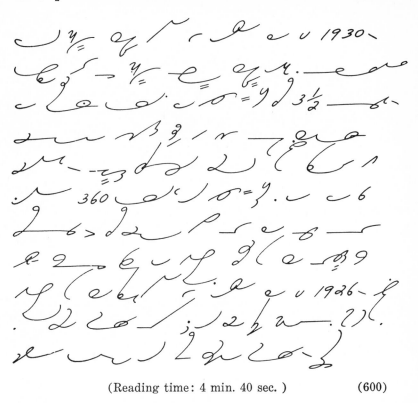

(Reading time: 4 min. 40 sec.)　　　(600)

PART 2. BUSINESS INFORMATION

Vocabulary Preview

ac/cu/racy
ac/tively
Ad/dres/so/graph

apart/ment
booths
cab/i/net

cir/cu/lar/iz/ing
clas/si/fi/ca/tions
con/tests

doc/tors
dwell/ers
elim/i/nated

filler
has be/come
high school

hint
li/cense
ly/ing

mar/riage
neg/lect
new/ly/weds

pri/mary
re/lied
tax

no mat/ter
post/age
Post Of/fice
De/part/ment

us/able
use/less
ves/ti/bules
worse than

Mailing Lists

Repetition plays an important part in advertising. **This is** just as true of circularizing as of [20] any other **form of** publicity. An element that contributes much to the success of a circularizing [40] campaign is the mailing list. Yet in some business offices there is no greater field of neglect than in [60] the keeping of the mailing list.

A mailing list is simply the names and the addresses of businesses and [80] individuals, arranged in some usable form. Such a list may be kept on cards in a file, on Addressograph [100] plates in a cabinet, or on a series of address stencils. No matter what the form of the list may be, a [120] factor of primary importance is to keep the list up to date. A mailing list is worse than useless when its [140] accuracy can no longer be relied upon. New names should be added as occasion arises; old names [160] should be eliminated as necessity dictates. For various reasons the Post Office Department sometimes [180] is unable to deliver mail to the addressee. As soon as such letters are returned to the senders, [200] the names of the addressees should be removed from the mailing list. If they are not, losses in postage, in stationery, [220] and in printed forms may result.

There are numerous sources of information for the building of a [240] proper mailing list. The names and the addresses of automobile owners can be obtained from license bureaus; [260] those of homeowners, from tax offices; those of apartment dwellers, from mail boxes in vestibules; and those of [280] newlyweds, from marriage columns in newspapers. General lists can be prepared from city directories and [300] telephone directories, from answers to contests, and from registrations at exhibition booths at fairs. In [320] fact, the sources are too numerous for more than a hint at the possibilities. The demand for classified [340] lists has become so great that mailing-list companies have been established. These companies sell lists of names of high-school [360] seniors, doctors, and teachers, as well as of businesses and persons belonging to other classifications.[380] They furnish names for any territory or combination of territories.

The value of a mailing [400] list depends upon its use. Lying idle in the office, it serves no purpose other than that of a [420] space-filler; but, actively used in a well-planned mailing campaign, it can be a valuable business-getter.   (439)

PART 3. BUSINESS CORRESPONDENCE

between

PRESTON STAINED SHINGLE COMPANY
177 National Street
Buffalo 5, New York

and

ROBBINS LUMBER CORPORATION
River and Second Streets
Henderson, Kentucky

Directions. The letters in this part are arranged for timed dictation for speed building. Practice the previews and the letters as instructed in previous dictation studies of this type.

LETTER 229

ab/sorb	per/ma/nent	
ad/vise you	res/i/dent	
com/pare	River	
free/dom	Rob/bins	
Hen/der/son	short no/tice	
or/gan/ized	stucco	
paint/ing	we do not	

April 2, 19—

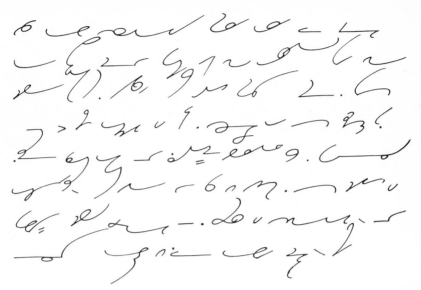

PRESTON STAINED SHINGLE COMPANY, Wm. M. Lloyd, Sales Department

(Reading time: 2 min. 20 sec.)   (297)

LETTER 230

abey/ance car/ried   two or three

April 10, 19—

Preston Stained Shingle Company
177 National Street
Buffalo 5, New York

Gentlemen

The interests in building material here in Henderson **are** now considering a modernizing [20] campaign. We should know definitely within the next two or three weeks whether the campaign will be carried [40] through. Until that time we prefer to hold your proposition in abeyance.

We suggest that you write us again [60] about the middle of next month.

Yours truly   (68)

ROBBINS LUMBER CORPORATION

HGW:AD   President

LETTER 231

as well	not only
bul/le/tins	tells
en/er/get/i/cally	you can do
have done	

May 10, 19—

PRESTON STAINED SHINGLE COMPANY, Wm. M. Lloyd, Sales Department

(Reading time: 50 sec.)   (115)

LETTER 232

setup

this may not be

to the full/est ex/tent

un/prof/it/able

May 14, 19—

Preston Stained Shingle Company
177 National Street
Buffalo 5, New York

Gentlemen

We are, of course, interested in any proposition that **will** increase our volume of sales on [20] a profitable basis. If **your** modernizing campaign will actually do this, we shall be willing to [40] co-operate to the fullest extent.

One difficulty we have found with modernizing propositions is [60] that, in some instances, the expense involved **is** so heavy that the resulting sales are unprofitable. This [80] may not be true of your proposition, but we should have to study the matter thoroughly and to analyze [100] your setup before we could determine our ability to carry a campaign through.

We do not want you to [120] go to any expense in laying your plan before us; but, if you can explain the details by mail, or [140] economically through your representative, **we** shall be glad to give the matter every consideration.[160]

Yours truly   (162)

ROBBINS LUMBER CORPORATION

HGW:AD   President

LETTER 233

cool

ex/cep/tional

let's

main/te/nance

mod/ern/izes

out/lay

we could not

May 21, 19—

[shorthand outlines]

PRESTON STAINED SHINGLE COMPANY, Wm. M. Lloyd, Sales
Department

(Reading time: 2 min. 15 sec.)   (291)

LETTER 234

at/tracts	*[outline]*	Gree/ley	*[outline]*	
by the way	*[outline]*	mod/ern/iz/ers	*[outline]*	
car/loads	*[outline]*	pop/u/la/tion	*[outline]*	
con/test	*[outline]*	pro/por/tion	*[outline]*	
do you want	*[outline]*	Ran/kin	*[outline]*	
eight thou/sand	*[outline]*			
fig/ure	*[outline]*			

June 11, 19—

[shorthand outlines]

PRESTON STAINED SHINGLE COMPANY, Wm. M. Lloyd, Sales Department

(Reading time: 1 min. 30 sec.)   (199)

LETTER 235

adapt

an/noy

con/sum/er's

cre/a/tive

just as well

ra/dio

speak/ing

July 14, 19—

(shorthand outline)

PRESTON STAINED SHINGLE COMPANY, Wm. M. Lloyd, Sales
Department

(Reading time: 2 min.)   (250)

LETTER 236

| in/ter/fere | *(shorthand)* | to of/fer | *(shorthand)* |
| slow | *(shorthand)* | va/ca/tions | *(shorthand)* |

July 17, 19—

Preston Stained Shingle Company
177 National Street
Buffalo 5, New York

Gentlemen

We certainly are interested in your sales promotion program and are now working along lines [20] that we hope will
produce some modernizing business. This work, however,
has been slow because of summer vacations,[40] which inter-
fere materially with any campaign at this time of the year.

We shall appreciate any [60] suggestions you may have to
offer from time to time.

Yours truly   (72)

ROBBINS LUMBER CORPORATION

HGW:AD   President

LETTER 237

el/e/va/tions	*(shorthand)*	side-/wall (adj.)	*(shorthand)*
ex/te/rior	*(shorthand)*	snap/shot	*(shorthand)*
panel	*(shorthand)*	sup/ple/mented	*(shorthand)*

July 24, 19—

(shorthand outline)

PRESTON STAINED SHINGLE COMPANY, Wm. M. Lloyd, Sales
Department   (Reading time: 1 min. 40 sec.)   **(213)**

LETTER 238

cou/pled
if you will have
in/var/i/ably

re/sist
temp/ta/tion
to join

August 14, 19—

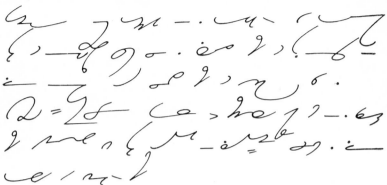

PRESTON STAINED SHINGLE COMPANY, Wm. M. Lloyd, Sales
Department

(Reading time: 1 min. 40 sec.)   **(217)**

LETTER 239

can/vass
fruit/ful

hur/ried
we shall give you

August 23, 19—

Preston Stained Shingle Company
177 National Street
Buffalo 5, New York

Gentlemen

Since receiving your letter of August 14, we have made
a rather hurried canvass of Henderson,[20] the result of which
is the enclosed list of names. While this list by no means
represents all the possibilities [40] in our territory, it does
represent what appear to be the most fruitful possibilities
at this [60] time.

We shall give you full co-operation in this trial campaign.

Yours truly   **(74)**

ROBBINS LUMBER CORPORATION

HGW:AD   President
Enc.

LETTER 240

fol/lowed   you will be given

August 28, 19—

PRESTON STAINED SHINGLE COMPANY, Wm. M. Lloyd, Sales Department

(Reading time: 35 sec.)   (76)

PART 4. BUSINESS PRACTICES

This part has been omitted from this dictation study.

PART 5. PROGRESS CHECKUP

See page 475.

DICTATION STUDY XXXIV

PART 1. BASIC SKILLS

Brief-Form Review

Directions. The following letter contains **79** different brief forms and brief-form derivatives. These are repeated until they represent about one in every two words. Some material has an even greater per cent of brief forms. If you know them well, you will not need to hesitate when you meet them. Hesitation in writing retards speed. Read the letter until you can read easily. Then make two shorthand copies of the letter.

(Reading time: 4 min. 40 sec.)   (600)

PART 2. BUSINESS INFORMATION

Vocabulary Preview

ap/proved
budg/ets
de/part/men/
  tal/ized

or/dered
pol/i/cies
re/ceipted
req/ui/si/tions

de/ter/mi/na/tion
ex/ec/u/tives
fis/cal
of the goods

sig/nif/i/cance
spec/u/la/tion
un/of/fi/cial

Budgets, Requisitions, and Purchase Orders

As *budgets, requisitions,* and *purchase orders* are familiar terms in the business office today, the student [20] stenographer should become acquainted with their significance.

In addition to other items a budget [40] includes a list of estimated needs, expressed in dollars, for a certain period of time. It usually [60] covers a fiscal year. It helps a business organization to get some idea of the amount of [80] money needed to run the business, and it serves as a basis for the determination of business policies.[100] The requirements expressed in the budget may be based on the needs of previous years, or they may be the result [120] of careful thought or speculation on the part of business executives. In a departmentalized business [140] the manager of each department is required to submit a budget for his department. The general [160] budget is prepared from these departmental budgets.

After a budget has been approved, the individual [180] departments may draw against the items listed in the budget.

Requisitions, or written requests, are used for [200] this purpose. A requisition includes the name or the number of the department or the person wishing the [220] supplies, the date of the requisition, and the kind and the quantity of materials needed. This requisition [240] is then passed along to the supply department or to the purchase department or agent. The requisition [260] is usually receipted upon the delivery of the goods to the department or the person [280] that placed the form. The use of this form acts as a check against the requesting of unnecessary items [300] and prevents the overstepping of the budget.

If the materials requested in a requisition are [320] not already in stock, but their purchase is authorized by the budget, the purchase agent prepares a special [340] form, or purchase order, for the buying of the goods. The original copy of the order is sent out from [360] the purchase department, and a carbon copy often serves as authority for the payment of the invoice.[380] The use of the purchase order prevents the unofficial buying of goods in the name of the company. Some [400] purchase orders carry a printed line to the effect that no goods will be paid for except when they have been ordered [420] on a properly signed purchase order.

(428)

PART 3. BUSINESS CORRESPONDENCE

between

TALLEY BROTHERS, INC.　　　　CARLTON TYPEWRITER EXCHANGE
2430 Olympic Street　　*and*　151 Fairmont Avenue
Seattle 7, Washington　　　　Seattle 2, Washington

and

MESSRS. COLLINGS, MARTIN & BOYDE
802 Professional Building
Seattle 2, Washington

Directions. The following letters will give you further practice in handling office-style dictation that includes corrections and insertions. Punctuation marks are not shown, as no punctuation is to be dictated in these letters. End-of-sentence punctuation, even though not dictated, can and should be written. Medial punctuation and paragraphs can be determined during transcription. Practice the vocabulary previews and the letters as previously instructed.

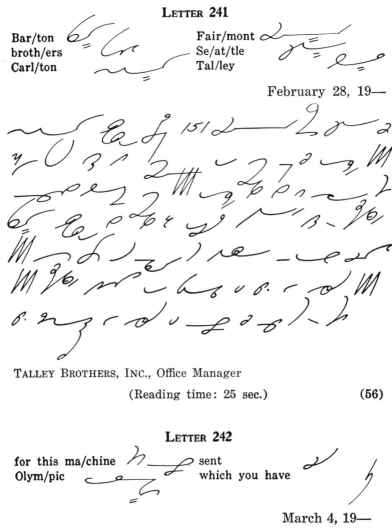

LETTER 241

Bar/ton
broth/ers
Carl/ton

Fair/mont
Se/at/tle
Tal/ley

February 28, 19—

TALLEY BROTHERS, INC., Office Manager

(Reading time: 25 sec.)   **(56)**

LETTER 242

for this ma/chine
Olym/pic

sent
which you have

March 4, 19—

Talley Brothers, Inc., 2430 Olympic Street, Seattle 7, Washington Gentlemen (pause) In your letter of February

28 you wrote (pause) make that you write that the Barton typewriter which you have was sent to you for trial (pause) We hold however your signed order (pause) make that your signed purchase order indicating a legitimate sale on our part (pause)

We therefore request that you send us (pause) change to remit for this machine accordingly Very truly yours

(57)

Dictated by Treasurer of Carlton Typewriter Exchange

LETTER 243

dis/close

March 6, 19—

TALLEY BROTHERS, INC., Office Manager

(Reading time: 40 sec.) (84)

LETTER 244

Boyde
Col/lings
for col/lec/tion

in ac/cord/ance
Mar/tin
paid

March 13, 19—

Talley Brothers, Inc., 2430 Olympic Street, Seattle 7, Washington Gentlemen Our client the Carlton Typewriter Exchange (pause) has placed in our hands (pause) an outstanding account (pause) insert for collection after hands (pause) against you for $112.50 the amount due on the purchase of a typewriter (pause)

This account should have been paid (pause) change that to as this account (pause) some weeks ago we must insist upon your remittance by return mail (pause) otherwise we shall be compelled (pause) to resort to legal proceedings (pause) insert after compelled in accordance with instructions given us Very truly yours   (81)

Collings, Martin & Boyde, Collection Department

LETTER 245

at any time
false
judg/ment

prem/ises

pur/chased
re/fused
re/peat/edly

we have been

March 15, 19—

[shorthand]

TALLEY BROTHERS, INC., Office Manager

(Reading time: 1 min. 20 sec.)   **(174)**

LETTER 246

heard   *[shorthand]*   lat/ter's   *[shorthand]*

March 25, 19—

Talley Brothers, Inc., Office Manager

(Reading time: 1 min.)   (134)

LETTER 247

con/cern/ing
mes/sen/ger
sup/plied
sur/ren/der

Wednes/day
morn/ing
we hope this

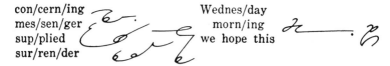

April 1, 19—

Talley Brothers, Inc., 2430 Olympic Street, Seattle 7, Washington Gentlemen (pause) After a thorough investigation of the records concerning the Barton typewriter (pause) that you received from the Carlton Typewriter Exchange on January 20 (pause) we have advised our client to accept the return of the machine and to close (pause) make that and to consider the matter closed (pause)

The Carlton Exchange has agreed to send a truck for the typewriter (pause) on next Wednesday morning (pause) We hope this arrangement will be satisfactory to you (pause) before that last sentence insert The messenger will be supplied with a properly signed receipt (pause) which will be given to you when you surrender the machine Yours very truly   (104)

Collings, Martin & Boyde, Collection Department

PART 4. BUSINESS PRACTICES

This part has been omitted from this dictation study.

PART 5. PROGRESS CHECKUP

See page 475.

DICTATION STUDY XXXV

PART 1. BASIC SKILLS

Theory Review

Directions. Confidence in your shorthand is essential for truly successful work. From time to time, you may find it necessary to record material that seems unusually difficult —an experience that tends to destroy confidence. Assuming that the speed of dictation is not too great, material will seem difficult to you if you do not know the shorthand outlines needed and/or if you do not understand the meaning of the language used. The following numbers, words, and phrases are all used in the shorthand plate in this part. Practice them until you thoroughly know the outlines for them. If you are unfamiliar with the meanings of any of the words, refer to your dictionary.

Expressions Containing Numbers

Key: $1,195,000; $2,998,000; $4,193,000; $37,528,672; $4,309,666; $41,240,070; $7,131,016; $6,145,900; $3,502,100; $993,800; 11 per cent; 25 per cent; 31 per cent; 4½ cents; 3½ cents; $2.40; $51.16; $3.80; $61.12; five years.

Do you know these words?

Key: contributed, central, decline, circumstances, paradox, transportation, reflects, reflected, resulted, efficiencies, capacity, stockholder, supplement, financial, fiscal, revenues, payloads, unprecedented, despite, curtailment, accrued, accent, executive, emphasize, benefits, operations, operating, structure, competitive, approaching, depreciation, preceding, equivalent, common, preferred.

Common Phrases

Key: to the, in the, with the, for the, when the, that the, of the, through the, that is, you will be, has been, to put, to pass, to begin, to get, in such, more than, were not, which would have, would have been, any other, during the past, last year, as a result.

Directions. Read the following shorthand plate until you can read easily at your goal rate and until you thoroughly understand the message that the letter is trying to express. Then make two shorthand copies of the plate. You may be surprised to find that so-called difficult material may seem very easy material after proper practice.

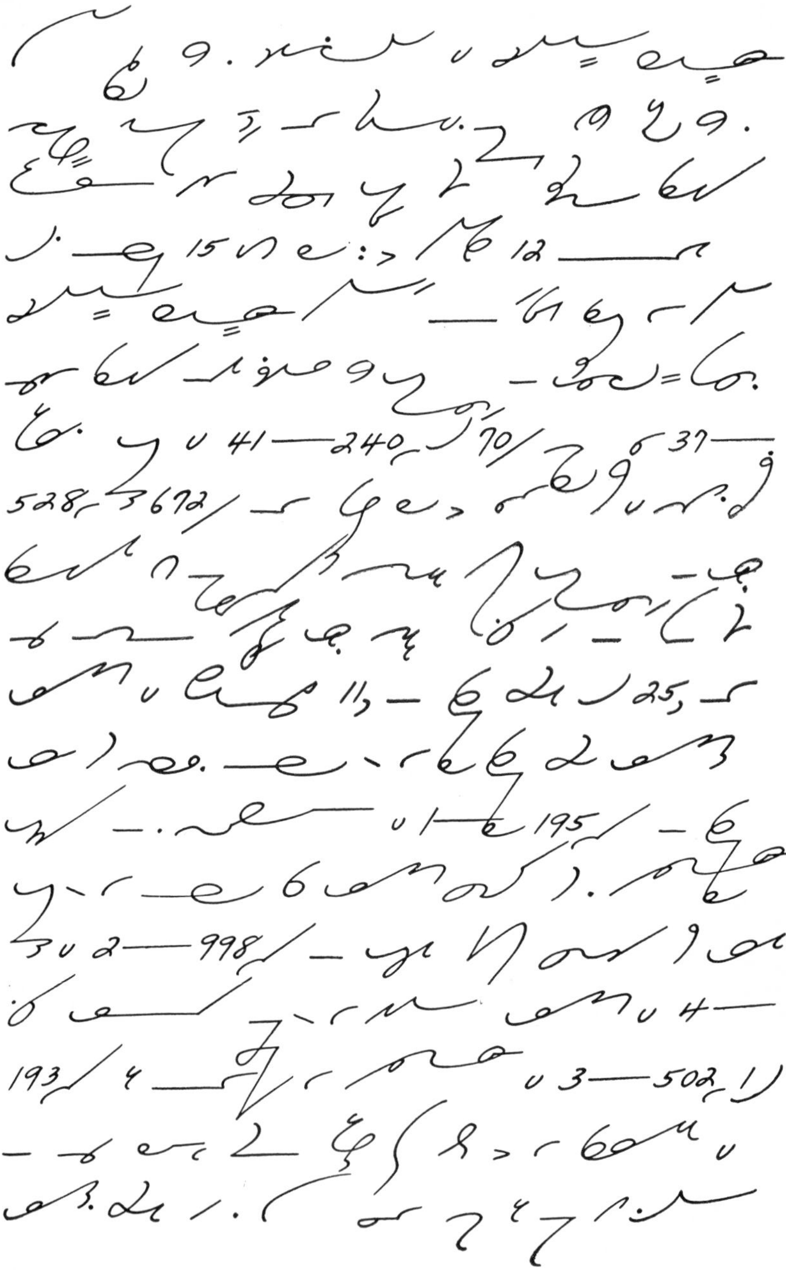

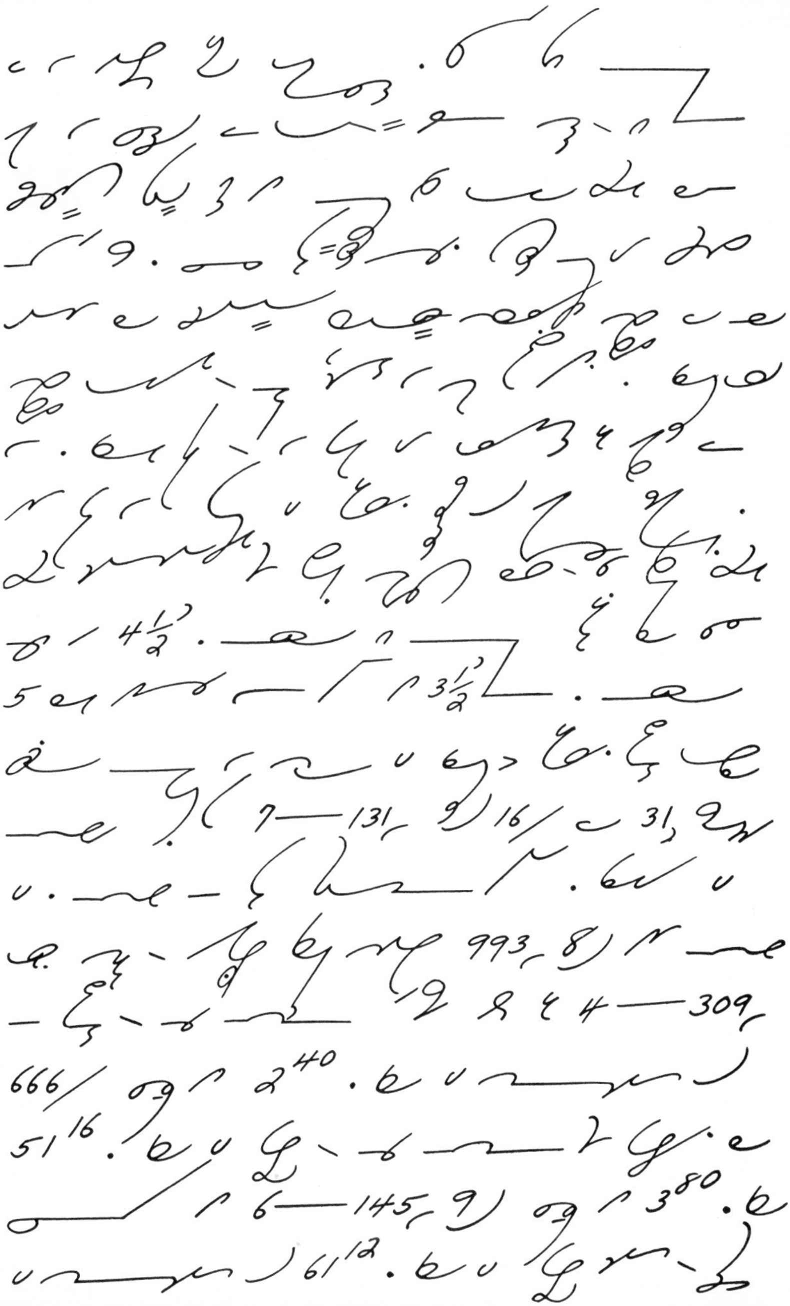

(Reading time: 4 min. 40 sec.) (600)

PART 2. BUSINESS INFORMATION

Vocabulary Preview

backs	how well
clothed	in/fe/rior
con/structed	nov/ice
dic/ta/tor's	post/script
fin/est	pre/dicts
home of/fice	re/ceive

Correspondence Opportunities

The following set of letters is an excellent example of what can be accomplished by a wide-awake [20] selling department. The first letter, an inquiry, opens the way; then the selling department starts to work. Notice [40] the action indicated in the second letter. The salesman has been requested both to write and to visit [60] the prospect, but the home office backs up the work of the salesman by well-planned sales letters.

The third letter has [80] two interesting features: First, it shows how well the home office keeps in touch with the work of the field representative; [100] second, it shows a turning of sales effort in another direction just as soon as the salesman appears [120] to be gaining his point.

Letter four continues the hammering, but introduces a new point of attack [140] in the postscript. Letter five shows that the sales effort is beginning to have effect. The salesman has closed his [160] particular sale; the letter campaign has apparently succeeded in one of its efforts; and the promise of [180] serious consideration fairly predicts a complete surrender.

Every business letter, in some way [200] or other, offers the dictator and the stenographer an excellent opportunity of serving their [220] company. The stenographer should see that the letter is clothed in the best possible dress so that the dictator's [240] message may receive the full attention and interest that it deserves. Of course, the foundation of a letter [260] must be well constructed; but a finishing touch of inferior quality may make the finest foundation [280] look like the work of a novice.   (286)

PART 3. BUSINESS CORRESPONDENCE

between

DUMONT TRANSPAR COMPANY		NU-WAY DISTRIBUTORS, INC.
52 Park Avenue	*and*	Pershing Square
New York 9, New York		Meadville, Pennsylvania

Directions. The letters in this part are arranged for timed dictation for speed building. Practice the material as previously instructed.

LETTER 248

ad/vis/a/bil/ity
blan/kets
com/forts

dis/trib/ute
Du/mont
ho/siery

mail or/der
Mead/ville

men's
Nu-Way
Trans/par

un/der/wear
ways and means
wom/en's

won/der/ing
wrap/ping

May 26, 19—

Dumont Transpar Company
52 Park Avenue
New York 9, New York

Gentlemen

In considering the advisability of wrapping our various products in Transpar, we [20] are wondering whether you can arrange to send to Meadville a man to go over this entire matter with us [40] and to suggest ways and means for the wrapping of our merchandise.

The items we have in mind are men's and women's [60] hosiery, men's shirts, men's and women's underwear, bed blankets, bed comforts, and probable additions as time goes [80] on. If we adopt Transpar wrapping, we shall use large quantities because we distribute articles throughout the [100] United States to more than a million mail-order customers.

We suggest that you set a definite time for [120] your representative to call and let us know the time.

Yours very truly   (134)

NU-WAY DISTRIBUTORS, INC.

RHE:EA   Purchasing Agent

LETTER 249

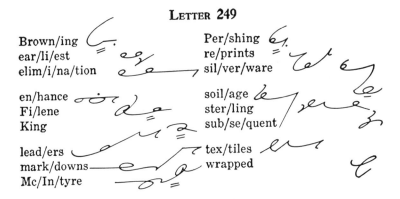

Brown/ing
ear/li/est
elim/i/na/tion

en/hance
Fi/lene
King

lead/ers
mark/downs
Mc/In/tyre

Per/shing
re/prints
sil/ver/ware

soil/age
ster/ling
sub/se/quent

tex/tiles
wrapped

June 3, 19—

[Shorthand outlines]

Dumont Transpar Company, Sales Service Section

(Reading time: 1 min. 30 sec.)   (203)

Letter 250

Chat/ham	pro/tect/ing
en/dorse/ments	pro/tec/tion
hand/bags	sev/eral hun/dred
hand/ker/chiefs	shop/wear
Horne	spot/lessly
hourly	trans/par/ent
Jo/seph	tune

DUMONT TRANSPAR COMPANY

52 PARK AVENUE — NEW YORK 9, NEW YORK

August 24, 19--

Nu-Way Distributors, Inc.
Pershing Square
Meadville, Pennsylvania

Gentlemen

We have just read one of the letters telling of your special offering of broadcloth shirts. Why not wrap these shirts in Transpar? Your customers associate this transparent protective wrapper with a product of better-than-average value.

Thirty-two million advertisements are telling the story of Transpar and are building consumer acceptance. The more Transpar you use, the greater will be your benefit from this nation-wide campaign. Thousands of your customers have read the accompanying advertisement. Many of them now give preference to shirts wrapped in Transpar.

May we suggest for your own retail stores a market test similar to the one described in a recent issue of Printers' Ink? A reprint is enclosed. Figure out just what your own extra profits would be if you tripled your sales and cut down on finger smudging and shopwear.

If you will tell us whether you will need Transpar for long-fold or short-fold shirts, quotations will be gladly furnished.

Very truly yours

DUMONT TRANSPAR COMPANY

Elmer Wagner

Sales Service Section

EW:CD

Enc. 3

P. S. Have you considered putting swatches in envelopes like the one attached?

MODEL 17—MODIFIED BLOCK LETTER WITH A POSTSCRIPT

The blocked address and signature and the ten-space indention of paragraphs represent a popular style of letter arrangement.

July 8, 19—

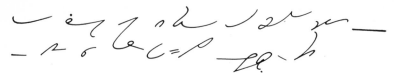

DUMONT TRANSPAR COMPANY, Sales Service Section

(Reading time: 1 min. 50 sec.)   (235)

LETTER 251

as/so/ci/ate	quo/ta/tions
broad/cloth	swatches
de/scribed	thirty-two mil/lion 32
fold	tri/pled
na/tion	wrap/per
print/ers'	

August 24, 19—

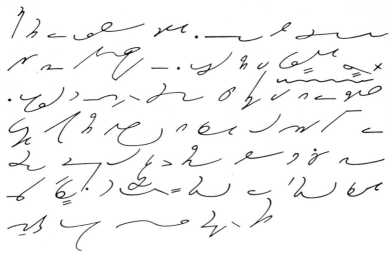

Dumont Transpar Company, Sales Service Section

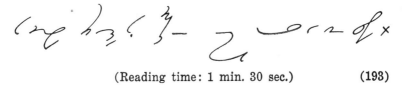

(Reading time: 1 min. 30 sec.) (193)

Letter 252

life/time   realm

mil/lion   so large as

out/put   will you give us

August 26, 19—

Dumont Transpar Company
52 Park Avenue
New York 9, New York

Gentlemen

    Following the recommendation of Mr. McIntyre, we have decided to wrap 20,000 [20] blankets in Transpar and shall place our order for this material at once. This same plan may be carried out [40] with the rest of our fall and winter output.

Your idea of a little Transpar envelope for our shirt samples [60] is new to us, but excellent. Will you give us the approximate cost of a thousand envelopes in million [80] lots. The envelopes need not be so large as the one you submitted. To bring the cost within the realm of [100] possibility, we should probably figure on envelopes of the quality of No. 300.

Serious [120] consideration will be given to your suggestion that we use Transpar for the wrapping of our Lifetime [140] broadcloth shirts.

Yours very truly   (146)

Nu-Way Distributors, Inc.

RHE:EA   Purchasing Agent

Letter 253

sa/lon   stim/u/lant

August 28, 19—

(shorthand symbols)

Dᴜᴍᴏɴᴛ Tʀᴀɴsᴘᴀʀ Cᴏᴍᴘᴀɴʏ, Sales Service Section

(Reading time: 55 sec.)   (118)

PART 4. BUSINESS PRACTICES

Vocabulary Preview

at all times	land	
at/ti/tudes	largely	
ce/les/tial	laugh	
East Hamp/ton	liz/ard	
en/vi/ron/ment	much time	
ex/trav/a/gant	neigh/bor's	
foot/stool	out/door	
fresh	pro/pose	
God's	re/al/i/ties	
grasp/ing	scru/pu/lously	
ha/bit/ual	sense	
healthy	sting/ing	
heart	strive	
I can get	su/per/la/tive	
I do not	to like	
I may be	un/chang/ing	
in/tend	uni/ver/sally	
in the past	wise enough	
in/sti/tu/tion	with him	

Employment studies show that wrong attitudes and other personality defects—not lack of skill—account for more than 85 per cent of the dismissals from jobs.

Business Attitudes

(Selected from *My Covenant*, published by The B. F. Goodrich
Company, of Akron, Ohio.)

I do not propose to live in the past. I intend to be so
busy grasping the realities of the present [20] and building
for the future that I shall not have much time left to live
over again the happy days of old.[40] What I have been is
of value and of interest to me now only as it contributes
to what I am and [60] to what I am going to be.

I fully realize that my ability to get what I go after
depends [80] largely upon being fit and looking that way. I
intend to sleep, eat, work, and play in a manner as nearly [100]
regular and habitual as possible. I expect to take as much
outdoor exercise as I can [120] get. At all times my effort will
be to feel like and look like a real representative of a sound,
healthy,[140] prosperous institution.

I do not expect to find one standard of living and one
set of customs [160] universally accepted by all men. Different
points of view and different ways of doing things are what
make the [180] world interesting. When I find myself in a
new environment, I am going to like it. I propose to [200] be
one of the home folks in any community in which I may
be established. Somewhere down in my heart I [220] may
cherish the idea that State Street in Chicago, East Hampton in Massachusetts, or Stinging Lizard in [240] Oklahoma
is "God's own footstool"; but I am going to be wise enough
to find other pieces of celestial [260] furniture anywhere I
may land.

In dealing with other persons, I will always observe the
rule of [280] unchanging courtesy. I will scrupulously avoid
extravagant claims and superlative statements. In order [300]
that I may at all times make my meaning clear to others,
I will make it a habit to seek and use the right word.[320]
Above all, I will strive to cultivate and keep fresh within
me a sense of humor that will enable me to [340] get my neighbor's point of view, to laugh with him instead of at him,
and to see myself as others see me.   (359)

PART 5. PROGRESS CHECKUP

LETTER PC-35

Collings Department Store
135 Filene Street
Chatham, New Jersey

Gentlemen

Leading retail department stores, such as Marshall Field in Chicago and Joseph Horne in Pittsburgh, have [20] been using Transpar successfully for the merchandising of their products. They find that Transpar guarantees clean [40] merchandise to customers because it gives complete protection against ordinary soilage, finger smudging,[30] and other types of shopwear with their consequent markdowns.

You know that a customer, when buying at your counters,[80] always says, "Give me a clean one." That is when Transpar comes to your assistance. Merchandise wrapped in Transpar is always [100] clean. Can't you figure just what this will save you in protection against loss?

Aside from its protective feature,[120] Transpar will serve as a business asset. Packages wrapped in Transpar are automatically classified by [140] customers as quality materials. Just as sterling in silverware suggests the best obtainable, so the [160] Transpar wrapper on your merchandise suggests quality products and points to your store as a quality store.[180]

Transpar is a transparent wrapping material that actually has a wide variety of uses. It [200] can be obtained in large sheets to serve as a wrapper for your biggest article, and it can be obtained in the [220] form of envelopes small enough to accommodate neatly your smallest samples. If you could visit our display [240] salon here in New York, you would see for yourself the thousands of products for which Transpar coverings have been [260] adopted. Here you would see little packages that could be carried in your pockets, and you would also see a [280] beautiful piano in its Transpar wrapper ready for a Christmas display.

For your own merchandise, we should like [300] to suggest a market test similar to the one described in the article enclosed with this letter. This [320] article first appeared in *Printers' Ink* and was so popular that we have had numerous requests for reprints.[340] Over and over again, merchants have expressed their interest in the experiment outlined in it. You will learn [360] from the article just how Transpar served Browning King & Company in a merchandising program that resulted [380] in an unusual increase in retail sales receipts. Won't you read the article carefully and then let [400] us work with you on a merchandising program for your own products.

If you will send us any item of your [420] stock with which you wish to experiment, we shall have it wrapped in the most attractive manner possible and [440] return it to you with suggestions for marketing. In this way, you will get, not only the assistance of a group [460] of expert artists, but also the help of a merchandising department that can offer you the accumulated [480] experience of years spent in successfully guiding the merchandising plans of retail department [500] stores.

While we are awaiting an answer from you, we are asking Mr. McIntyre, our representative in [520] your territory, to call on you to explain our service and to tell you some of the possibilities in [540] the use of Transpar. He will show you samples of clear and colored Transpar; he will be in position to quote prices [560] on many of your requirements; and he will suggest ways in which we can aid you with retail problems. We know that [580] you will find Mr. McIntyre's visit worth every minute you are willing to grant him.

Very truly yours [600]   (600)

DUMONT TRANSPAR COMPANY

EW:CD   Sales Service Section
Enc.

DICTATION STUDY XXXVI

PART 1. BASIC SKILLS

Theory Review

Directions. Wherever possible, the stenographer in business should learn to write in shorthand the names of cities that appear in her dictation. Of course, it is natural to suppose that the larger cities may appear oftener in dictation than the smaller cities and towns; but, in certain lines of business, the smaller cities prove to be the more important. For that reason, instead of practicing long lists of city names, the stenographer should make a list of those she uses most often and should then develop satisfactory shorthand outlines for them.

All the following outlines appear in the letter in this part. Read the outlines until you can read them easily without the aid of the key. Then write each outline at least once.

Names of Cities

Key: Boston, New York, Washington, Philadelphia, Vancouver, Seattle, Portland, San Francisco, Los Angeles, San Diego, London, Honolulu

Disjoined Prefixes and Suffixes

Key: interior, interested, interchange, international, internationally, intercontinental, transoceanic, steamship, theatrical

539

Do you know these words?

Key: inaugurated, expansion, competitive, maximum, promotional, profitable, extensive, vigorous, solicit, solicitation, carriers, neutral, certified, packaged, participating, activities, representation, scheduled, charter, forecasting, divert, generate, constitute, accomplishment, compete, mileage, presages, negotiations, furtherance, aggressively, domestic, multiplication

Directions. All the foregoing words appear in the following letter. Read the letter until you can read easily at your goal rate. Then make two shorthand copies of the letter.

(Reading time: 4 min. 40 sec.)   (600)

PART 2. BUSINESS INFORMATION

Vocabulary Preview

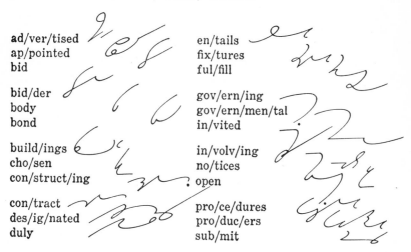

ad/ver/tised	en/tails
ap/pointed	fix/tures
bid	ful/fill
bid/der	gov/ern/ing
body	gov/ern/men/tal
bond	in/vited
build/ings	in/volv/ing
cho/sen	no/tices
con/struct/ing	open
con/tract	pro/ce/dures
des/ig/nated	pro/duc/ers
duly	sub/mit

Sealed Bids

Whenever any governmental department wishes to place an order that entails an expenditure greater [20] than a certain minimum set by the governing body, that order must be open to public bid. If [40] the order concerns equipment, furniture and fixtures, or supplies, some existing standard is usually [60] chosen to serve as a basis of comparison. Specifications are then drawn up to show exactly the [80] needs. The better-known manufacturers or producers of the materials are invited by letter to [100] submit bids on the requirements set forth in the specifications. Meanwhile newspaper notices give other [120] interested persons or businesses a chance to submit bids.

Sealed bids must be delivered to some designated [140] office on or before the advertised closing date. The bids are opened by a duly appointed body; [160] the offerings of each bidder are considered; and a satisfactory bidder is selected on the basis [180] of the quality of his goods, the fairness of his price, and his ability to fulfill the contract. The [200] order is not always given to the lowest bidder. Sometimes, when all bids appear too high, the requirements are [220] open to new bids.

In the case of an order involving a large sum of money, the successful bidder may [240] be required to furnish a bond to ensure his delivery of goods of the proper quality and at the [260] right time.

Business houses frequently follow similar procedures in buying materials and in constructing [280] buildings. They are not required, however, by law to do so, as is the case with governmental departments.[300]   (300)

PART 3. BUSINESS CORRESPONDENCE

between

DEPARTMENT OF PUBLIC SAFETY		BUILDING EQUIPMENT COMPANY
Rockville		245 Austin Street
Tennessee	*and*	Knoxville 3, Tennessee

Directions. The letters of this part have been arranged for office-style dictation. Letters 254 and 256 show the type of dictation you may expect, and Letters 255 and 257 show how the stenographer may have recorded the dictation.

When words, sentences, or paragraphs are to be deleted, or canceled, from the notes, it is just as well to indicate that fact as you have already been indicating other changes to be made in the notes. It often happens that a dictator may tell you to strike out a sentence and then immediately decide to leave the sentence as it is. Any special effort to mark out the material will only necessitate its rewriting in such a case. Of course, it will be necessary in either case to edit your notes very carefully before starting to transcribe. You should be sure that you know what changes are to be made in the letters and that the letters make sense and express the thoughts that your dictator intended.

When letters are to be sent by special delivery, registered, or air mail, you should make note of that fact at the beginning of the letter. Longhand abbreviations (Sp. Del., Reg., Air), as shown in Letter 257, will serve this purpose. "Register this letter and request a return receipt" may be indi-

cated by the longhand abbreviations *Reg. Ret. Rec.* (See
Letter 289, page 610.) A similar practice should be used to
indicate extra carbon copies or special carbon copy instructions, as 4CC, 6CC, or CC Mr. Miller. It is a serious office
mistake to fail to follow instructions.

LETTER **254**

as/sem/ble	ply/wood
au/di/to/rium	re/placed
ex/cep/tion/ally	Rock/ville
fas/ten	safety
guar/an/teed	sales/man's
in ev/ery re/spect	your/selves

*In order to indicate clearly the insertion dictated at the
end of this letter, label the insertion with a capital A and,
if time permits, use a similar label at the point at which
the insertion is to be made. This practice is illustrated in
the shorthand plates of Letters 272 and 274, pages 578 and
581.*

August 15, 19—

Department of Public Safety, Rockville, Tennessee Gentlemen (pause) This is to confirm the price (pause) make
that our salesman's price of $3.10 f.o.b. Rockville on audi-
torium chair No. 140 paragraph

This chair is of exceptionally good value (pause) is well
made in every respect and is guaranteed to give satisfaction
(pause) entire satisfaction for a period of twenty years
paragraph (pause)

If you wish us to fasten (pause) make that assemble
and fasten the chairs to the floor (pause) there will be an
additional charge of 30 cents a chair (pause) If however
you expect to take care of the installation yourselves
(pause) we shall furnish a blueprint showing the proper
layout (pause) Shipment can be made in approximately
twenty-five days paragraph

The installation of chair No. 140 (pause) Strike out chair will give you an auditorium of which Rockville may well be proud Very truly yours (pause) Read the second paragraph of that letter (pause) All right. Add to the end of the second paragraph (pause) If the plywood back or seat should split or open of its own accord during this time the chair will be replaced free of charge to you.   (161)

Dictated by Sales Manager of Building Equipment Company.

Letter 255

Aus/tin
bid/ders

bids
Knox/ville

August 29, 19—

CITY OF ROCKVILLE, Director of Public Safety
(Reading time: 50 sec.)   (115)

LETTER 256

de/fect   sturdy
in/sures   will place

September 2, 19—

Department of Public Safety, Rockville, Tennessee Gentlemen Thank you for your letter of August 29 giving us an opportunity of bidding on the chair equipment for the new auditorium in the Community Center of your city (pause) We are submitting our bid today paragraph

Some time within the next few days our representative will place on display one of our No. 140 chairs (pause) make that will place on display in the office of your city manager one of our No. 140 chairs (pause) We know that these chairs will serve you well and that you will be highly pleased with them (pause) Strike out that last sentence May we again direct your attention to the sturdy construction of these chairs and to our twenty-year guarantee that insures you against any possible defect paragraph

We shall appreciate the privilege of serving you Very truly yours   (117)

Dictated by Sales Manager of Building Equipment Company.

LETTER 257

awarded   with the least
orig/i/nally   pos/si/ble de/lay
to a great   you have been able
  ex/tent

In the last paragraph of this letter, the dictator indicated a deletion and then changed his mind by saying, "Strike that out. No that's all right. Leave it." The stenographer simply crossed out the "strikeout" that she had already indicated.

September 24, 19—

CITY OF ROCKVILLE, Director of Public Safety

(Reading time: 40 sec.)   (95)

LETTER 258

af/fected	she would
an/swered	un/cer/tain/ties

October 6, 19—

[shorthand notation]

CITY OF ROCKVILLE, Director of Public Safety

(Reading time: 1 min.) (131)

LETTER 259

next week *[shorthand]* this or/der *[shorthand]*

October 7, 19—

Department of Public Safety
Rockville
Tennessee

Gentlemen

A telegram received from our factory this morning indicates that the chairs for your new auditorium [20] will be shipped by the first of next week.

The delay in shipping this order has been caused by circumstances [40] beyond our control; but we are requesting the factory to rush the chairs to you and not to hold them for [60] a carload shipment.

We believe that the shipment will be started at the time specified.

Very truly yours   (79)

BUILDING EQUIPMENT COMPANY

DS:JH   Sales Manager

LETTER 260

fac/tors
fur/ther/more
have not yet

in/a/bil/ity
read/ily

October 10, 19—

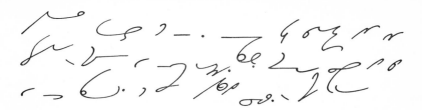

CITY OF ROCKVILLE, Director of Public Safety

(Reading time: 1 min. 10 sec.)   (160)

LETTER 261

desks	in our let/ter	
else	rushed	
fault	Sun/days	
hol/i/days	10,000 pounds	

October 15, 19—

Department of Public Safety
Rockville
Tennessee

Gentlemen

We have made every effort to effect prompt delivery of your order and have just learned that [20] the chairs left our factory at Grand Rapids on October 11. As the chairs weigh approximately [40] 10,000 pounds, about two-thirds carload capacity, they are being sent to Knoxville along with some desks that were [60] used to complete the carload. The car should reach us by Tuesday, October 18; and the chairs will then be rushed to [80] Rockville. We shall be able to complete our installation by Friday, October 21.

Of course, we regret [100] any inconvenience that you have experienced; however, we feel that we are not entirely at fault [120] in this matter. In our letter of August 15, we wrote that shipment, not delivery, could be made in [140] approximately twenty-five days. Such a time limit usually means actual working days, exclusive of [160] Sundays and holidays, after the receipt of an order. Allowing three days for the order to go through our [180] factory routine, you will find that we have kept our promise fairly well.

This explanation does not greatly improve [200] your situation; so we are planning to give you an installation so satisfactory that your pride [220] in a beautiful auditorium will help you to forget all else except the fact that the attractive chairs [240] were furnished by the Building Equipment Company, of Knoxville.

Very truly yours   (255)

BUILDING EQUIPMENT COMPANY

DS:JH   Sales Manager

PART 4. BUSINESS PRACTICES

Vocabulary Preview

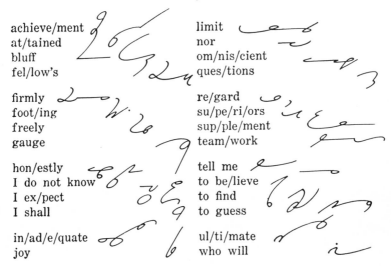

achieve/ment	limit
at/tained	nor
bluff	om/nis/cient
fel/low's	ques/tions
firmly	re/gard
foot/ing	su/pe/ri/ors
freely	sup/ple/ment
gauge	team/work
hon/estly	tell me
I do not know	to be/lieve
I ex/pect	to find
I shall	to guess
in/ad/e/quate	ul/ti/mate
joy	who will

Business Attitudes
(Continued)

I have sufficient confidence in myself not to judge myself by the other fellow's standards nor to limit [20] myself by his measure of achievement. I expect to meet many men who will try to gauge my future by their [40] past and will tell me that what I hope for can never be attained; but I have faith enough in myself to believe [60] that I can get an ultimate return that will justify any sacrifice made to secure it.

I [80] appreciate the necessity for organization and leadership in any concern. Discipline, with me, will [100] always be a thing to be taken for granted. I shall regard the opportunity to take orders from others [120] as a step toward fitting me for the larger responsibility that I am seeking up ahead. From [140] contact with my superiors, I expect to learn that it is always better to ask a man to do something [160] than it is to order him to do it.

I believe in the possibility of clean, organized effort. I [180] know what teamwork can accomplish. I am here with heart, head, and hands, to get the most and to give the most. I expect [200] to find some pleasure in everything I do and aim to make the joy of achievement increase with each step that [220] I take on the way in which I have set my feet.

I expect never to be omniscient. I realize that I [240] may occasionally be put in a position where I must supplement what I am sure of with a bluff about [260] something that I have to guess at. In this connection, however, I firmly believe that no man is ever [280] justified in bluffing twice on the same subject. The only wise course to follow is the one that will lead me to [300] an immediate, thorough investigation of the question or questions concerning which my knowledge is hazy [320] or inadequate. If I am dealing with any matters of vital importance and get into a [340] position where I am not sure of my footing, I intend to admit freely and honestly that I do not know,[360] and to set myself at once to finding out.   (368)

PART 5. PROGRESS CHECKUP

See page 475.

DICTATION STUDY XXXVII

PART 1. BASIC SKILLS

Theory Review

Directions. As you have already learned, not all dictation consists of easy, short letters. Sometimes the dictation will prove highly technical, and many strange words will be included in the material. Sometimes, although individual words may be easily understood, the manner in which the words are combined may make the material appear exceedingly difficult. In the letter in this part, many reasonably common words are combined in a discussion of stocks and dividends. If you have had bookkeeping, the subject matter may appear understandable; if you haven't, you needn't be frightened. Whenever you meet so-called difficult material, either in print or in shorthand plate, read it carefully several times, refer to the dictionary for any unfamiliar words, and you may be surprised how clear and easy the material will become.

Proceed in the usual manner.

Do you know these words?

Key: distribution, distributed, transfer, paragraphs, control, instrument, facilities, accumulation, cumulative, stockholder, wholehearted, accord, financial, dynamic

Key: inception, expenditures, hangars, totally, adequate, inadequate, remodeled, airway, communications, substantial, historic, conservative, dividend, proportion, tendered, conversion, converted, retention, redemption, accrued, management, disappeared, defray

Directions. All the foregoing words are used in the letter that follows. If you have practiced the words properly, the letter should be easy for you. Read the shorthand plate until you understand the message that it carries and until you can easily reach your goal rate. Then make two shorthand copies of it.

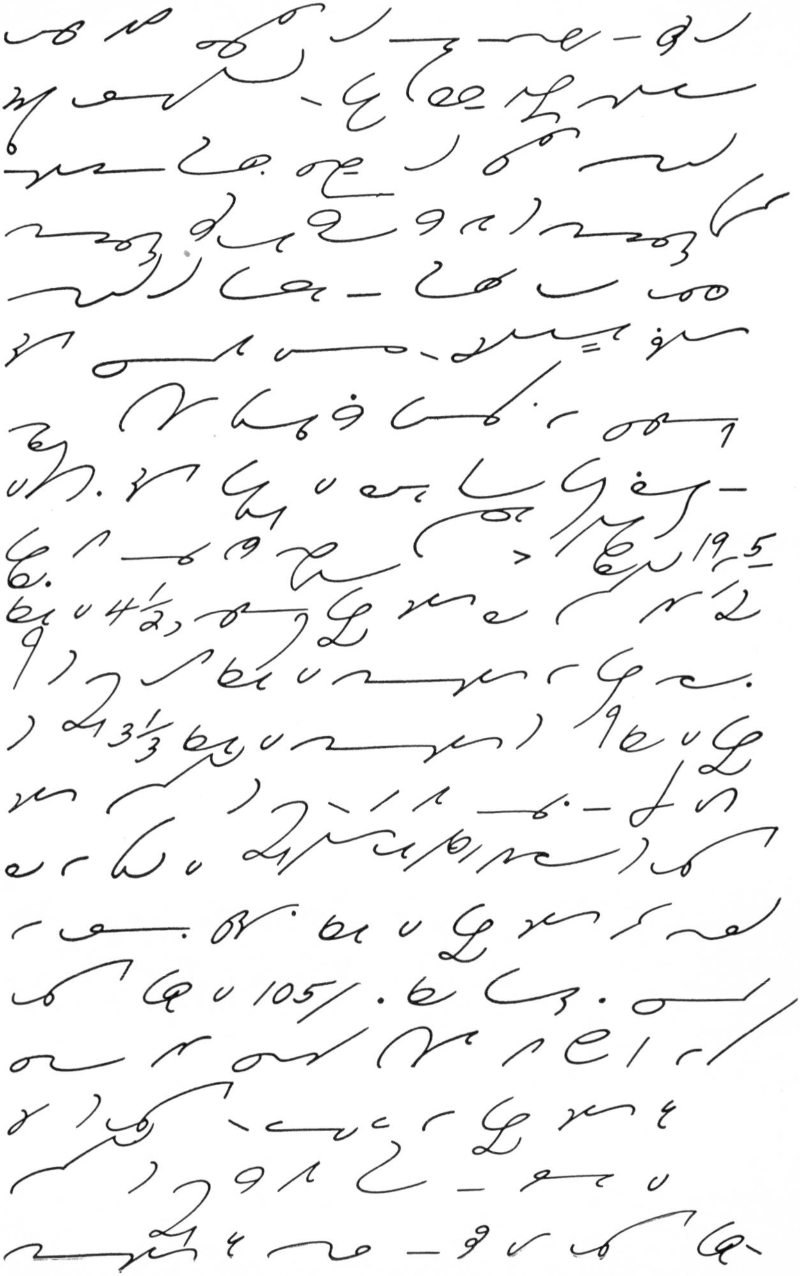

(shorthand)

$850,557\tfrac{2}{3}$

$39,150$

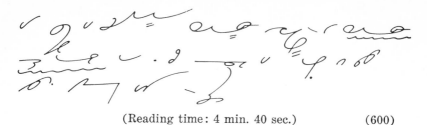

(Reading time: 4 min. 40 sec.)   (600)

PART 2. BUSINESS INFORMATION

Vocabulary Preview

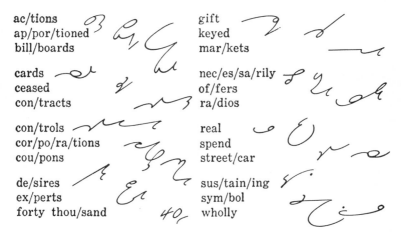

ac/tions	gift	
ap/por/tioned	keyed	
bill/boards	mar/kets	
cards	nec/es/sa/rily	
ceased	of/fers	
con/tracts	ra/dios	
con/trols	real	
cor/po/ra/tions	spend	
cou/pons	street/car	
de/sires	sus/tain/ing	
ex/perts	sym/bol	
forty thou/sand	wholly	

Advertising

Advertising is almost wholly responsible for the development of some markets for certain products;[20] and it is, in a large measure, the sustaining factor in markets already developed. Many a product,[40] made popular by advertising, has died when advertising ceased. A glance through newspapers of ten years ago[60] will show examples of this fact. Consequently, fields of advertising have continued to grow until the[80] supervision of advertising and the placing of contracts demand the services of experts. Newspapers and[100] magazines, billboards, streetcar cards, radios, and electric signs represent fields so extensive that corporations [120] find it necessary to employ advertising agencies to conduct their national advertising [140] campaigns.

The amount of money to be spent in advertising by a large company is usually [160] determined by the gross sales, either real or estimated. The total amount to be spent is then apportioned [180] among the various fields, not necessarily in equal sums. Tests are used from time to time to determine [200] the "pulling power" of any particular type of advertising. In newspapers and magazines the [220] advertisements are often keyed; i.e., the address in an advertisement is given a department number, a [240] room number, or some other identifying symbol, to indicate the source of information to be used [260] when persons write to the company. Sometimes coupons to be clipped act as keys. Other advertisements consist of [280] gift offers and trick announcements.

The advertising agencies that have charge of placing the many contracts required [300] usually work on the basis of cost plus a percentage. In other words, they are paid a percentage [320] of what they spend.

The extent to which advertising controls the actions and the desires of the people of this [340] country may be at least indicated by the fact that one company received forty thousand letters in answer [360] to a single radio announcement.

(368)

PART 3. BUSINESS CORRESPONDENCE
between

GOLDEN GATE BINDING COMPANY
978 Fairmont Street
San Francisco 4, California

and

NORTHWEST ADVERTISING CORPORATION
504 McGill Street
Carson City, Nevada

Directions. The letters in this part are arranged for timed dictation for speed building. Practice the material as previously instructed.

Golden Gate Binding Company

978 FAIRMONT STREET ● SAN FRANCISCO 4, CALIFORNIA

November 30, 19--

Northwest Advertising Corporation
504 McGill Street
Carson City, Nevada

Attention of Mr. Wall

Gentlemen

Pyramid Sales Portfolio

The enclosed folder gives a full description
of this novel selling device, about which you ask
in your letter of November 27; and the accompanying
price list shows illustrations of three standard
sizes that are carried in stock ready for immediate
delivery.

You write in your letter that these portfolios
are to be used in connection with displaying streetcar advertising. In the past we have built numerous
oblong portfolios and have found them extremely satisfactory. Just now, however, we have on file no
samples of the size you need; and, not knowing how
many displays your portfolio must contain or how
many portfolios you may require, we cannot estimate
a price on this material.

If you will send us your specifications, we
shall gladly quote prices that we know will be attractive.

Very truly yours

GOLDEN GATE BINDING COMPANY

S. D. Leonard
Secretary

SDL:EZ

Enc. 2

MODEL 18—MODIFIED BLOCK LETTER CONTAINING AN ATTENTION LINE AND A SUBJECT LINE

Although there are several acceptable arrangements of the attention line
and of the subject line of a letter, the arrangement shown here is practical and widely used.

LETTER 262

branch /   port/fo/lio /
golden /   pyr/a/mid
north/west   so/lic/i/ta/tion

of this na/ture

November 27, 19—

Golden Gate Binding Company
978 Fairmont Street
San Francisco 4, California

Gentlemen

Please send us descriptive matter and prices on your Pyramid sales portfolio.

Representatives [20] of the Northwest Advertising Corporation need something of this nature for convenience in presenting [40] streetcar-advertising facts during solicitation.

A prompt answer may lead to some good business.

Very truly [60] yours   (61)

NORTHWEST ADVERTISING CORPORATION

GOW:MC   Branch Manager

LETTER 263

built /   Ne/vada
Car/son   novel
il/lus/tra/tions   ob/long

in con/nec/tion   port/fo/lios
Mc/Gill

November 30, 19—

504

GOLDEN GATE BINDING COMPANY, Secretary

(Reading time: 1 min. 15 sec.)   (166)

LETTER 264

large enough   sev/eral weeks ago

January 5, 19—

Golden Gate Binding Company
978 Fairmont Street
San Francisco 4, California

Gentlemen

With regard to our correspondence of several weeks ago
on Pyramid sales portfolios,[20] it is possible that we may

need from 100 to 250 portfolios large enough to hold [40] 15 or 20 streetcar cards, the dimensions of which are 11 by 21 inches.

Please quote us your [60] best prices on these specifications.

Very truly yours   (71)

NORTHWEST ADVERTISING CORPORATION

GOW :MC   Branch Manager

LETTER 265

binder

January 12, 19—

GOLDEN GATE BINDING COMPANY, Secretary

(Reading time: 40 sec.)   (90)

LETTER 266

De/troit
en/amel
erected

flat
loop
loose-leaf

proofs
re/in/forced
serv/ice/able

snap
un/fas/ten

January 23, 19—

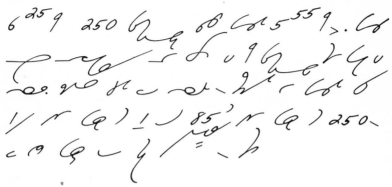

GOLDEN GATE BINDING COMPANY, Secretary

(Reading time: 1 min. 50 sec.)   (241)

LETTER 267

at this time
cre/ated
de/pend/ing

to us
writes

February 6, 19—

Golden Gate Binding Company
978 Fairmont Street
San Francisco 4, California

Gentlemen

The sample card portfolio that you prepared and sent to us has been submitted to our home office [20] in Seattle. It created a very favorable impression there. Our general sales manager,[40] however, writes that a maximum of fifty portfolios would be all we could use at this time, the order [60] depending upon the price.

Will you please quote prices on quantities of forty, forty-five, and fifty.

Very [80] truly yours   (82)

NORTHWEST ADVERTISING CORPORATION

GOW:MC   Branch Manager

Letter 268

iden/ti/cal
pre/vi/ously

rings

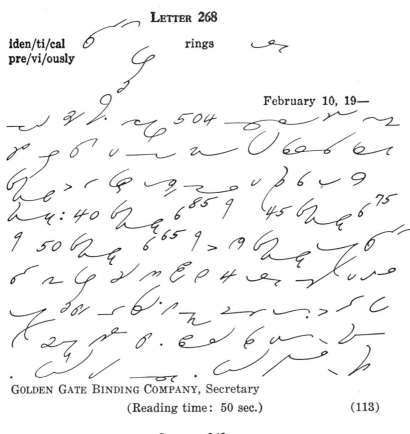

February 10, 19—

Golden Gate Binding Company, Secretary

(Reading time: 50 sec.)　　　　(113)

Letter 269

if these can be
Kilby

re/dis/tri/bu/tion
Trent

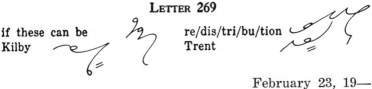

February 23, 19—

Golden Gate Binding Company
978 Fairmont Street
San Francisco 4, California

Gentlemen

Please enter our order for fifty portfolios, like the sample recently submitted, at your [20] quotation of $6.65 each. This order should be distributed as follows:

15 to Northwest [40] Advertising Corporation
1219 Kilby Building
Portland 2, Oregon

20 to Northwest [60] Advertising Corporation
612 Trent Building
Seattle 3, Washington

15 to Northwest Advertising [80] Corporation
504 McGill Street
Carson City, Nevada

If these can be sent in separate [100] boxes or containers for redistribution, that method will be helpful to us.

The invoice for this [120] equipment should be mailed to our Seattle office.

Very truly yours   (132)

Northwest Advertising Corporation

GOW:MC   Branch Manager

Letter 270

di/vided   two weeks
parts

February 28, 19—

GOLDEN GATE BINDING COMPANY, Secretary

(Reading time: 1 min.)   (134)

PART 4. BUSINESS PRACTICES

This part is omitted from this dictation study.

PART 5. PROGRESS CHECKUP

See page 475.

DICTATION STUDY XXXVIII

PART 1. BASIC SKILLS

Theory Review

Directions. The ability to prepare an accurate transcript of shorthand notes is an essential qualification for successful stenographic work. It is important, therefore, to understand what the dictator is trying to say in the message that he is dictating. If your transcript does not make sense to you, it is not likely to make sense to others. Be sure that you understand what you type. If necessary, ask questions until you are sure that you know what you are doing. The letter in this part contains many words that you have met before, but it is possible that many of the words are new to you. If you are not sure about them, use your dictionary.

Proceed in the usual manner.

Expressions Containing Numbers

Key: 8,000; 18,000; $10,000,000; $45,000,000; $60,000,000; $100,000,000

Do you know these words?

Key: parallel, constructing, restrictions, instrument, electronic, uninterrupted, regularity, utility, facilities, flexibility, accordingly, technical, governmental, domestic, leadership

And these words?

Key: twofold, forecast, fulfilled, personnel, pursuing, adventure, complimentary, personalized, projecting, conscious, spacious, pressurized, cabins, niceties, annals, segment, expanded, explore, differentials, nonstop, economic, deadweight, accelerate, elimination, feasible, renaissance, practicable, procedures, adaptation, devices, radio, frequencies, communications, systems, navigational, terminal, research, sacrifice, perfection, techniques, fuse, objectives, spur

Directions. All the foregoing words are used in the following letter. Read the shorthand plate until you understand the message that it carries and until you can easily reach your reading rate; then make two shorthand copies of it.

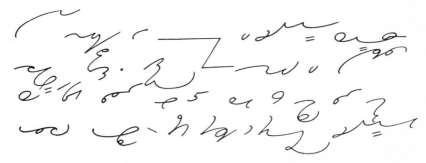

[Page of shorthand notation — not transcribable as text]

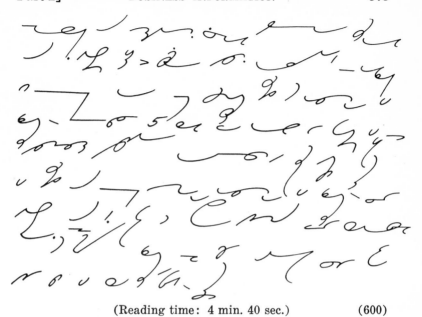

(Reading time: 4 min. 40 sec.) (600)

PART 2. BUSINESS INFORMATION

Vocabulary Preview

a dol/lar		he was	
an/gle		hea/then	
ashamed		life/long	
asleep		lis/tened	
awoke		log/i/cal	
be/nighted		or/a/tor	
breth/ren		painted	
deep/est		pas/sion	
el/o/quent		plead/ing	
fa/vor/ably		pro/ceeded	
fif/teen cents		re/solved	
five dol/lars		se/quence	
from my		speaker	
ful/filled		stole	
gos/pel		story	

sup/ple/ments　　　　　　　　twenty dol/lars
too many　　　　　　　　　　usher
to say　　　　　　　　　　　wrought

Follow-Up Letters

The follow-up letter is usually one of a series in which each letter supplements the preceding [20] one, the entire series having been planned to accomplish some definite purpose. The series may be used to [40] stimulate the future patronage of customers; it may be used to collect money; or it may be intended [60] to close a sale.

Although the purpose of a follow-up series may be fulfilled before the entire series has [80] been used, a well-planned series should show a logical sequence. Too many follow-up letters do nothing except follow [100] up. If a series is to be worth the effort and cost, it must be written so that each succeeding letter [120] presents new thoughts, or gives a new angle on previously used points, or makes suggestions that will cause the reader [140] to act favorably.

There is no set rule as to the number of letters required for a follow-up series.[160] The best plan is to end the series when its purpose has been accomplished. This idea is well illustrated [180] by the following story from Mark Twain:

"He was the most eloquent orator I ever listened to. He [200] painted the benighted condition of the heathen so clearly that my deepest passion was aroused. I resolved to [220] break a lifelong habit and contribute a dollar to teach the gospel to my benighted brethren. As the speaker [240] proceeded, I decided to make it five dollars, and then ten. Finally, I knew it to be my duty [260] to give to the cause all the cash I had with me—twenty dollars. The pleading of the orator wrought upon me [280] still further and I decided not only to give all the cash I had with me, but to borrow twenty dollars [300] from my friend who sat at my side. That was the time to take up the collection. However, the speaker proceeded [320] and I finally dropped asleep. When the usher awoke me with the collection plate, I not only refused to [340] contribute but am ashamed to say that I actually stole fifteen cents!"　　　　　　　　　　　　(353)

PART 3.　BUSINESS CORRESPONDENCE

between

EVERLASTING BLACKBOARD COMPANY
729 East Ohio Street
Chicago 10, Illinois

and

MR. CHARLES YANCEY, **Architect**
Trade Exchange Building
Casper, Wyoming

Directions. The following letters are arranged for office-style dictation and give practice in handling long insertions and "cut-in" margins. Not all changes or corrections are clearly indicated by a dictator, and it is therefore very important for the stenographer to be constantly on the alert to distinguish between instructions and actual dictated material.

Sometimes, several insertions are dictated after a letter is completed. In order to place the insertions properly, full instructions should be recorded; each insertion should be labeled by an alphabetic letter, as instructed in Letter 254 on page 545; and, if time permits, the same label should be placed in the notes at the point at which the insertion is to be made. This practice is illustrated in Letters 272 and 274.

Occasionally, in order to obtain a more attractive arrangement or greater emphasis of material on the typewritten page, certain parts of some letters or other transcription material should be typed with "cut-in" margins. Many employers leave questions of arrangement to the typist, but some dictators prefer to give instructions or, at least, suggestions. Experience shows that, over and over again, typists forget to set margins for "cut-in" paragraphs and to reset them after the "cut-in" material has been completed. It is wise, therefore, to use some signal in shorthand notes as a reminder that "cut-in" margins are to be used. Such a signal is shown in Letters 271, 272, and 274. The parallel lines may be drawn whenever convenient. If the lines are drawn during dictation, no other record of the instructions need be made; otherwise, it might be advisable to record the instructions of the dictator and to draw the lines at some time prior to actual transcription. It is not particularly important that the lines be accurately drawn, as the nature of the material should tell the typist at what points the changes in arrangement are to be made. The instructions may be given at any time—before, after, or during the dictation—and concern arrangement rather than content.

In this part, shorthand plates show letters with changes, corrections, and special instructions.

LETTER 271

af/firm/a/tive		ev/er/last/ing
ar/chi/tect		ex/am/ine
black/board		Lock/ett
com/men/su/		pro/duced
rate		sci/en/tif/i/cally
de/pend/able		Yan/cey

Notice how the stenographer, when instructed to use "cut-in" margins for a certain part of this letter, indicates that fact by the use of vertical lines through that part of her notes. The employer simply said, "Cut in the margins here." Model 7, page 157, and Model 12, page 367, show applications of "cut-in" margins.

March 2, 19—

EVERLASTING BLACKBOARD COMPANY, Sales Manager

(Reading time: 1 min. 30 sec.)   (194)

LETTER 272

as/sist		pur/chaser	
backed		risk	
basic		side-step (v.)	
cen/tury		spe/cial/ists	
chem/ists		squarely	
de/pend/a/bil/ity		un/der/ly/ing	
for/mu/las		un/tried	

March 9, 19—

EVERLASTING BLACKBOARD COMPANY, Sales Manager

(Reading time: 2 min.)   (260)

LETTER 273

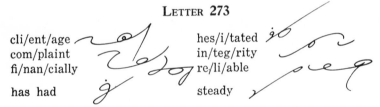

cli/ent/age	hes/i/tated
com/plaint	in/teg/rity
fi/nan/cially	re/li/able
has had	steady

In the last paragraph of this letter, the dictator indi-cated a deletion and then changed his mind by saying, "Strike that out. No, leave it." The stenographer simply crossed out the "strike out" that she had already indicated.

March 16, 19—

EVERLASTING BLACKBOARD COMPANY, Sales Manager

(Reading time: 1 min. 10 sec.)   (154)

LETTER 274

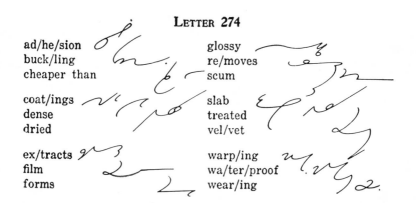

ad/he/sion
buck/ling
cheaper than

coat/ings
dense
dried

ex/tracts
film
forms

glossy
re/moves
scum

slab
treated
vel/vet

warp/ing
wa/ter/proof
wear/ing

March 23, 19—

Everlasting Blackboard Company, Sales Manager

(Reading time: 1 min. 45 sec.)   (229)

Letter 275

facts   slight/est

men/tal

March 30, 19—

EVERLASTING BLACKBOARD COMPANY, Sales Manager

(Reading time: 50 sec.)   (112)

PART 4. BUSINESS PRACTICES

Vocabulary Preview

af/fairs	pro/cras/ti/na/tion
afraid	rea/son/ably
com/pre/hen/sive	rid
dives	stronger
door	su/per/fi/cial
in/com/plete	thor/ough/ness
lis/tener	to ask
of my	who gets
out/sid/ers	who knows

Business Attitudes
(Concluded)

I am not going to be afraid to ask questions. It will be my constant effort, however, to make those questions [20] intelligent. I do not propose to be satisfied with a superficial or incomplete grasp of any [40] important subject.

In whatever I do, I know that the results obtained will depend upon the thoroughness [60] and the accuracy of my method of operation. I have had the occasion to observe that the [80] man who gets the best results is the man who knows where to find things when he wants them. It is my plan to keep reasonably [100] comprehensive notes and records in connection with the most important phases of my work.

I have already [120] learned that the only way to get rid of a day's work is to do it. I intend to clean up every [140] day's work as I come to it. So far as it is possible to do so, I expect to have a place for everything.[160] I know that when procrastination comes in at the door efficiency dives out through the window. Even [180] for my own simple personal affairs, I intend to keep some sort of follow-up system.

I intend to be [200] a good listener, but to have little or nothing to say when it comes to discussing with outsiders the details [220] of my business. There are many occasions when it is better to hear everything and see everything,[240] but to say nothing.

I expect to grow bigger and stronger every day; and, as the best help to getting [260] things, I intend never to lose my fresh, genuine interest in everything that goes on in the world.   (279)

PART 5. PROGRESS CHECKUP

See page 475.

DICTATION STUDY XXXIX

PART 1. BASIC SKILLS

Theory Review

Directions. High-speed shorthand writing requires the use of shorthand forms abbreviated to a greater extent than the outlines ordinarily used in office dictation. For those interested in developing high shorthand speed, there are numerous special vocabularies available. The stenographer who does not need high speed is advised to confine his or her efforts to the standard forms already learned. In many lines of business, however, there are phrases and expressions that can be written with short, easy outlines. If such expressions are used often, the stenographer would do well to prepare short forms for them. If the expressions are not used often, the longer forms are recommended, as the burden on the memory hardly justifies the use of the shorter forms. The following illustrations will show the short and the long forms of several expressions that appear in the shorthand plate in this part. You will note, however, that the shorthand plate uses only the longer form for each expression.

	Long	Short
Reconstruction Finance Corporation		
automatic pilots		
air pressure		

Directions. Read the following words until you can read them easily without the aid of the key. Then write each word at least once in shorthand.

585

Expressions Containing Numbers

Key: 300's; $90,000; 2,000 pounds; 6,000 pounds; 5,000 feet; 16,000 feet; $9,000,000; $20,000,000

Do you know these words?

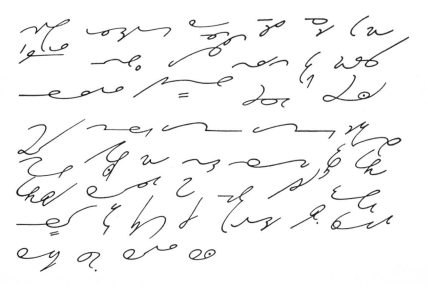

Key: contributory, reconstruction, electronic, intercity, intrastate, postwar, short-term, increasingly, automatic, critical, population, subordinated, military, Douglas, finance, valiant, converted, commercial, augment, augmentation, stopgap, completion, depreciation, war, cruise, cargo, spacious, pressure, pressurized, altitudes, upper, noticeable, descent, sleepers, Martin, option, justify, jet, thrust, deicing, pilots, aloft, accompanying, artery, area

Directions. All the foregoing words are used in the following shorthand plate. If you have practiced the words carefully, you should be able to read the plate easily. Read

the shorthand plate until you can reach your reading goal.
Then make two shorthand copies of it.

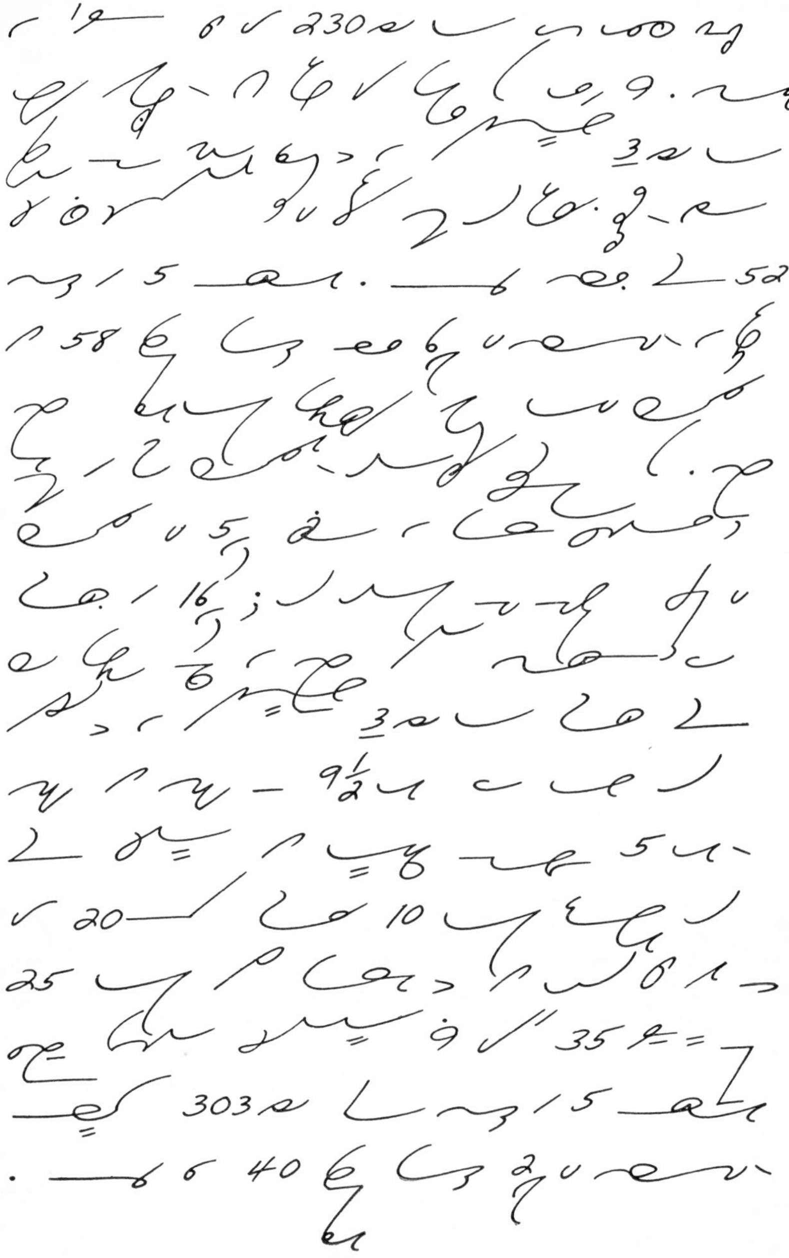

[Shorthand outlines]

(Reading time: 4 min. 40 sec.)   **(600)**

PART 2. BUSINESS INFORMATION

Vocabulary Preview

ap/pli/cant
be/fore/hand
can/di/date

in/flu/ence
in/ter/view
out/line

cau/tion
del/i/cate
dig/nity

po/si/tions
re/fine/ment
re/stricted

ex/er/cised
gram/mat/i/cal
im/ag/i/nary

same/ness
un/im/por/tant
un/ruled

The Letter of Application

There are two factors to be considered in connection with applications for positions: the letter of [20] application and the personal interview. Each of these requires particular attention.

In some cases the [40] preliminary application is a letter of application. The letter of application should be [60] free from both mechanical and grammatical errors. It should give all necessary information and, above [80] all, should reach the prospective employer's desk without delay. In order to avoid delay in mailing the [100] letter, one who intends to apply for a position at some future time may do well to write several letters [120] of application for imaginary positions and to use one of these letters, with necessary [140] changes, as a model for the real application when opportunity arises.

White unruled paper of [160] letterhead size is preferred for the letter of application because it carries a mark of dignity and [180] refinement. Sometimes, however, a paper of a delicate, attractive color has an advantage over [200] white. In the hundreds of letters received daily by a business, there is a great deal of sameness in general [220] appearance. Colored stationery is outstanding and may therefore give an applicant the benefit of an [240] early reading—a time element that often bears weight. Caution and good judgment, however, should be exercised [260] in the use of colored stationery; otherwise the very advantage desired may be lost.

Copies of letters [280] of recommendation are often used, but good references have a stronger influence. As letters of [300] recommendation are usually open letters, the information given is restricted. If references [320] are to be used, the applicant should obtain permission from the persons concerned. This matter, too, can be [340] attended to beforehand and need not delay the letter of application.

The personal data sheet is [360] a simple statement in outline form of the qualifications of the candidate for a position. It should [380] include the name, the address, and the age of the applicant; it should describe briefly the general education [400] and the commercial training; and it should list any positions previously held. Apparently unimportant [420] work, if mentioned on the data sheet, may sometimes influence the employer. The personal data sheet [440] is not always necessary; but when it is used, the information should not be repeated in the letter [460] of application.   (464)

PART 3. BUSINESS CORRESPONDENCE

between

SOUTHERN LUGGAGE COMPANY   MR. RAYMOND C. COLEMAN
809 Brook Street   *and*   778 Maymont Avenue
Tampa 3, Florida   Nashville 12, Tennessee

and

POWER EQUIPMENT CORPORATION
110 Jefferson Street
Birmingham 4, Alabama

and

AMERICAN HARVESTER COMPANY
219 Lafayette Street
Lexington 2, Kentucky

and

THE CENTRAL NOVELTY COMPANY
578 Grand Avenue
Cleveland 5, Ohio

Directions. The letters in this part are arranged for timed dictation for speed building. Practice the material as previously instructed.

LETTER 276

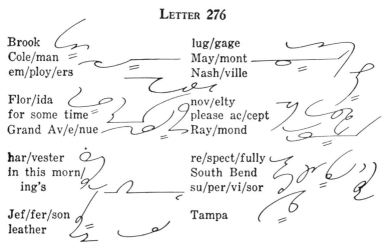

Brook	lug/gage
Cole/man	May/mont
em/ploy/ers	Nash/ville
Flor/ida	nov/elty
for some time	please ac/cept
Grand Av/e/nue	Ray/mond
har/vester	re/spect/fully
in this morn/	South Bend
ing's	su/per/vi/sor
Jef/fer/son	Tampa
leather	

778 Maymont Avenue
Nashville 12, Tennessee
January 16, 19—

Southern Luggage Company
809 Brook Street
Tampa 3, Florida

Gentlemen

Please accept this letter as my application for the position advertised in this morning's issue [20] of *Progress*.

I am twenty-seven years old and have had two years of college training. I have been connected [40] with sales work for the past seven years. Two years of this time have been spent on the road.

Although I have never sold leather [60] goods, my selling experience has been varied. My employers have been

Power Equipment Corporation [80]
110 Jefferson Street
Birmingham 4, Alabama

American Harvester Company
219 [100] Lafayette Street
Lexington 2, Kentucky

The Central Novelty Company
578 [120] Grand Avenue
Cleveland 5, Ohio

I have also worked for some time as district supervisor for [140] the Newton Magazine Distributors, of South Bend, Indiana. To all of these companies I respectfully [160] refer you for information about my ability and my character.

I am confident that, if [180] given a chance, I can produce good results for you.

Yours very truly   (193)

Raymond C. Coleman

LETTER 277

check/ing   will re/ceive
one or two weeks

January 19, 19—

SOUTHERN LUGGAGE COMPANY, Sales Manager

(Reading time: 25 sec.)   (60)

LETTER 278

we shall   *(shorthand)*   your name   *(shorthand)*

January 19, 19—

(shorthand outlines)

SOUTHERN LUGGAGE COMPANY, Sales Manager

(Reading time: 35 sec.)   (75)

(Similar letters were also sent to the American Harvester Company and The Central Novelty Company.)

LETTER 279

at the time   *(shorthand)*   re/signed   *(shorthand)*
com/mis/sion   *(shorthand)*   staff   *(shorthand)*
ef/forts   we can/not as/sist   *(shorthand)*

January 22, 19—

Southern Luggage Company
809 Brook Street
Tampa 3, Florida

Gentlemen

Mr. Raymond C. Coleman, about whom you ask, was employed on our sales staff about five years ago.[20] Reference to his sales records shows practically no business resulting from his efforts. As he was paid on [40] a commission basis, he consequently resigned his position after a few weeks.

Our investigation [60] of his character at the time of employment proved satisfactory, and we have no reason to believe he [80] has changed.

We regret that we cannot assist you further in this matter.

Very truly yours   (97)

POWER EQUIPMENT CORPORATION

LEW:AC   Sales Department

LETTER 280

by this com/pany   let us hear
if you can send us   from you
in our files   per/son/nel

January 22, 19—

Southern Luggage Company
809 Brook Street
Tampa 3, Florida

Gentlemen

We have no record of Mr. Raymond C. Coleman in our files.

If you can send us Mr. Coleman's [20] address in Lexington at the time he was employed by this company, we may be able to give you some [40] information about him.

If we can help you in any other way, let us hear from you.

Yours very truly   (59)

AMERICAN HARVESTER COMPANY

RHP:MM   Personnel Manager

LETTER 281

de/parted
first week
for less than

from him
that would be

January 23, 19—

Southern Luggage Company
809 Brook Street
Tampa 3, Florida

Gentlemen

About two years ago Mr. Raymond C. Coleman was in our employ for less than one week. During [20] his first week of employment he came into the office, left his price book and samples, and departed without saying [40] anything to anyone. We received no explanation from him later.

We therefore feel that we are in [60] no position to give you any opinion as to his ability or other personal qualifications [80]—at least, no opinion that would be satisfactory to you.

Very truly yours   (96)

THE CENTRAL NOVELTY COMPANY

SDW:GA   Sales Supervisor

LETTER 282

of our
to you

we thank you for the

January 25, 19—

SOUTHERN LUGGAGE COMPANY, Sales Manager

(Reading time: 30 sec.) (66)

PART 4. BUSINESS PRACTICES

This part is omitted from this dictation study.

PART 5. PROGRESS CHECKUP

See page 475.

DICTATION STUDY XL

PART 1. BASIC SKILLS

Brief-Form Review

Directions. The article in this part contains 92 brief forms and brief-form derivatives. The three letters that are quoted are famous letters in English literature. All were written before the invention of the typewriter. The language of these letters is somewhat different from the language of ordinary present-day business letters, but even so-called difficult language has a fairly high per cent of brief forms. Some of the following words, all of which appear in the article, may be new to you in shorthand.

Do you know these words?

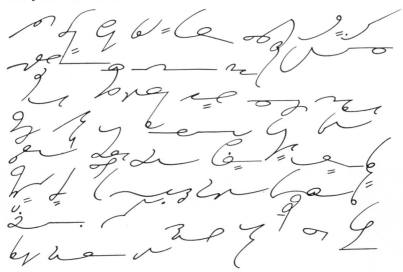

Key: diction, Benjamin, approached, point-blank, inadvisable, empty-handed, courtliness, naivete, uncommon, unknown, gentleman, civilities, stranger, Thomas, namesake, counsels, affectionate, disposition, reverence, murmur, Providence, portal, eternal, ineffable, farewell, Abraham, Lincoln, Bixby, Adjutant-General, gloriously, fruitless, beguile, overwhelming, tendering, consolation, republic, assuage, anguish, bereavement, cherished, solemn, altar

Directions. All the foregoing words are used in the following article. If you have practiced the words carefully, the reading of the article should be easy for you. When you are able to reach your reading goal, make two shorthand copies of the shorthand plate.

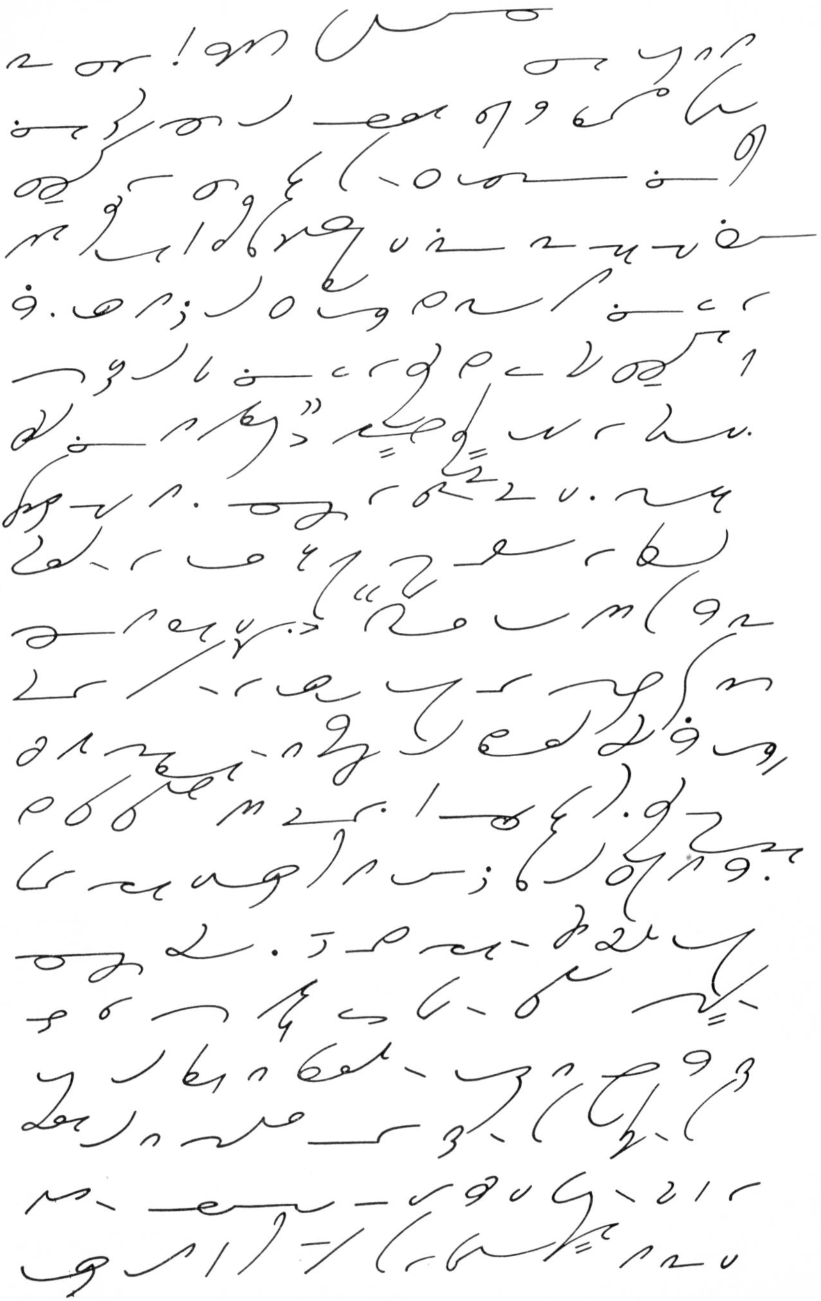

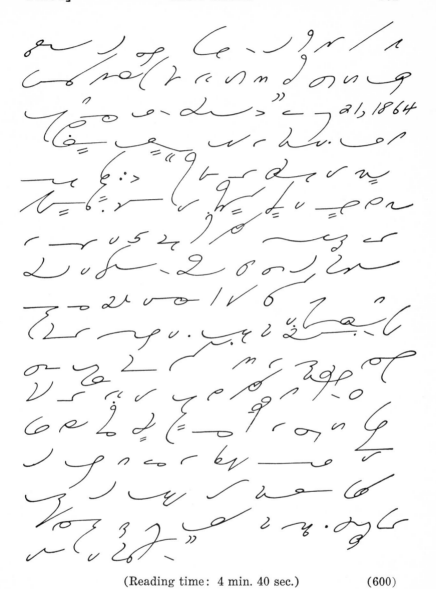

(Reading time: 4 min. 40 sec.)   (600)

(Adapted from *Making Business Letters Produce*, published by the Dennison Manufacturing Company, of Framingham, Massachusetts)

PART 2. BUSINESS INFORMATION

Vocabulary Preview

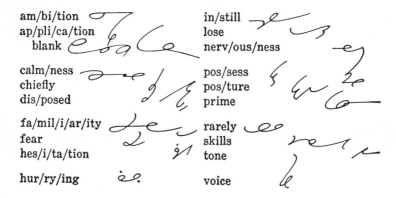

am/bi/tion

ap/pli/ca/tion

blank

calm/ness

chiefly

dis/posed

fa/mil/i/ar/ity

fear

hes/i/ta/tion

hur/ry/ing

in/still

lose

nerv/ous/ness

pos/sess

pos/ture

prime

rarely

skills

tone

voice

The Personal Interview

The personal interview is usually accompanied by a feeling of nervousness or excitement [20] on the part of the applicant for the position. To prevent such a feeling, it is of prime importance that [40] whatever skills the applicant may possess should be such as to instill confidence. There is no more satisfying [60] realization than to know a thing and to know that you know it. The ability to take good dictation [80] and to transcribe it rapidly and accurately, a thorough familiarity with the proper method [100] of using carbon paper, and a systematic manner of handling the notebook should leave no fear in the [120] mind of the inexperienced applicant. Additional confidence will arise from the ability to [140] use well several makes of typewriters.

The early part of the personal application may be devoted [160] to conversation between the employer and the applicant. At this time style of dress, posture and carriage, tone [180] of voice, and other personal qualities are important. Interest, ambition, calmness, judgment—all play their [200] part. If the interview creates a favorable impression, the applicant may be asked to take a short test.[220] This will probably consist chiefly of dictation and transcription. The applicant should have her own notebook

During the personal application for a job, the applicant's style of dress, posture, carriage, and tone of voice play an important part. Interested, intelligent attention to the interview should be apparent in manner and expression.

and [240] pencil ready. This test should be taken with the feeling that there is everything to gain and nothing to lose.[260] Employers rarely try to embarrass applicants or to make them feel ill at ease. The completed test should be [280] disposed of according to directions, and the applicant should then quietly await the report.

At some time [300] during the interview, the applicant may be asked to fill out an application blank. This blank is often used,[320] not so much to obtain information from the applicant, as to give the employer a chance to observe the [340] applicant's manner of working. With this in mind, the applicant should go directly to work, but without hurrying; [360] she should read the blank carefully and calmly; and she should write without hesitation. A personal data [380]

603

sheet helps materially in supplying information for an application blank.

If no report about [400] the position is received within two weeks, that fact does not necessarily indicate that the position [420] has been filled. A letter asking whether a decision has been made may well be sent to the business office. Such [440] a letter sometimes results in prompt action. (448)

PART 3. BUSINESS CORRESPONDENCE

between

SOUTHERN LUGGAGE COMPANY		MR. ROBERT E. PENNINGTON
809 Brook Street	*and*	1142 Monument Avenue
Tampa 3, Florida		Macon, Georgia

and

ATLANTA STORE FIXTURE COMPANY
117 Trotter Street
Atlanta 2, Georgia

and

MR. ARTHUR L. TOWNSEND, President
Arthur Townsend & Company
Macon, Georgia

Directions. The letters in this part are arranged for office-style dictation. Prepare the vocabulary previews and the letters as previously instructed.

Letter 283 is a letter of application. Such letters are usually not dictated to stenographers. In this case, however, the writer, already employed, makes use of stenographic help in applying for another position.

LETTER 283

ac/cred/ited		en/abled	
Ar/thur		fix/ture	
as/so/ci/ated		friendly	
ath/let/ics		Geor/gia	
At/lanta		grad/u/ate	
de/sign/ing		health	

into this mat/ter ⟋⟍⟍⟍ Pen/ning/ton ⟍⟍⟍
jour/nal ⟍⟍⟍ Town/send ⟍⟍⟍
Ma/con ⟍⟍ Trot/ter ⟍⟍⟍
of this year ⟍ ⟍⟍⟍ trunks ⟍⟍⟍

August 14, 19—

Miss White, may I ask you to help me with a letter of application. I want it set up on blank paper. Use my home address (1142 Monument Avenue, Macon, Georgia) in the heading and type only my name in the signature. The letter goes to Southern Luggage Company, 809 Brook Street, Tampa, Florida Gentlemen (pause) Your advertisement in the Macon *Journal* interests me because conditions in the store-fixture industry require me to leave my present position on September 1 of this year (pause) paragraph

For nearly five years (pause) change that to For the past five years I have been associated (pause) with the sales department of the Atlanta Store Fixture Company period (pause) In addition to selling comma (pause) my duties have been concerned with the planning (pause) and designing of stores period (pause) This work as you know (pause) means more than simply furnishing fixtures made of wood and glass period (pause) It includes (pause) strike that out (pause) It means a knowledge of merchandising (pause) period (pause) It requires an understanding of the basic principles (pause) connected with the selling of varied stocks period (pause) I have never (pause) make that Although I have never sold trunks or bags comma (pause) my suggestions have enabled many merchants to increase their luggage sales period (pause) Such friendly contacts should enable me (pause) to give you a good volume of business (pause) in this territory paragraph

I am a high-school graduate (pause) and a graduate of an accredited private commercial school period (pause) My health is good comma and I have (pause) No just a minute strike that out make it I am twenty-eight years old and single period (pause) now let's go on (pause) My health is good comma and I have always taken (pause) an active interest in athletics period (pause) For information about my ability and character comma (pause) I refer you (pause) make that I am permitted to refer you to Atlanta Store Fixture Company 117 Trotter Street Atlanta 2 Georgia (pause) and Mr. Arthur L. Townsend President Arthur Townsend & Company Macon Georgia (pause) set those up in address form (pause) new paragraph

If you think it worth while (pause) change that (pause) If you should deem it advisable comma (pause) I could make arrangements to see you in Tampa so that (pause) for the purpose of going into this matter in detail Yours very truly   (276)

Dictated by Robert E. Pennington

LETTER 284

Car/o/lina   ter/ri/to/ries
in/con/ven/ient

August 16, 19—

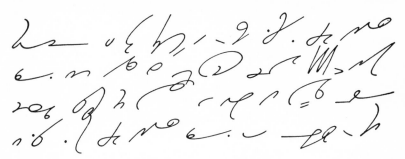

SOUTHERN LUGGAGE COMPANY, Sales Manager

(Reading time: 1 min.)   (129)

LETTER 285

con/fi/den/tial   em/ployee

August 16, 19—

SOUTHERN LUGGAGE COMPANY, Sales Manager

(Reading time: 30 sec.)   (74)

LETTER 286

home life *(shorthand outline)*   re/spon/si/bil/i/ties *(shorthand outline)*

August 16, 19—

(shorthand outlines)

SOUTHERN LUGGAGE COMPANY, Sales Manager

(Reading time: 50 sec.) **(116)**

LETTER 287

ev/ery/where *(shorthand outline)*   re/duc/ing *(shorthand outline)*
pleas/ing *(shorthand outline)*

August 17, 19—

Southern Luggage Company, 809 Brook Street, Tampa 3, Florida Gentlemen (pause) Mr. Robert E. Pennington has been in the employ of this company (pause) for the past five years (pause) We are turning off (pause) change that (pause) We are reducing our forces everywhere semicolon (pause) and we find it necessary to drop some old employees (pause) comma (pause) no matter how much we may regret (pause) we may personally regret to do so paragraph (pause)

Mr. Pennington has a pleasing personality (pause) and will make a good (pause) will make an acceptable representative for you (pause) He is a hard worker semicolon (pause) he takes his work seriously semicolon (pause) and he gives his employer full co-operation (pause) We should like to see you give him a chance Yours very truly (100)

Dictated by General Manager of Atlanta Store Fixture Company

LETTER 288

cit/i/zens	in/ti/mately	
friends	oc/ca/sions	
he will make	re/spected	
I have known	ties	

August 18, 19—

Southern Luggage Company, 809 Brook Street, Tampa 3, Florida Gentlemen (pause) I have known Mr. Robert E. Pennington and his family intimately for a number of (pause) for many years They are respected citizens of our community (pause) paragraph

For the past five or six years (pause) Robert has been on the sales staff (pause) of the Atlanta Store Fixture Company Throughout (pause) no During this time he has been able to serve us on numerous occasions semicolon (pause) and we have found him helpful reliable and capable (pause) reverse the order of those words (pause) period He is quick to make friends (pause) and he keeps them after he makes them paragraph (pause)

I am confident that he will make a good man for you (pause) and I know of no family responsibilities (pause) make that family ties that would prevent his giving your work (pause) the attention that it deserves Yours very truly   (115)

Dictated by Arthur L. Townsend, President, Arthur Townsend & Company

LETTER 289

Car/o/li/nas   or/der blanks
each month   states

August 21, 19—

<small>Southern Luggage Company, Sales Manager</small>

(Reading time: 1 min. 15 sec.)   **(171)**

PART 4. BUSINESS PRACTICES

This part is omitted from this dictation study.

PART 5. PROGRESS CHECKUP

Directions. The following letter is arranged for office-style dictation. It will give you practice in handling the various types of corrections and changes that you have learned to indicate in previous dictation studies, and it will serve as a further checkup on your ability to handle your shorthand vocabulary. When all changes and corrections have been made in this letter, the final letter will be **exactly** 600 standard words in length.

Letter PC-40

Mr. Robert E. Wilson Principal, Macon Technical High School Atlanta 14, Georgia Dear Mr. Wilson You have asked me to give some suggestions to your graduates (pause) change that to your graduating class (pause) on how to find the most desirable type of employment (pause) I can say very little that you have not already said to your students over and over again semicolon but maybe I can say the same thing in a different way paragraph

At first (pause) make that at the outset comma we must assume that jobs are either easy to find or hard to find period (pause) If jobs are easy to find comma there is no problem about which to be concerned semicolon but if jobs are not so numerous comma a definite campaign may be needed (pause) change that to necessary period I shall consider only the latter situation paragraph

It seems essential that applicants for jobs should know Strike out (pause) It seems essential for applicants for jobs to know very definitely what they can do period The school may be (pause) Strike out (pause) It may be the responsibility of the school to help them establish a basis for a decision of this kind (pause) At any rate comma the standards should be based on the ability of the worker (pause) make that should be based comma not on so many words a minute in either shorthand or typewriting comma but on the ability of the worker to produce a given amount of work in a specified time (pause) Standards of this sort can be arrived at by studying the local employment market (pause) If we may believe that the student has been prepared for a position in the local market comma then we may proceed to the next step (pause) make that steps paragraph

Some time ago comma the director of the personnel bureau of a large college in New York published a set of rules on how to get a job (pause) I am permitted to use these rules comma although I shall not quote (pause) attempt to quote exactly (pause) This director wrote colon paragraph

1. Keep clearly in mind that the basis (pause) insert the fact after mind (pause) that the basis of all success in any field is hard work (pause) Above all comma the work should be interesting paragraph

2. Keep clearly in mind the fact that there is a good job waiting for you (pause) There are several employers who will be able to use your services paragraph

3. Consider yourself as something to sell (pause) Regard your appearance your personality your education your character and your skills as products to be sold in a highly

There is always one best job for every person, one best way of getting that person into the job, and one best way of advancing in that job. Promotional opportunity should be an important consideration in choosing a job.

(pause) make that in an open and highly competitive market paragraph

4. Remember that the first rule of selling (pause) make that good selling is to know the article that you are selling paragraph

5. Don't accept the first job that is offered to you (pause) unless it is what you want semicolon unless you feel that you can be happy in it semicolon and (pause) unless you are confident that you can do the job well paragraph

6. Match up your ability desire and interest with the needs of the business and the employer (pause) Strike out that paragraph (pause) No leave it as it is paragraph

7. Don't give your prospective employer the hard job of finding out (pause) insert during the first minute of your interview after employer (pause) finding out for himself just what you can do (pause) or just what you want period This will (pause) Strike out (pause) This makes it easy for him to give you a courteous refusal by saying comma quote Leave your name and address (pause) We will call you if we need you period and end of quote paragraph

8. Show the prospective employer that you have made a careful analysis of yourself semicolon that you understand his needs semicolon and that he needs you as much as you want the job paragraph

Cut your margins in on those numbered paragraphs (pause) Maybe you had better read them to me (pause) Just a minute (pause) read No. 2 again (pause) All right (pause) Add as a final sentence to No. 2 Find them and sell yourself to them (pause)

Now read on (pause) Hold it a moment (pause) After No. 4 add a new No. 5 (pause) Remember that you must know thoroughly the market for the article that you are selling (pause) Renumber the items.

Read on (pause) Just a minute (pause) After old No. 5 add a new number (pause) Don't say that you will take any job at any salary under any working conditions (pause) You had better check your numbering very carefully (pause) I believe you have ten items now.

Let's go on with the letter (pause) Start a new paragraph

These rules have expressed more clearly than I could the solution to the job-getting problem comma and they can be equally applied to the problem of promotion on the job (pause) All I need add as a final word to your students is quote Success to you exclamation and end of quote Very sincerely yours (600)

Dictated by Arthur L. Townsend, President, Arthur Townsend & Company

The finished letter should appear as follows:

Mr. Robert E. Wilson, Principal
Macon Technical High School
Atlanta 14, Georgia

Dear Mr. Wilson

You have asked me to give some suggestions to your graduating class on how to find the most [20] desirable type of employment. I can say very little that you have not already said to your students [40] over and over again; but maybe I can say the same thing in a different way.

At the outset, we must [60] assume that jobs are either easy to find or hard to find. If jobs are easy to find, there is no problem [80] about which to be concerned; but if jobs are not so numerous, a definite campaign may be necessary. I [100] shall consider only the latter situation.

It seems essential for applicants for jobs to know very [120] definitely what they can do. It may be the responsibility of the school to help them establish a [140] basis for a decision of this kind. At any rate, the standards should be based, not on so many words a [160] minute in either shorthand or typewriting, but on the ability of the worker to produce a given [180] amount of work in a specified time. Standards of this sort can be arrived at by studying the local employment [200] market. If we may believe that the student has been prepared for a position in the local market, then [220] we may proceed to the next steps.

Some time ago, the director of the personnel bureau of a large college [240] in New York published a set of rules on how to get a job. I am permitted to use these rules, although I shall [260] not attempt to quote exactly. This director wrote:

1. Keep clearly in mind the fact that the basis of all [280] success in any field is hard work. Above all, the work should be interesting.

2. Keep clearly in mind the fact that [300] there is a good job waiting for you. There are several employers who will be able to use your services. [320] Find them and sell yourself to them.

3. Consider yourself as something to sell. Regard your appearance, your [340] personality, your education, your character, and your skills as products to be sold in an open and highly [360] competitive market.

4. Remember that the first rule of good selling is to know the article that you are [380] selling.

5. Remember that you must know thoroughly the market for the article that you are selling.

6. Don't [400] accept the first job that is offered to you unless it is what you want; unless you feel that you can be happy [420] in it; and unless you are confident that you can do the job well.

7. Don't say that you will take any job [440] at any salary, under any working conditions.

8. Match up your ability, desire, and interest, [460] with the needs of the business and the employer.

9. Don't give your prospective employer during the first [480] minute of your interview the hard job of finding out for himself just what you can do or just what you want. This makes [500] it easy for him to give you a courteous refusal by saying, "Leave your name and address. We will call you [520] if we need you."

10. Show the prospective employer that you have made a careful analysis of yourself; that [540] you understand his needs; and that he needs you as much as you want the job.

These rules have expressed more clearly than I [560] could the solution to the job-getting problem, and they can be equally applied to the problem of promotion [580] on the job. All I need add as a final word to your students is "Success to you!"

Very sincerely yours [600]   (600)

Arthur L. Townsend, President
ARTHUR TOWNSEND & COMPANY

HW

GENERAL VOCABULARY

This vocabulary contains a complete alphabetic list of the words and the phrases for which the shorthand outlines have been given in the dictation studies. The numbers following the words and the phrases indicate the pages on which the shorthand outlines may be found. Wherever more than one number follows a word or phrase, it means that the shorthand outline for that word or phrase appears in more than one type of situation; for instance, such an outline may appear in a vocabulary preview, and it may also appear in a review of theory principles.

In order to make this vocabulary as useful as possible, many of the commoner phrases have been cross-referenced. Thus, "has been able" will be found under "has"; but it will also be found under "able."

A

abey/ance, 499
abil/ity, 78, 279
able, 427
able, has been, 468
able, have been, 274
able, should be, 97
able, we may be, 425
able, we shall be, 434, 456
able, we should be, 114, 434
able, you have been, 547
able, you may be, 245
able, you will be, 319
aboard, 479
about, 35
about the, 32
about this, 433
about which, 433
above, 162
above the, 335
above them, 85
Abra/ham, 598
abroad, 479
ab/sence, 11
ab/sent, 218
ab/so/lutely, 270
ab/sorb, 497
ab/surd, 325
abun/dant, 104
ac/cel/er/ate, 570
ac/cent, 523
ac/cept, 61, 62
ac/cept, please, 592
ac/cept/able, 218
ac/cept/ance, 121
ac/cept/ances, 452

ac/cepted, 224
ac/cept/ing, 20
ac/com/mo/date, 198
ac/com/mo/da/tion, 80
ac/com/mo/da/tions, 483
ac/com/pa/nied, 224
ac/com/pa/ny/ing, 230, 586
ac/com/plish, 428
ac/com/plished, 368
ac/com/plishes, 297
ac/com/plish/ment, 490, 540
ac/cord, 554
ac/cord, in, 178
ac/cord/ance, in, 518
ac/corded, 67
ac/cord/ingly, 80, 569
ac/count, 5
ac/count, on this, 114
ac/count/ing de/part/-ment, 423
ac/counts, 328
ac/cred/ited, 604
ac/crued, 523, 555
ac/cu/mu/late, 473
ac/cu/mu/lated, 387, 425
ac/cu/mu/la/tion, 473, 554
ac/cu/racy, 495
ac/cu/rate, 75
ac/cu/rately, 318
ac/cus/tomed, 96
achieve/ment, 552
achieves, 490
ac/knowl/edge, 125
ac/knowl/edg/ing, 348

ac/knowl/edg/ment, 358
ac/quaint, 162
ac/quaint/ances, 464
ac/quainted, 235, 443
ac/quaints, 49
acres, 492
across, 77
acted, 479
ac/tion, 80
ac/tions, 558
ac/tive, 18
ac/tively, 495
ac/tiv/i/ties, 162, 540
ac/tiv/ity, 198
ac/tual, 172
ac/tu/ally, 8, 209
Ad/ams, 392
Ad/ams's, 390
adapt, 38, 504
adapt/a/bil/ity, 279
adapt/able, 147
ad/ap/ta/tion, 570
adapted, 235, 423
add, 180
added, 266
ad/di/tion, 336
ad/di/tion, in, 266
ad/di/tional, 24
ad/di/tion to the, in, 228
ad/dress, 3
ad/dressed, 61
ad/dressee, 192
ad/dresses, 25
Ad/dres/so/graph, 495
adept, 38
ad/e/quate, 555
ad/he/sion, 580
ad/ja/cent, 343

clean, 93
cleaned, 26
cleaner, 346
clean/ers, 347
clean/ing, 345
clean/li/ness, 239
clear, 38
cleared, 473
clear/ing/house, 172
clearly, 96
Clem/ens, 253
cler/i/cal, 473
clerk, 192
clerks, 172
Cleve/land, 53
clever, 202
cli/ent, 95
cli/ent/age, 579
Clif/ton, 22
climb/ing, 161
Clin/ton, 313
clipped, 205
clip/ping, 191
clock, 453
close, 12, 15
closed, 68
closely, 120
clos/est, 339, 420
cloth, 26
clothed, 526
clothes, 392
cloth/ing, 5
cloud, 297
clue, 15
coaches, 489
coarse, 104
coast, 332
coastal, 330
coated, 104
coat/ings, 580
colder, 228
Cole/man, 592
col/lat/eral, 36
col/lect, 3
col/lected, 178
col/lect/ing, 15, 275
col/lec/tion, 90
col/lec/tion, for, 518
col/lec/tion
    de/part/ment, 20
col/lec/tions, 328
col/lege, 467
Col/lings, 518
color, 104
col/ored, 155
col/or/ful, 200
col/or/ing, 107
col/umn, 57
col/umns, 12

com/bi/na/tion, 49
com/bine, 153
com/bined, 313
co/me/di/ans, 293
com/fort, 129
com/fort/able, 479
com/fort/ably, 485
com/forts, 527
com/ing, 456
com/mended, 346
com/men/su/rate, 576
com/ment, 348
com/mer/cial, 266, 586
com/mis/sion, 594
com/mon, 26, 523
com/mon/est, 131
com/mu/ni/cate, 348
com/mu/ni/ca/tions,
    555, 570
com/mu/nity, 174, 279
com/pa/nies, 137
com/pany, by this, 595
com/pa/ra/ble, 243
com/pare, 497
com/pared, 205
com/par/i/son, 479
com/part/ment, 444
com/pelled, 83
com/pete, 271, 540
com/pete, to, 138
com/pe/tent, 286
com/pe/ti/tion, 49
com/pet/i/tive, 164,
    523, 540
com/pet/i/tor, 275
com/plain, 120
com/plaint, 579
com/plaints, 120
com/plete, 131
com/pleted, 11
com/pletely, 12
com/ple/tion, 112, 586
com/pli/ance, 382
com/pli/ment, 202
com/pli/men/tary, 570
com/pli/ments, 146
com/ply, 124
com/pos/ite, 343
com/pre/hen/sive, 583
com/pro/mise, 61
con/ceived, 242
con/cen/trated, 249, 274
con/cern, 124
con/cerned, 49, 169, 325
con/cern/ing, 520
con/cerns, 224
con/ces/sion, 62
con/ces/sions, 138
con/clude, 23

con/cluded, 347
con/crete, 376
con/cur/ring, 69
con/den/sa/tion, 410
con/densed, 410
con/di/tion, 26
con/di/tions, 23
con/duct, 437
con/ducted, 479
con/fi/dence, 120
con/fi/dent, 25
con/fi/den/tial, 607
con/fined, 258
con/firm, 311
con/fir/ma/tion, 311
con/firmed, 311
con/firm/ing, 227
con/flicted, 409
con/form, 206
con/fronted, 59, 120
con/fu/sion, 73, 301
con/grat/u/late, 387
con/grat/u/late, I, 180
Con/gress, 127
con/nected, 98
Con/nect/i/cut, 253
con/nec/tion, 12
con/nec/tion, in, 561
con/sci/en/tious, 84
con/sci/en/tiously, 70
con/scious, 570
con/sent, 120
con/se/quence, 120
con/se/quent, 172
con/se/quently, 25
con/serv/a/tive, 555
con/sider, 5
con/sid/er/able, 145
con/sid/er/ably, 228
con/sid/er/ate, 101, 297
con/sid/er/a/tion, 400
con/sid/er/a/tion,
    care/ful, 433
con/sid/ered, 66
con/sid/ers, 62
con/signee, 224
con/sign/ees, 229
con/sisted, 230
con/sist/ent, 141
con/sists, 44
con/so/la/tion, 598
con/spic/u/ous, 44
con/stant, 75
con/stantly, 49
con/sti/tute, 540
con/sti/tutes, 177
con/strains, 249
con/structed, 526
con/struct/ing, 543, 569

dead/weight, 570
deal, good, 443
deal, great, 38
dealer, 153
deal/ers, 137
deal/ing, 75
deal/ings, 18
deals, 224
dear, 169
dearly, 9
Dear Miss, 107
Dear Mrs., 217
debtor, 452
debts, 8
De/cem/ber, 78
de/cep/tive, 266
de/cided, 32
de/cided, we have, 127
de/cid/edly, 101, 104
de/cides, 11
de/cid/ing, 445
de/ci/sion, 159
de/ci/sive, 445
dec/la/ra/tion, 239
de/clared, 437
de/cline, 523
de/duct/ing, 333
de/duc/tion, 266
de/ducts, 266
deems, 68
deep/est, 573
de/feat, 101
de/fect, 547
de/fec/tive, 382
de/fends, 101
de/fense, 62
de/ferred, 213
def/i/nite, 49
def/i/nitely, 62
def/i/ni/tions, 293
de/fray, 136, 555
de/gree, 445
de/grees, 293
de/ic/ing, 586
de/lay, 177
de/lay, with the least
  pos/si/ble, 547
de/layed, 229
del/e/gate, 420
del/i/cate, 590
de/light, 180
de/lighted, 270
de/light/ful, 255
de/lin/quent, 75
de/liv/ered, 129
deliv/ery, 53
de/liv/ery, spe/cial, 111
de/mand, 49
dem/on/strate, 392

dem/on/stra/tion, 269
dem/on/stra/tor, 420
dense, 580
de/parted, 596
de/part/ment, 159
de/part/ment,
  ac/count/ing, 423
de/part/ment, art, 32
de/part/ment,
  book/keep/ing, 273
de/part/ment,
  col/lec/tion, 20
de/part/ment, credit, 93
de/part/ment, fil/ing,
  218
De/part/ment, Post
  Of/fice, 496
de/part/ment, sales, 18
de/part/ment,
  ship/ping, 5
de/part/men/tal, 490
de/part/men/tal/ized,
  514
de/part/ments, 18
de/part/ments,
  ed/u/ca/tional, 239
de/part/ments,
  em/ploy/ment, 468
de/par/ture, 418
de/pend, 349
de/pend/a/bil/ity, 577
de/pend/able, 576
de/pend/ably, 358
de/pend/ent, 151
de/pend/ing, 565
de/pends, 321
de/pos/ited, 174
de/pot, 489
de/pre/ci/a/tion, 523,
  586
de/pressed, 245
dep/uty, 177
de/rived, 117, 283
de/scent, 376, 586
de/scribed, 532
de/scribes, 360
de/scrib/ing, 224
de/scrip/tion, 242
de/scrip/tive, 104
de/serves, 83
de/sign, 106
des/ig/nated, 543
de/signed, 241
de/sign/ing, 604
de/signs, 217
de/sir/able, 56
de/sired, 202
de/sires, 558
de/sir/ous, 38

desk, 358
desks, 551
Des Moines, 188
de/spite, 523
de/stroyed, 249, 445
de/tail, 65
de/tailed, 71
de/tails, 486
de/tec/tive, 345
de/ter/mi/na/tion, 514
de/ter/mine, 419
de/ter/mined, 162
de/ter/mines, 186
de/ter/min/ing, 98
de/tracts, 249
det/ri/men/tal, 249
De/troit, 563
De/troit 6, Mich/i/gan,
  106
de/vel/oped, 101
de/vel/op/ing, 148
de/vel/op/ment, 101,
  257
de/vel/op/ments, 186
de/vice, 166
de/vices, 101, 253, 570
de/vote, 101
de/voted, 101, 148
di/ag/o/nally, 57
di/a/gram, 212
dic/tate, 364
dic/tated, 3
dic/tates, 206
dic/ta/tion, 11
dic/ta/tor, 90
dic/ta/tor's, 526
dic/tion, 598
dic/tion/a/ries, 283
dic/tion/ary, 85
did not, 346
did not, I, 400
did not, you, 114
didn't, 5
died, 441
diet, 195
dif/fer, 11
dif/fer/ence, 9, 101
dif/fer/ences, 452
dif/fer/ent, 70
dif/fer/en/tials, 570
dif/fers, 266, 293
dif/fi/cult, 9, 101
dif/fi/cul/ties, 166
dif/fi/culty, 101, 232
dig/nity, 279, 590
dil/i/gent, 151
di/men/sions, 320
di/rect, 141
di/rected, 480

from those, 218
from which, 218
from you, 374, 433
from your let/ter, 129
front, 35
frozen, 225
fruit, 330
fruit/ful, 509
fruit/less, 598
fuel, 36, 73
ful/fill, 543
ful/filled, 570, 573
full, 289
full, in, 437
Fuller, 50
fully, 40
Ful/ton, 65
fun/da/men/tally, 452
fur/nish, 75
fur/nished, 188
fur/nish/ing, 466
fur/ni/ture, 188
fur/ther, 32
fur/ther/ance, 540
fur/ther/more, 550
fuse, 570
fu/ture, 44
fu/ture, in the, 334

G

gained, 425
gainer, 365
gal/ley, 283
gal/lons, 476
gal/lons, five, 136
ga/rages, 374
gar/dener, 106
gar/den/ing, 106
gar/dens, 400
Gary, 213
gas/o/line, 268
gath/er/ing, 75
gauge, 552
gauged, 318
gave, 283
gen/eral, 11
gen/er/ally, 209, 274
gen/er/ate, 540
gen/er/os/ity, 279, 304
gen/er/ous, 70
gen/tle, 151
gen/tle/man, 151, 598
gen/tle/men, 20
gen/tly, 393
gen/u/ine, 276
gen/u/inely, 469
ge/o/graph/i/cal, 371

ge/og/ra/phy, 371
George, 138
Geor/gia, 604
Ger/trude, 107
get, I can, 535
get, can you, 374
get, to, 523
gets, who, 583
get/ter, 49
gift, 558
girls, 343
give, will, 76
give, you can, 39
give me, 485
given, 420
given, have, 480
given, it is, 452
given, may be, 57
given, you will be, 510
given you, we have, 125
gives, 293, 488
give us, to, 216
give us, will you, 533
give you, to, 456
give you, we shall, 509
give your, to, 383
glad, I may be, 397
glad to re/ceive, 434
glad, we shall be, 112
glad/i/o/lus, 226
gladly, 212
glance, 161
glo/ri/ously, 598
glossy, 580
God's, 535
go/ing, I am, 40
golden, 561
golf, 147
good deal, 443
good-/naturedly, 101
goods, 358
goods, of the, 514
goods, of these, 125
Good/win, 155
Gor/don, 120
gos/pel, 573
gothic, 411
gov/erned, 420
gov/ern/ing, 543
gov/ern/ment, 356
gov/ern/men/tal, 543, 569
grade, 114
grades, 129
grad/u/ally, 18, 209
grad/u/ate, 604
grad/u/ates, 468
grad/u/at/ing, 482
grad/u/a/tion, 73

gram/mat/i/cal, 590
Grand Av/e/nue, 592
Grand Cen/tral, 254
Grand Rap/ids, 299
grand/stands, 147
grant, 9
granted, 59, 66
Grant/wood, 482
grasp/ing, 535
grate/ful, 241
grate/fully, 304
grat/i/fy/ing, 101, 425
grav/ity, 358
great deal, 38
great enough, 437
greater, 3
greater than, 97
great/est, 206, 339
greatly, 107
great many, 62
greedy, 191
Gree/ley, 503
Green/vale, 106
greet, 473
Greg/ory, 136
Grif/fin, 299
grip/ping, 276
gro/cers, 330
gross, 50
grounds, 445
group, 285
grow/ers, 330
growth, 313
guar/an/tee, 155
guar/an/teed, 545
guar/an/tees, 420
guard, 169
guarded, 325, 397
guess, 98
guess, to, 552
guide, 480
gummed, 349
Gu/ten/berg, 283
Guth/rie, 397

H

habit, 56
hab/its, 445
ha/bit/ual, 535
ha/bit/u/ally, 209
had, has, 579
had, he, 374
had, I, 253, 433
had, I have, 145
had, we, 5
had, we have, 40

had been, 433, 480
had not, we, 472
hadn't, we, 125
half tone, 104
Ham/il/ton, 77
ham/mer, 390
ham/mer/ing, 368
ham/pered, 490
hand, at, 98
hand, on, 18
hand/bags, 529
hand/i/cap, 455
hand/ker/chiefs, 529
han/dle, 53, 59
han/dled, 32, 236
han/dles, 313
hand/writ/ing, 44
Han/ford, 330
hang/ars, 555
hap/haz/ard, 154
hap/pen, 275
hap/pened, 151, 390
hap/pily, 209
hap/pi/ness, 40
happy, 148
hard/est, 339
hardly, 206
hard/ware, 268
harm, 169, 174
harm/ful, 325
har/mony, 169
Har/ring/ton, 410
Har/ris, 268
Har/ri/son, 79
Hart/ford, 253
Hart/ley, 226
har/vester, 592
has be/come, 495
has been, 62, 523
has been able, 468
has been made, 121
has given, 433
has had, 579
has not been, 174
has not yet been, 52
haste, 358
has/ten, 190
hasty, 269
haul/ing, 480
have, as we, 302
have, as you, 434
have, if you could, 40
have, if you will, 508
have, I may, 38
have, I should like to, 113
have, it will, 285
have, let us, 159
have, must, 356

have said, I, 434
have, seems to, 44
have, should like to, 244
have, that might, 97
have, they must, 490
have, we should, 5
have, we should like to, 36
have, which would, 523
have, which you, 516
have, would, 433
have, you may, 472
have, you might, 376
have been, 131
have been able, 274
have done, 500
have given, 480
have never, 232
have not, if you, 159
have not been, 439
have not yet, 550
have not yet, we, 411
haven't, 394
have you, 445
have you, to, 472
Ha/zen, 120
hazy, 186
head/ings, 420
head/quar/ters, 411
health, 604
healthy, 535
heaps, 445
heard, 519
heard, we have not, 80
hear from you, 20
hear from you, let us, 595
heart, 325, 535
heart/ily, 209, 347
hearty, 439
hea/then, 573
he had, 374
held, 175, 236
helped, 198
help/ful, 57
Hen/der/son, 497
Her/bert, 173
here is, 90
here's, 49
her/self, 98
hes/i/tancy, 269
hes/i/tate, 39
hes/i/tated, 235, 579
hes/i/ta/tion, 602
he wants, 297
he was, 573
he will make, 609

hex/ago/nal, 11
hick/ory, 313
high enough, 266
higher than, 136
high/est, 206, 339
highly, 382
high school, 495
high/ways, 374
him, to, 66
him/self, 76
hinges, 8
hint, 495
Hin/ton, 188
his/toric, 555
hold, 84
holder, 409
hold/ing, 53
holds, 203
hol/i/day, 122
hol/i/days, 551
home life, 608
home of/fice, 526
home/own/ers, 32
home/work, 15
"hom/ier," 40
hon/est, 69
hon/estly, 552
Ho/no/lulu, 539
hood, 449
hooked, 242
hope/lessly, 84
hope that, I, 434
hope that, in the, 441
hope that, we, 23
hope that the, we, 227
hope that this, we, 297
hope this, we, 520
hope you can, we, 467
hope you will, we, 303
hope you will be able, we, 434
hop/ing, 106
hor/i/zon/tal, 104
Horne, 529
hor/ror, 347
horse/power, thou/sand, 476
horses, 147
hose, 393
ho/siery, 527
ho/tel, 480
hour, 57
hourly, 529
hours, 229
house, 35
how/ever, 3, 73
how much, 20
how soon, 287
how well, 526

mod/ern/izes, 501
mod/ern/iz/ing, 32
mo/hair, 214
mois/tened, 349
mois/tener, 349
mois/ten/ing, 356
mois/ture, 313
molds, 186
mo/ment, 93
mo/ment, at the ear/-
  li/est pos/si/ble, 66
mo/ment, at the
  pres/ent, 488
Mon/day, 216
Mon/day morn/ing, 488
Mon/i/tor, 400
mon/o/graph, 371
mon/o/graphs, 371
Mon/roe, 77
Mon/tana, 155
month, each, 610
month, of this, 82
monthly, 20
months, 154
month's, 464
months, few, 437
months, six, 402
mon/u/ment, 376
mood, 390
mops, 345
more, 106
more and more, 401
more than, 159, 433,
  523
morn/ing, 172
morn/ing, Mon/day,
  488
morn/ing, next, 473
morn/ing, this, 114
morn/ing, to/mor/row,
  374
morn/ing, Wednes/day,
  520
morn/ing's, 40
morn/ing's, in this, 592
Mor/ris, 331
most, 15, 22
most, one of the, 188
mo/tions, 97
motor, 489
mount/ings, 285
mov/able, 283
move, 268
moved, 80
move/ment, 245
mov/ing, 22
Mrs., 217, 293
Mrs., Dear, 217
much, how, 20

much, just as, 62
much, too, 76
much, very, 172
much time, 535
Muir, 410
Mul/ti/graph, 200
mul/ti/graphed, 3
mul/ti/ple, 305
mul/ti/pli/ca/tion, 540
mul/ti/tude, 258
Mun/cie, 77
Mun/son, 466
mur/mur, 598
mu/seum, 239
must, they, 212
must be, 192
must be done, 490
must have, 356
mu/tual, 127
mu/tu/ally, 209
my/self, 175
my under/stand/ing,
  127

N

na/ivete, 598
name, 90
name, your, 594
namely, 484
names, 25
name/sake, 598
nar/row, 12
Nash/ville, 592
na/tion, 532
na/tional, 32
na/tion/ally, 138
nat/u/ral, 8
nat/u/rally, 18, 209
na/ture, of this, 561
nav/i/ga/tional, 570
near, 169
near/est, 172, 339
nearly, 83
nec/es/sar/ily, 209, 558
ne/ces/si/tate, 3
ne/ces/si/ties, 358
ne/ces/sity, 266
needed, 235
need/lessly, 443
neg/a/tive, 285
neg/lect, 496
neg/li/gence, 122
ne/go/ti/a/tions, 428,
  540
neigh/bor/hood, 449
neigh/bor's, 535

nei/ther, 68
Nel/son, 77
neon, 195
nerv/ous/ness, 602
neu/tral, 540
Ne/vada, 561
never, 68
never, have, 232
never, I have, 383
nev/er/the/less, 22
new, 108
New/ark, 122
New Bern, 376
new/est, 339
New Jer/sey, 122
new/ly/weds, 496
New Mexico, 64
New Ro/chelle, 173
news/boy's, 343
news/pa/per, 53
news/pa/pers, 154
New/ton, 173
New York, 35, 539
New York City, 254
New York 15, New
  York, 410
next, 228
next day or so, 395
next few weeks, 269
next morn/ing, 473
next time, 433
next week, 549
next year, 433
ni/ce/ties, 570
night, last, 145
night, to/mor/row, 114
night let/ter, 311
$993,800, 522
$9,000,000, 586
90 per cent, 492
$90,000, 586
no, 15
no charge, 142
noise/less, 343
noises, 117, 343
no longer, 239
no mat/ter, 496
non/sense, 12, 15
non/stop, 570
non/tech/ni/cal, 470
nook, 159
noon, 120
no one, 347
nor, 552
nor/mal, 266
Nor/ris, 5
North Av/e/nue, 269
North Car/o/lina, 254
north/west, 561

op/ti/mis/tic, 147, 386
op/tion, 419, 586
or/a/tor, 573
Or/chard, 173
or/der, mail, 527
or/der, on your, 122
order, thank you for
   your, 110
or/der, this, 549
or/der, your, 142
or/der blank, 158
or/der blanks, 610
or/dered, 514
or/ders, 49
or/der that, in, 321
or/di/nar/ily, 98, 325
or/di/nary, 36, 325
Or/e/gon, 93
or/gan, 186
or/gan/i/za/tion, 18
or/gan/i/za/tions, 90
or/gan/ized, 497
ori/en/tal, 241
orig/i/nal, 5
orig/i/nally, 547
other, 315
other, any, 243, 433,
   523
other, in any, 467
other, some, 85
others, 131
oth/er/wise, 117, 395
ounce, 73, 255
our/selves, 95
out/door, 535
out/field/ers, 147
out/fit, 159
out/fits, 239
out/go/ing, 349
out/lay, 501
out/line, 590
out/lined, 53
out/lines, 11, 73
out/lin/ing, 273
out/put, 533
out/set, 420
out/side, 36, 117
out/sid/ers, 583
out/stand/ing, 3, 73
out/ward, 449
over, 268
over/come, 272
over/due, 273
over/haul, 420
over/heard, 169
Over/land, 20
over/lap/ping, 349
over/look, 365
over/looked, 52

over/night, 226
over/pay/ment, 304
over/pays, 303
over/step/ping, 402
over/stocked, 18
over/whelm/ing, 598
owe, 9
owes, 15, 329
ow/ing, 444
own, 180
owned, 402
owner, 40
ox/fords, 124

P

Pa/cific, 90
pack/age, 216
pack/aged, 540
pack/ages, 49
packed, 420
pack/ing, 301
page, 155
pag/eants, 151
paid, 227, 518
pains, 158
paint, 36
painted, 573
paint/ing, 497
pairs, 124
pam/phlet, 283
pam/phlets, 243
Pam/plin, 226
panel, 506
pa/per, 27
par/a/dox, 523
par/a/graph, 143
par/a/graphs, 554
par/al/lel, 569
par/cel, 427
parcel-/post (adj.), 200
par/don, 169
park, 147
part, 5
part, on our, 304
par/tic/i/pat/ing, 540
par/tic/u/lar, 68
par/tic/u/larly, 410
partly, 245
parts, 293, 567
party, 329
pass, to, 523
passed, 57, 235
pas/sen/gers, 476, 492
passes, 83
pas/sion, 573
past, 57
past, dur/ing the, 434,
   523

past, in the, 158, 535
past-/due (adj.), 93
paste, 457
pas/tor, 299
pas/tures, 147
pa/tience, 76
pa/tient, 439
pa/tron/age, 411
pat/tern, 243
pat/terns, 293, 320
payee, 329
pay/loads, 523
pay/ment, 24
peak, 124
Pear/sall, 393
Pear/son, 483
pe/cul/iarly, 73, 402
pen, 155
pen/alty, 279
pen/cil, 107
pen/ciled, 214
pend/ing, 457
pen/hold/ers, 445
pen/nant, 148
Pen/ning/ton, 605
Penn/syl/va/nia, 51
peo/ple, 25
per cent, 125, 492, 522
per cent, fifty, 476
per cent, hun/dred, 125
per/cent/age, 464
per/fect, 382
per/fec/tion, 207, 570
per/fectly, 66
per/form/ance, 83
per/form/ers, 293
per/haps, 212
pe/riod, 18
per/ma/nent, 497
per/mis/si/ble, 321
per/mis/sion, 188
per/mits, 11
per/mit/ted, 235, 321
per/pet/u/ally, 209
per/se/cute, 91
Per/shing, 528
per/sist, 473
per/son, 484
per/sonal, 3
per/son/al/ity, 398
per/son/al/ized, 570
per/son/ally, 66, 209
per/son/nel, 570, 595
per/sons, 49, 293
per/tain, 356
per/tain/ing, 169, 457
per/ti/nent, 12
pes/ter/ing, 402
Pe/ters/burg, 173

Sam/uel, 18
San An/to/nio, 398
San Di/ego, 539
San/dusky, 136
San Fran/cisco, 539
San Fran/cisco,
   Cal/i/for/nia, 330
san/ity, 279
sat/is/fac/tion, 3
sat/is/fac/to/rily, 136,
   209
sat/is/fac/tory, 112
sat/is/fac/tory,
   en/tirely, 488
sat/is/fied, 110
sat/isfy, 62
Sat/ur/day, 120
Sav/age, 35
saved, 229
sav/ings, 173
saw/dust, 147
say, to, 433, 574
scale, 232
scarcely, 415
scarc/est, 339
scar/city, 279
sched/ule, 213
sched/uled, 540
schemes, 360
scho/las/tic, 386
school, 15, 420
school, high, 495
sci/ence, 195
sci/en/tific, 239
sci/en/tif/i/cally, 576
score/boards, 147
scores, 464
scout, 313
scratched, 23
screen, 104
scrib/bled, 12
scru/pu/lously, 535
scum, 580
sealed, 349
sealer, 349
seal/ing, 349
search, 464
sea/son, 125
sea/sons, 49
seated, 485
Se/at/tle, 516, 539
sec/ond, 35
se/cret, 397
sec/re/tary, 241
se/crets, 466
sec/tion, 138
se/curely, 489
se/cu/rity, 62, 279
Se/da/lia, 467

see, to, 253
seek/ing, 464
seemed, 59, 93
seems to be, 272
seems to have, 44
seen, you've, 394
seg/ment, 570
sel/dom, 29
se/lect, 11
se/lected, 158
se/lec/tion, 361
self-/addressed, 439
self-/explanatory, 379
self/ish, 8
self-/preservation, 212
sell/ing, 18
sem/i/per/sonal, 62
sender, 364
send/ing you, we are,
   287
send us, if you can, 595
send us, if you will, 419
send us, please, 410
send us, to, 32
sen/ior, 466
sense, 535
sen/si/ble, 200
sent, 516
sent, we have, 227
sen/tence, 84
sen/tences, 297
sep/a/rate, 56
sep/a/rated, 192
sep/a/rately, 232
sep/a/ra/tion, 276
Sep/tem/ber, 35
se/quence, 573
ser/geant, 151
se/rial, 415
se/ries, 3
se/ri/ously, 343
served, 257
serve you, to, 39
serv/ice, 43
serv/ice/able, 564
serv/ices, 91
set/tle, 20
set/tled, 136, 236
set/tle/ment, 24
set/tling, 3
setup, 501
$7,131,016, 522
seventy-/five dol/lars,
   374
79,000 pounds, 476
sev/eral, 166
sev/eral hun/dred, 529
sev/eral weeks, 400
sev/eral weeks ago, 562

sev/eral years, 437
se/ver/est, 339
shade, 147
shades, 293
shad/ing, 186
share, 169, 456
sharp/ened, 11, 151
sharp/ens, 445
sharp/est, 339
she, 97
she can, 84
sheer, 445
sheets, 202
she is, 84
shelves, 124
she would, 548
shield, 413
shift, 136
shift/ing, 445
shin/gle, 35
shin/gles, 32
ship/ments, 122
ship/per, 224
ship/ping
   de/part/ment, 5
shirts, 5
shoes, 120
shop/wear, 529
short, 8
short-/circuits, 445
short/hand, 12, 59
shortly, 216
short no/tice, 497
short-/term, 586
short time, 356
short while, 335
should be, 44
should be able, 97
should be done, 232
shoul/der, 40
should have been, 331
should like to have, 244
should not be, 12
shouldn't, we, 125
show, 15
showed, 226, 343
show/ing, 230
shown, 32
shows, 20
shrink/age, 313
shut, 343
shut/tle, 413
side-/step (v.), 577
side-/wall (adj.), 506
side walls, 40
sid/ing, 39
sight-/seeing, 484
sign, 444
sig/nal, 258

sig/na/ture, 193
sig/na/tures, 218
signed, 390
sig/nif/i/cance, 514
signs, 376
silk, 393
sil/li/est, 339
Sil/ver Lake, 226
sil/ver/ware, 528
sim/i/lar, 64
sim/ple, 32
sim/pler, 131
sim/plest, 339
sim/pli/fies, 297
sim/plify, 57
sim/ply, 27
sin/cere, 297
sin/cerely, 38
sin/cer/ity, 279, 297
since that time, 43
sin/gle, 44
sirup, 255
sis/ters, 169
sit/u/ated, 138
sit/u/a/tion, 9
sit/u/a/tions, 466
six hun/dred, 202
$6,145,900, 522
six months, 402
16,000 feet, 586
6,000 pounds, 476, 586
$60,000,000, 569
$61.12, 522
size, 56
sized, 287
sizes, 104
sketch, 106
sketches, 32
skilled, 313
skills, 602
skin, 49
slab, 580
slack, 313
sleep, 297
sleep/ers, 586
sleep/ing, 35
slide, 245
slides, 473
slid/ing, 27
slight, 257
slight/est, 582
slightly, 228
slip, 193
slipped, 56
slot, 413
slow, 506
slow/ing, 172
slowly, 22, 195
small, 44

smaller, 51
small/est, 320, 339
smart, 169
smart/est, 217, 339
Smith, 217
smooth, 361
smoth/ered, 490
smudged, 364
smudg/ing, 231
snap, 564
snap/shot, 506
so, 15
soap, 200
so/cial, 207
so/cially, 209
so far as, 79
soft, 27
soil/age, 528
so large as, 533
sold, 18, 236
sole, 397
sol/emn, 598
so/licit, 378, 540
so/lic/i/ta/tion, 540,
  561
so/lu/tion, 427
so many, 297, 433
some/how, 40, 73
some of the, 25
some of this, 239
some/one, 297
some/one else, 8
some other, 85
some/thing, 70
some time, 276
some time ago, 22
some/times, 18, 29
some weeks ago, 318
some/what, 154
some/where, 331
so much, 433
soon, how, 287
sorry, I am, 173
sorry, we are, 79
sort, 18, 325
sound, 257
sounds, 32
sources, 76, 325
South Adams, 254
South Bend, 592
South Da/kota, 20
south/ern, 345
South Spring, 65
space, 215
spa/cious, 570, 586
Spain, 93
span, 346
spar/ingly, 18

speaker, 573
speak/ing, 504
spe/cial, 32
spe/cial at/ten/tion,
  345
spe/cial de/liv/ery, 111
spe/cial/ists, 577
spe/cially, 209, 243
spe/cials, 49
spe/cific, 49
spec/i/fi/ca/tions, 313
spec/i/fied, 137
spec/ify, 313
spec/i/fy/ing, 27
spec/i/men, 420
spec/u/la/tion, 387,
  514
speed, 84
spell/ing, 98
spell/ings, 293
spend, 558
spend, to, 402
spent, 38, 151
spick, 346
Spill/man, 10(
spin/dle, 412
spirit, 120
spir/it/u/ally, 209
spite, in, 76
splen/did, 127
split, 226
split/ting, 376
spoil, 117
spoiled, 236
spoil/ing, 245
spoke, 66
sponge, 349
spool, 368
sport, 124
spot/lessly, 529
spots, 290
spread, 349
spread/ing, 347
spring, 35
Spring, South, 65
Spring/dale, 122
Spring/field, 214
sprin/kled, 147
spur, 84, 570
spurn, 325
square, 128
square feet, 136
square inch, 104
squarely, 577
stacked, 349
staff, 594
Staf/ford, 466
stages, 239
stained, 32

sus/tain/ing, 558
swatches, 532
sweep/ing, 158
swing, 159
switch, 393
sworn, 438
Syc/a/more, 438
sym/bol, 558
syn/o/nyms, 293
sys/tem, 91
sys/tem/atic, 57, 386
sys/tems, 570

T

ta/ble, 166
tab/u/lated, 387
tackle, 360
tact, 297
take care, to, 445
taken, 205
taken, we have, 53
tal/cum, 49
talked, 137
Tal/ley, 516
Tampa, 592
tan/gled, 418
tap/es/try, 299
tax, 496
tax/i/cabs, 489
Tay/lor, 254
teacher, 84
teach/ers, 483
team/work, 552
tear (v.), 349
tech/ni/cal, 224, 569
tech/ni/ques, 570
tel/e/gram, 114
tel/e/grams, 311, 371
tel/e/graph, 311, 371
tel/e/graphed, 122
te/leg/ra/phers, 371
tel/e/graphic, 311, 371
te/leg/raphy, 371
tel/e/phone, 122
tel/e/phoned, 59, 120
tell him, to, 382
tell/ing us, 39
tell me, 552
tells, 500
tell us, 244
tem/plates, 320
tem/po/ra/rily, 8
tem/po/rary, 9, 29
temp/ta/tion, 508
tend, 346
tend/ency, 11, 29

ten/dered, 555
ten/der/ing, 598
tend/ing, 95
tends, 329
$10,000,000, 569
Ten/nes/see, 313
Ten/nes/see,
  Mem/phis, 376
tenses, 293
10,000 pounds, 551
term, 198
ter/mi/nal, 254, 570
terms, 24
ter/ri/to/ries, 606
ter/ri/tory, 25
Terry, 62
test, 313
tested, 257
tests, 239
Texas, 393
text/book, 466
text/books, 457
tex/tiles, 528
than, 94
than, bet/ter, 11
than, cheaper, 580
than, faster, 84
than, for less, 596
than, for more, 257
than, greater, 97
than, higher, 136
than, less, 272, 433
than, more, 159, 433,
  523
than, rather, 140
than, worse, 496
thanks, 198
thanks, many, 177
Thanks/giv/ing, 203
thank you, I, 38
thank you for, we, 381
thank you for the, 43
thank you for the, we,
  596
thank you for your, 130
thank you for your, we,
  382
thank you for your
  let/ter, 485
thank you for your
  let/ters, 470
thank you for your
  or/der, 110
that can be, 36
that could be, 376
that is, 18, 523
that it is, 319
that it was, 434

that may be, 32
that might be, 376
that might have, 97
that might have been,
  76
that's, 394
that the, 289, 433, 523
that there is, 254
that there was not, 433
that they were, 124
that will, 49
that will be, 243
that would be, 596
the/a/ter, 486
the/at/ri/cal, 539
them, 467
them, one of, 141
theme, 154
them/selves, 18
then, 93, 94
the/o/ret/i/cal, 386
there are, 452
thereby, 259
there/for, 22
there/fore, 22
there may be, 321
there was not, 433
there wasn't, 433
there will be, 467
there would be, 84
these, from, 32
these, to, 32
these mat/ters, 334
these will be, 161
they may be, 154
they must, 212
they must be, 445
they must have, 490
they're, 394
they will be, 374
thick, 305
thicker, 12
thick/nesses, 356
thin, 231
things, 420
think, if you, 286
think/ing, 490
third, 91
$35,000, 443
31 per cent, 522
$37,528,672, 522
30,000 feet, 476
thirty-/two mil/lion,
  532
this can be done, 192
this claim, 440
this does not, 85
this may be, 84

this may be done, 193
this may not be, 501
this morn/ing, 114
this or/der, 549
this was done, 331
this year, 482
Thomas, 598
Thomp/son, 18
thor/oughly, 98
thor/ough/ness, 583
those, 3
though, 9
thought, 15, 38
thought, I, 376
thoughts, 97
thou/sand, 569
thou/sand, eight, 503
thou/sand, forty, 558
thou/sand, one, 316
thou/sands, 91
threat/en/ing, 76
three, 299
three, two or, 499
3½ cents, 522
3½ min/utes, 492
$3.80, 522
300 miles, 476
300 per cent, 125
300's, 586
360 land/ings, 492
$3,502,100, 522
three months ago, 203
3,000 air/ports, 492
through, 3
through/out, 44
through/out the, 158
through the, 57, 523
through this, 433
throws, 224
thrust, 586
thumb/ing, 44
Thurs/day, 217
thus, 91
tick/ets, 486
tick/ler, 457
tie, to, 158
ties, 609
tile, 241
time, 216
time, at any, 518
time, at that, 43
time, at the, 594
time, at the pres/ent,
  18
time, at the same, 49
time, at this, 565
time, at which, 82
time, by this, 198
time, for some, 592

time, for the, 444
time, long, 442
time, much, 535
time, short, 356
time, since that, 43
time, some, 276
timely, 198
time/pieces, 455
times, 492
times, at all, 434, 535
tis/sue, 111
to, 15
to a great ex/tent, 547
to any kind, 269
to any one of the, 413
to ask, 583
to be, 390, 433
to be done, 409
to be/gin, 523
to be/lieve, 552
to be made, 287
to be sure, 205, 434
to bore, 162
to carry, 393
to charge, 255
to com/pete, 138
to con/tain, 214
to cover, 175
to/day, 53
to/day's, 198
to do, 409, 433
to do it, 409
to do so, 5
to do this, 27
to find, 552
to get, 523
to/gether, 95
to/gether, all, 303
to/gether with the, 53
to give us, 216
to give you, 456
to give your, 383
to guess, 552
to have, 433
to have been, 38
to have you, 472
to him, 66
to im/press, 420
to join, 117, 508
told, I, 433
told, we, 226
To/ledo, 138
to lend, 244
tol/er/ances, 321
to let us have, 241
to let us know, 216
to like, 535
to lis/ten, 402
to make, 38

to me, 113
to meet, 120
to/mor/row, 29
to/mor/row morn/ing,
  374
to/mor/row night, 114
to my at/ten/tion, 331
tone, 602
tons, 253
too, 15
to of/fer, 506
took, 24
took, we, 274
tools, 490
too many, 574
too much, 76, 433
top, 468
to pass, 523
To/peka, 228
top-/notch, 161
to pre/clude, 95
to pro/ceed, 110
to produce, 433
to pro/mote, 257
to pro/tect, 95
to provide, 433
to push the, 198
to put, 523
to rec/tify, 122
to re/duce, 80
to re/ject, 319
to re/lieve, 125
to re/mind you, 453
to ren/der, 138
to rest, 274
to re/vive, 269
To/ronto, 411
to say, 433, 574
to see, 253
to send us, 32
to serve you, 39
to spend, 402
to sub/mit, 229
to sup/ply, 98
to take ad/van/tage,
  266
to take care, 445
to/tal, 175
to/tally, 555
to tell him, 382
to the, 433, 523
to the full/est ex/tent,
  501
to these, 32
to this, 224
to tie, 158
touch, 43
tour, 480
tour/ist, 480

to us, 565
to/ward, 18, 169, 449
to/wards, 445
tow/els, 457
to which, 301
town, 155
Town/send, 605
to work, 322
to write us, 39
to you, 596
to your at/ten/tion, 8
trace, 143
tracer, 144
trade, 419
traf/fic, 136
trag/edy, 180
train, 288
trained, 212
train/ing, 97
trans/act/ing, 224
trans/ac/tion, 179
tran/scribed, 11
tran/scribes, 258
tran/scrip/tion, 218
trans/fer, 554
trans/ferred, 283
trans/fer/ring, 104
transit, 224
trans/mit/ted, 311
trans/o/ce/anic, 539
Trans/par, 527
trans/par/ent, 529
trans/port, 485
trans/por/ta/tion, 141, 523
travel, 480
trav/el/ers, 480
trav/el/ing, 155
treas/urer, 145
treated, 580
treat/ment, 79
Tre/mont, 331
Trent, 566
Tren/ton, 200
trial, 283
Trib/une, 145
tried, 361
tri/pled, 532
trip/li/cate, 311
trol/ley, 288
Trot/ter, 605
trou/ble, 79
trou/bles, 358
trou/ble/some, 85
truck, 142
true, 331
trunks, 605
trust, 438
trus/tee, 437

truth, 40
try/ing, 204
tube, 51
Tues/day, 318
tulip, 226
tune, 529
turn, 325
turned, 24
turn/ing, 97
turn/o/ver, 24
Twain, 253
12 cents, 492
20 acres, 492
$20, 476
twenty dol/lars, 574
$25, 476
25 miles, 492
$25,000,000, 476
25 per cent, 522
25 years, 492
20,000,000, 492
$20,000,000, 492, 586
twice, 155
twirl, 335
two, day or, 143
two, one or, 35
two, week or, 419
$2,000,000,000, 492
2,501,074,036, 492
$2.40, 522
two/fold, 570
$250,000,000, 212
$2,998,000, 522
two or three, 499
2,500 feet, 492
2,000 horse/power, 476
2,000 pounds, 586
two weeks, 567
two weeks ago, 200
type, 202
typed, 154
types, 3
type/set/ting, 104
type/writer, 27
type/writ/ers, 423
type/writ/ten, 91
typ/i/cal, 62
typ/ing, 412
typ/ist, 3
typ/ists, 420
typ/ist's, 335
ty/po/graph/i/cal, 231, 371

U

ul/ti/mate, 29, 552
un/able, 51
un/a/void/able, 361

un/cer/tain/ties, 548
un/cer/tainty, 437
un/chang/ing, 535
un/com/mon, 598
un/con/sciously, 445
un/der, 11
un/der/ly/ing, 577
un/der sep/a/rate cover, 489
un/der/stand, 93
un/der/stand, please, 95
un/der/stand, we, 53
un/der/stand/ing, 272
un/der/stand/ing, my, 127
un/der/stood, it is, 314
un/der/take, 360
un/der/tak/ing, 283
un/der/took, 428
un/der/wear, 527
un/de/sir/able, 83
un/dis/turbed, 297
un/doubt/edly, 51, 73, 101
un/e/qualed, 158
un/ex/pect/edly, 101
un/fair, 62
un/fas/ten, 564
un/folded, 207
un/for/tu/nate, 3
un/for/tu/nately, 18, 29
un/guarded, 169
uni/form, 73
uni/formly, 365
un/im/por/tant, 590
un/in/i/ti/ated, 253
un/in/ten/tional, 304
un/in/ter/rupted, 569
un/ion, 188
unit, 73
United States, 212
units, 51
uni/ver/sally, 535
uni/ver/sity, 285
un/known, 598
un/less, 83
un/nec/es/sary, 300
un/of/fi/cial, 514
un/paid, 83
un/pleas/ant, 83
un/prec/e/dented, 523
un/pro/duc/tive, 361
un/prof/it/able, 501
un/rea/son/ably, 442
un/rolled, 236
un/ruled, 590
un/safe, 232

weave, 242
web, 413
Web/ber, 20
we be/lieve, 227
Web/ster, 173
Web/ster's, 293
we can, 289
we can do, 18
we can/not as/sist, 594
we could not, 501
we did, 333
Wednes/day, 122
Wednes/day morn/ing, 520
we do not, 497
we do not wish, 82
week, first, 596
week, next, 549
week, of next, 81
week, of this, 81
weekly, 198
week or two, 419
Weeks, 93
weeks, few, 18
weeks, next few, 269
weeks, one or two, 593
weeks, sev/eral, 400
weeks, two, 567
weeks ago, 397
weeks ago, sev/eral, 562
weeks ago, some, 318
we en/close, 426
we ex/pect, 18
we give, 433
we find, 289
we had, 5
we had not, 472
we hadn't, 125
we have, 433
we have been, 518
we have de/cided, 127
we have done, 125
we have given you, 125
we have had, 40
we have not heard, 80
we have not yet, 411
we have sent, 227
we have taken, 53
we have your let/ter, 427
we hope that, 23
we hope that the, 227
we hope that this, 297
we hope this, 520
we hope you can, 467
we hope you will, 303
we hope you will be able, 434

weight, 3
we in/fer, 332
wel/come, 242
wel/fare, 361
well, as, 500
well, how, 526
well, just as, 504
well-/known, 242
we may be able, 425
we may be sure, 36
we must, 433
we no/tice, 23
were, 455
were, that they, 124
were, we, 22
were, you, 304
we re/gret, 243
we re/gret the, 127
were not, 433, 523
were not, if it, 468
we shall, 594
we shall be, 276
we shall be able, 434, 456
we shall be glad, 112
we shall give you, 509
we should ap/pre/ci/ate, 77
we should be, 198
we should be able, 114, 434
we should have, 5
we should like, 439
we should like to have, 36
we should like to know, 20
we should like to see, 200
we shouldn't, 125
west, 332
west/ern, 64
West/min/ster, 411
West/o/ver, 257
West/side, 374
West Vir/ginia, 242
we thank you for, 381
we thank you for the, 596
we thank you for your, 382
we told, 226
we took, 274
we under/stand, 53
we want, 8
we were, 22
what, 15
what/ever, 301
wheel, 374

Wheeler, 376
when/ever, 343
when I was, 40
when the, 97, 523
where, 57
where are you, 374
wher/ever, 313
whether, 8
whether or not, 80
which, about, 433
which, at, 84
which, from, 218
which would have, 523
which you have, 516
while, 97
while, short, 335
whirls, 393
whis/tle, 343
white, 114
who gets, 583
who knows, 583
whole, 277
whole/hearted, 554
whole/sale, 330
wholly, 558
whom, 230
whose, 207
who will, 552
why not, 9
wicks, 358
wide-/awake (adj.), 198
widely, 358
will, if you, 173
will, who, 552
will be, 287
will be made, 322
will find, 85
will give, 76
Wil/liam, 128
will/ing, we are, 22
will/ingly, 314
will/ing/ness, 95
will make, 131
will place, 547
will re/ceive, 593
Will Rog/ers, 148
will you give us, 533
will you please, 159
will you please see, 213
Wil/son, 254
Wind/lay, 438
win/dow, 125
win/ter, 36
wire, 315
Wis/con/sin, 200
wis/dom, 29, 297
wise, 311
wise enough, 535

wish, 15
wish, I do not, 68
wish, if you, 146
wish, we do not, 82
wished, 347
wishes, 65
wish/ing, 62
with/draw, 331
with him, 433, 535
with/hold/ing, 442
within, 106
within the, 25
with/out, 11
with re/gard, 174
with the, 192, 523
with the least
    pos/si/ble de/lay, 547
with this, 277
with us, 285, 433
with you, 440
woman, 347
wom/an's, 390
women, 390
wom/en's, 527
won, 148
won/der/ful, 393
won/der/ing, 527
won't, 5
wood, 313
wooden, 299
Wood/son, 345
word, 329
words, 40, 293, 325
words, in other, 457
work, to, 322
worked, 120, 235
worker, 104
work/ing, 79
work/man/ship, 113
work/men, 239
world, 15, 136
world, busi/ness, 425
world, in the, 283
worn, 427
worry, 325

worse, 79
worse than, 496
worth-/while, 5, 6
worth while, 6, 117
wor/thy, 363
would have, 433
would have been, 229,
    523
wouldn't, 395
wo/ven, 242
wrapped, 528
wrap/per, 532
wrap/ping, 527
wringer, 393
writer, 3
writ/er's, 122
writes, 565
write us, to, 39
writ/ing, 40
writ/ing, I am, 127
writ/ing, we are, 382
writ/ten, 3
wrong, 181
wrought, 574
Wynne, 65
Wy/o/ming, 158

Y

Yan/cey, 576
yards, 142
yarn, 243
year, dur/ing the past,
    158
year, last, 523
year, of this, 605
year, this, 482
years, 293, 492
years ago, 360
years, five, 522
years, for many, 67
year's, last, 82
years, sev/eral, 437
yes, 200
yes/ter/day, 148

yet, 8
yet, has not, 52
yet, have not, 550
yielded, 236
Yon/kers, 254
yoke, 413
you, 15
you can be, 227
you can do, 500
you could not be, 434
you can give, 39
you could not be, 434
you did not, 114
you'd like to know, 395
you gave me, 434
you have, 433
you have been able, 547
you have done, 127
you have made, 382
you'll, 161
you may be able, 245
you may be sure, 128
you may find, 216
you may have, 472
you might have, 376
you must be, 148
Young, 300
your, 15
your in/quiry, 393
your in/ten/tion, 23
your let/ter, 130
your name, 594
your or/der, 142
your re/mit/tance, 83
yours, 5
your/self, 8
your/selves, 545
you've seen, 394
you were, 304.
you will be, 51, 523
you will be able, 319
you will be given, 510
you will find, 242
you will not be, 148
you will note, 177

INDEX